The
WILEY
advantage

Dear Valued Customer,

We realize you're a busy professional with deadlines to hit. Whether your goal is to learn a new technology or solve a critical problem, we want to be there to lend you a hand. Our primary objective is to provide you with the insight and knowledge you need to stay atop the highly competitive and ever-changing technology industry.

Wiley Publishing, Inc., offers books on a wide variety of technical categories, including security, data warehousing, software development tools, and networking — everything you need to reach your peak. Regardless of your level of expertise, the Wiley family of books has you covered.

- For Dummies – The *fun* and *easy* way to learn
- The Weekend Crash Course –The *fastest* way to learn a new tool or technology
- Visual – For those who prefer to learn a new topic *visually*
- The Bible – The *100% comprehensive* tutorial and reference
- The Wiley Professional list – *Practical* and *reliable* resources for IT professionals

The book you hold now, *Storage Security: Protecting SANs, NAS, and DAS,* provides a comprehensive guide for protecting the mission-critical data that is in your storage system. Best-selling author John Chirillo and storage expert Scott Blaul cover everything you need to know to build security into your storage systems, defend existing storage systems, and test your defenses, making this book a must-have for network engineers and admins, security analysts and engineers, and anyone responsible for protecting the valuable data in a storage system.

Our commitment to you does not end at the last page of this book. We'd want to open a dialog with you to see what other solutions we can provide. Please be sure to visit us at www.wiley.com/compbooks to review our complete title list and explore the other resources we offer. If you have a comment, suggestion, or any other inquiry, please locate the "contact us" link at www.wiley.com.

Finally, we encourage you to review the following page for a list of Wiley titles on related topics. Thank you for your support and we look forward to hearing from you and serving your needs again in the future.

Sincerely,

Richard K. Swadley
Vice President & Executive Group Publisher
Wiley Technology Publishing

Visual

Bible

DUMMIES

WILEY

***more information
on related titles***

Also Available from John Chirillo

Hack Attacks Revealed, 2nd Edition, 0471232823

UNIX and Windows security from the hacker's perspective

Hack Attacks Denied, 2nd Edition, 0471232831

Fortify your networks against the next generation of intruders

Hack Attacks Encyclopedia, 0471055891

A complete history of hacks, cracks, phreaks, and spies

Hack Attacks Testing, 0471229466

Put your network's security to the test

Storage Security: Protecting SANs, NAS, and DAS

Storage Security: Protecting SANs, NAS, and DAS

John Chirillo, CISSP, ASE, CCDA, CCIE, CCNA, CCNP
and Scott Blaul, CISSP, ASE, CCIE, CCNA, CCNP, CNE

WILEY

Wiley Publishing, Inc.

Storage Security: Protecting SANs, NAS, and DAS

Published by
Wiley Publishing, Inc.
10475 Crosspoint Boulevard
Indianapolis, IN 46256
www.wiley.com

ISBN: 0-7645-1688-4

Manufactured in the United States of America.

10 9 8 7 6 5 4 3 2 1

1B/RY/RS/QS/IN

For general information on our other products and services or to obtain technical support, please contact our Customer Care Department within the U.S. at (800) 762-2974, outside the U.S. at (317) 572-3993 or fax (317) 572-4002.

Wiley also publishes its books in a variety of electronic formats. Some content that appears in print may not be available in electronic books.

Library of Congress Control Number: 2002114682

About the Authors

John Chirillo began his computer career at the age of 12, when he spent a year teaching himself the basics of computers and then wrote several software pieces that were published. He went on to become certified in numerous programming languages, including QuickBasic, VB, C++, Pascal, Assembler, and Java. John later developed the PC Optimization Kit (increasing speeds up to 200 percent of standard Intel 486 chips).

After running two businesses, Software Now and Geniusware, John became a consultant (specializing in security and analysis) to prestigious companies, where he performed security analyses, sniffer analyses, LAN/WAN design, implementation, and troubleshooting. During this period, John acquired numerous internetworking certifications, including Cisco's CCNA, CCDA, CCNP, Intel Certified Solutions Consultant, Compaq ASE Enterprise Storage, UNIX, CISSP, and pending CCIE. He is currently a Senior Internetworking Engineer at a technology management company. John is the author of several security and networking books, including the Hack Attacks series from John Wiley & Sons.

Scott Blaul has been in the electronics industry since 1981, when he started as an electronics repair technician in the United States Marine Corps. As an instructor in the USMC, Scott taught electronics for five years. After leaving the Marines in 1989, Scott went to work for Inacomp Computer Corporation, which was ultimately acquired by ValCom. During his thirteen years there, he has been involved in many facets of the computer service industry, including Field Services (desktop-related technology and services) and Professional Services (server-, infrastructure-, storage-, and security-related services). His services included support for many Fortune 1,000 companies. Scott has obtained certifications as well as internetworking experience. These certifications include CNE, ASE, CCNA, CCNP, CISSP, and CCIE (pending).

Credits

Acquisitions Editor
Katie Feltman

Project Editor
Mark Enochs

Copy Editor
Gabrielle Chosney

Technical Editor
Tom Brays

Editorial Manager
Mary Beth Wakefield

Vice President and Executive Group Publisher
Richard Swadley

Vice President and Executive Publisher
Bob Ipsen

Executive Editor
Carol Long

Executive Editorial Director
Mary Bednarek

Project Coordinator
Nancee Reeves

Supervisor of Graphics and Design
Shelley Lea

Proofreading
Kim Cofer

Indexing
Virginia Bess

Preface

Many books have been written about security, giving countless accounts of security breaches. The intent of this book is not to duplicate those books, but rather to show how to leverage and apply much of their content to help you create a more secure centralized storage network, while focusing specifically on why a given storage network technology might be a better security choice in a given situation. Inevitably, some of the general security topics must be covered (as they relate to storage security), along with specific storage network security solutions.

The goal of implementing a storage network must not be lost when considering how to protect it. After all, when determining what type of storage network to use, you should base your decisions on essential business needs or requirements. Once you have chosen the type of storage network technology appropriate to these needs, you can decide on the appropriate level of security based on the sensitivity of the data. However, we show you how to use security as a method of choosing which device(s) may best suit your environment.

> **SECURITY THOUGHT:** Data that is so secure that it can't be accessed can produce the same result as having no data at all. Consequently, although the primary focus of this book is storage, storage networks, and more specifically, security as it relates to storage networks, we will not lose sight of the need to access data.

Who Should Read This Book

Implementing centralized storage can allow companies to gain a greater level of control over their data, while potentially saving real dollars in equipment costs and administration. However, it can also be a scary proposition if it is not met with the utmost concern for security. Therefore, anyone interested in creating a more secure centralized storage environment should read this book. It contains valuable information for IT personnel, consultants, CIOs, and technical sales personnel.

What This Book Provides

In a nutshell, this book covers storage network technologies as well as storage backup technologies, while focusing on potential data security and protection issues, including possible breaches, redundancy strategies (within the DAS/NAS/SAN framework), intrusion detection, availability, data protection, monitoring, testing, and countermeasures—all from a granular perspective. Data replication strategies and techniques as they relate specifically to NAS and SAN architectures are discussed, including RAID, cloning, snapping, remote data replication, multiple platform access security requirements, and backup strategies and technologies. We outline a sound security planning process to help ensure the integrity of centralized data, including procedural and technology answers to security issues and ways to help protect against such menaces as social engineering threats aimed at your data repository.

Keeping all these factors in mind and using the Ten Domains of Computer Security (CISSP) as a guideline, this book provides you with:

♦ A general foundation for the different types of storage technology

♦ Information about general storage network technology strengths and weaknesses

♦ Information about the security strengths and weaknesses of each type of storage network technology

♦ Assessment materials to help you select the technology that's right for your company

♦ The means to choose the right solution based on security needs

♦ The means to choose secure backup solutions

♦ Information about secure methods of implementation

♦ The framework to create, implement, and test a sound storage network security policy

♦ Information about data encryption technologies

♦ A discussion of countermeasures you can take

Because the evaluation phase, the planning phase, and the testing phase are so vitally important to the selection of, and ultimately the successful implementation of, a secure storage network, we not only cover the necessary information, we also provide samples within the text. The book's companion Web site (`www.wiley.com/compbooks/chirillo`) also provides these documents, which you can use as a baseline for your storage network security needs.

Icons Used in This Book

Icons appear in the text throughout the book to indicate important or especially helpful items. Here's a list of the icons and their functions:

NOTE: This icon provides additional or critical information and technical data on the current topic.

TIP: This icon points out useful techniques and helpful hints.

CROSS-REFERENCE: This handy icon points you to a place where you can find more information about a particular topic.

SECURITY THOUGHT: Security thoughts are simply items to think about during the security process. Sometimes this icon warns you about side effects you should watch out for or precautions you should take before doing something that may negatively impact your network or systems.

To be successful, one must surround oneself with the finest people. With that in mind, I would like to thank my wife Kristi, first and foremost, for her continued support and patience during this book's development. Next I thank my family and friends for their encouragement and confidence.

- John Chirillo -

I would like to dedicate this book to my wife Cherrie and my daughter Kyra, without whose support and understanding this project would not have been possible. I would also like to thank my family and friends for their support, encouragement, patience, and understanding during the development of this book.

- Scott Blaul -

Acknowledgments

We would also like to thank the many folks from the different manufacturers and consulting companies that contributed information to the writing of this book. We are especially grateful to Carol Long, Katie Feltman, Mark Enochs, Kevin Kent, Gabrielle Chosney, and anyone else we forgot to mention from John Wiley & Sons, Inc., David Fugate at Waterside, and technical reviewer Tom Brays.

Contents

Chapter 1
Storage Evolution

Before we dive into storage security, we take you on a brief journey back in time that allows you to reflect for a moment on where technology has been and where it is today, and why storage and storage network security are so vitally important to a company's livelihood. Accordingly, this chapter sets out definitions of key terms and explanations of key concepts and historical storage technologies, all as a starting point for a discussion of storage and storage network security.

General Terminology

Before we go any further with our discussion, it is useful to define a few key terms:

- **Storage network:** Our choice of the term *storage network* is no accident. Because storage can be implemented in different ways using different technologies (that is, DAS, NAS, SAN, and iSCSI), the term *storage network* is used to refer generically to storage implementations that provide access from many devices (homogeneous or heterogeneous) within an environment to a multiple hosts. For example, multiple storage subsystems attached directly to multiple (individual) servers using SCSI technology purely to provide shared file access can be considered as much a storage network as a network attached storage (NAS) or a storage area network (SAN) solution. It is also important to note that when the term *storage network* is used throughout this text, it includes the components of the storage network, as well as the storage device(s). For example, a SAN storage network could include host-attached, fiber arbitrated loop, or Fibre Channel switch technology. The specific hardware components, configuration, software components, and security components will be described as appropriate.

- **Direct attached storage (DAS):** In the context of this material, *direct attached storage (DAS)* is storage attached directly to a given host for the purpose of sharing data. When we refer to DAS (unless otherwise specified), assume a single host with internal storage or attached to an external storage device (not a NAS or SAN), such as a server connected to a SCSI storage subsystem.

- **Network attached storage (NAS):** *Network attached storage (NAS)* generically refers to storage that is shared over a network connection (typically Ethernet) via TCP/IP. Most often NAS devices allow files to be shared between heterogenous hosts over a network using a common file protocol. For example, files can be directly shared over a TCP/IP network without the intervention of a separate host device such as a file server.

♦ **Storage area network (SAN):** *Storage area aetwork (SAN)* generically refers to storage that is shared by multiple connected hosts typically over a fiber connection. These hosts may connect directly to the SAN, or through a fiber hub or switch. SANs are fast subnetworks, containing storage disks (and other devices such as SAN tape libraries), and SANs storage devices allow more storage space to be added that will be shared by the entire LAN and/or WAN, often without affecting services or productivity.

Why NAS or SAN?

One of the main reasons companies use NAS or SAN solutions is to "centralize" the data to get better control over their data assets. In doing so, multiple devices may connect to, have access to, or be able to "see" the NAS or SAN. The effect can be likened to a drop of water hitting a pool and causing a ripple effect (see Figure 1-1). Each ripple can contain vulnerabilities from any direction and must, therefore, be taken into account from a security perspective. Using *ripple security logic* in planning your storage network security goes a long way toward ensuring that your data is secure. Ripple logic is the backbone of secure storage.

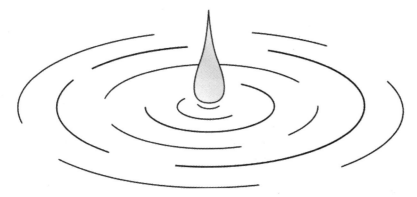

Figure 1-1: The ripple effect

From Mainframe to Distributed

In the 1980s and early 1990s, there was a movement to decentralize many of the computing resources and processes of the "big iron" mainframes in favor of distributed processing architectures as shown in Figure 1-2. Some of the distributed network architectures during that time were 3Com 3Plus Open, Appleshare/Apple Talk, LAN Manager, Novell Netware, Banyan Vines, LANtastic, MS Windows for Workgroups, and Windows NT, as well as the many derivations of UNIX, including AIX, True-64 UNIX, HP-UX, SCO, SUN Solaris, and Linux from various sources. However, some of these operating systems have all but ceased to exist. Some of the more common distributed networking architectures in use today are Novell Netware, Microsoft Windows NT4 and 2000, SUN Solaris, HP-UX, AIX, and Linux.

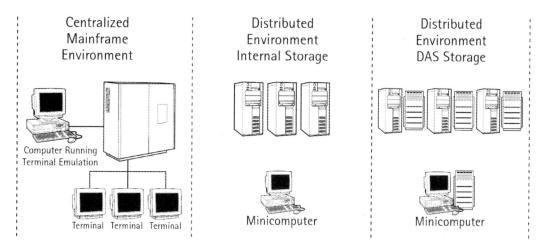

Figure 1-2: Mainframe to distributed to distributed with DAS

Hardware manufacturers leveraging the technology of distributed computing environments initially leveraged both internal and external direct attached storage (DAS) because of technical limitations (that is, distance limitations inherent in SCSI), the speed DAS could provide, the relative ease with which it could be deployed, lower cost (as compared to other available technologies), market acceptance, and many other factors. However, as companies began to overrun the capabilities of DAS, manufacturers began looking for alternatives. EMC and other companies such as IBM and Digital Equipment Corporation (DEC) had already established themselves in the mainframe market with their own large-scale storage devices. For example, according to Exodus (a cable and wireless service):

> "In 1990, EMC introduced its Symmetrix product line, becoming the first company to provide intelligent information storage systems based on arrays of small, commodity hard disk drives for the mainframe market." EMC was able to establish its Symmetrix product in the mainframe space, and subsequently, a portion of the distributed market. This was possible because "EMC extended its Symmetrix technology in 1995 to create the first-ever platform-independent storage system, capable of simultaneously supporting all major computer operating systems."

However, the Symmetrix product line required a substantial initial investment. During the late 1990s of this timeframe, Digital Equipment Corporation was struggling in the marketplace. The fact that DEC had technologically sound products like the VAX and Alpha product lines and had made a commitment to storage technology as far back as the 1970s motivated the Compaq Computer Corporation to acquire DEC for the small sum of $9.6 billion in January 1998. The reasoning behind this maneuver was as much to compete with the HPs and IBMs of the world as it was to secure DEC's products, including their storage technology. These types of scenarios play out even today, as the computer industry allows only the strongest, biggest, and most fit to survive. Note the acquisition of Compaq by Hewlett Packard Corporation in September of 2001 to form the new HP.

Distributing resources

One reason that the centralized mainframe computing model shifted to the distributed computing model (refer to Figure 1-2) was the belief that decentralization would distribute the administration throughout an organization and thus reduce the use of high-priced, outside firms to manage mini- and mainframe implementations. In some cases, the move to a distributed computing model did provide cost relief, but in many cases, it had the opposite effect. Many factors contributed to the increase in costs, but much of this increase was caused by the additional administration needed at multiple locations to handle the distributed environment.

In general, mainframe development was slow and tightly controlled. Many companies started to look for ways to develop software for the new distributed network environments that would allow them to leapfrog in front of their competition. This became obtainable because companies could now develop specific "point applications" based on a distributed platform rather than having to wait for development to occur on the mainframe. For this reason also, many companies began to migrate (not always fully) to distributed environments.

Distributing the computing resources decentralized the data, as illustrated in Figure 1-3. This shift caused the emergence of new issues concerning management (how to control the data assets), protection (how to ensure that data is protected in the event of a failure), remote availability (how to make data available remotely), and security. These issues were compounded by many contributing factors, including financial structures within organizations (departments with their own budgets, and so on), hardware limitations, and corporate politics (that is, control of the assets).

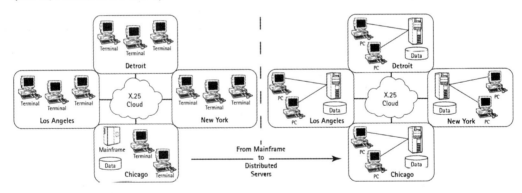

Figure 1-3: The shift from mainframe centralized data to distributed data

Corporations were also struggling with how to better control and manage their data and intellectual property, which, in a distributed environment, could be allocated among several workgroups, departments, and business units. If, for example, the accounting department has its own server with direct attached storage, its data can become "segmented" from the rest of the company's. In some cases, such segmentation may be the preferred security method, but in many cases, it causes an "out of sight, out of mind" scenario that may lead to the disclosure of sensitive information. Human resources are another good example of where this could happen. It is no secret that corporations want to (and should) keep their employee information confidential as well. In many cases this too has been accomplished by segmentation. Once the HR data network has been segmented from other networks, greater flexibility in control of data flow to the HR network/information can be obtained.

Centralized data was a byproduct of the mainframe computing model, while distributed data storage solutions came with its own risks. Those two models together gave rise to the question, "How can corporations leverage the best of both the centralized and distributed worlds?" The answer is network attached storage (NAS) and storage area network (SAN).

NAS and SAN emerge as viable alternatives to DAS

Because of the boom in storage technology, and the fact that manufacturers tout their strengths and try to mitigate their weaknesses, the terms NAS and SAN have become somewhat confusing. In other words, they can mean different things depending on which consultant, vendor, or manufacturer you talk to.

We discuss the technology and security needs of DAS, NAS, and SAN in Chapters 2, 3, and 4, respectively. For now, we merely provide a brief general description of NAS and SAN that builds on the definition we offered at the beginning of this chapter.

   ♦ NAS is generally the less expensive of the two types of centralized storage options. Depending on the vendor, NAS may support only a limited number of operating systems (one manufacturer's device may support only two platforms, Windows NT/2000 and Netware, for example), or it may support any operating system that can access it using a standard protocol/file system (TCP/IP and CIFS, for example). Because of these discrepancies from manufacturer to manufacturer, it's important to thoroughly understand the features and benefits, as well as the strengths and weaknesses, of a given NAS device.

   ♦ SAN, on the other hand, typically costs more than its NAS counterpart. In addition, a SAN is often more robust, offers more redundancy features, options, scalability, can be implemented using some type of "SAN network architecture" (very often fiber), and can usually support multiple operating systems. A SAN can oftentimes be configured to replicate data over long distances (that is, when disaster recovery is used).

In the past, many organizations could not afford to implement a NAS or SAN. With recent changes in the marketplace, however, the price of many NAS devices and some SAN devices has plummeted, making them viable alternatives for many organizations. These reduced costs allow companies to leverage the features NAS and SAN solutions offer, and the technologies are thus becoming much more commonplace. Subsequent chapters discuss how to choose the right solution based on one's security needs.

As with any new technology, the new features, requirements, and potential security issues of NAS and SAN must be dealt with while your organization fulfills its original business needs.

For these and many other reasons we discuss in subsequent chapters, the need to ensure data security and availability has become even more critical. Some key issues raised by NAS and SAN are as follows:

♦ **Renewed centralization concerns:** Many times, the phrase "putting all your eggs in one basket" has been used to downplay the role NAS or SAN can play and the cost reductions NAS and SAN technology can provide to an organization. However, if companies make the decision to "recentralize" their data using NAS or SAN without taking the proper measures to secure, back up, and replicate the data, the cliché becomes true: All the data resides in one potentially insecure, unprotected basket.

♦ **Backup windows:** Another issue that arises with NAS and SAN implementations is the available time to back up all the data (termed the *backup window*). Centralizing data means that larger amounts of data exist on a single device. It is not uncommon today for organizations to have from half a terabyte to many terabytes of data on a single device. It is also not uncommon for these same organizations to use only a small backup window (especially with global companies). Using the right tools and methodologies for data backup within the backup window has become crucial. Ensuring that the backup process is done securely is also a very important part of the equation.

♦ **New distribution issues:** The events of September 11, 2001, have forever changed the face of information and technology security. Since that date, more and more companies are looking toward NAS/SAN to protect and replicate their data. NAS and SAN implementations can go a long way toward that end by providing tools that allow data to be duplicated locally and remotely. However, doing so can require that the "centralized" data now be distributed to at least one other location, raising additional security concerns and needs.

Riding the Technology Wave

Arguably, the overall growth of the computer technology sector and its associated technological advances has been nothing short of phenomenal. If you look back to the 1980s, for example, you find that a standard IBM PC/XT computer came with an 8088 processor running at 4.77 MHz, 128 to 640K of memory, a 10 or 20MB hard drive, and a monochrome monitor. In contrast, some of today's desktop models contain 2.53 GHz processors, 3GB of memory, 120GB hard drives, AGP graphics, and a whole host of other peripherals that can be added—all at prices that boggle the mind. One of the best ways to depict this phenomenal growth is by using simple mathematical equations.

In the 1980s, a PC base unit running at 4.77 MHz (no monitor, graphics card, floppy, or hard drive) sold for approximately $1200. The following equations show that the price of a comparable system today is $60,113.

```
$1200/4.77 MHz = $25.58 per MHz
$25.58 x 2530 MHz = $60,113
```

At that price, manufacturers would not be selling anywhere near the volume of computer systems that are sold today.

> **NOTE:** Although we used the processor speed for our computation, the general concept holds true if you use memory size and speeds and hard drive size and speeds to perform the computation as well.

Not only did technology advancements take place during the 1980s and 1990s, but they took place incrementally/exponentially. As more resources were made available, less low-level programming (machine language, for example) was required to make applications perform new functions. By programming in higher-level languages, the application development and testing process was shortened, allowing software products to reach the market sooner. This shortened software-development time only added fuel to the technology growth fire.

We affectionately refer to these technology advancements as "waves" of technology. As given waves rolled into the computer technology arena, the computer industry also saw a boom in the number of computer service providers and consultants. Many companies providing these services entered the cycle late (riding on top of the wave rather than starting out when the swell began), yet touted themselves as experts. Some of these "experts" performed sub-par work for very low rates. As a result, many companies that were burned made a conscious effort to bring these services in-house. Using in-house technology services is a good idea for day-to-day operations, but can be imperfect when adopting new technology or applications.

> **NOTE:** In-house technology staff often finds that day-to-day operations take precedence over keeping up with new technologies. When this occurs, even very sound, conscientious people may not be fully prepared to deal with the issues associated with a storage network. Make sure you have the proper talent for this type of implementation. Perform tests and validation using outside firms.

As more and more applications were developed, more and more uses for these applications were identified, and needs for future application development were and continue to be identified. One common thread within applications is the need for storage: storage to install, configure, and manage the application itself, and storage for the data the application creates, evaluates, manages, and manipulates. These applications (in many cases) were placed on their own distributed platforms.

The Internet has also added to the need to store more and more data. Whether the "dot.coms" hit it big or went bust, they all had storage requirements in some form or another. In fact, this data is the only tangible asset possessed by many Internet-based businesses. For example, some Internet-based companies acquire, profile, and sell as many qualified e-mail addresses as they can get their hands on to would-be marketers. To make these addresses appealing, such companies try to get as much information as they can on the sender. The quality of the data is as important as the data itself. You can imagine the storage requirements that this type of company might have.

Past history has taught businesses many things. Internet companies learned, for example, that data can be king and that whoever has the best data can "rule"—but only as long as the data remains king.

As a result, companies are continually on a quest for the best data, which means that their storage requirements continue to grow. Even with hierarchical storage management solutions, the rate at which storage is growing makes it difficult at best to archive data (especially if the data is accessed frequently or must be available quickly, as it is in the insurance industry). It appears that a seemingly endless storage growth cycle has emerged.

So why is all this so important to the storage network explosion?

A large number of manufacturers, analysts, consultants, industry experts, and the like are saying that centralized storage is the way to go. And centralizing storage assets where possible is one way in which those assets can be better secured, controlled, and managed. However, it is also a well-known fact that once assets are centralized, the company is also vulnerable to catastrophic losses. Companies may sometimes overlook this fact in the process of centralizing data because the data is considered to be internal.

Beware: The analyst, consultant, or industry expert is often not the best choice for ensuring that your data is secure. These are the same people that may simply be "riding the wave". It's best to choose a known entity that has a storage security practice, and validate them with the services of another if possible. This may seem like overkill, but if your data is king, you can bet the revolution has begun.

To illustrate the preceding concept, the next two sections look at a fictitious, but not implausible, scenario.

The rise to the top

In this scenario, imagine that you are the MIS director of a major corporation. Company revenue per annum is $4.5 billion. Thirty percent of this revenue is generated from Web sales, with over 45,000,000 distinct transactions per year. The current infrastructure is comprised of distributing platforms with distributed data structures (assume separate servers with direct attached storage, although this scenario could be distributed in other fashions as well). Due to the current design of the environment, each new requirement for increased storage (assuming DAS has been maxed out) results in the addition of more storage as well as a new server, Network Operating System (NOS), storage subsystem, tape backup system (to accommodate the backup window), tape backup software, anti-virus software, and any other specialized devices or software used on the server or to manage the server, such as remote access devices and monitoring software. Once purchased, the equipment must be configured, tested, and integrated into the environment. Even in the most automated of environments, the costs mount up pretty quickly (not to mention the additional administration that is needed).

Because of these recurring cost factors, and because your favorite equipment provider and/or consultant is telling you that centralization is the wave of the future, you decide that centralizing your data is the way to go. You do your homework and start to look at the possible technologies that fit your company's needs. You enlist the assistance of your favorite equipment provider and/or consultant, and the barrage of options comes pouring in.

The pure equipment provider talks about features, options, pricing, availability, installation/rollout, and maintenance, while the consultant usually discusses speeds, feeds, topologies, bells and whistles, compatibility, scalability, ubiquity, backup solutions, and integration (the really good ones also discuss security in great detail). You can now begin the process of building your evaluation plan.

You've evaluated technology-related products several times before, so you pull out one of your old templates and start to revise it to accommodate your new storage network project. You are careful to make sure that you modify areas to ensure that devices that connect to the storage network and their associated data are taken into account. About midway through the revision, you realize that you need to incorporate security concerns into your new plan. Using a copy of your server security plan as a template, you begin to incorporate security information into your project plan. Realizing that it is probably a good idea to get some assistance because you need to ensure proper security, you turn to your favorite commodity equipment provider (after all, they've done great work in the past). You send them the documents to be reviewed and modified.

When you receive the documents back from the equipment provider, you notice that several security items were added. They appear to be well thought out and complete. You decide to use these items to begin the evaluation process. An evaluation matrix is created to summarize the responses for each question in the evaluation, as well as a rating scale to keep track of the pros and cons of each product.

You meet with vendor after vendor, manufacturer after manufacturer, and consultant after consultant. As you go through the evaluation with each of them, you carefully place their answers into the appropriate category. The rating associated with each answer is placed into the rating scale previously created. The matrix and rating scale are tallied, and the top four respondents are selected.

Round two begins. The evaluation criteria and matrix are once again modified to ensure compatibility, supportability, ease of use, and the like within your environment. You tour the facilities of each of the top four respondents, where they demonstrate their prospective solutions to your needs. Using the new matrix, each respondent is re-evaluated. Based on the current needs of the company, the features, speeds and feeds, management tools, and the other bells and whistles each vendor touts, you decide that a SAN is the best solution for your company's data centralization needs.

Assuming that price is no object (which is seldom the case), you choose the product that most closely fits your technology needs. That product is XYZ Company's "Invisible SAN." The vendor has provided good pricing on both the equipment and installation services. You provide the vendor with the necessary quote and installation information to include training and documentation requirements. You begin the procurement process.

Once the vendor receives the order, they inform you that the equipment should arrive in a few weeks and tentatively schedule an installation date. The equipment arrives, and the scheduled installation begins. The installation team does an excellent job of installing the equipment and addressing the few minor issues that arise. Each of the devices that required access to the SAN are set up, connected, and tested. The configuration and management utilities are installed and tested. Your provider ensures that you receive the training, documentation, and maintenance information as required by the original quote. Furthermore, they verify that the security measures (as outlined in the evaluation criteria) have also been met by providing you with the documentation on how they were addressed. You review the installation process with your team, ensure they have received all the necessary training and documentation, and collectively agree that the installation is complete. Congratulations—you are now the owner of a new SAN, which was implemented on time and even slightly under budget.

But don't start working on that employee-of-the-year speech just yet!

The bottom falls out

The CEO, executive staff, and board of directors applaud your effort. After all, a SAN can be a huge investment for a company, and you were able to pull it off on time and under budget. Everything is going great, until you get a call from the CEO indicating that he just got a call from one of the shareholders. It seems that an e-mail was sent to one of the company's competitors that contained some of the company's (confidential) data. Among this data were client records, including purchasing habits, invoicing requirements, payment methods, and in many cases, credit card information. The CEO wants you to find out ASAP how they got this information. (Remember that the chance of the CEO being calm is highly unlikely in a situation as serious as this.) You assemble your team, call in a security expert, and begin to research how this could have happened.

The first order of business is to ensure that the breach does not continue to occur. At this point you don't know how or where the breach occurred, so your only course of action may be to bring down the services that are pertinent to this data. Yes, this means downtime. In fact, the seriousness of the situation will probably require a consultation with the CEO (not a fun position for anyone to be in).

The next step is to determine the best way to get at the root of the problem. With the help of your security expert, you begin to build a step-by-step action plan in which you examine all logs that may contain pertinent information. This process could take weeks, given the potential number of logs that may have to be searched.

While you are searching through the logs, you must also determine if specific accounts were used to gain access to the hijacked information, and if so, which ones. You have your administration team search for anomalies in the user authentication process. Since your customers order merchandise off your Web site, you assemble another group to look specifically at Web access, Web accounts, and potential holes in the security.

You meet with the appropriate officers within the company to determine if this breach should be reported. Once the report has been filed, it will very likely become public knowledge, which means that it may affect the confidence your customers have in purchasing products electronically (and other methods) from you. For now, the officers determine not to disclose the breach until its method and scope have been identified. However, the general consensus is to report it once the source has been determined and protected against.

Because legal action may occur, additional "cyberinvestigators" are brought in. Throughout the process you, your team, and the cyberinvestigator(s) compile all the information, taking care to ensure that the evidence is documented, provable, and remains available for future reference.

This process continues for several months. The cost of the investigation continues to mount. The losses in revenue, customer confidence, and productivity continue to add to the cost incurred, and the CEO and board of directors start looking for someone to blame.

Who do you think the most likely candidate will be?

Now, instead of working on your employee-of-the-year speech, you're trying to ensure you won't be looking for a new job.

> **NOTE:** Realize that the preceding scenario is not a scare tactic. This type of situation happens time and time again to very good people with the best of intentions. They are only guilty of not having the knowledge and the right tools (for whatever reason) to minimize the risk of a security breach.

The plan has to work

The MIS director in our scenario was only performing what he thought were the proper steps to protect the company by using a proven plan. However, applying a proven plan that doesn't fully take into account storage security concerns is an all too common error. An astute security professional would realize that our MIS director could have addressed certain areas more thoroughly. Some of the "holes" he left include:

- Minimal business needs validation
- Missing preplanning technical requirements phase
- Missing preplanning security requirements phase
- No standards definitions
- No risk assessment
- No selection criteria for the security team(s)
- No presite security audit
- No presite technical audit
- No findings review
- No revalidation of business, technical, and security needs
- Not choosing the right help
- No data classification procedures
- Lack of identified countermeasures and procedures
- Lack of environment security procedures

- Lack of data protection procedures
- Missing disaster plan and what security requirements it entails
- No standards of security methodology used
- No testing program
- No outside validation
- Failure to assess legal ramifications (for example, government requirements or potential litigation exposure)

This is just a representative sampling of some of the areas that were not addressed, but this is representative of typical behavior and issues that often occur when implementing centralized storage. We cover more of these areas as they relate to storage network and data security in subsequent chapters of this text.

Real-world examples

Do you think that our hypothetical example is too far-fetched? Consider this real-world example from the book *The CISSP Prep Guide* published by John Wiley & Sons, Inc. (2001):

"One day last year, the CEO of a large media company received an alarming e-mail. The sender said he had gained access to the computer system of the CEO's company. If the CEO were willing to pay a large sum of money, the sender would reveal the weaknesses that he had found in the company's computer system. Just to ensure that he was taken seriously, several sensitive files (including photographs) that could only have come from the company's network were attached to the e-mail."

Sound familiar?

The account goes on to describe the months of effort it took to arrest the culprits. By that time, a great deal of damage had been incurred, and the cost in terms of both money and resources was substantial. For example, while the security breach was being resolved, the company most likely ceased implementations of any new products and features. Also, much of the normal work process was likely interrupted, causing a backlog. These kinds of events could cause a company to miss a small window in a given market, resulting in even more lost revenues. It's no secret that the cost of a breach can be exponential compared to the cost of the data itself.

> **SECURITY THOUGHT:** Just as an accounting company should not audit itself, the company that helps you protect your data should not perform security audits on its own work. Select a separate company to perform the security audits.

Numerous companies have experienced security breaches, and more of these breaches occur every day. Oftentimes, we don't hear about these incidents because companies are reluctant to report them, fearing the potential publicity and negative impact they will almost certainly have on their business operations. At the very least, such publicity results in a loss of consumer confidence, and ultimately, in lost revenue.

Mark Lewis, a site editor at www.searchStorage.com, posted an article titled "Unsecure SANs Invitation for Hackers" on March 26, 2002. In that article, Lewis discusses weaknesses in SANs configurations and cites Himanshu Dwivedi, managing security architect at @stake, Inc., as saying, "Ninety-nine percent of unauthorized users get into the network because of bad configuration, not by some elite, super method." The article goes on to suggest solutions offered by Dwivedi and by Ray Drake, who manages a 200-server data center for Lincoln Electric System in Lincoln, Nebraska, that is in the midst of a SAN implementation and security audit. Dwivedi and Drake suggest segmentation, layering, and proactive security auditing as vital approaches to securing a SAN.

Example article 1

Originally published on SearchStorage.com, a TechTarget community. Copyright 2002, TechTarget, Inc.

Unsecure SANs Invitation for Hackers

By Mark Lewis, Site Editor
March 26, 2002, SearchStorage

Storage Area Networks (SANs) may be the future of networked storage, but the networking technology could be an open invitation for hackers to access your data.

According to Himanshu Dwivedi, managing security architect at @stake, Inc., and a speaker at the SearchStorage.com Storage Management 2002 conference held in Chicago last week, SANs are a gateway for hackers to tap into a businesses' network.

The weakest link: The Fibre Channel connection.

"Hackers will try to gain access through the path of least resistance," said Dwivedi. "We are seeing the same problems in the Fibre Channel that you saw in the IP networked–based world in the late 80s."

One of the things storage administrators do have going for them, notes Dwivedi, is that they know exactly how their networks are configured.

"Ninety-nine percent of unauthorized users get into the network because of bad configuration, not by some elite, super method," said Dwivedi. "The biggest problem a hacker has is figuring out what your SAN looks like."

There are some short-term solutions that were recommended by Dwivedi. He says there are two major areas where administrators can shore up their SANs. The first is by segmentation. This means a logical segmentation of management traffic from data traffic. Most hackers, Dwivedi said, will logically be going after a company's most prized data.

The second is in the switch configuration. Under this umbrella, there are three areas to secure the network; Simple Name Server hard and soft zoning, port binding and port type controls.

Aside from these solutions, users break it down to a more simple solution.

"The main thing about security is just being proactive," said Ray Drake from Lincoln Electric System in Lincoln, Neb.

Drake, who manages a 200-server data center, is also in the middle of a major SAN implementation and security audit with an outside consulting firm.

"We are in the middle of a SAN implementation, but at the same time we are also in the fifth or sixth month of a security analysis. Once we complete that, we'll have a better idea where the holes are," said Drake.

Dwivedi also recommends that storage professionals consider the amount of layers internal and external users see.

"You have to make it difficult for the hackers. Six or seven layers may not be enough; a single compromised server may open the gateway to a SAN," said Dwivedi. "One to two layers is also not enough for the internal network."

Example article 2

Published on The Register.co.uk.

Myth of Storage Security Savaged

By John Leyden
Posted January 24, 2002

Storage security will become an "imperative" this year as the adoption of Internet technologies undermines the comforting notion that storage networks are safe from hacker attacks.

In an analysis of storage security, the Yankee Group concludes that security will become an essential aspect of deployment strategies as users expand disaster recovery planning or roll out storage networks that mix multiple network protocols.

Yankee is seeking to dispel the impression that dedicated, Fibre Channel storage networks are "closed" networks, i.e., not subject to security breaches. As mixed IP-Fibre Channel storage networks or IP storage networks become deployed, security will be even more important, the research house argues.

"Customers have used a combination of zoning and LUN masking to segregate how users and servers connect to SANs, but both methods still can offer holes to hackers by being difficult to configure and manage as the number of network nodes increases," Yankee analyst Jamie Gruener writes.

"The emergence of IP-based storage networks will increase the need for specific storage security policies, due to increased complexity of managing these mixed networks."

Vendors have announced products which protect the integrity of data through software management tools, at the storage array levels, within the storage network switch, and in dedicated function storage security processors.

Brocade, the largest storage networking vendor, has promised to deliver new security features through its Fabric OS management software. Emerging firms are also carving a niche. For example, FalconStor is offering key-based encryption as part of its virtualisation software and NetOctave, an IP chip vendor, has launched a security processor designed specifically for the storage market.

Yankee adds a caveat to this by saying there isn't a standard way to solve the storage security problem and the market hasn't got beyond the delivery of point products. Storage vendors need to take an active role in promoting storage security best practices and technologies—or risk a backlash, Yankee warns.

Gruener said: "Without adequate strategies to help customers deal with the emerging storage security problem, vendors will likely be susceptible to customer scrutiny in the longer term as the level of complexity and exposure for breaches increases."

Example article 3

Published on ChannelSuperSearch.com.

How Secure Is IP-Based Storage?

By Sonia R. Lelii
VARBusiness
Posted January 31, 2002

Wayne Lam, co-founder and vice-president of FalconStor Software in Melville, N.Y., has a word of caution for administrators toying with the idea of putting storage data on an Internet protocol (IP) network where hackers, viruses and denial-of-service attacks are a daily threat: "Mimicking or hijacking an IP address is child's play," he says. "My 6-year-old can do it. IP is very easy to hack, unfortunately."

By and large, in the past few years, the storage world has been immune from such security threats. Built-in capabilities such as zoning, host masking, and logical unit numbers (LUNs) have kept the peace among servers by designating disk space. Consolidating storage into Storage Area Networks (SANs) has paved the way for less distributed storage, thereby reducing access.

But Fibre Channel's shortcomings, including its expense and lack of interoperability, have opened the door for companies such as Cisco Systems, FalconStor, IBM, Nishan Systems, and SANValley Systems to design switches and solutions using IP and Ethernet networks to transport storage. IP's best attribute is that it is ubiquitous and less costly: More than 90 percent of networks are based on it. But by bringing IP back into the storage environment, are VARs opening the door to all the security concerns that come along with it?

"Remember, an IP-based storage server is just as vulnerable as anything else on IP," says Michael Karp, an analyst with Enterprise Management Association, Boulder, Colo. "All the security problems associated with IP don't go away. Once data is out there in transmission, anything can capture it."

Trying to stay one step ahead of the naysayers, companies including FalconStor and Nishan have installed security mechanisms within their IP storage products before the iSCSI protocol is even standardized. For instance, Nishan staged a demonstration last year in which the company simulated a wide area IP-based SAN and used SonicWall GX–series Internet security appliances to encrypt data flowing through an exposed link. Meanwhile, FalconStor has installed a key-based authentication mechanism in its IP Stor software that creates virtualized SANs and NAS. In addition, SANValley Systems' SL1000 IP-SAN gateway has software-based authentication and authorization security capabilities, and the San Jose, Calif.–based company plans to add hardware-based encryption as well.

"Security requires backward thinking," says Pete Lindstrom, an analyst with the Hurwitz Group. "It's not about 'How do I make things work?' It's about 'How do I break it?' People assume technology will be used the way it was intended. But in security, the idea is how to use it in completely unintended ways," he says. "Security often has taken a back seat to functionality. That's the traditional challenge we face."

Fibre Channel Not Bulletproof

In a recent interview, James Staten, director of strategy at Sun Microsystems, revealed Fibre Channel's dirty little secret: A protocol designed specifically for storage traffic, Fibre Channel security is limited to zoning, host masking, and LUNs. "If you think IP has holes, wait until you see Fibre Channel," Staten says. "It has almost no security."

The masking and LUN capabilities are in place to keep the peace among servers by blocking off portions of disk space, instead of letting each server think it controls all the storage. It's the equivalent of limiting what you can see by covering your left eye.

Fibre Channel was designed with the presumption that storage would exist on a dedicated network, far removed and isolated from the reach of most end users, except for a few IT managers. More stringent security mechanisms were not incorporated into the protocol because it was assumed that storage would be isolated from typical messaging traffic making its way through the Internet.

"How do you secure a Storage Area Network in today's environment?" FalconStor's Lam asks. "Quite frankly," he answers, "there is no security. And that is why people don't talk about it."

The issue is particularly thorny for those in the storage service-provider market, where data from 20,000 companies may be in colocations across the country. Proponents of IP storage use that to their advantage to build a case for putting storage on an IP network. Unlike Fibre Channel, IP networks have at least 20 years of practical experience. The IP security (IPSec) protocol standard, which includes authentication, authorization, and encryption, is prevalent in many existing products, making it easy for companies like Nishan Systems to add security functions into their products through partnerships.

"Today, the chipsets that do IPSec encryption are available, and you can integrate them right into your products," says Tom Clark, director of technical marketing at Nishan Systems. "The encryption functionality is already stable. It's standards-based, so we don't have to go through the arduous task of engineering a security solution from scratch."

Encryption may be one of the highest levels of security out there, but even that technology can't protect environments from the nefarious e-mail carrying a virus. The only way to ensure against that is to make sure end users are on high alert for any e-mail with an unusual attachment.

"I'm not sure there are easy solutions to this," says Sandy Helton, CTO and executive vice-president of SANValley Systems.

"You can only attack certain problems with certain solutions. Traffic may be authorized, but it may also be malicious. And once it's inside, it can wreak havoc."

Too much hype?

Even if you don't subscribe to the likelihood of being hacked, there are many other facets of storage security (data protection) that you must consider. (We use the term *data protection* because that's the overall goal of storage security: to keep your data safe and secure.)

A case can be made for almost any scenario, but the fact is, no matter how unlikely the odds, if you have considered it you should document it and address it or rule it out as a viable risk. Later in this book during our discussion on data protection, we outline a solid security plan that helps you select and secure the right storage technology for you. For now, consider the following scenarios and think about the likelihood that one of these events could occur within your environment.

♦ Flood

♦ Fire

♦ Equipment-damaging electrical surge (lightning, for example)

♦ Accidental erasure of data (storage management)

♦ Unauthorized access (not a hacker) to data (internal or external)

♦ Transported backup tapes falling into the wrong hands

♦ Employee burning a CD with account data so they can work at home

♦ Improperly configured storage device

♦ Using NAS running IP and CIFS/NFS without proper IP security

♦ Using a Fibre Channel infrastructure with no zones (or zones that are improperly configured)

♦ Serving up LUNs to multiple or the wrong devices

♦ Creating multiple tape backup copies (on-site and off-site storage)

♦ Virus attacks

♦ Improperly configured management and/or monitoring software

♦ Installation documentation

♦ Redundancy

This list is just a very small sample of some of the storage network security concerns that must be addressed. Some could be considered true disasters; others are matters of general security, and some matters of storage security. However, the likelihood of each of these events occurring can play a critical role as you select your storage solution and ultimately create a secure storage network.

Plans to mitigate or prevent each of these events (and others to be discussed in later chapters) should be incorporated into your security plan.

SECURITY THOUGHT: The process of designing a secure storage network should be thought of primarily as a reverse engineering process. The goal of a hacker or malicious code may not be to disclose the data; it may be simply to break the storage network—in other words, prevent authorized individuals from using it.

The Ten Domains of Computer Security

Many individuals and companies make the potentially fatal mistake of looking at security from a technology-only standpoint. Many of the companies we have dealt with still base their sense of security on the quality of their firewall and anti-virus protection. Although such measures are vital components in creating a secure network and ultimately a secure storage network, they are simply not enough. In environments where the customer is not technology-savvy, even firewalls that perform their jobs flawlessly could make potential losses worse because these devices may provide the user with a false sense of security (through no fault of the product or manufacturer).

A similar potentially fatal mistake argument can be made for organizations that realize that security planning and process are vital, but fail to adopt a sound methodology as a measuring stick.

In our travels, the most secure organizations combine the best security practices and technology and use a sound methodology as a measuring stick. These organizations realize the importance of using a methodology such as the Ten Domains of Computer Security.

Throughout the computer technology industry, one of the most commonly accepted validations of security competence is the Certified Information Systems Security Professional (CISSP) program. This program validates that the individual who possesses the certification has achieved competency in the Ten Domains of Computer Security, and has the support of others validating that claim.

The Ten Domains of Computer Security are:

1. Security Management Practices
2. Access Control Systems
3. Telecommunications and Network Security
4. Cryptography
5. Security Architectures and Models
6. Operations Security
7. Applications and Systems Development
8. Business Continuity and Disaster Recovery Planning
9. Law, Investigation, and Ethics
10. Physical Security

As we discuss DAS, NAS, and SAN security, we correlate the different security components to these domains to ensure they can be applied within your environment. Numerous materials and books can be found on the Ten Domains of Computer Security and the CISSP program, so we do not include them here. However, we do include relevant portions of each domain as they pertain to storage network security.

This is an important distinction from many other materials as we depart from much of the philosophical security outlines and topics, and apply security using a standard methodology (using a how-to approach where possible) to your storage network needs, allowing us to demonstrate actual use versus philosophical use.

SECURITY THOUGHT: It is not possible to achieve 100 percent security and still provide access to the data! For this reason, you should use a formal process to classify data, perform a risk analysis, and evaluate risk versus cost of security. There will likely be scenarios where the cost to secure a component dramatically outweighs the risk. When this is the case, it may be necessary to accept the risk.

Summary

Our first chapter starts out by discussing the general differences between DAS, NAS, and SAN. Because much of the marketplace has blurred the distinction between these technologies, we provide more complete definitions for each.

Next, we provide some history on where technology and more specifically storage technology has been, where it is today, and where it is going, including why companies are centralizing data on NAS and SAN platforms. This history is supplemented by several scenarios (fictitious and real) and examples of security issues and breaches. These examples highlight the critical importance of storage network security to you and your company.

Security is only as good as the program behind it. Although no one can provide a 100 percent guarantee that security will never be breached, using sound security practices, processes, procedures, and technology, coupled with a sound industry standard methodology, provides the best means of protection available today.

In subsequent chapters, we apply these concepts to storage network security and try to give you a much better understanding of the potential risks, the methods of mitigating those risks, and the ways to ensure that your decisions not to address the risks do not come back to haunt you.

Chapter 2
Direct Attached Storage (DAS)

In Chapter 1, we mentioned that "multiple storage subsystems attached directly to multiple (individual) servers using SCSI technology, purely to provide shared file access, can be considered as much a storage network as a network attached storage (NAS) or a storage area network (SAN) solution." This is an important fact to remember when creating a secure storage network environment. It is also important to note that in most environments that use NAS or SAN solutions, there will likely be hosts that contain or are connected to their storage directly. In many of these cases, the devices remain because they serve a very specific role within the environment and/or because they aren't capable of attaching to the storage network device (due to lack of device driver support, for example). Oftentimes, you find "standalone" hosts—with associated storage—and/or multiple directly attached storage devices located in remote sites.

As with most technologies, using DAS may provide better security than a NAS or SAN in some situations, while in other situations it may not. This can and should be an important— maybe the ultimate—determining factor when selecting a DAS, NAS, or SAN. Gaining "security advantages" wherever possible should be the main goal.

If we eliminate political motivations and cost/price from the equation, we can better focus on the technology and security factors of a given solution. Once these factors have been outlined, we can add them back into the equation to determine if a given solution is right for your environment.

Finally, as we progress through this book, we build on the information and security factors outlined in each chapter to provide a comprehensive methodology for selecting a secure storage solution. Chapter 7 covers the culmination of these building blocks.

What Is Direct Attached Storage?

Although *direct attached storage (DAS), direct access storage device (DASD),* and *server attached storage (SAS)* are terms that are often used interchangeably, their meanings aren't exactly the same. For example, *DASD* was a common term used in the mini- and mainframe computer world to describe magnetic disk media that was directly accessible by the mini- or mainframe, whereas *SAS* was used to generically describe storage that was attached to a "server" rather than a mainframe. The term *DAS* can create even more confusion because it can refer to either. For our purposes, the term DAS will refer to storage that is either internal or directly connected to a single host for the primary purpose of sharing the storage with other devices.

> **NOTE:** We do not include cases where a NAS may be used for a single host or a SAN may be connected to a single host. These are covered separately in Chapters 3 and 4. Data backup solutions are also covered in Chapter 6.

When most people hear the term DAS, they usually think of a single host connected to an external storage device—sometimes called a storage subsystem. However, it is equally important to include internal storage housed in a host in most DAS discussions because many manufacturers have integrated the same features and functionality for either/both internally or externally connected drives.

Since the term *DAS* is generic in nature, it can also be used to refer to other types of storage devices that can be directly attached, such as magnetic tape devices and optical devices. When discussing DAS, therefore, it is important to clearly understand the context and use of the term. For now, the primary components of our DAS discussion focus on DAS technology and connection methods.

Understanding DAS Technology

Storage devices can be directly attached to a host in a variety of ways. Although the prevalent thinking within the computer industry is that DAS is a SCSI subsystem technology of some sort (SCSI-1 through UltraX SCSI), connected to a host using a SCSI controller, it is important to note that many technologies can be used as DAS, including:

- Serial Storage Architecture (SSA)
- Universal Serial Bus (USB V1.1, USB V2.0)
- IEEE 1394 (Firewire)
- High Performance Parallel Interface (HiPPI)
- Integrated Drive Electronics (IDE)/Advanced Technology Attachment (ATA)
- The many versions and variations of Small Computer System Interface (SCSI) (for example, SCSI-1 through Ultra3 SCSI or differential SCSI)
- Ethernet
- iSCSI
- Fibre Channel

Not only can these technologies be used as DAS, but you must also consider the additional features available in a given manufacturer's implementation of the technology. Such features may include Redundant Array of Inexpensive (or Independent) Drives (RAID) with varying RAID levels (0-53 for example) or even High Voltage Differential (HVD) or Low Voltage Differential (LVD) SCSI technology. Considering such features may move a standard implementation to a nonstandard or proprietary implementation. This is often favorable from a security perspective.

> **NOTE:** A good description of RAID levels can be found by searching for "RAID levels defined" on your favorite search engine. This will bring up both vendor and generic definitions.

In addition to considering the various features, you must also consider the administrative, management, and monitoring options that may accompany each technology. However, if you place these items "on the back burner," remember that the underlying selection criteria is generally performance, and performance is most often judged by data throughput (in other words, by how quickly data can be read/written).

There certainly is no shortage of material available to help you choose a DAS technology to suit your performance needs, and since performance is such a critical factor when evaluating storage requirements, oftentimes the technology that provides the "best performance" will win—possibly at the expense of security considerations.

How many storage decisions concerning DAS involve a good quality security evaluation as part of the storage technology selection process? Where do the security concerns of selecting a specific technology come into play? If two DAS technologies provide similar performance (and features), would it make sense to include security as part of the DAS storage evaluation criteria (or any other storage evaluation criteria)? We certainly think so! But the sad fact is that most storage decisions are based almost exclusively on speeds, feeds, features, benefits, and cost (and not necessarily in that order). In addition, many times inherent security is a lessor factor because there are tangent solutions available and third-party options such as encryption.

In order to answer the preceding questions, you must understand a little bit about the DAS technologies and how they interact with both the host and the storage media. We will discuss different versions of SCSI, IDE, SSA, USB, Firewire, and HiPPI in the following sections. Although it is possible to use Ethernet, iSCSI, and Fibre Channel technologies to directly attach a storage device to a host, they are more often used as storage network devices and will thus be discussed later in the chapters on NAS and SAN technologies, respectively.

Serial Storage Architecture

Serial Storage Architecture (SSA) is a high-performance open storage interface with the following features:

- SSA is a high-speed (up to 160 Mbps) serial connection technology.
- SSA uses a 4-wire connection rather than multiple wire connections like those of SCSI (parallel connection) and other parallel technologies.
- SSA is typically connected in a loop configuration similar to that of FDDI, and can support up to 128 devices using either copper or fiber cabling.
- Transmissions on the loop can occur bidirectionally.
- Distances between devices can range from 15 meters to 10 kilometers.

♦ SSA was originally designed by IBM as an alternative to the SCSI architecture.

♦ SSA has not yet gained widespread acceptance, and will probably lose out to some of the other up-and-coming technologies.

♦ SSA provides higher fault tolerance through multiple path design and early error detection.

On an SSA topology, data is transmitted using frames. SSA uses Control, Application, and Privileged frames. The frame and field format is listed as follows:

Flag	Control	Address	Data	CRC	Flag
	2 to 6 bits	1 to 6 bytes	Up to 128 bytes	4 bytes	

SSA will automatically create a logical web when initialized using *configurators* and *responders*. For example, devices that are aware of the SSA web—such as the SSA host adapter—are configurators. A disk device would be a responder. Figure 2-1 illustrates a sample SSA topology. Much like FDDI used for network connectivity, this design reduces single points of failure. Each SSA adapter also has split/independent circuitry. SSA can also be configured using switch technology.

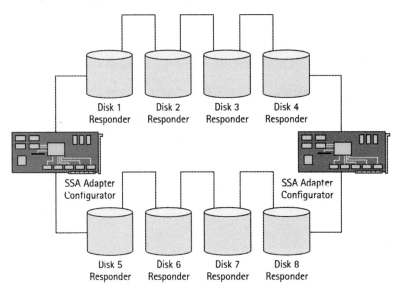

Figure 2-1: Serial Storage Architecture (SSA) redundancy

Universal Serial Bus

Beginning in 1996, USB was developed by Compaq, DEC, IBM, Intel, Microsoft, NEC, and Nortel primarily to allow multiple peripherals to be connected using a higher speed, more flexible serial technology. They were successful, as can be evidenced by the fact that there are adapter types that include USB to SCSI, USB to parallel, USB to serial, and USB to RJ-45. Devices can be added and removed without powering down the computer.

Storage devices are being created to use USB because of its flexibility including CD-R and CD-RW drives, USB hard drives, USB tape drives, with more to come. Although the performance is not there yet, some companies have leveraged USB to create smaller, multidisk storage networks using software to share the devices. USB has also been used in some environments (in similar fashion) to create portable images. For these reasons, USB warrants discussion.

♦ Two versions of Universal Serial Bus have been developed: V1.1 and V2.0. USB V1.1 operates in a range from 1.5 Mbps to 12 Mbps, and V2.0 operates at up to 480 Mbps (although the single device sustained rate is about 53 Mbps).

♦ USB uses a 4-wire connection (2 for data and 2 that carry 5-volt DC).

♦ Up to 127 devices can be connected. Low port density (4, for example) USB hubs have become quite common and inexpensive.

♦ Transmissions occur serially.

♦ Distance specified device-to-device or device-to-hub is 3 to 5 meters or 10 to 16.5 feet. Up to 5 hubs can be chained together to achieve longer distances.

♦ USB has gained widespread acceptance, and with additional advancements in speed and performance will likely continue to do so.

On a USB topology, data is transmitted using four packet types: Start of Frame, Handshake, Token, and Data. Host-to-device communication is used. Figure 2-2 illustrates a logical USB host device configuration using four USB ports.

Firewire

Firewire (IEEE 1394) was originally developed by Apple to allow multiple peripherals to be connected using a higher-speed, more flexible serial technology. Unlike USB however, Firewire was designed with devices that needed more bandwidth in mind. Such devices as camcorders, hard disk drives, and high-speed printers are prime candidates for Firewire. Devices can be added and removed without powering down the computer.

As with USB (V2.0), devices such as CD-R, CD-RW, and DVD-RW can leverage the speed and flexibility of Firewire. Firewire hard drives have also been used in some larger Apple environments (similar to how USB was used in larger environments) to create shared storage and portable images. One of the unique differences between Firewire and USB is that Firewire devices can communicate peer-to-peer, whereas USB devices must communicate to a host. Therefore, Firewire devices can communicate directly without host intervention. Firewire features are summarized as follows:

♦ Firewire can handle speeds up to 400 Mbps, with plans to handle over 3 Gbps in future releases.

- It uses a 6-wire connection (4 for data and 2 that carry 5-volt DC).
- Up to 63 devices can be connected.
- Transmissions occur serially.
- Distance specified using standard cables is up to 4.5 meters or 14.85 feet. Repeaters allow a device to be up to 236 feet from the source.
- Firewire has gained "good" acceptance because its initial release had higher speeds than USB. If it continues to stay ahead of USB in the speed category, it could become even more widespread.

Firewire uses four protocol layers to transfer data: the serial bus management layer, the physical layer, the link layer, and the transaction layer. Figure 2-3 illustrates an IEEE 1394 configuration.

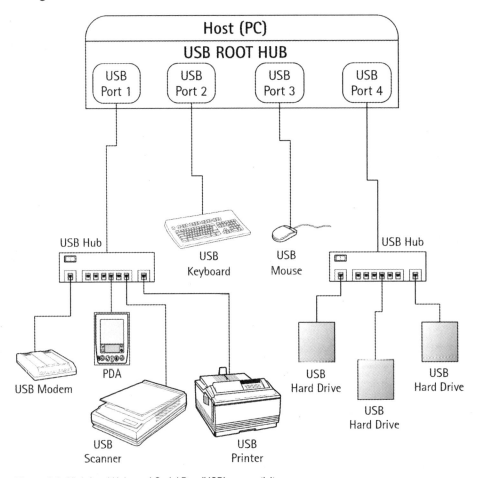

Figure 2-2: High-level Universal Serial Bus (USB) connectivity

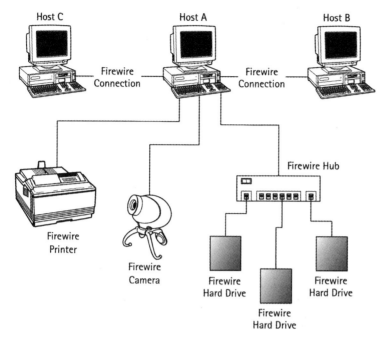

Figure 2-3: IEEE 1394 Firewire network

Since Firewire can establish relationships on a peer-to-peer basis, each of the hosts at the top of Figure 2-3 can communicate with the devices at the bottom of the figure. Devices can also communicate directly—from a camera to a hard drive or printer, for example.

High Performance Parallel Interface/Gigabyte System Network

Relating to storage, High Performance Parallel Interface/Gigabyte System Network— otherwise known as HiPPI/GSN—is an ANSI X3T9.3 standard that has been used primarily to connect high-speed storage (DAS) to mainframe and supercomputers. HiPPI technology is expensive, and its use is not considered widespread when compared to other technologies.

NOTE: HiPPI is also well-suited for network backbone connections and for clustering devices that need high-speed connections. However, its expense can cause it to be prohibitive as an alternative.

HiPPI's flexibility extends beyond simply allowing parallel connections for DAS. Because of its speed, it can be used in many forms, including HiPPI serial (Fiber) and HiPPI-SC (Switch Control).

♦ Currently, HiPPI can handle speeds up to 1600 Mbps, with development of 6400 Mbps or SuperHiPPI underway. Thirty-two parallel data bits are used to yield up to 800 Mbps throughput, while 64 parallel data bits are used to yield up to 1.6 Gbps.

- ◆ HiPPI uses a 50-pin connector for 800 Mbps HiPPI and a 100-pin connector (actually two 50-pin connectors) for 1.6 Gbps HiPPI.

- ◆ Transmission occurs using 32- or 64-bit parallel connections.

- ◆ Distance specified using standard cables is up to 25 meters, or 82.5 feet. Fiber extenders enable a device to be up to 10 kilometers, or 6.2 miles, from the source.

- ◆ HiPPI is a proven technology that has gained acceptance. However, HiPPI's cost has typically restricted its use—outside of some mainframe and supercomputers—to high-speed, fault-tolerant hosts like Alpha, Tandem, and Sun Microsystems (for example, PCI HiPPI cards). Keep in mind that HiPPI is not as widely accepted as other less expensive technologies. Nonetheless, it is considered widely used in its given market segment and, given that it provides speeds up to 6.4 Gbps, it could become a viable alternative for other markets if costs become more competitive.

HiPPI technology uses different protocols to provide different functionality. The physical layer protocol that defines the mechanical, electrical, and signaling characteristics of HiPPI are defined in HiPPI-PH. HiPPI uses the HiPPI Framing Protocol (HiPPI-FP) to build its frames, while HiPPI-SC defines the switching protocol. HiPPI-LE, HiPPI-FC, and HiPPI-IPI define ways to allow HiPPI to map to other protocols.

Figure 2-4 illustrates some of the ways HiPPI can be used to connect both internal devices and remote locations using fiber extenders.

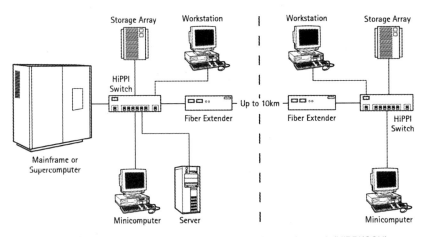

Figure 2-4: High Performance Parallel Interface/Gigabyte System Network (HiPPI/GSN) usage

Integrated Drive Electronics/Advanced Technology Attachment

Integrated Drive Electronics (IDE) technology is used in the majority of today's PC-based systems. It is less expensive than some of the other technologies and provides good (though not fabulous) performance. Advanced Technology Attachment (ATA) is an extension of the IDE bus and is the official name used by ANSI. Each IDE controller can connect to two IDE devices in a master and slave configuration.

Many manufacturers produce devices—including (but not limited to) hard drives, CD-Rs, CD-RWs, DVDs, and DVD-RWs—that can connect to IDE controllers.

Some of the key features of IDE/ATA are as follows:

♦ IDE throughput rates vary dramatically depending on bus implementation and configuration, but speeds of 65 Mbps to 1 Gbps are possible using striping techniques.

♦ IDE devices use a 40-pin connection.

♦ Two devices per IDE channel are possible. In fact, two IDE channels are common in today's machines.

♦ IDE transmissions occur in parallel rather than serially.

♦ The maximum cable length specified in the ANSI standard is 18 inches (even less for ULTRA-66/100 devices).

♦ IDE has gained widespread acceptance due to its low cost and good performance, and with additional advancements in speed and performance will likely continue to do so.

Due to limited device support and cable distances, using IDE as a storage network itself presents certain limitations. Nonetheless, with RAID and striping technologies, devices employing IDE technology can contribute to an overall storage network. Figure 2-5 is a logical illustration of a standard IDE (4-device) configuration.

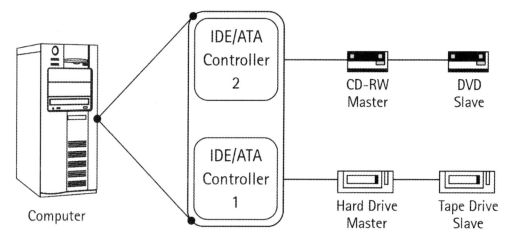

Figure 2-5: High-level Integrated Drive Electronics/Advanced Technology Attachment (IDE/ATA) usage

Although Figure 2-5 shows multiple devices, a 4–hard drive configuration is possible. With the low cost of IDE drives, high-capacity (160+GB) drives with relatively high speeds (7200

RPM), and striping technology, some companies have used such a configuration much like they would an appliance-type NAS device.

Small Computer System Interface

Small Computer System Interface (SCSI) has existed for more than 15 years and is the most widely accepted DAS technology in today's market, as evidenced by its relative low cost compared to other technologies, its development backing, multiple iterations of the technology, variations of the technology, and many other factors. It is successful partly because it can support multiple devices on a single bus.

SCSI is similar to USB and Firewire in that it can support multiple types of devices, but at a reduced number (0-7 for 8-bit and 0-15 for 16-bit). It has been used to allow connectivity to hard drives, scanners, printers, CD-R, CD-RW, WORM, and many other types of devices.

Some key SCSI features are as follows:

- ◆ SCSI throughput rates vary depending on the type of SCSI implementation that is used. The transfer rates can thus be anywhere from 4 Mbps to 80 Mbps.

- ◆ Multiple connections are used based on the version of SCSI that is being used. For example, SCSI-1 uses IDC-50, DB-25, centronics 50, or DB-50, whereas Ultra SCSI uses IDC HPD68, HPCEN68, and VHDCEN68.

- ◆ Although SCSI cards typically contain one SCSI bus that can be used internally or externally, dual SCSI bus cards are available today. With these types of adapters, up to 30 hard drives (or other devices) can be connected to a single card.

- ◆ SCSI transmissions occur in parallel rather than serially.

- ◆ Single cable lengths can range from 3 to 25 meters (10 to 82.5 feet). Most often, ten-foot lengths are used and can be chained together up to 80 feet if the cabling is sound and maintained.

- ◆ SCSI requires termination of the SCSI chain. This can be done actively or passively.

- ◆ SCSI has gained widespread acceptance due to its low cost for multiple device support and good performance.

If you use multiple SCSI controllers in a single host with high-speed drives, you can create a storage appliance of sorts. For example, assuming there are no performance issues, if four dual SCSI bus controllers were used in a single host, it would be possible to support up to 120 hard disks. Figure 2-6 illustrates such an example.

In Figure 2-6, each SCSI adapter card supports two SCSI buses, and each drive subsystem can support up to 15 devices.

> **NOTE:** The information provided on the preceding technologies is by no means all-encompassing. The outline of each technology will simply be used to build our evaluation criteria.

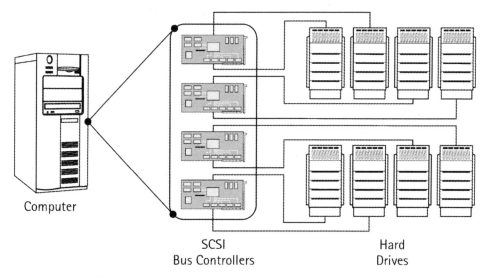

Figure 2-6: Storage appliance based on Small Computer System Interface (SCSI) controllers

Fault tolerance

No discussion of DAS technology would be complete without some discussion of DAS redundancy and fault-tolerant features. Fault-tolerant features (relating to storage) include RAID 0-53, redundant power supplies, snap shotting (explained in more detail in Chapter 3 and Chapter 4), data replication, and clustering. Fault tolerance produces a significant reduction in downtime and, if all is tallied, countless amounts of money worldwide. Unfortunately, many people simply don't think of some of the additional security concerns posed by redundancy. We describe one such cost here, and others throughout this book. Just listen to the following brief, but eye-opening, account of an Internet-based company.

PQR (a fictitious company) was a booming Internet-based company. As with many Internet companies, PQR's livelihood depended not only on having the most current data possible, but also on keeping it safe from their competition. Everyone in the organization knew the importance of the data and data availability. PQR spent millions of dollars building redundancy throughout their environment. Within their cost controls, they ensured there were no single points of failure for the devices that fit within the budget. Data was replicated to an off-site facility. Devices were clustered and RAID was used, mirroring for some applications and RAID 5 for others. Furthermore, they spared no expense when it came to security technology. The company was doing quite well, putting some distance between themselves and their competition. They were starting to realize some of the fruits of their labors. All in all, it was a very impressive setup.

The operative word here is *was*.

Without warning, PQR's competition caught up (seemingly overnight). Everyone struggled to find the reason. How could they have lost ground? How could the competition have gained an advantage so quickly? Without any obvious answers, PQR started to investigate. None of the security logs showed any breaches. There were no backdoors, no unprotected outside connections, and no compromised user accounts. In short, none of the evidence suggested that outsiders had gained access to their data. Thus, PQR started an internal investigation.

After auditing hundreds of pieces of equipment, talking to hundreds of employees, and looking at countless logs, only one thing seemed amiss: a file server log showed that during a maintenance window, all the drives in a RAID set had been replaced. Probing further, PQR noticed that the interval at which each drive was replaced would have been sufficient to allow the data to be automatically rebuilt on each drive because RAID 5 was used. When they reviewed the maintenance log, nothing indicated that the drives had been replaced.

Ultimately, PQR determined that one of their employees had replaced each drive in the RAID set, allowed the RAID set to rebuild, and simply walked out of the facility with the customer data in his laptop. The data made its way to their competition. Since PQR was using SCSI technology, which is inexpensive and readily available, PQR's competition easily accessed the data on the drives by replicating the setup. But how much damage would have been done if PQR were using HiPPI or even SSA technology?

> **SECURITY THOUGHT:** Security does not simply entail protecting against known threats; it also entails preparing for unknown menaces.

Using Technology Matrix Criteria to Determine DAS Security

What determines whether a given technology is considered "secure?" Moreover, how do you know which technology to choose over another when basing your decision on security? The answer to these questions is often murky. Fortunately, you can use certain methods to help you select the right technology—from a security perspective.

The security of a given technology is typically graded relative to the technology's availability at a given point in time. Nevertheless, it is important to establish a security baseline, or standard, by which each technology is gauged. The following sections use such a security baseline to help you determine which DAS technologies are most secure in a given environment.

In this chapter and some of the chapters to follow, we use a series of matrices to grade the security aspects of these DAS technologies. Keep in mind that many variables, outside of technology alone, can change the overall security rating of a given solution. The evaluation criteria incorporate many of the variables and can be used as a gauge to assist toward that end. The security evaluation criteria within a given technology can be the same or different for each major storage segment (for example, DAS evaluation criteria may differ from that of NAS, which in turn may differ from that of SAN). However, when evaluating for the type of storage requirement, the evaluation criteria should be static so an "apples to apples" comparison can be made.

> **SECURITY THOUGHT:** Creating a secure environment may require trading some performance to increase security.

The matrix shown in Figure 2-7 is used to evaluate each of the DAS technologies. This matrix can also be downloaded from the www.wiley.com/compbooks/chirillo Web site and modified to suit your environment. In particular, the matrix helps you evaluate each technology on its security strengths rather than on its performance. We recommend that you use this type of logic outside of the performance evaluation criteria so you understand which technology makes the most sense from a security perspective. Once you have the information from your security evaluation, you can combine it with your performance evaluation and chart the results. The best possible result is a technology that provides the highest security rating as well as the best performance. Assuming that cost is not a factor, such a technology should be your choice.

The DAS technology/security matrix

Because the components of a certain technology may not apply across technology boundaries, the scope of a technology/security matrix should relate to the type of technology (DAS, in this case) being evaluated.

It is also important to understand the components of the data to be protected. Data classification is one of the most common ways to determine the data's "value."

> **CROSS-REFERENCE:** We discuss data classification in more depth in Chapter 8. For now, we briefly define the evaluation criteria used to support our discussion of creating a baseline.

The following criteria can be used to evaluate DAS technologies. We employ a numbering scheme from 1 to 5 for each criterion (with 1 indicating least preferred and 5 indicating most preferred). For example, the 1 to 5 numbering scheme for the Acceptance factor represents the technology's level of widespread use. A rating of 5 indicates that the technology has not been widely adopted, and a rating of 1 means that it is very prevalent in the marketplace. In terms of the Connection criterion, a rating of 1 means Proprietary and a rating of 5 means Very Common. When performing technology security evaluations, it is wise to evaluate technologies as they relate to the overall computing industry.

The eleven factors used in our technology/security matrix are defined as follows:

♦ **(A) Acceptance:** Acceptance is a relative evaluation criterion. Market acceptance/ penetration (in other words, how many installations of and the availability of a certain technology) can no doubt be a huge factor in determining the number of potential vulnerabilities in this technology. If the target is small (not widely accepted or widely installed), it stands to reason that the bull's-eye should be small (the knowledgebase and number of threats will most likely be small making it harder to breach). A less popular technology oftentimes equates to less security risk (if it's not widespread, there aren't as many hackers trying to break into it); thus, a technology with a "not accepted" rating may be a better security choice than one that is "widely accepted." A technology in widespread use may be the target for any would-be hacker. For this reason, a technology with a lower acceptance level gets a higher rating.

- **1 = Widely accepted:** Technologies with a rating of 1 are used, implemented, or available in a very high percentage of machines. A good example of a widely accepted technology is Ethernet; it is the most prevalent networking topology today, and is being shipped/integrated with many x86-based platforms, including laptops, desktops, and many servers. It does not come with all computing platforms, but on a per-piece basis, it is very prevalent.

- **2 = High acceptance:** Technologies that fall into the high acceptance category are typically used on many platforms, but are not as prevalent as those that are widely accepted.

- **3 = Average acceptance:** Technologies with a rating of 3 are typically gaining some ground in their acceptance level. USB has widespread use, but Firewire is currently in the average acceptance category.

- **4 = Low acceptance:** Technologies with a low acceptance level are newer technologies or ones that are more specialized. Examples in this category include HiPPI and SSA.

- **5 = Not accepted:** Although these technologies are used in some venues, they have not been widely adopted.

♦ **(B) Breachability:** Breachability is the ease with which a prospective attacker can gain access to information using a given technology. For example, an attacker could connect directly to a given DAS technology and then use widely available tools to easily view/capture the data. The original data need not be completely compromised on initial connection, but if the data can be captured, it can be compromised offline. If, say, a host connects to the DAS technology for the purpose of mirroring logical drives, the data is breached once it is captured, even if the capturer has not yet broken additional data security measures.

- **1 = Very easily breached:** In the case of these technologies, you only need connect to DAS to access the data. Once a physical connection has been established, very easily breached technologies may only require access to the drive(s) to allow access to the data, without modification of any physical or logical configuration of the existing DAS. In this scenario, the host (and clients) may only be aware of degradation in performance.

- **2 = Easily breached:** With these technologies, you must connect to the DAS technology to gain access to the data. Once a physical connection has been established, technologies with a rating of 2 can be breached using widely available tools. No modification of any physical or logical configuration of the existing DAS occurs. In this scenario, the host (and clients) may only be aware of degradation in performance.

- **3 = Breachable:** Breachable DAS technologies only require disconnection of the DAS from one host and reconnection to another host. No special configuration tools or software are needed.

- **4 = Hard to breach:** Hard-to-breach DAS technologies not only require disconnection of the DAS from the host, but also the use of special configuration software and specific equipment, to achieve the breach. An example of special equipment is a product that is only available from the manufacturer.

- **5 = Very hard to breach:** DAS technologies with a rating of 5 require disconnection of the DAS from the host, special configuration software, specific manufacturer's hardware, and an in-depth knowledge of the original configuration. Technologies that do not allow for autoconfiguration make the breach more difficult.

♦ **(C) CISS Compliance:** CISS compliance is a weight based on how well a given technology complies with the pertinent CISS domains. These security domains are primarily security architecture and physical security.

- **1 = No compliance:** DAS technologies that fall into this category maintain no compliance with CISS.

- **2 = 25% or less compliance:** DAS technologies in this category maintain 25% or less compliance to the pertinent CISS domains.

- **3 = 50% compliance:** DAS technologies in this category maintain 50% or less compliance to the pertinent CISS domains. It is possible to be fully compliant in one category and have no compliance in another category.

- **4 = 75% compliance:** The pertinent CISS domains are between 75% and 99.xxxxx% compliance.

- **5 = 100% compliance:** Only a technology with perfect CISS compliance can be given a rating of 5. However, this does not mean that the technology can never be compromised.

> **NOTE:** Throughout this book, we discuss CISS (Computer Information Systems Security) and how it can be leveraged to create more secure storage networks. For now, it is important to know that a CISS compliance measure is used.

♦ **(D) Common Knowledgebase:** If the general population knows a given technology well, you can bet there are many ways to use that knowledge maliciously. Many times, using a good "complicated" not-so-well-known technology provides you with a security advantage.

- **1 = General knowledge:** The basic usages of level 1 technologies are generally known by most of the computing population, including end users.

- **2 = Well-known:** DAS technologies in the well-known category are prevalent. You can find quality support for them within a corporation as well as from external sources, even across general platform technologies.

- **3 = Common:** Technologies in this category are common knowledge. They are generally understood at an average level.

- **4 = Not-so-well-known:** The knowledgebase regarding these technologies is somewhat limited. DAS technologies can also fall into this category when they are only prevalent in a given technology segment.

- **5 = Uncommon:** In this category, the number prevalant within the overall computing technology industry is very low.

♦ **(E) Connection:** The Connection criterion assesses the ease of connecting to a given technology and then using it to compromise data. For example, USB technology would rate low on the Connection scale because it would be very easy to connect to and use the bus and potentially compromise data because compromise can be as simple as plugging into a USB port or hub.

- **1 = Very common:** If the connection type has a very high install base compared to the overall computing industry, it is considered very common. Additionally, if the connection technology has been widely adopted by a very high number of manufacturers, it is also considered very common and easy to duplicate.

- **2 = Common:** These DAS technology connectors have been adopted by many manufacturers and are prevalent within the industry.

- **3 = Accepted:** This type of connector is generally accepted within the industry.

- **4 = Limited:** Limited connectors are typically used across some platforms, and may have more than one application.

- **5 = Proprietary/Uncommon:** These types of connectors are generally synonymous with only one type of technology.

♦ **(F) Data Protection:** Data protection as it pertains to security refers to a given technology's ability to provide fault tolerance. This helps ensure against data loss due to failures. However, fault tolerance can also be a security risk, as noted in the Hardware Fault Tolerance Exposure (H). This component should be judged solely on its ability to protect the data when a hardware failure occurs. The ability to include redundant power supplies, split buses, and dual controllers adds to the data protection rating.

- **1 = No protection:** This category encompasses DAS devices with no inherent ability to provide built-in data protection and no software support for data fault tolerance. They simply provide storage.

- **2 = Single DAS-level protection:** This category includes DAS technologies that do not have manufacturer support for built-in data protection but are supported by a software fault tolerance option. Software mirroring is an example.

- **3 = RAID-level protection:** Many companies integrate different levels of RAID (0-53) technology into their products. Configuration of hardware-level RAID is most often accomplished using a configuration tool.

- **4 = Three-level protection:** This category encompasses DAS technologies that provide three levels of fault tolerance, with additional features such as online sparing of drives. This provides greater protection than hardware-level RAID alone.

- **5 = Highly protected:** DAS devices with other integrated features such as redundant power supplies, split communications buses, dual controllers, and battery backed-up cache are considered highly fault-tolerant and therefore highly protected. Many of these technologies can even provide local, data replication.

♦ **(G) Framing/Protocol:** The method used to transfer data between a controller and DAS device typically uses a "frame or a protocol." If this method is considered proprietary or very uncommon, it can provide a security advantage. As noted earlier, an uncommon method is less likely to possess the same level of vulnerability as some of the more common types. Many of the tools available for hacking, whether it be ethical or immoral, may not support those protocols that are uncommon.

  • **1 = Standard/Very common:** This category comprises standards that are widely prevalent—many people know about them, technicians use them, and programmers write code for them. Much of the source is open source in the public domain, and is therefore available for both valid and unauthorized purposes.

  • **2 = Common framing:** Common framing is still in the mainstream but is generally considered more secure.

  • **3 = Very common protocol:** In general, a protocol can provide somewhat better security protection than using framing only. But much like very common frames, very common protocols are widely used, and the tools for them are very much available.

  • **4 = Common protocol:** As with common framing, common protocols are still in the mainstream, but not quite as prevalent.

  • **5 = Proprietary/Very uncommon framing/protocol:** Once again, you are less likely to see people trying to crack items that are proprietary and/or very uncommon than their mainstream counterparts; however, propriety might have to be judged relatively. For example, HiPPI may be prevalent in the supercomputer marketplace, but when all technologies are considered, it is not the most widely used.

♦ **(H) Hardware Fault Tolerance Exposure:** Fault tolerance is good technology for protecting your data, but it can also be used against you. From a pure data lockdown point of view, fault tolerance can result in increased vulnerability to a security threat or exposure. However, from the standpoint of data protection (in other words, ensuring that you do not lose your data), fault tolerance is a must. The trick to remember is that this portion of the security/technology matrix evaluates the relative exposure of the data based on the type of fault tolerance used. In other words, hardware fault tolerance as it relates to data exposure is the criterion. The data fault tolerance is evaluated for risk and for how the data is "contained," or kept from getting into the wrong hands.

  • **1 = High fault tolerance:** This category comprises an infrastructure with more than three methods of making the data fault-tolerant. The more replicated the data is, the more risk will be involved in keeping it secure. This is the highest level of redundancy.

  • **2 = Three-level data fault tolerance:** This category comprises the next highest fault tolerance level. Three data fault-tolerant options somewhat reduce the risk, but three data touch points still exist.

- **3 = Two-level data fault tolerance:** This category comprises common redundancy. There are two methods of protecting the data in use, and therefore the exposure is not considered as great as when more are used.

- **4 = Single data level fault tolerance:** This category comprises a less frequent design where only one method of fault tolerance is used, and consequently, exposure is more limited.

- **5 = No fault tolerance:** This category comprises a design that lacks redundancy altogether. Consequently, there is only one data point (the minimum number of data points possible).

> **NOTE:** Some of the data protection methods used should not figure into this, as they are designed to increase uptime and are not necessarily data protectors (except where corruption is concerned). Therefore, they do not add to or detract from hardware fault tolerance exposure. For example, redundant power supplies do not further expose the data.

- **(I) Optional Security Measures:** Special configuration software may pose a security risk if it is used maliciously or improperly. Such configuration software may erase data or redirect it to an inappropriate source. Additionally, you may be able to run the configuration software remotely, a situation that often poses great security risks.

  - **1 = No security measures:** In this category, the special configuration software contains no security measures and can be configured locally or remotely with widely available connections (for example, using IP or serial port connections with no built-in security).

  - **2 = Minimal security:** Configurations can be performed locally or remotely using more secure means (for example, proprietary local connection and dial-up versus IP).

  - **3 = Average security:** Local configuration only. Configurations can be performed locally or remotely using encryption technologies.

  - **4 = Moderately secure:** Configurations can be performed locally or remotely using encryption technologies, proprietary connections, and reverse authentication.

  - **5 = Highly secure:** Configurations can be performed only locally using proprietary connections.

- **(J) Physical Security Issues:** Physical security can take many forms. For our purposes, we are concerned with physical security as it relates to DAS devices. If the DAS is entirely within the processing unit (host) and completely locked, it is thought to have complete protection from physical access. However, if the DAS device is external to the processing unit, where anyone could remove a drive, it is thought to be almost completely unprotected. An external DAS device in a locked cabinet might garner a 4 rating rather than a 5 if its associated host is not as secure. You should not be able to accidentally unplug power and cables, since this can cause data loss. Devices should be clearly (but generically) marked (Host to DAS). For example Host_A DAS_A. Doing this keeps some ambiguity in the data center for those devices that need it, and the personnel responsible for its maintenance are the only individuals who should understand its configuration, as well as use and have access to it. Even if the device is placed in a room with controlled access, it cannot be considered fully secure if it is not locked within the data center and labeled. It is important to conform to CISS physical security standards.

- **1 = Any physical access:** Anyone can gain unhampered physical access into the computer room and/or data center and thus gain physical access to the DAS device.

- **2 = Physical access to cabinet:** Anyone can gain unhampered physical access to a cabinet, rack, or other equipment housing device that is lockable. Level 2 is still a relatively low rating, because it is very possible to leave something unlocked. Tracking is limited when no access control is in place.

- **3 = Multiple access control without logging:** Access is controlled via a pushbutton locking system, nonlogged keypad, or a locked door and coupled with locking equipment cabinets, power cable protection, security connections, and other such features.

- **4 = Access control with logging:** Access is controlled using a logged system such as logged keycard access, logged keypad access, logged identity management (possibly biometric), along with locking equipment cabinets/racks, power cable protection, security connections, and other such features.

- **5 = Full conformance to CISS physical security standards:** Physical access is fully compliant with CISS standards, including such items as fire protection, environment protection, and standard physical security.

NOTE: Physical security and protection is a topic unto itself. For now, we have chosen only certain criteria for the evaluation matrix.

- ◆ **(K) Special Configuration Software Issues:** The way a DAS is configured can also affect its security. If a DAS device can be configured to use password protection before allowing configuration changes, it can definitely provide additional security protection against unauthorized configuration changes that could lead to loss of data or data compromise. The options of each manufacturer/vendor must be evaluated. One vendor may allow such an option, while another may not. Additional security features may also be possible, such as configuration protection and configuration backup. These features can protect data in the event of a device failure.

  - **1 = Not available:** DAS technologies that fall into this category are not provided any configuration protection.

  - **2 = Simple password protection:** In this configuration type, protection is achieved using a simple password scheme.

  - **3 = Simple authentication protection:** In this configuration type, protection is achieved using an authentication scheme (for example, a username/simple password).

  - **4 = Complex authentication protection:** In this configuration type, an authentication scheme can be set up for authentication with complex passwords.

  - **5 = Multiple levels of protection:** In this configuration type, multiple levels of configuration protection are provided. These can include password and authentication (simple and complex), as well as backup configuration options.

This list of criteria is meant to provide you with a solid baseline for DAS technology security evaluation. Keep in mind that some of the criteria used here may be more important in certain environments than in others; in your environment, for example, you may want to include some other influence. Therefore, you can add a weighting system to each category in order to perform a better evaluation.

Try to include as much detail in an evaluation as possible. It is better to evaluate and validate any possible determining factors, rather than not include them at all. Figure 2-7 shows a sample evaluation in a Microsoft Excel spreadsheet.

As stated previously, in certain cases a given evaluation will use some, all, or more than the criteria specified here. However, our list serves as a solid baseline for many evaluations. Since we are evaluating DAS technology only (no configuration software or options), we will use a modified evaluation form. The form shown in Figure 2-8 is filled out using the 1–5 rating scale, totaled and averaged using the previous criteria. Each score takes into account only the DAS technology itself.

You can take a look at how each technology scored in the matrix to authenticate the assessment.

USB

♦ **Acceptance:** There is no doubt at this point in time that USB is a widely accepted technology. It is being integrated into many computer-related products, which earns it a rating of 1.

♦ **Breachable:** USB technology—considered to be a plug-and-play technology—was designed to be easy to connect to. For this reason, USB scores a 1 in the Breachable category.

♦ **CISS Compliance:** Because USB is protocol based and requires host-to-device communication, it meets some of the requirements of CISS and as such scores a 3 in this category.

♦ **Common Knowledgebase:** USB is very prevalent in today's computer marketplace and has rapidly been accepted by most people—at least to the extent of usage and device connection. It earns a rating of 2.

♦ **Connection:** It has become difficult to find a company without USB connections. Most computer stores, warehouses, vendors, manufacturers, and customers have USB throughout (and at the very least, in a few areas). USB's popularity is expected to expand even further very rapidly. Thus, USB is rated a 1 in the Connection category.

♦ **Data Protection:** By itself, USB does not have any built-in hard drive fault tolerance functionality; however, with the use of software, it can be configured to use RAID, giving it a weight of 2 in the Data Protection category.

♦ **Framing/Protocol:** USB is protocol-based. This is apparent by the fact that using computers running DOS, special protocol stacks are needed to access USB devices.

These stacks, however, are very common and thus USB receives only a 3 in this category.

♦ **Hardware Fault Tolerance Exposure:** Although USB does not have its own fault-tolerant features (relating to DAS), it is capable of being leveraged for software fault tolerance. This, coupled with its ease of connection and its ability to insert devices and capture data, gives it a rating of only 3.

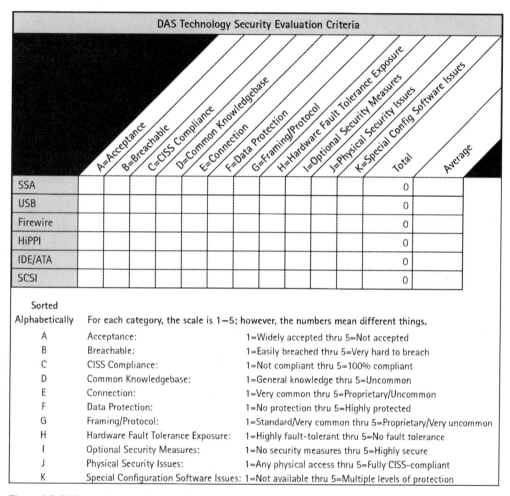

Figure 2-7: DAS security evaluation matrix

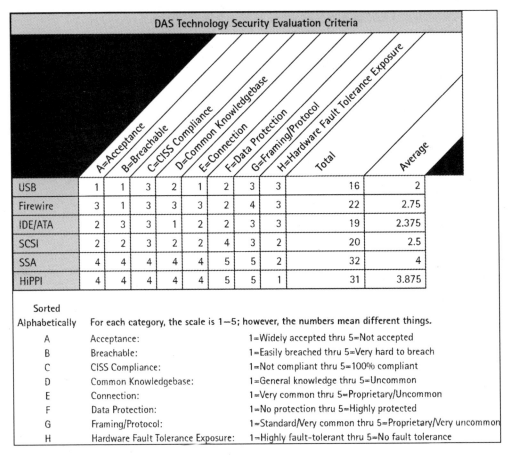

DAS Technology Security Evaluation Criteria										
	A=Acceptance	B=Breachable	C=CISS Compliance	D=Common Knowledgebase	E=Connection	F=Data Protection	G=Framing/Protocol	H=Hardware Fault Tolerance Exposure	Total	Average
USB	1	1	3	2	1	2	3	3	16	2
Firewire	3	1	3	3	3	2	4	3	22	2.75
IDE/ATA	2	3	3	1	2	2	3	3	19	2.375
SCSI	2	2	3	2	2	4	3	2	20	2.5
SSA	4	4	4	4	4	5	5	2	32	4
HiPPI	4	4	4	4	4	5	5	1	31	3.875

Sorted Alphabetically	For each category, the scale is 1–5; however, the numbers mean different things.	
A	Acceptance:	1=Widely accepted thru 5=Not accepted
B	Breachable:	1=Easily breached thru 5=Very hard to breach
C	CISS Compliance:	1=Not compliant thru 5=100% compliant
D	Common Knowledgebase:	1=General knowledge thru 5=Uncommon
E	Connection:	1=Very common thru 5=Proprietary/Uncommon
F	Data Protection:	1=No protection thru 5=Highly protected
G	Framing/Protocol:	1=Standard/Very common thru 5=Proprietary/Very uncommon
H	Hardware Fault Tolerance Exposure:	1=Highly fault-tolerant thru 5=No fault tolerance

Figure 2-8: Filling in the DAS security evaluation matrix

IDE/ATA

♦ **Acceptance:** IDE/ATA is widely accepted, but mostly on the desktop/laptop fronts. It is also by far where the highest physical number is sold. This technology has been around for some time. It scores only a 2 in this category.

♦ **Breachable:** Most IDE/ATA drives are internal, adding to their security, but the bus is easy to connect to and data can be readily captured. Thus, IDE scores a 3 in the Breachable category.

♦ **CISS Compliance:** IDE/ATA is protocol-based and generally conforms to about half of the pertinent CISS standards, giving it a rating of 3 in this category.

♦ **Common Knowledgebase:** IDE/ATA has a very large and diverse common knowledgebase, largely due to its use in many user-based PCs and the fact that it has been around for some time. For these reasons, it scores a 1 in the Common Knowledgebase category.

♦ **Connection:** Most IDE/ATA connections are a standard 40-pin connection that is readily available. In fact, most "computer people" have one or two IDE cables just lying around. Therefore, IDE/ATA only receives a 2 in the Connection category.

♦ **Data Protection:** Generally, IDE/ATA does not have built-in data protection like RAID. However, some solutions implement IDE using RAID 1. Since that is not the norm, IDE is rated a 2 in the Data Protection category.

♦ **Framing/Protocol:** IDE/ATA is protocol-based. There are many references and tools available when compared to USB. Although IDE/ATA is becoming more common, it currently warrants a rating of 4 in this category.

♦ **Hardware Fault Tolerance Exposure:** Although IDE/ATA does not have its own fault-tolerant features (relating to DAS), it is capable of being leveraged for software fault tolerance. This, coupled with its ease of connection and its ability to insert devices and capture data, gives it a rating of only 3 in this category.

Firewire

♦ **Acceptance:** Firewire has gained acceptance and is being implemented in many products that require higher speeds than USB. Video is one such example. However, when compared to the widespread acceptance of other available technologies, Firewire scores only a 3.

♦ **Breachable:** Firewire is very easy to plug into and operates on a peer-to-peer basis. In other words, devices can communicate directly with each other, bypassing hosts. For this reason, Firewire scores a 1 in this category when compared to other technologies.

♦ **CISS Compliance:** Firewire is protocol-based and does not require host-to-device communication. It does, however, use a strong Physical-to-Link layer conversion IEEE 1394.

♦ **Common Knowledgebase:** Although it is not as strong as USB, Firewire is gaining ground and is being implemented in many computer systems (with USB also). Its rating is 3 in this category.

♦ **Connection:** The Firewire connection is not as common as other connections, such as USB, but is gaining better acceptance in this area. It scores a 3 in this category.

♦ **Data Protection:** By itself, Firewire does not have any built-in hard drive fault tolerance functionality. However, with the use of software, it can be configured to use software RAID, giving it a weight of 2 in this category.

♦ **Framing/Protocol:** Firewire is protocol-based and considered a very common protocol, giving it a rating of 3.

♦ **Hardware Fault Tolerance Exposure:** With limited fault-tolerant support, the exposure is minimal. However, software RAID is often used and, for this reason, Firewire gets a rating of 3 in this category.

SCSI

- ◆ **Acceptance:** SCSI is very accepted in certain venues, including the storage arena. It provides support for multiple devices at a lower cost than some of the alternatives, making it a logical choice for multiple hard drive support. Its acceptance is rated a 2.

- ◆ **Breachable:** SCSI is very easy to plug into. It is possible to connect more than one device to SCSI and capture data. For this reason, it is rated a 2 in the Breachable category.

- ◆ **CISS Compliance:** SCSI is protocol-based and can be used to communicate with multiple and varying devices. It has been around for quite some time and is considered to be a mature product. It complies with more than 50 percent of the CISS recommendations. Thus, it achieves a score of 3 in this category.

- ◆ **Common Knowledgebase:** Lots of people know about SCSI. Although it has some special requirements (like terminations), you can easily find SCSI resources, products, and internal support. For this reason, SCSI scores a 2 in this category.

- ◆ **Connection:** The only thing that prevents SCSI from being lower than a 2 is that there are multiple types of SCSI connectors. There are varying levels of SCSI devices as well (SCSI-1 through Ultra SCSI-3 and beyond). SCSI connections are rated as a 2.

- ◆ **Data Protection:** Manufacturers commonly implement multiple hardware RAID levels into their SCSI offerings. Oftentimes, this includes online spares. For this reason, SCSI is rated high, with a 4.

- ◆ **Framing/Protocol:** SCSI is protocol-based. Although many versions of SCSI are available, adding to its complexity, it is still considered a very common protocol and is rated a 3.

- ◆ **Hardware Fault Tolerance Exposure:** Because SCSI has multiple data fault-tolerant options, it also has more potential fault-tolerant exposures. For this reason, it is rated a 2 in this category.

Serial Storage Architecture

- ◆ **Acceptance:** SSA is used primarily in IBM solutions, and since it is not highly leveraged by other manufacturers, it can only be described as not widely accepted when compared to the other technologies, causing its rating to be a 4.

- ◆ **Breachable:** SSA is considered difficult to breach because of its relatively low acceptance level, nonstandard connections, higher cost, and limited distribution. It is thus assigned a rating of 4 in this category.

- ◆ **CISS Compliance:** SSA is protocol-based. Its CISS compliance rating is based on a combination of the security factors affecting the pertinent domains of computer security, including availability, failure resistance, and protocols. It complies with greater than 75 percent of the pertinent CISS criteria, making its score a 4 in this category.

- ◆ **Common Knowledgebase:** When compared to other technologies, SSA's knowledgebase is thought to be relatively low (due to its comparatively low acceptance and high cost). It is assigned a value of 4 in this category.

♦ **Connection:** Because SSA's connection is considered proprietary (SSA uses a 4-wire serial cable), it has a rating of 4 in this category. Although it is considered proprietary, there are enough implementations in the market today to keep it from receiving a 5.

♦ **Data Protection:** SSA technology was designed by IBM as a means of connecting large storage devices. These devices can generally be implemented using data protection including multiple RAID levels. For this reason, SSA scores a 5 in this category.

♦ **Framing/Protocol:** SSA uses both protocols and manipulations of framing technology to achieve its mission and is considered more complex than many of the other technologies, primarily because the common knowledgebase is low. Even though it is used extensively in some markets, it can still be considered proprietary in nature. As such, it is rated a 5 in this cateogory.

♦ **Hardware Fault Tolerance Exposure:** Because of its use in high-performing data-intensive critical applications, SSA implements many fault-tolerant features. Like HiPPI, and due to multiple fault-tolerant features, SSA can only be rated a 1 in this category.

High Performance Parallel Interface

♦ **Acceptance:** Although HiPPI is used in supercomputers and some mini- and mainframes, its acceptance level can only be described as not widely accepted when compared to the availability of USB, Firewire, IDE/ATA, and SCSI technologies. For this reason, it is assigned a value of 4 in this category.

♦ **Breachable:** HiPPI is considered difficult to breach due to its relatively low acceptance level (compared to that of other technologies), high cost, and limited distribution. It is assigned a rating of 4 in this category.

♦ **CISS Compliance:** HiPPI is protocol-based. HiPPI's CISS compliance rating is based on a combination of the security factors affecting the pertinent domains of computer security, including availability, failure resistance, and protocols. It complies with greater than 75 percent of the pertinent CISS criteria, making its score a 4 in this category.

♦ **Common Knowledgebase:** When compared to other technologies, HiPPI's knowledgebase is thought to be relatively low. Just ask a few of your team members what "HiPPI" stands for and you'll be surprised at the response. This relative obscurity makes it a better security choice than some of the more common technologies. It is assigned a value of 4 in this category.

♦ **Connection:** Because HiPPI's connection is considered proprietary, it is assigned a value of 4. Although this technology is considered proprietary, there is enough popularity in the market today to keep it from receiving a 5.

♦ **Data Protection:** HiPPI technology is designed for supercomputers and offers tremendous features for data protection, including crossbar functionality, data replication, and the like. Although it is considered a direct attachment, it can also be used to create a highly resilient fault-tolerant storage network. For this reason, it scores a 5 in this category.

♦ **Framing/Protocol:** HiPPI uses multiple protocols to achieve its mission and is considered more complex than many of the other technologies. Even though it is used extensively in some markets, it can still be considered proprietary in nature, and as such is rated a 5 in this category.

♦ **Hardware Fault Tolerance Exposure:** Because of its use in high-performance data-intensive critical applications, HiPPI is very fault-tolerant. The technology is used to achieve high throughput and uptime. Because of these features, it can only be rated as a 1.

It is important to be as objective as possible when evaluating a technology. Your evaluation will not be legitimate if personal preference or bias plays a part.

> **SECURITY THOUGHT:** One of the chief components of data security is to protect data from deletion.

Tallying the results

Once each technology has been assigned the appropriate values, you can determine which technology makes the most sense from a security perspective. If that technology could fill your business needs—and you had an unlimited budget and available support—you might stop there. But that's not too realistic is it? So how can you achieve a good balance?

One of the best methods we have found is to perform a security/cost/performance analysis. We just showed you how to perform a security analysis on the technology (minus the information that needs to be evaluated for specific vendors' products). The next step is to perform a cost analysis and a performance analysis. The results of each should be charted and then compared with one another.

> **NOTE:** Many cost and performance evaluation tools are available. You can find some of them on this book's companion Web site at www.wiley.com/compbooks/chirillo.

As stated earlier, the "technology winner" (all things being equal) is the most secure, best performing, and lowest cost option. We have yet to see a technology that has the highest rating in all three of these areas. Therefore, you must begin the process of determining where the trade-offs will be. Thoroughly document your decisions and the possible repercussions of each decision (this process is detailed later in the book), ensure you have the backing where necessary on those decisions, and get signoffs as appropriate.

> **CROSS-REFERENCE:** Chapter 8 covers how to document your decisions and any repercussions.

Determining Which Storage Technology Meets Your Security Needs

When performing an evaluation to determine which storage technology is the right security choice, specific uses and quantity of data must also be considered. However, it is unlikely that one technology will suit all of an organization's needs.

Another logical approach is to classify all the data, sort the data by classification, and evaluate technologies to support that data both separately and collectively. If a common storage platform can appropriately handle all the data with common classifications, consider and evaluate it. Even though different technologies mixed within an environment can cause some confusion, it is our experience that if multiple technologies are evaluated for specific security uses, and are managed well, security risks can be greatly reduced.

It is also our experience that environments managed completely by internal staff introduce risks that could be avoided by augmenting with outside security professionals. The issue is not the quality of the staff, but the fact that they may not be privy to all the updates, upgrades, and in many cases how changes to something as simple as a server profile can affect overall security. Countless vulnerability assessments have been performed with great results, only to see the customer can be breached later because a patch was applied to a device that removed or mitigated a security measure. The bottom line is to classify the data and evaluate it separately and collectively.

It is possible, though not likely, to illicitly reach a single secure storage technology. This holds true if the data is not classified, and in some cases where there are multiple data classifications. This makes it possible to have all "Not Classified" data on the same technology (DAS for example) and all classified technology on another technology.

Moreover, the biggest predicament with a DAS solution is the inherent attached system vulnerabilities. System compromises through operating system flaws and such are common ailments for a DAS security solution. Peter Delle Donne, vice-president of storage sales and marketing for Compaq Computer Corporation stated, "Last year we grew external storage almost 83 percent year-over-year." People are migrating from DAS to SAN- and NAS-type solutions for centralized-security management and administration.

In a nutshell, DAS is simple and capable of delivering high performance at a low entry price, but it does not scale and is costly to manage. One security concern, among others mentioned in this chapter, is the unpredictable demand and the risk of downtime when adding new storage.

If you use ripple security logic with a DAS at the center, you can clearly see how using a DAS limits the potential scope of data loss. However, some very real touch points and security concerns remain, such as the following:

- **The technology itself:** As you have seen, the DAS technology you select dramatically affects the security of your data. If you must use a certain technology, follow the methods in this book to make it as secure as possible.

- **The hosts:** The cyberworld can be a scary place if you're not sure you are protected. Hosts—and more specifically, the operating systems they run—can pose some of the greatest risks. Choosing an operating system that is less prone to attacks is a sound security practice. If you don't have that option, do everything you can to make the host secure, and then call in some experts to validate your work. Keep a "change log," and make it a practice after every change to go through a security checklist, validation procedure, and test procedure to ensure that no vulnerabilities were introduced. Keep the hosts up-to-date as well. Many operating systems release patches and fixes on a consistent basis. Review and apply them as appropriate.

- **Remote locations:** Remote locations can become the forgotten few. DAS devices hooked up to remote locations may become one of the greatest storage security risks. Many times, these devices may have replications of highly classified data, yet they may not be using the same methodologies as the "central office."

- **Physical security issues:** Although unlikely, suppose for a moment that you have a host connected to a DAS device. The host software is locked down so tight it squeaks, but the host and DAS do not have any physical protection. The server is disconnected from the DAS and connected to another server; the data is copied, and then the DAS is reconnected to the original server. As a result, the device is compromised. Physical security would deter many potential compromises.

- **Clustering issues:** Clustering is often used to reduce business interruption in the event of a host failure (as well as other features). A host can only take over for a failed host if both have access to the same data. Thus, it is imperative that each host be secured separately. This is especially true when one host's primary function is to provide different services from the other host. Use the same practices listed in "The hosts" section above, but use them individually.

- **Administration:** Administration of hosts can either enhance or detract from data security. For example, the file system chosen to reside on a DAS can affect its security.

> **CROSS-REFERENCE:** File systems are discussed in more detail in Chapter 6.

- **Management software:** Management software for both the host and DAS device can also provide potential data risks. SNMP vulnerabilities, for example, can lead to data loss or data compromise (see Chapter 9 for more on SNMP).

- **Special configuration programs:** Configuration programs can pose some security risks. A DAS device with multiple channels that can be connected to multiple hosts (that is, a cluster) can be used to delete the data on the DAS device (either accidentally or intentionally). Controllers with built-in configuration software may be susceptible to attacks that could send configuration commands to the DAS device.

- **Justifying the wrong things:** By now, we hope you realize that you should look at the special security needs of your data devices. One of the real issues pertaining to DAS (and other storage network devices) is justifying away a given technology based on incorrect or incomplete findings or data. It is also important to challenge standards where appropriate. If a standard poses a much greater security risk than another DAS technology, and the data classification warrants it, make the recommendation for the appropriate DAS technology.

- **Identity management:** Many companies invest millions in storage and storage networks. Many of these same companies use identity management products (for example, biometric devices) to confirm and track *who* is authorized and authenticated to access "highly classified" data. They also use products that track what they do. And many of these companies do not require the same process when it comes to administrators, technicians, and engineers, all of whom can change or delete the same data. Identity management should be used on *any* and *all* devices that can affect highly classified data.

Providing a Secure DAS Foundation

To provide a secure DAS foundation for your storage system, carefully consider the following points:

♦ **Classify the data:** One of the most important (and most overlooked) facets of data security is building a classification scheme and using it to gauge the importance of the data. It is obvious that some data should be "highly classified," but there may be some supporting data (or development data) that is you don't immediately classify. If you build a sound classification scheme and evaluate all data against it, you have made a good start toward choosing the right storage technology.

♦ **Use standards:** Choose and use a security methodology as a guide. Computer Information Systems Security is one such standard.

♦ **Build a plan:** Put a plan together, starting with data classification(s), for the evaluation of the security attributes of different DAS technologies and how they relate to and can best secure your classified data.

> **CROSS-REFERENCE:** We thoroughly discuss DAS, NAS, and SAN planning in Chapter 8.

♦ **Use a matrix or two:** As you have seen, using a matrix can take bias out of the picture. In many cases, you may be surprised by the evaluation results. In fact, the criteria used in our security evaluation helped determine that HiPPI is the best DAS technology (although it can also be used as a SAN technology). As security options, security criteria, and DAS technologies change, keep the matrices up-to-date to ensure the most accurate evaluation criteria.

♦ **Chart the results of your evaluation:** Chart the results and use them to ensure that your performance criteria are tempered with security criteria.

♦ **Identify the most secure technology:** Whenever possible, choose the most secure DAS technology. If all the other security components are in place, using that selection as a solid foundation will help you create the most secure storage solution.

♦ **Stay away from mainstream products if possible:** This warning is a big source of debate. Many argue that mainstream products have more support, more development, more options, and so on. They also argue that because of their popularity, the security support is better also. However, it is also a known fact that the technologies with the largest market penetration are also targeted the most by hackers. We argue that if a technology is endowed with good support, shows adequate performance, and is affordable, it makes the best choice.

♦ **Fault-tolerant options:** Understand the security issues relating to fault tolerance.

♦ **Require identity management:** If you consider your data critical, use identity management and usage tracking. Be mindful of how identity management is performed and ensure it is included in your evaluation criteria.

♦ **DR options:** Data is an asset and the primary means by which many companies are differentiated from their competition. In other organizations, (such as the government), it may be the means by which democracy is protected. As such, it must be protected at all costs. Disaster Recovery (DR) is becoming more and more common; however, some organizations make the mistake of protecting the "live data" while missing security holes at the replicated site. Evaluate each site and each component with the same vigor as the data at the live site(s).

♦ **Limitations:** Make special notes of any security limitations in the evaluation. These limitations may be the deciding factor between technologies. Also note data protective mechanisms, and protective measures inherent to the DAS-attached server.

> **NOTE:** Limitations should be based on security merit, not performance or cost. Also on the whole, DAS is only as secure as the server it is attached to.

Summary

This chapter discusses how different direct attached storage (DAS) technologies can add to overall security. These technologies are outlined and evaluated using a set of basic criteria. You now have a basic evaluation form and scheme that can be built upon to encompass all of your DAS technology evaluation criteria. Keeping the evaluation criteria pertinent is also critical to the success of the evaluation.

Although many of the exposures listed in this chapter might seem somewhat obscure and in some cases controversial, remember that many of them have already been used to take down several companies. We'll talk more about compromises in each chapter.

It is impossible to overemphasize the importance of proper planning and technology evaluation in the interest of sound security. The chapters that follow continue to build on this philosophy.

Chapter 3
Network Attached Storage (NAS)

With our discussion on DAS complete, we can now move into a detailed discussion on NAS technologies and general NAS security issues. NAS is compared and contrasted to DAS and SAN, and its native security strengths and weaknesses are evaluated. As you progress through this book, you build on the information and security factors outlined in each chapter to provide a comprehensive methodology that allows you to select a secure storage solution. The culmination of these building blocks occurs in Chapter 7.

What Is Network Attached Storage?

If you were to ask ten tech-savvy people to define network attached storage (NAS), you'd almost certainly get ten different answers. However, you would find one common element in each response—that NAS is a network storage device that can be shared over a network topology, often referring to NAS as an *appliance*. NAS devices come in several different forms, each with various features from many different manufacturers. The range of NAS definitions is partly the result of this diversity of features and the fact that product manufacturers implement NAS devices differently. Also, many manufacturers, in an effort to compete with SANs, are implementing features previously leveraged in SAN environments. In order to better understand NAS, we now take a look at NAS technology.

Understanding NAS technology

As you review NAS technology, you will start to see the reasons for the ambiguity. Not only do some features and options cross NAS and SAN technology boundaries, but certain NAS implementations fit the general definition of a SAN (as discussed in Chapter 4). For now, some of the more common aspects of NAS technology are outlined and described. You will see both similarities and differences between NAS technology components and those of DAS and SANs. Since DAS was discussed in the previous chapter, that baseline of knowledge is used to describe similarities between DAS and NAS technologies. Although SAN is discussed in the next chapter, similarities between SAN and NAS are briefly pointed out as well.

In our discussion on DAS, the importance of the connection methods that DAS uses and how each can affect security were emphasized. Since NAS is not directly connected to a host (with some exceptions), NAS security concerns and evaluation criteria are different from those of DAS. To better comprehend these concerns, thus enabling the implementation of sound security measures, a good understanding of NAS technology is a must. The following list outlines many of the common NAS technology properties:

◆ NAS is often IP-based, but native support exists for IPX/SPX and AppleTalk on some NAS devices.

◆ Whereas SAN devices are block-based, NAS access is file-based, very often using Common Internet File System (CIFS)/Server Message Block (SMB) protocol, Network File System (NFS), Network Control Protocol (NCP), or even Hypertext Transfer Protocol (HTTP).

◆ An operating system, oftentimes referred to as *embedded* or *hardened*, is typically used on a NAS device.

◆ A NAS device may have the ability to be accessed by clients, servers, or both.

◆ Some NAS devices are server-based products that can attach to a DAS or SAN.

◆ Many NAS products are supported using RADIUS configurations.

◆ Some NAS devices contain *snap*, clone or data replication functionality.

◆ Other fault-tolerant features, such as RAID and data replication, can vary widely based on the product.

◆ Many devices, including NAS devices, leverage BIOS and/or Flash ROM.

◆ SNMP/CMIP provide management options.

◆ Most confusing is the fact that a NAS can be configured to operate like a SAN.

NOTE: Many companies manufacture NAS, and the different products reflect a variety of features, options, and configurations. It is not our intention to cover each product here, but rather to outline many of the common NAS features. Specific features must be evaluated on individual merit. Include them in your evaluation matrix.

From this list, you can see not only that NAS and SAN options cross boundaries, but also that NAS and SAN contain some of the features of DAS. Like DAS, most NAS and SAN devices provide fault-tolerant options such as RAID. Similar to the file-sharing component of a host in a DAS implementation, a NAS device contains a gateway type device that allows for file sharing. Figure 3-1 illustrates a NAS device broken down into three main components: storage, operating system, and file system.

So how does NAS actually work?

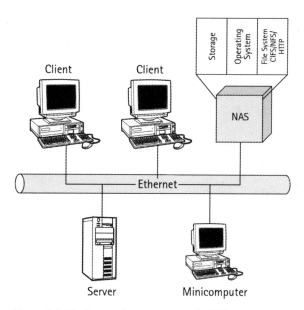

Figure 3-1: The three main components of a NAS device: storage, operating system, and file system

NAS properties

In this section, we break down the list of NAS technology properties and discuss how NAS operates. Using the material from this discussion, you can begin to build your NAS evaluation matrix to better understand NAS technology security issues and concerns.

- ◆ **IP-based:** Using IP as a basis for their communication, NAS devices allow disparate systems to access them either locally or over long distances. Because most devices today can use IP to communicate, NAS devices offer a relatively easy migration from distributed data environments to more centralized data networks. However, this flexibility comes with a cost. Using ripple security logic, it becomes apparent that IP-based NAS solutions can pose significant security risks. When the data is centralized and potentially accessible from anywhere, the security measures of literally every device on the cascading rings must be taken into account.

NOTE: Some NAS devices support the IPX/SPX and AppleTalk protocols natively, allowing direct connection from devices running IPX/SPX or AppleTalk. This is an important security consideration when choosing a NAS device.

- ◆ **File-based access:** One of the appealing features of NAS is that it is based on a file access system; it is not block-based. If you need a high-performing transactional database, NAS is not the way to go. However, if you want flexibility in terms of who can access the data using diverse platforms such as Microsoft Windows, Novell NetWare, Linux, UNIX, or any system that leverages HTTP, NAS may be the best option. Most NAS devices support at least CIFS/SMB and NFS; however, you can find NAS devices that support Hypertext Transfer Protocol (HTTP), File Transfer Protocol (FTP),

NetWare Core Protocol (NCP), and even AppleTalk File Protocol (AFP). The type of file-based access used can greatly affect security concerns. There is another file system to consider when implementing a NAS. The operating system on the NAS device may use a block method to read and write files directly to the disk, while using a file format like those discussed in this chapter to share files with other clients. This can become an important security factor when determining how to provide adequate security for the NAS device. Figure 3-2 illustrates general IP-based communications with a NAS device using multiple platforms.

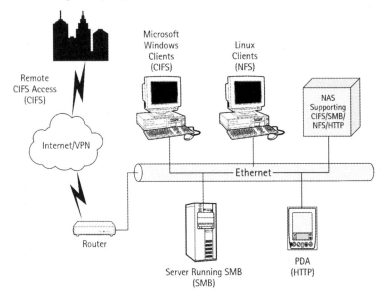

Figure 3-2: NAS IP-based communciations

NOTE: CIFS is based on SMB and provides enhancements to the SMB protocol. Since SMB was introduced in the 80s, it has been enhanced several times.

♦ **OS:** To provide file-based services, NAS devices implement some form of operating system (OS). These come in various forms, including standard or "off-the-shelf" Microsoft Windows, UNIX, and Linux, as well as modified versions of each (frequently referred to as embedded, or hardened, versions). Some NAS devices even leverage Microsoft Windows CE, VxWorks, or QNX. VxWorks and QNX are real-time operating systems (RTOSs); they often reside entirely in flash memory. Whether off-the-shelf, hardened, or embedded, almost all of these implementations are modified to improve (speed up) the file sharing and file access processes, as well as provide improved security measures.

♦ **Client/server:** The way devices gain access to a NAS may also depend on whose NAS it is. Some manufacturers support file access directly from hosts including end-user work-stations, while other implementations use a front-end device like a file server. Still other implementations require client software to be loaded on each device that will access the

NAS. Although each device may reside on the same network, direct access may only be gained if the appropriate conditions are met. Figure 3-3 generically illustrates each type of configuration just discussed.

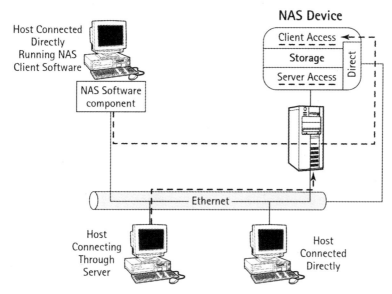

Figure 3-3: NAS configurations

♦ **Server-based or integrated:** Not only do features and operating systems of NAS devices vary, the physical NAS design also varies. NAS devices can be integrated, which means they contain both the NAS operating environment as well as the storage. Typically, this style of NAS device is relatively economical compared to a SAN and may be called a *NAS appliance.* Conversely, NAS devices come in "optimized" server-based models without their own mass storage (usually, they have internal storage for the operating system), oftentimes referred to as a *NAS server* or *NAS head.* Many of these devices were developed to allow connection to a SAN to provide NAS functionality in SAN environments.

> **SECURITY THOUGHT:** Environments with both NAS and SAN implementations are often more than twice as susceptible to security breaches as environments with only a NAS or SAN.

♦ **Connection method:** How a connection is established varies depending on which file access system is used. The selection of the file system can impact security as much as the type of operating system used. Each file system and authentication mechanism should be weighed heavily when evaluating security requirements. Connections that are established solely at the client without requiring authentication to the server (such as native NFS) are considered to be stateless connections. Authentication occurs as the client and its ID is compared at the server to determine file rights. Such connections are relatively easy to breach using readily available and well-documented techniques. For this reason, many NAS devices implement their own authentication mechanism in addition to the client-side authentication. Stateful connections are considered to be more secure because they require authentication with the device being accessed. This authentication process may occur directly at the NAS device or using some other form of authentication, as is the case with Microsoft Windows and domain controllers or RADIUS. Stateful connections can therefore leverage two or more levels of authentication and oftentimes include client-level, network-level, and NAS-level authentication. Additionally, devices using stateful connections periodically check the connection to verify the authenticity of the communicating device.

♦ **RADIUS:** Some of the more security-conscious companies producing NAS devices allow authentication to occur using Remote Authentication Dial-In User Service (RADIUS). RADIUS servers are client/server-based devices that can provide central authentication. Features within RADIUS devices and NAS devices today allow RADIUS to be used as a central authentication point for NAS devices. The RADIUS server acts as an authentication gateway to the NAS device. This provides an extra level of security protection when NAS devices are used. Figure 3-4 illustrates this type of authentication. The client originally authenticates locally, then to the domain controller. If access to the NAS device is required, the client will then be authenticated by the RADIUS server and allowed to access the NAS device.

♦ **Clone/snap:** As more and more data becomes centralized, customers, manufacturers, and vendors alike have realized that data availability is more critical than ever. Maintenance, backup windows, hardware failures, and corruption are some of the factors that affect data availability. With the price of disk storage coming down (respectively on a per-GB basis), and in order to address some of the data availability issues, local data duplication technologies have been integrated into both NAS and SAN devices. The logic behind cloning technology has been around for a long time. After all, a clone can be achieved by simply mirroring data or using a disk imaging tool. However, on today's networks, cloning is most commonly thought of as the process of creating a duplicate of a volume. Snap technology, also referred to as *snapping* or *snap shotting,* is the process of creating a point-in-time copy of data. One of the major benefits of snap technology is that snap technology does not require the same amount of physical space as the original production data, depending on how long the snap will be available, and is very quick compared to cloning. Both technologies can be used to address some of the previously mentioned data availability issues.

CROSS-REFERENCE: Cloning and snap technology are discussed further in Chapter 5.

♦ **RAID and data replication:** As with DAS, many NAS devices contain features such as RAID and data replication. These options function very similarly to those in DAS technology. Data replication is typically easier to accomplish, since NAS leverages IP. This means that, bandwidth permitting, data can be replicated over great distances.

♦ **SAN-like configuration:** One of the reasons NAS and SAN often get confused is that a NAS device can be configured to operate like a SAN—that is, on a separate network or topology. This concept is discussed in more depth in a later section, "Providing a Secure NAS Foundation."

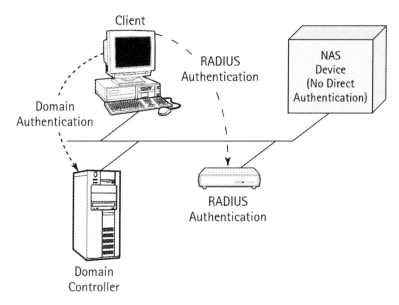

Figure 3-4: RADIUS authentication

- ◆ **NAS application software:** This is the area in which many of the NAS products attempt to favorably differentiate themselves from their competitors. It includes items such as authentication mechanisms, permissions/rights, and various configuration and management tools. This is one area to focus particular attention on when performing a security evaluation of NAS products.

- ◆ **SNMP/CMIP management:** SNMP management has been the mainstay of network management for some time. A simple Internet search for "SNMP vulnerabilities" will no doubt prove that serious security concerns must be addressed if SNMP is going to be used as a management tool for NAS devices. Common Management Information Protocol (CMIP), on the other hand, is not as well known. It was developed by the government and certain corporations to address issues in SNMP. Since it was designed for use on the ISO protocol stack, it is commonly used in the telecommunications industry. Although there is some support for CMIP on networks, this support is limited at best. For these reasons, how a NAS device is managed must be considered and scrutinized.

- ◆ **BIOS issues:** One additional issue that can affect a NAS and ultimately NAS security is how different manufacturers implement a Basic Input/Output System (BIOS). Much like the configuration issues described in DAS technologies, NAS BIOS implementation can affect NAS security. For example, if a BIOS can be flash upgraded remotely, it is possible to alter the BIOS instruction set and then send it to the NAS device, altering its operation. This may have an adverse effect on data integrity.

You already know that NAS devices can communicate using protocols such as TCP/IP, IPX/SPX, and AppleTalk, but gaining an in-depth understanding of this process can help you create more secure NAS environments. TCP/IP, IPX/SPX, and AppleTalk basics are not discussed here, so a solid understanding of these protocols and the seven layers of the OSI model are necessary.

File systems

File systems are a fundamental component of NAS. They operate by leveraging the seven layers of the OSI model. Because different operating systems may only be able to use certain types of file systems, you may not be able to choose between file systems. However, many of the operating systems are providing alternatives to their native file system access methodologies. Where this is the case, you should choose the most secure file system.

♦ **CIFS/SMB:** CIFS/SMB is a client-server-based protocol designed to allow the sharing of resources, including serial ports, mail ports, printers, and, for our purposes, files. CIFS/SMB operates at the Presentation and Application layers of the OSI model. This allows it to function over many protocols, including TCP/IP, IPX/SPX, AppleTalk, Decnet, and/or NetBEUI. Figure 3-5 shows two common protocols and how CIFS/SMB is used on them.

OSI MODEL	TCP/IP	IPX
Application	CIFS/SMB	CIFS/SMB
Presentation		
Session	NETBIOS	NETBIOS
Transport	TCP/UDP	SPX
Network	IP	IPX
Data Link	Topology (Ethernet)	Topology (Ethernet)
Physical	Physical	Physical

Figure 3-5: CIFS/SMB usage

♦ **NFS:** NFS uses file handles and three components to determine which files are to be accessed. Only one of these components is secret and has been proven to be relatively easy to breach. For this reason, many NAS devices implement additional security measures when NFS is used.

♦ **NCP:** NetWare Core Protocol (NCP) allows the sharing of files in a similar fashion to NFS but uses IPX/SPX rather than TCP/IP. SPX can be compared to TCP functionality in that it resides at the Transport layer, and communicates with the upper layers.

♦ **HTTP:** Because Hypertext Transfer Protocol (HTTP) is so widely used on the Internet and intranets, many manufacturers of NAS devices have built HTTP support into their NAS product offering. On many of these NAS devices, enhanced security is used to reduce the potential for data loss.

♦ **FTP:** File Transfer Protocol (FTP) is used widely for transferring files between devices, with the result that many NAS manufacturers have provided native FTP support.

SECURITY THOUGHT: Most people purchase NAS devices for the flexibility they can offer. Many times, features are not needed and not used. When this is the case, be sure to shut down or lock down unneeded features.

Limitations

Although NAS addresses many of the heterogeneous file-sharing issues that can arise on a network (including over long distances), it still provides a specific solution and as such does not address centralized data needs in their entirety.

File sharing or database access

By their nature, NAS devices can provide a great deal of flexibility, especially in environments that need extremely long-distance communications such as the Internet. That said, NAS devices are not the right choice in every situation from both a functional and security perspective. Because NAS devices are file-system-based rather than block-based (as is the case in a SAN), they are not a good choice for database applications. Such applications may require multiple read/write functions to occur at a very rapid rate to keep up with multiple requests. For this reason, a block-based storage system, as is most commonly the case with a SAN, is a better choice than a NAS device.

File sizes

Another mitigating factor when evaluating NAS versus DAS versus SAN is the nature and size of the file transfers. NAS devices are usually best suited for many small duration (size) file transfers, whereas DAS and SAN devices handle large duration file transfers more efficiently. When this is the case, a DAS or SAN is probably a better choice.

Network speed

Another area of concern or potential limitation for a NAS implementation is the network itself. An environment that is still running 10 Mbps shared Ethernet without 100 Mbps or 1 Gbps connectivity is not a good candidate for a NAS device. A NAS device adds many requests/ responses to the network; thus, depending on the volume of traffic destined for the NAS device, the network may become saturated with traffic, causing such communication issues as collisions, retransmissions, and disconnects. If the network cannot be redesigned, an alternative storage solution might be a better choice, one that limits the read/write traffic over the production network.

Network composition

In addition to the speed of a network (for example, 10/100/1000 Mbps), the topology, physical layout, and current security state of a network can determine a given NAS implementation's level of security. Because NAS devices are most often used to allow heterogeneous access to files, the NAS device is very often implemented directly on a production network. If the current production network is not using sound security practices, processes, and procedures, then the NAS device cannot be considered secure.

Features/options

Another very important factor in determining the limitations of a NAS is in the available features. Because the market frequently perceives a NAS device as the "cheaper" alternative to a SAN, many companies have been forced to reduce the built-in features of a NAS in order to provide a cost-competitive NAS solution. Most NAS devices have available fault-tolerant options, such as redundant power supplies and RAID. And although it is not true across the spectrum of products, NAS products very often do not have the same types or levels of features when compared to a SAN. As noted previously, some NAS devices have integrated features that allow third-party devices to provide additional features like RADIUS authentication, which can greatly increase the overall security measures and should be considered during the security evaluation of a NAS product. Nonetheless, the break point is becoming grayer every day. This is only further confused by emerging technologies like iSCSI, FCIP, and iFCP. The primary differences between NAS devices and devices like iSCSI are that NAS is file based and iSCSI is block based. iSCSI, FCIP, and iFCP are briefly discussed in Chapter 4.

Security limitations

Some of the general security issues inherited with NAS devices are their inherent ability to enable applications to do the following:

- ◆ To enforce their own proprietary security through NAS
- ◆ To protect communication and data integrity within the system
- ◆ To provide secure scalability and aggregate bandwidth
- ◆ To protect the delivery channel communications
- ◆ To provide authentication and access control
- ◆ To provide encryption technologies

Since a NAS device uses an operating system to provide for the file storage, its operating system largely determines the preceding factors.

Using Technology Matrix Criteria to Determine NAS Security

NAS devices are part of the network framework, so the need to protect the data and devices is critical. Perimeter security, once again, is simply not enough to protect against malicious users and local/remote attackers; therefore, a corporate strategy and strong NAS security policy is necessary to adhere to the ripple security logic. What's more, both the strategy and the security policy should address the critical security risks inherited to and/or from NAS, such as unauthorized access, unauthenticated access, unprotected administrator access, vulnerable network access points (which can include exposed switches and routers), data hijacking, and sniffing. Later in this chapter, we talk more about these issues with a design implementation of a NAS foundation that covers access control, integrity, and privacy.

NAS topologies

Because most NAS devices, and more specifically the file systems used for NAS devices, conform to the OSI model (that is, CIFS/SMB or NFS), they can be configured to operate on many topologies using different protocols. Figure 3-5 showed two of these. NAS devices can also be configured to operate on Token Ring, FDDI, and even Fibre Channel, supporting protocols such as IP, IPX/SPX, AppleTalk, and Decnet.

Furthermore, since many NAS devices can be configured to operate using higher-level protocols such as HTTP and FTP, they can also be made very easy to access by any device that can communicate with the NAS device using that protocol. This allows a NAS device to fit well into long-distance file-sharing solutions. A good example of how this long-distance NAS solution might work would be any one of the numerous Internet-based online storage houses. Many of these companies allow users to purchase a specified amount of "Internet-based" storage to be used as needed. They are accessed using either HTTP or FTP (some actually require client software to be loaded on the user machine). Some of these companies use NAS devices because of their ability to communicate using HTTP or FTP, while others use a SAN-like connection approach that still allows communications to occur through a file-sharing device (typically a file-server-type device capable of the appropriate protocol) using HTTP or FTP. However when a SAN-style device is used it provides greater flexibility by allowing block transfers to occur as discussed in Chapter 4. Whether it's HTTP or FTP, these same companies make substantial investments in additional security.

One of the key factors that determines which topology a given NAS device will operate on is whether it supports multiple Network Interface Cards (NICs). An appliance-type NAS device may only contain an Ethernet connection, whereas a file-server-style NAS device that can connect to a SAN device may allow not only multiple client communication technologies/topologies, but several SAN connection technologies as well. An example would be a file-server-style NAS device that can be connected to Ethernet 100 Mbps or 1 Gbps, Token Ring or FDDI topologies for the client access side, and FDDI, ATM, or Fibre Channel for the SAN connection. This type of device offers a great deal of flexibility.

Sometimes, you may not even know that you're using NAS. Devices like CD-ROM, CD-RW, and WORM jukeboxes have leveraged NAS-style technology for many years. Such devices are often overlooked in the grand security scheme. This is a dangerous oversight, since many of these devices are used to archive files to conserve space. In some organizations, very high quantities of new data arrive daily, and these devices are archiving data that may be only weeks old to conserve valuable hard drive space. This data may still be considered active and could be very useful to competitors of a given company. For this reason, such devices should be considered, evaluated, and secured as part of a sound security strategy. They are further discussed in Chapters 6 and 7.

NAS's strengths and weaknesses

For most of us, data management is critical, and small- to medium-size networks require a cost-effective and reliable means to manage it. For this reason and others that are addressed shortly, a NAS solution may be the preferred method to share files and increase productivity. General NAS strengths are:

♦ File sharing over long distances

♦ Heterogenous operating system file sharing

♦ Minimally disruptive installation

♦ Can be independent of the operating system yet still share files

♦ Low cost

♦ Typically easy to install as they are often viewed (and built as) appliance-type devices

General NAS weaknesses are:

♦ File based versus block based, which may not be good for databases

♦ Unless a separate IP network is created, NAS over IP can be nondeterministic.

♦ Even if a database can leverage a file-sharing device, it may not be able to handle the nondeterministic nature of IP.

♦ Typically not as robust in features and functionality as a SAN

Slow file access and high network congestion are probably the result of an abundance of workstation shares and/or dwindling server space. These conditions can all be side effects of insufficient data storage. A NAS solution can alleviate many of the problems associated with the aforementioned symptoms. Application servers can begin to focus on serving applications and reducing bandwidth when storage requirements are eliminated. Network and network-segment congestion can decrease as well when shares are removed from workstations. With a NAS solution, data can be accessed quickly and reliably, since NAS is independent of your file servers and workstations. With a NAS RAID solution, you can create a fault-tolerant system using a combination of drive sets for performance and redundancy. In some cases, hardware-based RAID solutions are implemented for even better performance and reliability, especially with a fault-tolerant RAID subsystem (that is, dual power supplies) and hard disk hot-swapping (the capability to replace a faulty hard drive without shutting down the system). A software-based RAID solution cannot compete with the latter because it struggles with current system processing utilization.

These RAID configurations are broken into levels based on redundant features that are fundamentally uncomplicated. The four most common RAID levels are 0, 1, 3, and 5. (RAID Level 4 looks very much like Level 3, but the stripes are now much larger. Level 4 is rarely used because it has no advantages compared to the popular Level 5.)

♦ **Level 0: Data striping.** Blocks of each file are spread across multiple disks. This level delivers no redundancy, but it does improve performance.

- ♦ **Level 1: Disk mirroring.** A technique whereby data is written to two identical disks simultaneously. If one of the disk drives goes down, the system can instantly switch to the other disk without any data loss or interruption in service.

- ♦ **Level 3: Same as Level 0.** In addition, one dedicated disk is reserved for error correction data. Level 3 provides good performance and some level of fault tolerance.

- ♦ **Level 5:Byte-level data striping and error correction.** Delivers excellent performance and good fault tolerance but is not the best solution for performance when using certain databases.

Hardware-based fault-tolerant mechanisms offer much better RAID performance and reliability. The most critical advantages include less downtime, fully redundant subsystems, and hot-swappable disk drives—upon drive failure.

In addition to reliable data storage, a NAS system can provide cross-platform file sharing for your Windows, NetWare, *NIX, and Max platforms. Each client will have access to retrieve and store files in their native formats so that conversion is not necessary.

Smaller businesses that cannot afford to outsource consultants or train or hire technical-savvy engineers and network administrators can use a NAS solution to accommodate their storage needs. With a plug-and-play interface, setting up and configuring a NAS system is easy; in most cases, it is up and running in minutes.

Obviously, a strong security policy employed and enforced on the network and local workstations is necessary, since NAS weaknesses can be exploited and inherited from the LAN. With a cost-effective design, NAS typically includes weak proprietary security features that can almost always be bypassed with a simple segment sniffer or weak administrative access control. We talk more about NAS security in this chapter and in more detail in Chapters 7 and 8 later in this book.

Genevieve Ortegon of FIA Storage Systems Group said it best: "Network-attached storage is an attractive option for small to medium-size businesses due to its cost. For any business, it is important that dollars spent result in dollars earned. The proposed benefits of implementing a technology must be carefully evaluated to determine whether the investment will justify itself in the long run. Expanding servers is not a cost-effective way to increase storage capacity. Implementing a NAS system is. NAS, by virtue of being a single repository completely dedicated to storage, is clearly the smartest investment for ensuring the integrity, reliability, and accessibility of your data.

"These factors present a strong case to small or medium-size business owners looking for a simple and cost-effective way to experience what today's global enterprises are benefiting from: sophisticated technology; fast, reliable network access; improved productivity; and the peace of mind that comes with knowing that mission-critical data is safe…"

Using the Technology Security Matrix

You can use the following matrix to evaluate NAS technologies. This matrix can also be downloaded from the book's companion Web site (www.wiley.com/compbooks/chirillo) and modified to suit your environment. The matrix helps you evaluate the technologies on their security strengths rather than on their performance. The best possible result is a technology that provides the highest security rating as well as the best performance. Assuming that cost is not a factor, such a technology should be your choice.

Because the components of a certain technology may not apply across technology boundaries, the scope of a technology security matrix should be limited to the type of technology (NAS, in this case) that is being evaluated.

It is also important to understand the components of the data to be protected. Data classification is one of the most common ways to determining the data's "value." Data classification is discussed in more depth in Chapter 8. For now, we briefly define the evaluation criteria used to allow the creation of a baseline.

The following criteria can be used to evaluate NAS technologies. We employ a numbering scheme from 1 to 5 for each criterion (with 1 indicating the least desirable state and 5 indicating the most desirable state). For example, the 1 to 5 numbering scheme for the Acceptance criterion represents the technology's level of widespread use. A rating of 1 indicates that the technology has not been widely adopted, and a rating of 5 means that it is very prevalent in the marketplace. In terms of the Connection criterion, a rating of 1 means Proprietary and a rating of 5 means Very Common. When performing technology security evaluations, it is wise to evaluate technologies as they relate to the overall computing industry.

The eight factors used in our NAS technology security matrix are defined as follows:

- ◆ **(A) Acceptance.** Acceptance is a relative evaluation criterion. Market acceptance/penetration (in other words, how prevalent is the technology compared to other technologies and the availability of a certain technology) can no doubt be a huge factor in determining the number of potential vulnerabilities in the technology. If the target is small, it stands to reason that the bull's-eye should be small. A less popular technology oftentimes equates to less security risk (if it's not widespread, there aren't as many hackers trying to break into it); thus, a technology with a "not accepted" rating may be a better security choice than one that is "widely accepted." A technology in widespread use may be the target for any would-be hacker. For this reason, a technology with a lower acceptance level gets a higher rating on the evaluation matrix.

  - • **1 = Widely accepted:** Technologies with a rating of 1 are used, implemented, or available in a very high percentage of machines. A good example of a widely accepted technology is Ethernet; it is the most prevalent networking topology today, and is being shipped/integrated with many x86-based platforms, including laptops, desktops, and many servers. It does not come with all computing platforms, but on a per piece basis, it is very prevalent.

- **2 = High acceptance:** Technologies that fall into the high acceptance category are typically used on many platforms, but are not as prevalent as those that are widely accepted.

- **3 = Average acceptance:** Technologies with a rating of 3 are typically gaining some ground in their acceptance level. USB has widespread use, but Firewire is currently in the average acceptance category.

- **4 = Low acceptance:** Technologies with a low acceptance level are newer technologies or ones that are more specialized. Examples in this category include HiPPI and SSA.

- **5 = Not accepted:** Although these technologies are used in some venues, they have not been widely adopted.

♦ **(B) Breachability.** Breachability is the ease with which a prospective attacker can gain access to information using a given technology. For example, an attacker could connect directly to a given NAS technology and then use widely available tools to easily view/ capture the data. The original data need not be completely compromised on initial connection, but if the data can be captured/recorded, it can be compromised off-line. If, say, a host connects to the NAS technology for the purpose of mirroring logical drives, the data is breached once it is captured, even if the capturer has not yet broken additional security measures.

- **1 = Very easily breached:** In the case of these technologies, you only need connect to NAS to access the data. Once a physical connection has been established, very easily breached technologies may only require access to the drive(s) to allow access to the data, without modification of any physical or logical configuration of the existing NAS. In this scenario, the host (and clients) may only be aware of degradation in performance.

- **2 = Easily breached:** With these technologies, you must connect to the NAS technology to gain access to the data. Once a physical connection has been established, technologies with a rating of 2 can be breached using widely available tools. No modification of any physical or logical configuration of the existing NAS occurs. In this scenario, the host (and clients) may only be aware of degradation in performance.

- **3 = Breachable:** Breachable NAS technologies only require disconnection of the NAS from one host and reconnection to another host. No special configuration tools or software are needed.

- **4 = Hard to breach:** Hard-to-breach NAS technologies not only require disconnection of the NAS from the host, but also the use of special configuration software and specific equipment to achieve the breach. An example of special equipment is a product that is only available from a specific manufacturer.

- **5 = Very hard to breach:** NAS technologies with a rating of 5 require disconnection of the NAS from the host, special configuration software, specific manufacturer's hardware, and an in-depth knowledge of the original configuration. Technologies that do not allow for autoconfiguration make the breach more difficult.

♦ **(C) CISS compliance.** CISS compliance is a weight based on how well a given technology complies with the pertinent CISS domains. These domains are primarily security architecture and physical security.

- **1 = No compliance:** NAS technologies that fall into this category maintain no compliance with CISS.

- **2 = 25% or less compliance:** NAS technologies in this category maintain 25% or less compliance to the pertinent CISS domains.

- **3 = 50% compliance:** NAS technologies in this category maintain 50% or less compliance to the pertinent CISS domains. It is possible to be fully compliant in one category and have no compliance in another category.

- **4 = 75% compliance:** The pertinent CISS domains are between 75% and 99.xxxxx% compliance.

- **5 = 100% compliance:** Only a technology with perfect CISS compliance can be given a rating of 5. However, this does not mean that the technology can never be compromised.

♦ **(D) Common knowledgebase.** If the general population knows a given technology well, you can bet there are many ways to use that knowledge maliciously. Many times, using a good "complicated" not-so-well-known technology provides you with a security advantage.

- **1 = General knowledge:** The basic usages of level 1 technologies are generally known by most of the computing population, including end users.

- **2 = Well-known:** NAS technologies in the well-known category are prevalent. You can find quality support for them within a corporation as well as from external sources, even across general platform technologies.

- **3 = Common:** Technologies in this category are common knowledge. They are generally understood at an average level by the average IT professional.

- **4 = Not-so-well-known:** The knowledgebase regarding these technologies is somewhat limited. NAS technologies can also fall into this category when NAS technologies are only prevalent in a given technology segment.

- **5 = Uncommon:** In this category, the knowledgebase regarding uncommon technologies within the overall computing technology industry is very limited.

♦ **(E) Data authentication and encryption:** This criterion refers to the inherent ability of a given technology to employ identification and authentication techniques and compatibility with such schemes from knowledge-based techniques to characteristic-based.

- **1 = None:** If the type of device has an inherent lack of encryption acceptance or does not comply, it is considered to have no authorization or encryption.

- **2 = Some identification:** This category includes knowledge-based authentication techniques such as strong passwords.

- **3 = Some encryption:** This category includes the ability to encrypt data.

- **4 = Good identification and encryption:** This category includes a combination of strong identification and the ability to encrypt data.

- **5 = Advanced Authentication:** These types support authentication technologies such as tokens and tickets.

♦ **(F) Optional security measures.** Special configuration software may pose a security risk if it is used maliciously or improperly. Such configuration software may erase data or redirect it to an inappropriate source. Additionally, you may be able to run the configuration software remotely, a situation that often poses great security risks.

- **1 = No security measures:** In this category, the special configuration software contains no security measures and can be configured locally or remotely with widely available connections (for example, using IP or serial port connections with no built-in security).

- **2 = Minimal security:** Configurations can be performed locally or remotely using more secure means (for example, proprietary local connection and dial-up versus IP).

- **3 = Average security:** Configurations can be performed locally or remotely using encryption technologies.

- **4 = Moderately secure:** Configurations can be performed locally or remotely using encryption technologies, proprietary connections, and reverse authentication.

- **5 = Highly secure:** Configurations can be performed only locally using proprietary connections.

♦ **(G) Physical security issues.** Physical security can take many forms and is covered in many other security textbooks including those that cover CISSP. For the purposes of this book, we are concerned only with physical security as it relates to NAS devices.

- **1 = Any physical access:** Anyone can gain unhampered physical access into the computer room and/or datacenter and thus gain physical access to the NAS device.

- **2 = Physical access to cabinet:** Anyone can gain unhampered physical access to a cabinet, rack, or other equipment housing device that is lockable. Level 2 is still a relatively low rating, because it is possible to leave something unlocked. Tracking is limited when no access control is in place.

- **3 = Multiple access control without logging:** Access is controlled via a pushbutton locking system, nonlogged keypad, or a locked door, and is coupled with locking equipment cabinets, power cable protection, security connections, and other such features.

- **4 = Access control with logging:** Access is controlled using a logged system such as logged keycard access, logged keypad access, logged identity management (possibly biometric), along with locking equipment cabinets/racks, power cable protection, security connections, and other such features.

- **5 = Full conformance to CISS physical security standards:** Physical access is fully compliant with CISS standards, including such items as fire protection, environment protection, and standard physical security.

♦ **(H) Special configuration software issues.** The way a NAS is configured can also affect its security. If a NAS device can be configured to use password protection before allowing configuration changes, it can definitely provide additional security protection against unauthorized configuration changes that could lead to loss of data or data compromise. The options of each manufacturer/vendor must be evaluated. One vendor may allow such an option, while another may not. Additional security features may also be possible, such as configuration protection and configuration backup. These features can protect data in the event of a device failure.

- **1 = Not available:** NAS technologies that fall into this category do not have any inherent configuration protection.

- **2 = Simple password protection:** Configuration protection is achieved using a simple password scheme.

- **3 = Simple authentication protection:** Protection is achieved using an authentication scheme (for example, a username/simple password).

- **4 = Complex authentication protection:** An authentication scheme can be set up for authentication with complex passwords.

- **5 = Multiple levels of protection:** Multiple levels of configuration protection are provided. These can include password and authentication (simple and complex), as well as backup configuration options.

This list of criteria is meant to provide you with a solid baseline for NAS technology security evaluation. Keep in mind that some of the criteria used here may be more important in certain environments than in others; in your environment, for example, you may want to include some other influencing factor. Therefore, you can add a weighting system to your matrix in order to perform a better evaluation. It is better to evaluate and validate any possible determining factors, rather than not include them at all.

As stated previously, there are cases where a given evaluation will use some, all, or more than the criteria that were just discussed. However, the list we provide serves as a solid baseline for many evaluations. Since we are evaluating NAS technology only, we use a modified version of the evaluation form from Chapter 2. The form, shown in Figure 3-6, is filled out using the 1–5 rating scale, totaled and averaged using the previous criteria. Each score takes into account only the NAS technology itself.

Matrix assessment

Let's see how each of the technology factors shown in Figure 3-6 scored in the security evaluation.

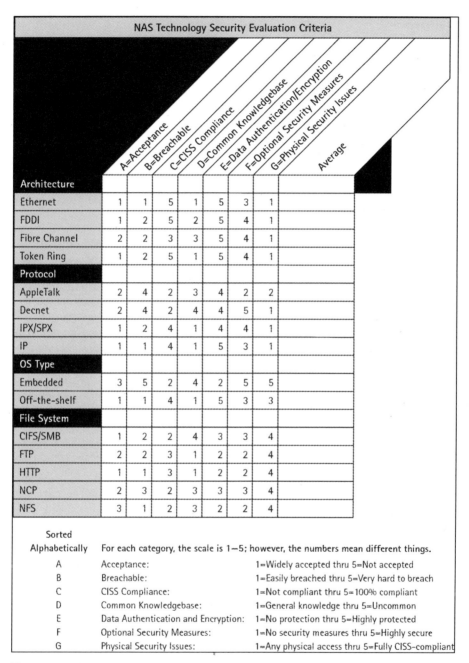

NAS Technology Security Evaluation Criteria	A=Acceptance	B=Breachable	C=CISS Compliance	D=Common Knowledgebase	E=Data Authentication/Encryption	F=Optional Security Measures	G=Physical Security Issues	Average
Architecture								
Ethernet	1	1	5	1	5	3	1	
FDDI	1	2	5	2	5	4	1	
Fibre Channel	2	2	3	3	5	4	1	
Token Ring	1	2	5	1	5	4	1	
Protocol								
AppleTalk	2	4	2	3	4	2	2	
Decnet	2	4	2	4	4	5	1	
IPX/SPX	1	2	4	1	4	4	1	
IP	1	1	4	1	5	3	1	
OS Type								
Embedded	3	5	2	4	2	5	5	
Off-the-shelf	1	1	4	1	5	3	3	
File System								
CIFS/SMB	1	2	2	4	3	3	4	
FTP	2	2	3	1	2	2	4	
HTTP	1	1	3	1	2	2	4	
NCP	2	3	2	3	3	3	4	
NFS	3	1	2	3	2	2	4	

Sorted Alphabetically	For each category, the scale is 1–5; however, the numbers mean different things.	
A	Acceptance:	1=Widely accepted thru 5=Not accepted
B	Breachable:	1=Easily breached thru 5=Very hard to breach
C	CISS Compliance:	1=Not compliant thru 5=100% compliant
D	Common Knowledgebase:	1=General knowledge thru 5=Uncommon
E	Data Authentication and Encryption:	1=No protection thru 5=Highly protected
F	Optional Security Measures:	1=No security measures thru 5=Highly secure
G	Physical Security Issues:	1=Any physical access thru 5=Fully CISS-compliant

Figure 3-6: NAS technology security evaluaton criteria

Architecture

This section reviews the security evaluation results for four of the most common LAN architectures: Ethernet, FDDI, Fibre Channel, and Token Ring.

Ethernet

Ethernet uses a bus or star topology whose specification is the basis for the IEEE 802.3 standard. This architecture operates on the physical and lower software layers, and with newer versions, supports data rates up to 1GB (1,000MB) per second. When a station on an Ethernet network is ready to transmit, it must first listen for transmissions on the channel. If another station is transmitting, it is said to be "producing activity." This activity, or transmission, is called a *carrier*. Thus, Ethernet came to be known as the *carrier-sensing communication medium*. With multiple stations, all sensing carriers on an Ethernet network, the mechanism was termed *Carrier Sense Multiple Access*, or *CSMA*.

If a carrier is detected, the station waits for at least 9.6 microseconds after the last frame passes before transmitting its own frame. When two stations transmit simultaneously, a *fused signal bombardment*, otherwise known as a *collision*, occurs. Ethernet stations detect collisions to minimize problems. This technology was added to CSMA to become *Carrier Sense Multiple Access and Collision Detection*, or *CSMA/CD*.

Stations that participate in the collision immediately abort their transmissions. The first station to detect the collision sends out an alert to all stations. At this point, all stations execute a random collision timer to force a delay before attempting to transmit their frames. This timing delay mechanism is called the *back-off algorithm*. And, if multiple collisions are detected, the random delay timer is doubled. After ten consecutive collisions and multiple double random delay times, network performance will not improve significantly. This is a good example of an Ethernet flooding exploitation.

Ethernet received the following ratings on the list of security evaluation criteria:

- ♦ **Acceptance:** Ethernet is among the most widely accepted technologies and is implemented as part of many network infrastructures. For this reason, Ethernet scores a 1 in this category.

- ♦ **Breachable:** Once an Ethernet connection is established on a local segment, passive sniffing deems a rating of 1 in this category.

- ♦ **CISS compliance:** Because this architecture is compatible with all of the CISS standards, although not inherently secure, it rates a 5 in this category.

- ♦ **Common knowledgebase:** Ethernet has a very large and diverse common knowledgebase and thus scores a 1 in this category.

- ♦ **Data authentication/encryption:** Ethernet has the inherent ability to comply with the strongest of identification and authentication techniques and therefore receives a 5 in this category.

- ♦ **Optional security measures:** With only specific connection implementations, specifically internetwork segmentation, Ethernet rates a 3 in this category.

- ◆ **Physical security measures:** The architecture rates a 1 in this category, since anyone can gain unhampered physical access when exposed to the network infrastructure.

FDDI

The American National Standards Institute (ANSI) developed the Fiber Distributed Data Interface (FDDI) around 1985. FDDI is like a high-speed Token Ring network with redundancy and failover using fiber optic cable. FDDI operates at 100 Mbps and is primarily used as a backbone network, connecting several networks together. FDDI utilizes Token Ring *token passing* technology, which, when fully implemented, contains two counter-rotating fiber rings. The primary ring data travels clockwise and is used for transmission; the secondary ring (traveling counterclockwise) is used for backup failover in case the primary goes down. During a failure, auto-sense technology causes a ring wrap for the transmission to divert to the secondary ring.

Because FDDI frame sizes may not exceed 4,500 bytes, FDDI is a feasible medium for large graphic and data transfers. The maximum length for FDDI is 200 kilometers with 2,000 stations for a single ring and one-half that for a dual-ring implementation. FDDI was designed to function as a high-speed transport backbone; therefore, FDDI assumes workstations will not attach directly to its rings, but to a Multistation Access Unit (MAU) or router, as they cannot keep up with the data transfer rates. Consequently, frequent station power cycles will cause ring reconfigurations, and it is recommended that directly connected MAUs be powered on at all times.

FDDI received the following ratings on the list of security evaluation criteria:

- ◆ **Acceptance:** FDDI is among the most widely accepted technologies and is implemented as part of many network infrastructures. For this reason, it scores a 1 in this category.
- ◆ **Breachable:** Although FDDI is typically not as exposed as Ethernet, when a connection is established on a local segment, passive intrusion deems a 2 rating.
- ◆ **CISS compliance:** This architecture is compatible with all of the CISS standards. Although not inherently secure, it rates a 5 in this category.
- ◆ **Common knowledgebase:** FDDI has a very large and diverse common knowledgebase, but it is not as widely accepted as Ethernet. Therefore, it scores a 2 in this category.
- ◆ **Data authentication/encryption:** FDDI has the inherent ability to comply with the strongest of identification and authentication techniques, therefore receiving a 5 in this category.
- ◆ **Optional security measures:** With only specific connection implementations, FDDI rates a 4 in this category. Fiber does not emit electrical signals and therefore cannot be tapped nor permit unauthorized access using typical measures.
- ◆ **Physical security measures:** The architecture rates a 1 in this category, because anyone can gain unhampered physical access when exposed to the network infrastructure.

Token Ring

Token Ring technology, originally developed by IBM, is standardized as IEEE 802.5. In its first release, Token Ring was capable of a transmission rate of 4 Mbps. Later, improvements and new technologies increased transmissions to 16 Mbps. To help understand Token Ring networking, imagine a series of point-to-point stations forming a circle. Each station repeats, and properly amplifies, the signal as it passes by, ultimately to the destination station. A device called a *Multistation Access Unit (MAU)* connects stations. Each MAU is connected to form a circular ring. Token Ring cabling may consist of coax, twisted pair, or fiber optic types.

In Token Ring, there are two prioritization fields to permit station priority over token utilization: the *priority* and the *reservation* fields. Stations with priority equal to or greater than that set in a token can take that token by prioritization. After transmission completion, the priority station must reinstate the previous priority value so normal token passing operation can resume. Intruders that set stations with priority equal to or greater than that in a token can control that token by prioritization.

Token Ring employs various methods for detecting and managing faults in a ring. One method includes *active monitor* technology, whereby one station acts as a timing node for transmissions on a ring. Among the active monitor station's responsibilities is the removal of continuously circulating frames from the ring. This is important, as a receiving station may lock up or be rendered temporarily out-of-service while a passing frame seeks it for processing. As such, the active monitor will remove the frame and generate a new token.

Another fault management mechanism includes station *beaconing*. When a station detects a problem with the network, such as a cable fault, it sends a beacon frame, which generates a failure domain. The domain is defined as the station reporting the error, its nearest neighbor, and everything in between. Stations that fall within the failure domain attempt to electronically reconfigure around the failed area. Beacon generation may render a ring defenseless and can essentially lock up the ring.

Token Ring received the following ratings on the list of security evaluation criteria:

◆ **Acceptance:** Token Ring is among the most widely accepted technologies and is implemented as part of many network infrastructures. For this reason, it scores a 1 in this category. However it continues to lose ground to Ethernet and will most likely score a 2 and possibly below in the not so distant future.

◆ **Breachable:** Although Token Ring is typically not as exposed as Ethernet, when a connection is established on a local ring, passive intrusion deems a rating of 2.

◆ **CISS compliance:** Token Ring architecture is compatible with all of the CISS standards. Thus, it rates a 5 in this category.

◆ **Common knowledgebase:** Token Ring has a very large and diverse common knowledgebase, therefore scoring a 1 in this category.

- ◆ **Data authentication/encryption:** Token Ring has the inherent ability to comply with the strongest of identification and authentication techniques. Thus, it receives a 5 in this category.

- ◆ **Optional security measures:** With only specific connection implementations, Token Ring rates a 4 in this category.

- ◆ **Physical security measures:** The architecture rates a 1 in this category, since anyone can gain unhampered physical access when exposed to the network infrastructure.

Protocol

This section discusses the most common protocols implemented within NAS designs, including AppleTalk, Decnet, IPX/SPX, and TCP/IP.

AppleTalk

AppleTalk was designed in the early 1980s in conjunction with the Macintosh computer. It was developed as a client-server, or "distributed" network system. Through AppleTalk, users share network resources, such as files and printers, with other users. Computers supplying these network resources are called "servers." AppleTalk identifies several network entities. The most common is a "node," which—simply stated—is any device connected to an AppleTalk network.

The most common nodes are Macintosh computers and laser printers, but many other types of computers are also capable of AppleTalk communication, including IBM PCs, DEC VAX, and numerous other types of workstations. A router maintains a node on each connected network. To avoid confusion, these are referred to as "ports." The next entity defined by AppleTalk is the "network." An AppleTalk network is simply a single logical cable. Finally, an AppleTalk "zone" is a logical group of one or more (possibly noncontiguous) networks.

The original implementation of AppleTalk is called *Phase I*; it was originally designed for local workgroups. With the proliferation of over 1.5 million Macintosh's in the first five years of its life, Apple found that some larger corporations were exceeding the "built-in" limitations of AppleTalk Phase I. Thus, they created *AppleTalk Phase II*. AppleTalk Phase II extends the number of nodes in an internetwork to over 16 million and the number of zones to 255. With AppleTalk Phase II, Apple also enhanced AppleTalk's routing capabilities.

AppleTalk received the following ratings on the list of security evaluation criteria:

- ◆ **Acceptance:** AppleTalk is a widely accepted protocol. However, it is not as commonly used as other protocols, so it scores a 2 in this category.

- ◆ **Breachable:** This protocol has always been less exploited, giving it a rating of 4 in this category.

- ◆ **CISS compliance:** AppleTalk is compatible with only a few of the CISS standards. Although it is not inherently compatible, it gets a rating of 2 in this category.

- ◆ **Common knowledgebase:** AppleTalk has a common knowledgebase, therefore scoring a 3 in this category.

♦ **Data authentication/encryption:** AppleTalk has the inherent ability to comply with some identification and authentication techniques. Therefore, it receives a 4 in this category.

♦ **Optional security measures:** With minimal security options, AppleTalk rates a 2.

♦ **Physical security measures:** The protocol rates a 2 in this category because an intruder can gain physical access to the infrastructure but hijack data with only specific technologies.

IPX/SPX

IPX, NetWare's original network (layer 3) protocol, is a *connectionless datagram* (a logical grouping of information sent as a Network layer unit over a communication medium) protocol, and, as such, is similar to unreliable datagram delivery offered by the Internet Protocol (IP). Also, like IP address schemes, Novell IPX network addresses must be unique; they are represented in hexadecimal format and consist of two parts—a network number and a node number. The IPX network number is an assigned 32-bit long number. The node number is a 48-bit long hardware or Media Access Control (MAC) address for one of the system's Network Interface Cards (NICs). The NIC manufacturer assigns the 48-bit long hardware or MAC address.

Because the host portion of an IP network address has no equivalence to a MAC address, IP nodes must use *Address Resolution Protocol (ARP)* to determine the destination MAC address. An ARP packet that is broadcast to all hosts attached to a physical network will contain the IP address of the node or station with which the sender wants to communicate. Other hosts on the network ignore this packet after storing a copy of the sender's IP/hardware address mapping. The target host, however, replies with its hardware address, which will be returned to the sender to be stored in its ARP *response cache*.

As a relative to IPX, the most common NetWare transport protocol is the *Sequenced Packet Exchange (SPX)*. The protocol transmits on top of IPX at layer 4 of the OSI. Like TCP, SPX provides reliable delivery service, which supplements the unreliable datagram service in IPX. For Internet access, Novell utilizes IPX datagrams encapsulated in UDP (which is ultimately encapsulated in IP) for transmission. SPX is a packet-oriented protocol that uses a transmission window size of one packet. Applications that generally use SPX include R-Console and P-Console.

SPX uses a reliable delivery connection establishment, whereby connection endpoints verify the delivery of each packet. During connection establishment, an SPX connection request must take place. These connection management packets incorporate the following sequence:

1. Connection request.
2. Connection request ACK.
3. Informed disconnect.
4. Informed disconnect ACK.

Using this connectivity, SPX becomes a connection-oriented service, with guaranteed transmission delivery and tracking. Note that, in addition to informed disconnect, there is another method of session called the *unilateral abort*, which is used for emergency termination.

After a NetWare client logs in to a NetWare server and begins sending requests, the server uses the watchdog process to monitor the client's connection. If the server does not receive any requests from the client within the *watchdog timeout period*, the server sends a watchdog packet to that client. A *watchdog packet* is simply an IPX packet that contains a connection number and a question mark (?) in the data portion of the packet. If the client's communications are still active, the client responds with a Y, indicating that the connection is valid. The *watchdog algorithm* is simply a technology that allows SPX to passively send watchdog packets when no transmission occurs during a session. Basically, a watchdog request packet, consisting of an SPX header with SYS and ACK bits set, is sent. The receiving station must respond with a watchdog acknowledgment packet to verify connectivity. If the watchdog algorithm has repeatedly sent request packets (approximately ten every three seconds for 30 seconds) without receiving acknowledgments, an assumption is made that the receiving station is unreachable, and a unilateral abort is rendered.

Advancements in SPX technologies took error recovery from an uncouth error detection abort to packet retries and windowing. If the receiving station does not acknowledge a packet, the sending station must retry the packet submission. If the sending station still does not receive an acknowledgment, the sender must then find another route to the destination or receiving station and start again. Worse case, if acknowledgments fail again during this process, the connection is canceled with a unilateral abort.

To avoid contributing to bandwidth congestion during attempted transmissions, SPX does not submit a new packet until an acknowledgment for the previous packet has been received. If the acknowledgment is delayed or lost because of degradation, SPX will avoid flooding the network by using this simple form of congestion control.

IPX/SPX received the following ratings on the list of security evaluation criteria:

- ◆ **Acceptance:** IPX/SPX is widely accepted, so it scores a 1 in this category.
- ◆ **Breachable:** This protocol, once an intruder gains access to the data, is easily breached using widely available tools. Thus, it receives a 2 in this category.
- ◆ **CISS compliance:** IPX/SPX, although not inherently secure, is compatible with many of the CISS standards. It receives a 4 in this category.
- ◆ **Common knowledgebase:** This technology and its general uses is generally known among most of the computing population, giving it a score of 1.
- ◆ **Data authentication/encryption:** IPX/SPX has the inherent ability to comply with some identification and authentication techniques, thus giving it a 4 in this category.

♦ **Optional security measures:** IPX/SPX is moderately secure because configuration can be performed locally or remotely using encryption technologies, proprietary connections, and reverse authentication. It rates a 4 in this category.

♦ **Physical security measures:** The protocol rates a 1 in this category because anyone can gain physical access to the infrastructure and hijack data,once exposed to the infrastructure.

IP

The Internet Protocol (or IP, described in RFC 791) part of the TCP/IP suite is a four-layer model. IP is designed to interconnect networks to form an Internet that passes data back and forth. IP contains addressing and control information that enables *packets* to be routed through this Internet. (A packet is defined as a logical grouping of information, which includes a header containing control information and, usually, user data.) The equipment—that is, the routers—that encounter these packets, strip off and examine the *headers* that contain the sensitive routing information. These headers are modified and reformulated as a packet to be passed along. Packet headers contain control information (route specifications) and user data. This information can be copied, modified, and/or spoofed (masqueraded) by intruders.

One of the IP's primary functions is to provide communications between two endpoints. IP is termed a *connectionless*, unreliable, best-effort delivery protocol that delivers datagrams through an internetwork. Another of IP's principal responsibilities is the fragmentation and reassembly of datagrams to support links with different transmission sizes.

IP datagrams are the very basic, or fundamental, transfer units of the Internet and are commuted between IP modules. IP datagrams have headers with fields that provide routing information used by infrastructure equipment such as routers.

Be aware that the data in a packet is not really a concern for the IP. Instead, IP is concerned with the control information as it pertains to the upper-layer protocol. This information is stored in the IP header, which tries to deliver the datagram to its destination on the local network or over the Internet. To understand this relationship, think of IP as the method and the datagram as the means. The IP header is the primary field for gathering information, as well as for gaining control.

It is important to understand the methods a datagram uses to travel across networks. To sufficiently travel across the Internet, over physical media, you want some guarantee that each datagram travels in a physical frame. The process in which a datagram travels across media in a frame is called *encapsulation*.

Ideally, an entire IP datagram fits into a frame and the network it is traveling across supports that particular transfer size. However, we all know that nothing is ideal. One problem with our traveling datagram is that networks enforce a maximum transfer unit (MTU) size, or limit, on the size of transfer. To further confuse the issue, different types of networks enforce their own MTU size; for example, Ethernet has an MTU of 1500, FDDI uses 4470 MTU, and so on. When datagrams traveling in frames cross network types with different specified size limits, routers must sometimes divide the datagram to accommodate a smaller MTU. This process is called *fragmentation*. Routers provide the fragmentation process of datagrams, and as such, may become vulnerable to passive and intrusive attacks.

IP received the following ratings on the list of security evaluation criteria:

♦ **Acceptance:** IP is widely accepted, so it scores a 1 in this category.

♦ **Breachable:** This protocol is easily breached using widely available tools. Thus, it rates a 1 in this category.

♦ **CISS compliance:** IP is compatible with many of the CISS standards but it is not inherently secure. It receives a 4 in this category.

♦ **Common knowledgebase:** This technology and its general uses are generally known by most of the computing population, giving it a score of 1 in this category.

♦ **Data authentication/encryption:** IP has the inherent ability to comply with most identification and authentication techniques, giving it a 5 in this category.

♦ **Optional security measures:** IP is partially secure and configuration can be performed locally or remotely using encryption technologies, proprietary connections, and reverse authentication. It scores a 3 in this category.

♦ **Physical security measures:** The protocol rates a 1 in this category because anyone can gain physical access to the infrastructure and hijack data, once exposed to the infrastructure.

OS type

Recall that NAS devices implement some form of operating system that comes in various forms, including standard or off-the-shelf Microsoft Windows, UNIX, and Linux, as well as modified versions of each that are oftentimes called *embedded,* or *hardened*, versions of these operating systems. In this section, we review the security evaluation results for these OS types.

Embedded

When a NAS device uses an embedded operating system, use the following evaluation criteria:

♦ **Acceptance:** This OS type has an average acceptance level and is gaining some ground in this area, giving it a score of 3.

♦ **Breachable:** This OS type is very hard to breach and is not typically exposed to auto-configuration exploits, making the breach more difficult. As a result, it receives a 5 in this category.

♦ **CISS compliance:** As an embedded software module, this OS type is only compatible with a few of the CISS standards, giving it a 2 rating.

♦ **Common knowledgebase:** This OS type is not very common, giving it a 4 rating in this category.

♦ **Data authentication/encryption:** Embedded OS types have the inherent ability to typically comply with only proprietary identification and authentication techniques. Thus, they rate a 2 in this category.

- **Optional security measures:** Being embedded on a chip, this OS type IP gets a 5 rating.
- **Physical security measures:** Since this OS is embedded and protected by perimeter containment, it rates a 5 in this category.

Off-the-shelf

When a NAS device uses an off-the-shelf operating system, use the following evaluation criteria:

- **Acceptance:** Standard OS types are among the most widely accepted, scoring a 1 in this category.
- **Breachable:** This OS type is easily breached using widely available tools, therefore giving it a 1.
- **CISS compliance:** This type is typically compatible with most of the CISS standards. However, it is not inherently secure, so it scores a 4 in this category.
- **Common knowledgebase:** This OS type and its general uses is generally known by most of the computing population, giving it a score of 1 in this category.
- **Data authentication/encryption:** Standard OS types have the inherent ability to comply with most identification and authentication techniques, therefore scoring a 5 in this category.
- **Optional security measures:** This OS type typically contains only average security, therefore requiring third-party fortifications. It scores a 3 in this category.
- **Physical security measures:** Most of the time, the standard OS type is exposed to multiple access control without logging. Therefore, it rates a 3 in this category.

File system

Recall that file systems are a fundamental component of NAS, operating in compliance with the seven layers of the OSI model. In Figure 3-6, CIFS/SMB, NFS, NCP, HTTP, and FTP have been rated according to the different security criteria, but their scores are still highly subject to opinion, preference, and implementation. You should score these file system types based on your own research and uses.

- **CIFS/SMB** is a client-server-based protocol designed to allow the sharing of resources including serial ports, mail ports, printers, and, for our purposes, files. CIFS/SMB operates at the Presentation and Application layers of the OSI model. This allows it to function over many protocols, including TCP/IP, IPX/SPX, AppleTalk,Decnct, and/or NetBEUI.
- **The Network File System (NFS)** uses file handles and three components to determine which files are to be accessed. Only one of these components is secret and has been proven to be relatively easy to breach. For this reason, many NAS devices implement additional security measures when NFS is used.
- **The NetWare Core Protocol (NCP)** allows the sharing of files in a similar fashion to that of NFS, but using IPX/SPX rather than TCP/IP. SPX can be compared to TCP

functionality in that it resides at the Transport layer and can communicate with the upper layers.

♦ Because **HTTP** is so widely used on the Internet and intranets, many manufacturers of NAS devices have built HTTP support into their NAS product offering. On many of these NAS devices, enhanced security is used to reduce the potential for data loss.

♦ Because **File Transfer Protocol (FTP)** is used widely for transferring files between devices, many NAS manufacturers have provided native FTP support.

Determining Which Storage Technology Meets Your Security Needs

As discussed in the previous chapter, the likelihood that one storage methodology will work throughout an entire organization is slim, at best. Our discussion of NAS has only served to strengthen the notion that you must use multiple storage technologies. However, when using multiple technologies, it is important to evaluate each specific technology including NAS security issues discussed in this chapter.

If you use ripple security logic with a NAS, you can see that using a NAS connected to a production network potentially allows access from virtually anywhere if the NAS and associated security issues are not implemented and addressed properly. Figure 3-7 illustrates this fact.

As the rings cascade outward, it becomes apparent that any device capable of creating a path to the NAS device becomes a potential vulnerability point and must be considered in the security plan. The following list outlines some of the factors that can affect NAS security as shown in Figure 3-7.

♦ **The technology itself:** The technology used for the NAS device can also affect the NAS device. For example, if a server-style NAS is used and an off-the-shelf operating system is used, all of the server's potential strengths and weaknesses—including how it connects (DAS or SAN)—must be considered.

♦ **The hosts:** The NAS device is also a host and must be evaluated as such. The host operating system greatly determines the security measures that must be taken to provide the necessary security based on the data classification. Similar methods to those discussed in Chapter 2 may apply, but because some of the operating systems may be embedded or hardened, these operating system issues must be taken into account as well. Contacting the manufacturer to determine the frequency at which patches are released and how to apply patches can greatly assist here.

♦ **Network security:** When deploying a NAS device, network security becomes paramount. After all, the network security is the sentry controlling access to the area that contains the data. Once in the area, access to the data can be further controlled by implementing additional security measures, including those inherent to the NAS device itself. With the data centralized, the potential for loss increases.

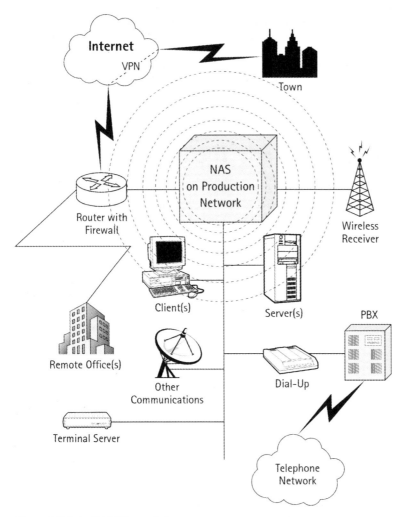

Figure 3-7: Potential NAS security issues

♦ **Internal weaknesses:** Network and local workstation security vulnerabilities aside, NAS devices may lack the ability to provide file manager access decisions in a scalable, secure, and efficient manner. We discuss the option of providing an external file manager (shown in Figure 3-8) to address these issues.

♦ **Remote locations:** When data is made readily available to remote locations, the security of each of these locations must be considered. As you can see in Figure 3-7, remote locations can cause data corruption, compromise, or loss. Suppose the remote location also allows users to dial into their network. An attacker might easily breach the dial-in security of the remote location and use that breach to gain access to the NAS. Therefore, remote location security, authentication, authorization, and access control must be strong.

♦ **Administration:** Administration of NAS devices can either enhance or detract from data security. For example, the file system chosen for use on a NAS device can determine if the connection is stateless or stateful, and if no other security exists, this can determine how easily a breach can occur.

♦ **Management software:** Because NAS devices are designed to centralize data, management software is oftentimes designed to allow management functions to occur from anywhere. While this provides great flexibility, it also provides multiple vulnerability points.

♦ **Special configuration programs:** As with management software, if the NAS configuration software can be accessed from anywhere, it can potentially be used for other than its intended purposes. Thus,configuration software should warrant specific attention in the security planning, implementation, and testing phases.

♦ **Identity management:** We cannot emphasize enough how important it is to control access to centralized data. At the very least, use a sound identity management technology to control access to the management and configuration options of your centralized data devices. If configuration of a NAS device can be accomplished remotely, you can greatly reduce the risk by employing a physical identity management scheme. Such a scheme may include using fingerprint, voice, face, retina, or other such physical identity management devices.

♦ **Topologies:** Because NAS devices use standard communication protocols to allow hosts to communicate directly to the NAS device, NAS devices can operate over most topologies, including Ethernet, Token Ring, ATM, FDDI, and Fibre Channel. Although this provides great flexibility, it can also make security much more challenging.

> **CROSS-REFERENCE:** Chapters 5 and 6 discuss how to make data more available, secure, and protected whether it resides on a DAS, NAS, or SAN system.

♦ **The "Big Filing Cabinet":** One additional security issue to consider when using a NAS device concerns the practice of segmenting data. Too often, companies implement NAS devices as a "Big Filing Cabinet." The issue here is that anyone needing access to the NAS can potentially access all the data. Segment the data and require separate security for different types of data. Using the user classification, data classification, and "need to know" methodologies can help outline who should have access to the data.

Providing a Secure NAS Foundation

Earlier in this chapter we employed and revised techniques of the Network Attached Secure Disk (NASD) system to provide a secure NAS foundation template. Later in this book, we examine the specific secure implementations in a step-by-step cookbook-like fashion, including outer perimeter security mechanisms. With that said, our cumulative NAS specific security methodology is based on the NASD system, and Figure 3-8 shows the overview, design goals, and capabilities of the system sourced from the studies of Howard Gobioff, Garth Gibson, and Doug Tygar of Carnegie Mellon University.

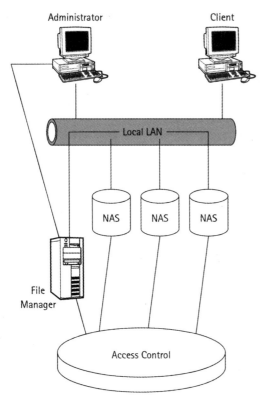

Figure 3-8: The NASD system with an external file manager making access decisions in a scalable, secure, and efficient manner

NASD fabric

A file system can only run securely if the policy maker (file manager) and enforcer (drive) exchange a minimum amount of information. When a file manager grants access to a user, the file manager must communicate the user's access rights to the drive. The drive must check that the information came from the file manager and is fresh. The goal of the NASD security system is to achieve this communication in a safe, flexible, and efficient way. One approach is to have the file manager inform the drive directly of a user's rights, which the drive will enforce when it later identifies the named user's requests. However, this approach requires that the drive be aware of the user's identity and implies a specific user authentication mechanism to the drive. It must maintain information on a per user basis, which requires more administration than a capability system.

One alternative, used in NASD, is to pass access rights to the drive through a cryptographic capability, which allows the authentication mechanism to be removed from NASD allowing a decision to be made by the file system implementer rather than being dictated by NASD.

Instead of being aware of the user's identity, the drive is only aware of a user's access rights, the capability arguments which describe a user's access rights, and a capability key, which is used by the user to prove that he is entitled to the rights he claims. The keys are derived from the capability arguments and a working key associated with the partition on which the object resides. Further details regarding the capability definition are explained later in this chapter.

How can the file manager efficiently and safely control access to the contents of a network attached drive? The file manager must be able to perform management functions on the drive and to control client access to storage. NASD's security infrastructure is designed to perform these functions while resisting attacks by an adversary with full knowledge of the NASD protocol.

Since your hypothetical adversary knows your protocol, the system's security ultimately rests on keeping the keys private (for example, key management). The NASD key management hierarchy balances flexibility of use and security. You support key management that can take advantage of tamper-resistant hardware when it exists, and in other cases affects key management through software control.

Keep the following goals in mind when designing the security for NASD:

♦ The NASD security system should explicitly separate the policy enforcement mechanism from the policy decision process so the file manager must be able to communicate policy decisions to the drive.

♦ The protocol should prevent unauthorized modification of client requests and capabilities while protecting the privacy of requests if dictated by the policies of clients or file managers.

♦ To minimize interaction with the file manager, the drive should be able to validate client operations without direct communication with the file manager.

♦ To allow for low memory drive implementations, there should be no long-term state shared between drive and client. Overall state requirements of the drive should be kept at a minimum, but additional memory should enhance performance.

♦ The security protocol should add as little overhead as possible in terms of computation and the number and size of messages.

The heart of the NASD security system is the capability architecture governing access to NASD objects. A NASD capability is composed of the capability arguments and a capability key. The *capability arguments* are a tuple (an ordered set of values) containing:

♦ Drive identifier

♦ Partition

♦ Object identifier

♦ Region (byte range)

♦ Access rights

♦ Expiration time

- ◆ Minimum protection requirements
- ◆ Basis key (black or gold)
- ◆ Audit identifier

The *capability key* is a cryptographic key used by a client to bind a specific NASD request to a capability through the use of a MAC. The MAC creates a relationship between the fields of the capability, the request, and the digest. If the drive generates the same MAC that was included in the request, the drive can be confident that the MAC, the capability arguments, and the request were all received without tampering.

The first four fields of the capability key identify the set of bytes for which the capability is valid:

- ◆ The *access rights* and *expiration time* limit the operations and time range for which the capability is valid. The lifetime of a capability cannot exceed the lifetime of the working key under which it was issued. Otherwise, the validity of the capability cannot be verified.

- ◆ The *basis key*, which is used to generate the capability key, indicates whether this capability was issued with the black working key or the gold working key.

- ◆ The *minimum protection* indicates a floor set of security options that the file manager requires of the client for all operations using the capability. This permits the file manager to require a higher standard of security than is required by the partition.

Finally, the *audit identifier* is a field where the file manager can associate arbitrary values with the capability. In auditing implementations of NASD, the drive records the audit identifier in a log record for an operation performed with the capability. This allows a log analyzer to later extract this information from the logs on the drive. With the audit identifier, you can easily integrate drive security with other applications, such as transaction management (by recording a transaction ID in the audit identifier) or audit trails (by recording the user's identity in the audit identifier).

NASD requires that the file-system-specific client/file manager protocol provide private transmission of capability keys to the clients, along with transmission of the capability arguments. You expect this to be performed as part of a directory lookup process, but it is not a requirement for NASD. The capability arguments are necessarily kept private. If an adversary can read the capability arguments, he still cannot access the object without a working key or the capability key. If an adversary modifies either the request or the response, he will, at best, execute a Denial-of-Service (DoS) attack. However, if the adversary can perform such an attack, he can probably interfere with any network traffic—a more general Denial-of-Service attack.

A client can prove it has the right to access an object by using a capability key to encrypt and/ or digest a request. The capability keys are derived from the capability arguments and a working key for the partition where the object resides. When the capability arguments are given to the drive, the drive can independently compute the capability key and verify the critical parameters for an access check.

If the capability arguments and capability key don't match, then the drive will be unable validate the request. Since clients know neither of the working keys, clients are unable to generate a forged key. If the working key changes, the drive will also be unable to generate the expected capability key. However, in this case, the changes correspond to expected invalidations of access rights.

Administrator-to-file management system security

You should consider employing specific administrative authentication and verification to provide control over the security configurations. Your security policy should enforce a marriage between management controls and the security functions. You should employ strong user identification and authentication, such as encryption and strong passwords. Password policies should be enforced and should contain conditions such as changing passwords at least every three to six months, immediately after a password is relinquished, and/or as soon as a password has been compromised or even suspected of a compromise.

When changing passwords or when passwords expire, the new password should contain at least eight characters; two of these characters must be letters and at least one must be a nonletter character. Any new passwords must differ from the old ones by at least three characters. Your password policy should follow the general password guidelines instituted by the U.S. government:

- ♦ Passwords must contain at least eight nonblank characters.
- ♦ Passwords must contain a combination of letters (preferably a mixture of upper- and lowercase letters), numbers, and at least one special character within the first seven positions.
- ♦ Passwords must contain a nonnumeric letter or symbol in the first and last positions.
- ♦ Passwords must not contain the user login name.
- ♦ Passwords must not include the user's own or a close friend's or relative's name, employee number, Social Security number, birthdate, telephone number, or any information about him or her that the user believes could be readily learned or guessed.
- ♦ Passwords must not include common words from an English dictionary or a dictionary of another language with which the user is familiar.
- ♦ Passwords must not contain commonly used proper names, including the name of any fictional character or place.
- ♦ Passwords must not contain any simple pattern of letters or numbers such as "qwertyxx."

Summary

Network attached storage can definitely provide some benefits in heterogeneous environments. However, because it can be implemented on most topologies using many protocols, it presents some unique security challenges. In order to address these issues, a good understanding of NAS technology and general security concerns is a must. Throughout this chapter, we list the general areas of concern. We also provide some valuable information on how to assess NAS products and add a valuable NAS matrix to your security toolkit. We point out specific areas to be aware of when implementing NAS devices.

Finally, we list NAS security concerns that can affect your choice of NAS over another storage technology. When NAS is a valid choice, it should be built on a solid foundation. For this reason, we have included information in this chapter that will help you begin to build a secure NAS foundation.

Chapter 4
Storage Area Network (SAN)

If DAS and NAS can handle databases and heterogeneous file sharing, respectively, what can a SAN offer? At first glance, it might appear that a SAN is nothing more than stacked storage devices that get connected to hosts just like DAS, and to a degree, this is true. However, storage area networks offer much more. Whereas DAS devices are limited in the amount of storage they can contain—primarily due to the devices that can be supported by the DAS technology used—SAN technologies support a larger number of physical devices over greater distances with faster speeds than many of the DAS technologies.

However, some DAS technologies, such as HiPPI and SSA, can be used to create SANs, and using the definition of a SAN, NAS devices can be configured in a SAN by segmenting a network so only storage traffic exists on the segment. It is also possible to use technology typically associated with a SAN in a DAS environment. So, what really defines a SAN? Moreover, what specific security concerns must be dealt with when implementing a SAN?

This chapter answers these questions by discussing storage area networks, how they differ from DAS and NAS technologies, and the special security issues that need to be evaluated when a SAN is the solution of choice.

What Is a Storage Area Network?

Unlike DAS or NAS, which are both devices that can share storage over a network, a storage area network (SAN) is primarily a high-speed network used to connect hosts with storage devices. As Figure 4-1 illustrates, this storage area network is often completely separate from the production network traffic in a deterministic fashion. These deterministic characteristics are often needed by applications such as databases.

> **NOTE:** The term *deterministic* refers to the predictability of a datagram arriving within a specified amount of time.

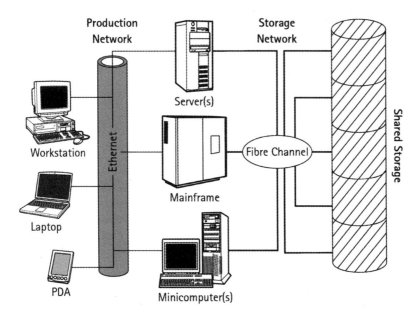

Figure 4-1: SAN segmented from a production network

In even more simplistic terms, a SAN is a network designed for the purpose of sharing storage. Defining a SAN in this way, it is clear how a NAS configured to operate on its own network, separate from any production network, could be considered a SAN. This creates some confusion between the two. To further cloud the issue, you are not required to have only storage traffic traversing the SAN topology (although where practical, this is a good practice). Protocols such as TCP/IP are capable of functioning on most network topologies, and in many cases coexist on a SAN topology.

> **SECURITY THOUGHT:** A SAN is not a device; rather, it is a collection of connected devices that communicate together for the primary purpose of sharing storage. Each connected device has specific security requirements and is therefore entered into the security equation.

Disk-based storage is not the only type of storage available for a SAN. SAN-based optical devices, as well as backup solutions, can be used. They are covered in the chapters to follow.

Understanding SAN technology

If you concede that both NAS and a storage area network cannot only coexist, but can in fact be configured to use the same segmented media, then what makes a SAN a SAN and a NAS a NAS? As discussed in the previous chapter, a NAS device is file system–based, and SAN communication is block-based. Additionally, SAN disk devices must ultimately be connected to a host or hosts, whereas a NAS device can function as a host.

You can see some of the differences by outlining a few of the more common SAN technology characteristics. It becomes apparent that there are both similarities and differences between SAN technology components and DAS and NAS components, as was the case in the two previous chapters, when you compared those technologies to a SAN. However, a SAN can be used to provide storage for each environment: DAS, NAS, and SAN. This makes it a very flexible technology. Since the DAS and NAS technologies have already been discussed, you can use them as reference points as we discuss SANs.

Fibre Channel has become the most prevalent SAN technology today. However, there are other options, some of which can provide enhancements to security, and in some cases, better performance.

A SAN can be compared to other networks in many ways. SAN devices can be directly attached to a host (similar to how you would connect two devices over Ethernet using a crossover cable), connected to a SAN hub or switch (most commonly Fibre Channel, but other SAN technologies exist), and may even support zoning (a technology that can be likened to a combination of virtual LANs and virtual private networks). To better understand these concepts, let's take a look at SAN technologies.

> **NOTE:** Many different companies manufacture SANs, and the features, options, and configuration can vary greatly from one product to another. This chapter doesn't attempt to cover each product; rather, it outlines many of their common features. Specific features must be evaluated on individual merit and should be included in the SAN security evaluation matrix.

- SANs today are most commonly Fibre Channel–based, but they can be created using DAS technologies, such as SSA and HiPPI.
- SAN access is block-based, and as such, requires the use of a host to be shared with other clients.
- A SAN contains many devices, including Host Bus Adapters (HBAs), hubs, switches, disk storage devices, magnetic tape backup devices, and even optical devices.
- The SAN does not determine which file system is used; the operating system of the connected host does.
- Hosts and NAS devices can be directly attached or network attached to SAN storage.
- SANs can use hubs or switches. Switches can provide an extra measure of security if they support zoning, a technology that can control access from host devices.
- Many SAN devices contain "snap," clone, or data replication functionality independent of the host-connected devices.
- Most SAN storage devices contain fault-tolerant features such as RAID, hot spare drives, split backplanes, multiple channel support, and "on the fly" allocation (and sometimes deallocation) of space.
- One of the many reasons to implement a SAN is to provide a foundation that can allow data replication to occur over the SAN topology.

♦ SANs can be configured using technologies such as SSA, HiPPI, and SCSI. Most often, this is accomplished by HBAs designed to communicate using one of these technologies connected to a hub or switch. This is how the host devices communicate with the storage device in its native block mode.

♦ Fiber or Fibre Channel connections are often leveraged because of their ability to carry communications over longer distances than their copper counterparts. Since fiber or Fibre Channel connections use light to communicate, and since generally only one line transmits and one line receives using light pulses, the transmission is considered to be serial in nature. When this is the case, it often requires the native communication method of a given technology to be "converted" to a serial type format. Serial HiPPI is one example when a parallel technology is converted to a serial transmission to allow serial transfers to occur. Some manufacturers mix technologies to provide a SAN fabric while using SCSI devices.

> **NOTE:** The term *SAN fabric* is used to generically refer to the devices of a Fibre Channel network that connect host devices to the storage devices.

♦ Storage is advertised (or made visible to hosts connected to the SAN) to host devices. For example, Logical Unit Numbers (LUNs) can be advertised to a host or multiple hosts. The ability to only allow a given host to see the LUN it is supposed to see is referred to as *LUN masking*. LUN masking provides an extra level of security for the SAN device.

For example, when a Windows server comes online, it actively searches for available LUNs. IF a LUN is available to the server, the server will write its signature. The writing of this signature can cause data loss because it has the potential to erase the current file system. For this reason (and other, more malicious, reasons), LUN masking is an integral part of any SAN security program.

♦ SANs are often used when clustering servers because the same storage can be shared by the cluster.

♦ SAN devices are designed to be peers of, rather than subservient to, a host.

♦ Manufacturers provide different SAN configuration tools and methods. A simple example would be using a Graphical User Interface (GUI) versus a command-line interface.

♦ Most often, the intelligence for a SAN is contained within the SAN device itself.

♦ Network configuration and management options also vary, sometimes even by model within a given manufacturer's SAN product line.

SAN properties

This section discusses the SAN technology properties and how a SAN operates. Using the material from this discussion, you can continue to add to your evaluation workbook and build your SAN evaluation matrix to better understand SAN technology security issues and concerns. Your focus is on SAN data storage or SAN-based hard disks.

♦ **Block-based:** Many SAN devices use block-style logic that stems from DAS technologies. This allows SAN devices to use commonly available communication methods to provide connectivity to these larger-scale storage devices. Among the most common of these transfer methodologies is the *block transfer methodology*. In very simple terms, technologies that use block-based transfer methods address the data by disk block number(s), and either transfer the data contained in the referenced block(s) to the accessing device (read) or place data into the referenced block(s) (write). Figure 4-2 illustrates a block read. On a SAN, this block-style communication is accomplished over the storage area network using an adapter or device that can communicate directly with the storage device, can reference the correct address, and can transmit and receive blocks in the correct format much like a direct attached storage device. This adapter must be able to convert communications into an understandable form for the storage area network block transfer mode required. Devices installed in the host are often called Host Bus Adapters (HBAs), or more generically, *SAN adapters*. Once inserted into the hosts, these adapters can be directly connected to the storage area network device or through a SAN hub or switch. Therefore, unlike in a DAS connection such as a parallel SCSI connection, a host need not be directly connected to a SAN storage device.

♦ Figure 4-2 illustrates a host making a request from a SAN disk at a given address location. The storage device responds with the data stored at the specified location.

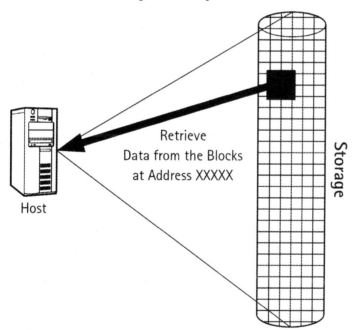

Host

Retrieve
Data from the Blocks
at Address XXXXX

Storage

Figure 4-2: A block transfer from SAN storage device to host

NOTE: SAN devices are often, though not always, configured in close proximity to their host devices.

♦ **Partitioned:** SAN storage devices are designed to centralize storage. In order to accomplish this, such devices can contain large quantities of raw storage. This storage can be provided on a one-to-one, one-to-many, or many-to-many basis. Since many devices can be attached to the SAN storage device, it must be divided up or partitioned. Figure 4-3 shows ten disks and four servers, illustrating a many-to-many scenario. Notice that the storage is divided, but not equally, to allow access by the four servers. Server 1 actually has access to four disks, two in each storage cabinet. Server 2 has access to three drives, Server 3 has access to two drives, and Server 4 has access to one drive. This partitioning is typically performed using the SAN storage configuration tools. Since these tools differ, it is important to evaluate each type of tool available for the possible SAN storage devices you are considering.

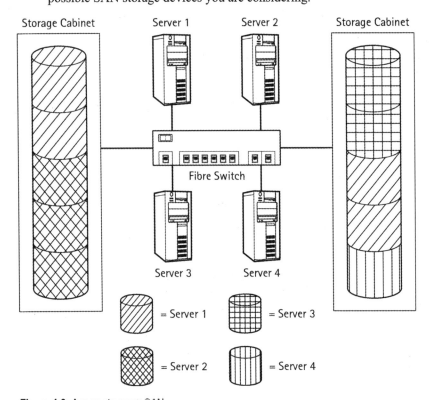

Figure 4-3: A many-to-many SAN

♦ **Operating system:** When a SAN is used, some sort of host must be configured to connect to the SAN. Since SAN adapters are needed in order to communicate with a SAN, the OS must support the SAN adapter (or else drivers must be available), and the equipment must support the SAN adapter. The host and OS therefore determine the file system used on the portion of the SAN storage device to which the host has access. If file sharing is required, the OS is responsible for providing this functionality. A NAS

device that can meet the criteria necessary to connect to a SAN can leverage the
functionality of a SAN and still be able to share files in NAS fashion.

♦ **Served up/LUNs:** Different SAN technologies provide access to storage devices using
different means. One of the most common methods today is to provide Logical Unit
Numbers (LUNs) that many operating systems can see. You can accomplish this using a
SAN configuration utility. LUNs can be made available to many devices or just one.
This is possible because each HBA (Host Bus Adapter) has an address, much like a
MAC address on a network interface card, and the storage can be served up to only that
address, multiple addresses, or all addresses.

♦ **SAN fabric:** Devices that connect other devices to a SAN comprise the SAN fabric.
This is typically accomplished through the use of a SAN switch.

♦ **Multiple layers (hubs/switches):** One of the many reasons SANs are attractive is that
they can provide access to a much greater number of storage devices than a typical DAS
technology. On a standard one-level (flat) SAN, 126 devices can exist. However, by
cascading switches and hubs, the theoretical physical number becomes limitless. As you
can see in Figure 4-4, continual cascading could allow access to a very large number of
devices. However, this flexibility carries a cost. The level of complexity involved in
designing, configuring, maintaining, and securing this configuration definitely increases.
It is also important to note here that switches do not only come in the Fibre Channel
variety. HiPPI, for example, uses switches with standard HiPPI connection interfaces as
well as serial HiPPI.

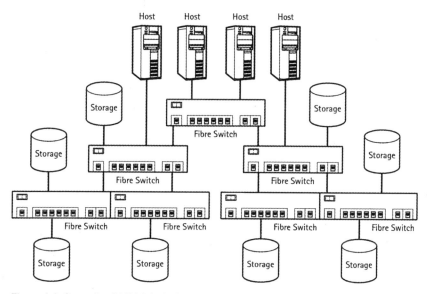

Figure 4-4: Cascading SAN fabric devices

♦ **Zoning:** Since a SAN is a network and the network can use switches, it stands to reason
that there should be a way to segment the network. On Fibre Channel, this segmentation
is called zoning. If you're familiar with virtual local area networks (VLANs) and virtual

private networks (VPNs), then the concept of zoning should be relatively easy to understand. Zoning allows devices to be placed into logical groups called *zones*. The zones of a SAN fabric can overlap, allowing a device to reside in more than one zone. In Figure 4-5, notice that Host A is outside the zones and can potentially access any zone, Host B can access storage in Zone 1 and Zone 2, and Host C can access storage devices in Zones 2 and 3.

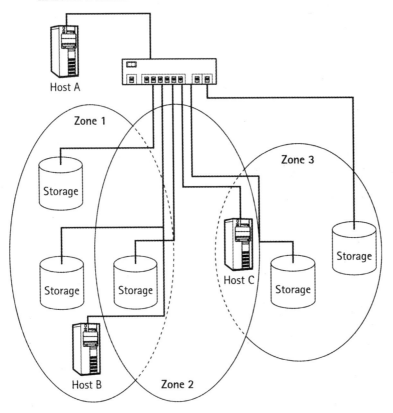

Figure 4-5: SAN zoning example

SECURITY THOUGHT: If you view security from a conventional standpoint, you may end up with only conventional security. Hackers, however, are unconventional.

♦ **Connection method(s):** Connection methods can vary greatly, depending on the type of technology implemented. Among the most common connection methods is Fibre Channel, which can be connected using ST-, SC-, or LC-style connections directly between the HBA and the SAN device, or via a hub or switch. However, other options also exist. HiPPI, for example, can be connected using fiber (serial HiPPI) or standard HiPPI (parallel connectors) switches.

♦ **Cloning/Snapping:** One of the most common reasons companies consider implementing a SAN, and specifically the network portion of a SAN, is to reduce the backup window of storage devices by implementing high-speed backup devices that can communicate directly to the SAN disk device(s) over the storage network. Cloning and snapping/snap shotting can be used to provide either a complete copy of the data (cloning) or a point-in-time snapshot of the data (snapping/snap shotting). These clones or snaps can be used to allow data to be backed up while production data continues to operate.

♦ **RAID, online hot spare, and data replication:** We know that SAN devices are designed to house large numbers of physical hard drives to create large data storage pools. We also know that the devices that fail most in electronics are devices that have moving parts. Just talk to any hard drive, tape drive, or jukebox manufacturer. Therefore, the probability of failure within a SAN increases with each drive added. For this reason, RAID, online hot spare drives, and data replication become even more important. Most SAN manufacturers have multiple RAID levels that can be implemented on their device(s). Additionally, most support online hot sparing of physical disk drives. When a hard disk fails, the SAN device senses the failure, and the online hot spare automatically inserts itself in place of the failed drive. If the failed drive was part of a RAID set, data begins to be rebuilt on the spare drive. Data replication is most often a component of a Disaster Recovery Plan. The primary difference between a snap or clone versus data replication is "live data." Data replication creates two copies of data, one local and one remote, and tracks changes. When the live data is changed, the replicated data is also changed. In this fashion, the data is kept up-to-date. To some extent, data replication can be thought of as long-distance mirroring.

♦ **Split bus, backplane, or channels:** Within the SAN disk device enclosure, the backplane, or bus, is where the physical hard drives get a connection. These backplanes may be split up into several backplanes to provide additional fault tolerance and to increase performance. By splitting the bus, a single operation can cause functions to occur on multiple devices simultaneously, in parallel rather than serially.

♦ **Architecture:** SAN devices operate differently depending on the manufacturer. Some manufacturers use Fibre Channel to the SAN device and SCSI within the device, whereas other manufacturers use Fibre throughout. A Fibre Disk drive is not as readily available as its SCSI counterpart.

♦ **Caching:** Memory access is definitely faster than hard drive access, so another performance-enhancing feature that many SAN devices employ is caching. In very simple terms, *caching* is a method of using memory to store recently accessed data and the adjacent block of that data into memory to allow faster access (a read cache). Many devices also have a cache that stores the data to be written to the storage device(s), which keeps the host from waiting for all the data to be stored before moving on to other processing functions. SAN devices that implement caching very often provide backup power to the cache in the event of power failure.

♦ **Clustering:** Clustering can also improve the availability of devices in the event of a failure. A *cluster* is two or more host devices configured as a team. Within a cluster, the team members can all be active participants, or some may be active and some only become active in the event of a failure. In any case, one of the primary purposes of the cluster is to provide redundancy. SANs provide an excellent medium for clusters.

Figure 4-6 illustrates a two-host cluster using redundant links. Servers A and B form the cluster. Each server contains two HBAs and is connected to both Fibre Switches. In addition, SAN A and SAN B are both connected to the Fibre Switches, which allows both servers to see both SAN storage devices, providing good redundancy.

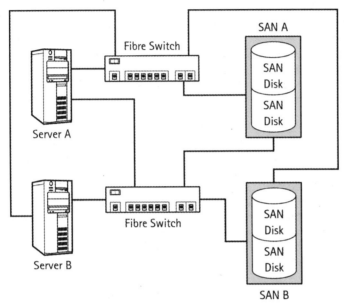

Figure 4-6: Dual SAN server cluster

♦ **Configuration software/options:** Because there are multiple components within a SAN, the configuration options and parameters for each should be evaluated. The two general methods of configuration for SAN devices are command line–based and graphical-based. Different manufacturers leverage different configuration tools and options. Even within a given manufacturer's product line, the configuration tools for different models may vary. Also, because SAN storage devices contain many options, SAN manufacturers have created SAN configuration/management tools to make the tasks more user-friendly. The strength of the authentication of both methods should be evaluated. Some SAN devices can be configured directly from a general host, and it is therefore possible for accidental or malicious reconfiguration to cause data loss. Most SAN devices can be configured to reduce this possibility.

♦ **SNMP/CMIP management:** As with DAS and NAS, most SAN devices can be managed using a management protocol. The security strengths and weaknesses of the management protocol and how it is used must be evaluated. This evaluation must include the ability of the management protocol and configuration application to alter configurations.

♦ **BIOS/Integrated software issues:** Because SAN devices can use BIOS as well as images that can be contained on removable media or flash memory, the tools, methods of upgrading, and strength of security inherent to these devices should also be considered. Devices that can be "flashed" over an IP connection can provide a potential vulnerability to DoS and even loss of data attacks, and should therefore be closely guarded.

♦ **Client communication:** Although it is possible to connect a client directly to a SAN and provide storage to devices individually, clients most often communicate to the SAN storage devices through another host device (for example, a server). This communication takes place in the same fashion as servers connected to DAS storage devices. Security concerns must be escalated, however, because more data is likely to be available through a single device attached to a SAN than it is with DAS. The communication method used to connect to the host or server depends on the configuration of the server and clients, rather than the SAN storage device. For example, a network running only AppleTalk could share files to other network devices using only AppleTalk if the server was configured to do so. This can be an important point where security is concerned.

> **NOTE:** Many servers connected to SAN storage devices are configured to share files in similar fashion to NAS. Some of these same servers provide additional services—not just file sharing. It is important to understand what services are being provided and the potential impact of these services if they are breached.

Limitations

One of the main purposes of a SAN is to reduce limitations. For this reason, many of the limitations associated with DAS or NAS do not exist within SAN technology. However, SANs are not totally boundless; they do have some limitations, as you will see in the following sections.

Functional use

Because SANs use block-based transfers, they require the use of a specialized adapter in order to communicate between a host and a SAN device, be it a switch, disk storage device, or tape device. The adapter varies depending on which SAN architecture is chosen. A Serial Storage Architecture HBA is different from a standard HiPPI SAN adapter, which is different from a Fibre Channel HBA.

Host-based file sharing and database access

SANs provide greater flexibility in use than that of a general NAS, because the storage in a SAN device can be connected to transactional-style devices (database servers), mail servers, multimedia servers, and NAS servers. Since a SAN's primary purpose is to provide storage to hosts, it is the host that determines the access to the data, and therefore the limitation.

Distances

In the case of a standalone host device (for example, without the use of a NAS), the distance between the host and the SAN device is limited. Because most NAS devices can communicate via TCP/IP, and can be implemented on a production network, the host-to-device communication can occur at almost any distance where end-to-end latency (the time it takes for a datagram to travel from point-of-origin to destination) is not an issue. However, SAN host devices must be able to physically connect to the SAN fabric. Because different technologies can be used with a SAN, and because different manufacturers' products vary, so do actual distance limitations. Standard HiPPI (the parallel version) defines a cable length of up to 25 meters, whereas Fibre Channel can support up to 10 kilometers.

Complexity

Another limitation, either real or perceived, is that SANs are complex. This belief is largely due to the fact that SANs are still not as widely understood as other technologies. When limited understanding is combined with multiple device options, hubs and switches, zoning, cloning, snapping, data replication, multiple RAID options, tape backup options, and the myriad of configuration, management, and monitoring options, it is no wonder that this perception is perpetuated. However, SANs can also be almost as simple as a direct attached storage device.

Device support

Some manufacturers' device drivers do not support some operating systems or platforms, such as clustering of those operating systems. When you need a large quantity of storage, and a SAN device does not support the platform, NAS may be required. However, if you choose a NAS server that is supported by the SAN, and the SAN supports the options and operating systems needed at a future date, a NAS server and SAN combined might be a good solution.

Features/options

Many SAN devices exhibit similar or duplicated features. However, some SAN manufacturers provide configuration devices that only operate on a single platform and/or operating system. Depending on the platform, how it's implemented, and the potential modifications made to the OS, this method can either provide a security advantage or can introduce additional security weaknesses.

This theory also holds true with additional features of a given SAN implementation. For example, the ability to modify a SAN configuration using only SNMP might pose a substantial security risk. A substantial risk could also be posed if configuration features or options have substandard or no built-in security.

Serially-based

Fiber and Fibre Channel technologies use light pulses to communicate data over optical cables. Since these transmissions occur serially, and even though high speeds are achieved over these technologies, the fact is that serial communication can still be considered a limitation relating to storage technologies. Just imagine, for a moment, parallel Fibre Channel connections where multiple fibers connect to a device in parallel for the purpose of increasing the bandwidth.

An example of this parallel theory exists in other network devices that can aggregate links or ports together. For example, many Cisco switches support Ether-Channels. This is accomplished by combining two links/ports together and aggregating the bandwidth to increase speeds.

Determining SAN Security

Because a SAN is an integral part of an infrastructure's framework and reliable data processing is a primary concern, the need to protect this data over a variety of delivery channels is key. With the explosion of SANs routing confidential enterprise information, perimeter security is simply not enough to protect against data hijackers, crackers, remote attackers, and malicious users. With that said, a corporate strategy and policy for a secure SAN is required to implement the necessary safeguards. Most of these safeguards originate within the internal foundation, spiraling out to the perimeter firewalling systems, adhering to the ripple security mentioned in a previous chapter. They should address the most critical security risks inherited to and/or from a SAN, including:

♦ **Unauthorized access:** Local users and remote attackers can access classified data.

♦ **Unauthenticated access:** Unprivileged users can access privileged data.

♦ **Unprotected administrator access:** Unencrypted local and remote administrator authentication and access can be achieved.

♦ **Idle host scanning and spoofing:** Advanced discovery and/or local trusted systems can be used to masquerade as a trusted device to retrieve sensitive information and/or compromise security.

♦ **Vulnerable delivery channel access points:** Exposed zones, islands, and remote networks can compromise security.

♦ **Data hijacking and sniffing:** Exposed data links and vulnerable operating systems can be exploited by external attackers.

SAN topologies

There are varying types of SAN technologies that can be used to build a SAN infrastructure. The following list comprises some of the more well-known SAN technologies.

♦ **Fibre Channel:** Fibre Channel is currently the media for which most SAN manu-facturers are designing products. As previously mentioned, devices can connect directly to each other using an FC-Hub, a Fibre Channel Switch, or combinations thereof. When devices are directly connected, the configuration is referred to as *point-to-point*. Devices can also connect in a logical loop using a hub or a physical loop by directly connecting several devices together to form a physical loop. This type of configuration can also be called a *Fibre Channel Arbitrated Loop (FC-AL)*. The loop functions in similar fashion to an FDDI ring, since the ring reconfigures itself as devices are added or removed, or if a device fails. Another important point is that as more and more devices are added, the size of the ring increases. When Fibre Channel switches are used to connect SAN de-vices, the network may also be referred to as a *SAN fabric*. Switches are used to create point-to-point connections that operate at high speeds. In contrast to FC-AL, as devices are added, there is no ring to increase.

♦ **HiPPI:** Another technology used for SANs, HiPPI can operate using its native parallel connectors, which are directly connected to devices (as discussed in Chapter 2) or used to create a SAN by connecting HiPPI parallel to HiPPI parallel switches. Additionally, HiPPI serial can be connected in point-to-point or switched fashion using fiber.

♦ **SSA:** Serial Storage Architecture can also be used in point-to-point or chained in linear fashion, loop, or using switches. The connections can be made using the standard four-wire copper connections or fiber optic.

♦ **Gigabit Ethernet:** Because of its prevalence in the marketplace, and its low cost when compared to Fibre Channel, some SAN manufacturers have designed SAN devices that use Gigabit Ethernet. The primary difference between these devices and NAS devices still remains in the transfer method. Although the communication may be encapsulated in IP, the transfer takes place in a block fashion.

Other SAN-style technologies

As enterprises grow, they must leverage current investments and also communicate over longer distances. To accomplish this, manufacturers have developed products that allow legacy storage devices to be connected to storage networks, as well as products that can extend the communication distances. Some of these storage network devices are Fibre Channel Bridges, multiplexers, repeaters, and routers. This area is still plagued by a great deal of ambiguity, as many terms are used interchangeably (bridge and router, for example), but devices such as these can extend the physical distance limitations and allow legacy storage devices, such as SCSI, to communicate over Fibre Channel.

♦ **iSCSI:** Internet SCSI (iSCSI) is one of the emerging technologies that allow SAN communication (block-style communication) over IP. The impetus behind iSCSI's development is largely the need for companies to leverage Gigabit Ethernet (and beyond) over copper. Since Ethernet technology is widely used, very well-known and less expensive than comparable fiber and Fibre options, creating a separate storage network could become as simple as creating a separate segment or another VLAN. This is very appealing to many organizations, especially when considering 10 Gbps Ethernet and beyond.

♦ **FCIP:** Fiber Channel over IP is a proposed standard that will permit multiple SANs to be connected over IP, allowing multiple SANs to communicate over much greater distances than pure Fibre Channel can support. In addition, FCIP can leverage the investment many companies have in Ethernet technology.

♦ **iFCP:** Internet Fibre Channel Protocol is geared towards allowing SAN devices to be linked to existing IP infrastructures. Fibre Channel switches, for example, could be replaced with Ethernet devices using iFCP.

♦ **iSNS:** Internet Storage Naming Service is a standard proposed by Nishan Systems. This protocol enables discovery and naming services for SAN storage devices running over IP. Because it resolves some of the compatibility issues of iSCSI, it is possible that iSNS along with iSCSI will be used together.

Each of these technologies can suffer from the same non-deterministic characteristics associated with TCP/IP. This means that even though they are capable of performing block data transfers over IP, if they are connected to applications that need deterministic connectivity, timeout issues may still arise. This can cause applications such as databases to time out, resulting in loss or corruption of data.

Because these technologies are still struggling with standards, we will not devote a great deal of time to them. It is important to note, however, that we anticipate they will begin to show up soon.

> **SECURITY THOUGHT:** Block-based transfers encapsulated in IP add an additional dimension to IP security measures because it becomes possible for an attacker to capture blocks of transferred information from applications like databases. Specific storage devices (similar to current firewalls) will most likely emerge in the future to address the potential threat.

Using the SAN security matrix

Keeping in mind the previously mentioned critical security risks, in this section you use another matrix to grade additional SAN security aspects. The evaluation criteria used incorporates the primary SAN security concerns that can be used as a gauge to assist toward developing a secure strategy, some of which are touched upon later in this chapter.

Two main categories of SAN storage options must be evaluated. The first category comprises the SAN technology options, which are evaluated in much the same way as DAS technology. The second category comprises device-specific features and limitations. Matrices for both categories are provided, in Figures 4-7 and 4-8. The criteria used in the DAS technology matrix have been discussed in Chapter 2. Since the SAN technology options use the same criteria, they will not be reviewed here. Instead, refer to Figure 4-7, which illustrates the SAN technology security matrix.

The device-specific security matrix shown in Figure 4-8 uses a different set of evaluation criteria. Note that options vary not only between competing SAN devices, but also within the models in a given manufacturer's product line. Therefore, features are not always implemented with the same emphasis on security.

SANs, much like other computing devices, can fall into many categories. For example, entry-level SAN storage devices are very inexpensive compared to their enterprise counterparts. For this reason, when you evaluate SAN devices, make sure that you are evaluating similar devices, but that there is some overlap in the evaluation criteria. General level categories are included within the matrix to show how the matrix can be used to evaluate different levels of different manufacturers' devices.

The matrix uses the following evaluation criteria:

♦ **(A) Scalability:** One of the primary reasons to implement a SAN is to provide storage scalability. Scalability is the ability of a storage device to grow. The level of scalability is oftentimes determined by the amount of physical storage that can be contained within the SAN device. However, the more physical storage available within a device, the more the potential for catastrophic data loss, or non-authorized data exposure. A device that can have many terabytes therefore rates lower than a device that cannot. The following list shows some relative breakpoints when considering individual products. Undoubtedly, if a company with 50 or more terabytes of storage were not able to access the data on that storage device, the failure would be considered catastrophic.

- 1 = More than fifty terabytes of storage.
- 2 = Twenty-five to forty-nine terabytes of storage.
- 3 = Five to twenty-four terabytes of storage.
- 4 = One to four terabytes of storage.
- 5 = Less than one terabyte of storage.

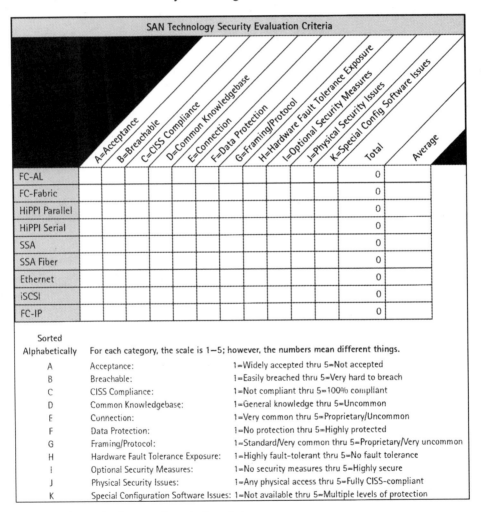

SAN Technology Security Evaluation Criteria												
	A=Acceptance	B=Breachable	C=CISS Compliance	D=Common Knowledgebase	E=Connection	F=Data Protection	G=Framing/Protocol	H=Hardware Fault Tolerance Exposure	I=Optional Security Measures	J=Physical Security Issues	K=Special Config Software Issues	Total	Average
FC-AL												0	
FC-Fabric												0	
HiPPI Parallel												0	
HiPPI Serial												0	
SSA												0	
SSA Fiber												0	
Ethernet												0	
iSCSI												0	
FC-IP												0	

Sorted Alphabetically	For each category, the scale is 1–5; however, the numbers mean different things.	
A	Acceptance:	1=Widely accepted thru 5=Not accepted
B	Breachable:	1=Easily breached thru 5=Very hard to breach
C	CISS Compliance:	1=Not compliant thru 5=100% compliant
D	Common Knowledgebase:	1=General knowledge thru 5=Uncommon
E	Connection:	1=Very common thru 5=Proprietary/Uncommon
F	Data Protection:	1=No protection thru 5=Highly protected
G	Framing/Protocol:	1=Standard/Very common thru 5=Proprietary/Very uncommon
H	Hardware Fault Tolerance Exposure:	1=Highly fault-tolerant thru 5=No fault tolerance
I	Optional Security Measures:	1=No security measures thru 5=Highly secure
J	Physical Security Issues:	1=Any physical access thru 5=Fully CISS-compliant
K	Special Configuration Software Issues:	1=Not available thru 5=Multiple levels of protection

Figure 4-7: SAN technology security evaluation criteria

	A=Scalability	B=Partitioning	C=Share Method	D=Security Domain Zoning	E=Snap/Clone/Data Replication	F=BIOS/Flash	G=Authentication/Encryption	Total	Average
Entry Level								0	
Workgroup Level								0	
Department Level								0	
Division Level								0	
Enterprise Level								0	

Sorted Alphabetically	For each category, the scale is 1–5; however, the numbers mean different things.	
A	Scalability:	1=More than 50TB thru Less than 1TB
B	Partitioning:	1=Non Secure partitioning thru 5=Command line
C	Share Method:	1=All pools any device thru 5=Secure 1-to-1
D	Security Domain Zoning:	1=Limited or none thru 5=All known
E	Snap/Clone/Data Replication:	1=DR no encryption thru 5=None
F	BIOS/Flash:	1=TCP/IP thru 5=Internal Replacement
G	Authentication/Encryption:	1=None thru 5=Advanced

Figure 4-8: Device-specific security matrix

♦ **(B) Partitioning:** The available storage on SAN storage devices is commonly divided up into smaller amounts and allowed to be accessed by different hosts. Devices commonly do this via software, but it can also be accomplished physically. Because the methods and ability to partition vary, theyshould be evaluated separately. A storage device that can achieve the most secure rating should be considered the best partitioning option from a security perspective.

- 1 = Partitioning can be accomplished remotely over potentially nonsecure transmission media.

- 2 = Partitioning can be accomplished remotely but has proprietary encryption.

- 3 = Partitioning can be accomplished locally via network tools.

- 4 = Partitioning can be accomplished only from the SAN storage device using a GUI tool.

- 5 = Partitioning can be accomplished only from the SAN storage device using only command-line options.

♦ **(C) Share method:** After the storage is logically divided into smaller amounts, it must also be made available (served up) to hosts. The way this is accomplished can dramatically affect security, data availability, and data integrity. If a device allows the least secure option, and that is its default configuration, it should be rated low. These sharing methods are partially configuration-based and partially feature-based.

  - 1 = All disk pools can be advertised to any connected device.
  - 2 = All disk pools can be advertised to all connected devices with some security—for example, using only the HBA IDs of the connected host.
  - 3 = A single disk pool is available to any connected device.
  - 4 = A single disk pool can be advertised to all connected devices with some security—for example, using only the HBA IDs of the connected host.
  - 5 = A single disk pool is available to a single device securely.

♦ **(D) Security domain zoning:** Some industries establish strict regulations on how data must be protected, such as allowing devices to only see certain other devices containing data. One method of addressing this requirement is through zoning (security domain zoning is discussed later in this chapter). There are multiple components of security domain zoning. Some of those can be related to VLANs and VPNs, while others are more closely related to access control lists. The greater the flexibility of security support, the higher the security domain zoning rating.

  - 1 = Limited or no security domain zoning support.
  - 2 = Strong authentication.
  - 3 = Strong encryption.
  - 4 = Strong authentication and encryption.
  - 5 = Support for all known security domain zoning exists, including items such as ACLs.

♦ **(E) Snapping/cloning/data replication:** Snapping, cloning, and data replication are technologies designed primarily to enhance data availability and protect the data from loss. However, the ability to support these technologies means that multiple copies of data exist, which can create additional security risks. Of the available options, snapping is considered the most secure because without access to the original data, the snap is not very useful. However, a clone or replicated data provides duplicate information that can be compromised. The strength of the security used to achieve each of these clones or snaps can have a dramatic effect on risk.

  - 1 = Remote data replication without encryption or other security measures.
  - 2 = Remote data replication with encryption or other security measures.
  - 3 = Snapping and cloning.
  - 4 = Snapping.
  - 5 = No inherent snapping, cloning, or data replication.

CROSS-REFERENCE: Snapping, cloning, and data replication are more thoroughly discussed in Chapters 5 and 6.

♦ **(F) BIOS/Flash:** The ability to update or change firmware on a device is important because that allows it to be flexible for future needs. However, the method in which these updates are performed can vary by device and manufacturer. Devices that can only be upgraded by replacing an internal device are considered to be the most secure, whereas devices that can potentially be configured to allow the update/upgrade to occur over the Internet, for example, are considered least secure.

  • 1 = An update or upgrade can be performed via TCP/IP or SNMP.

  • 2 = An update or upgrade can be performed only by devices that can attach to the storage network.

  • 3 = An update or upgrade can be accomplished by replacing an externally located device such as a Flash Memory card.

  • 4 = Proprietary software or devices must connect directly to an upgrade/update port on the SAN storage device to allow an update to occur.

  • 5 = The BIOS is internal and can only be updated or upgraded by gaining physical access to the internal device, and by removal or replacement of the BIOS.

♦ **(G) Authentication/Encryption:** This category refers to the inherent ability to employ identification and authentication techniques and compatibility with several schemes from knowledge-based to characteristic-based techniques.

  • 1 = None: If the type of SAN technology has an inherent lack of encryption acceptance or does not comply.

  • 2 = Some identification: This rating includes knowledge-based authentication techniques such as strong passwords.

  • 3 = Some encryption: This rating includes the ability to encrypt data.

  • 4 = Good identification and encryption: This rating includes a combination of strong identification and the ability to encrypt data.

  • 5 = Advanced authentication: These types of SAN technologies support authentication technologies such as tokens and tickets.

Providing a Secure SAN Foundation

Face it: the best defense for a SAN framework security strategy is a good offense. In other words, if you identify the vulnerable points in your SAN infrastructure and implement reliable security solutions, you can lock down and control the infrastructure, thereby ensuring a reliable, secure foundation. Your goal at this juncture is to provide a secure SAN foundation template that addresses the critical SAN security risks, including device manageability, access control management, administration, authentication, custom scalability and flexibility, security domains, security controls, and security auditing.

Manageability

One of the most important control factors for a secure SAN framework is the capability to manage every SAN device throughout the infrastructure, including local and remote SANs and SAN islands. Next in line is the ability to manage trusted switches, routers, and any other internetworking equipment throughout the framework. A local client/server-based SAN management system can deliver centralized control for all enterprise-wide devices.

Access control management

Administrative accessibility and exposed interfaces require strict management in a secure SAN environment. Encryption, passwords, and access control systems should be implemented and monitored. A variety of access control techniques and combinations thereof can be implemented for different environments, including:

- **Discretionary access control (DAC):** This control restricts access to data based on the user and/or access levels to which they belong. A user or process given discretionary access to information is capable of passing that information along to another user.

- **Mandatory access control (MAC):** This multilevel security technique prevents a user from making information available subjectively. All users and data resources are classified with a security label where access is denied if the user's label does not match that of the resource.

- **Lattice-based access control:** Every user and data resource is associated with an ordered set of classes. Resources of a particular class may only be accessed by those whose associated class is as high as or higher than that of the resource.

- **Rule-based access control:** Every access request is compared to the user's rights in order to grant or deny access.

- **Role-based access control:** Every user is assigned a role, and each role is assigned specific levels of access privileges that are inherited by the user.

- **Access control lists (ACLs):** A database or table that contains individual access rights for each resource and each user (for example, a collection of users who have been given permission to use an object and the types of access they have been permitted).

These access control techniques have been theorized into several models for representations of each, as follows:

- **The Bell-LaPadula Model** includes mandatory access control by determining access rights from different security levels, and discretionary access control by cross-referencing access rights from a matrix.

- **The Clark-Wilson Model** achieves data integrity with both a well-formed transaction that prevents users from manipulating data and a separation of duties that prevents users from making unauthorized changes.

- **The Biba Model** protects data integrity by specifying that a subject cannot execute objects with a lower level of integrity, modify objects that have a higher level of integrity, and request service from other subjects that have a higher level of integrity.

♦ **The U.S. Defense Department's National Security Agency Orange Book**
specifications account for the attached system's security policy, accountability
mechanisms in the system, and the operational and life cycle assurance of the system's
security.

Access administration

Upon approval, accounts should be created, and access rights and permissions should be
implemented by way of the file and data owner's method (each data resource is assigned an
owner, or administrator, who is responsible for its rights and permissions), the principle of
least privilege (every user is granted the minimum level of permissions—just enough to do his
or her job), and/or a separation of duties and responsibilities (a power control where the same
person who creates accounts shouldn't also approve the creation of accounts, or grant access
rights, and so on). Upon activation, account usage or accesses should be logged, journaled,
and monitored.

Authentication

User identification and authentication is also an important factor for a secure SAN framework.
The most common methods include strong passwords, biometrics, tickets, and tokens.

Strong passwords

Passwords and accounts should not be shared and should be actively managed separately.
Password policies should be enforced and should also specify that a password be changed
initially and on a recurring basis. More specifically, passwords should be changed:

♦ At least every 3 to 6 months.

♦ Immediately after the password is relinquished.

♦ As soon as password has been compromised or even suspected of a compromise.

Password guidelines

A password should contain at least eight characters. At least two of these characters must be
letters and at least one must be a nonletter character. Any new passwords must differ from the
old ones by at least three characters. Use the following general password guidelines instituted
by the U.S. government:

♦ Passwords must contain at least eight nonblank characters.

♦ Passwords must contain a combination of letters (preferably a mixture of upper- and
lowercase letters), numbers, and at least one special character within the first seven
positions.

♦ Passwords must contain a nonnumeric letter or symbol in the first and last positions.

♦ Passwords must not contain the user login name.

♦ Passwords must not include the user's own or a close friend's or relative's name, employee number, Social Security number, birth date, telephone number, or any information about him or her that the user believes could be readily learned or guessed.

♦ Passwords must not include common words from an English dictionary or a dictionary of another language with which the user is familiar.

♦ Passwords must not contain commonly used proper names, including the name of any fictional character or place.

♦ Passwords must not contain any simple pattern of letters or numbers such as "qwertyxx."

Biometrics

In the world of security, biometrics is the study of measurable biological characteristics. In the computer security world, biometrics refers to authentication techniques that rely on measurable physical characteristics that can be automatically checked, such as computer analysis of fingerprints or speech. Though the field is still in its infancy, many people believe that biometrics will play a critical role in the future of security. Personal computers may someday include a fingerprint scanner on which you would place your index finger to access the computer. The computer would analyze your fingerprint to determine who you are and, based on your identity, authorize different levels of access. Access levels could include the ability to use credit card information to make electronic purchases, change your profile, and so on.

Biometrics also refers to the automatic identification of a person based on his/her physiological or behavioral characteristics. This method of identification is preferred over traditional methods involving passwords and PINs for two main reasons:

♦ The person to be identified is required to be physically present at the point-of-identification.

♦ Identification based on biometric techniques obviates the need to remember a password or carry a token.

With the increased use of computers as vehicles of information technology, it is necessary to restrict access to sensitive/personal data. By replacing PINs, biometric techniques can potentially prevent unauthorized access to or fraudulent use of ATMs, cellular phones, smart cards, desktop PCs, workstations, and computer networks. PINs and passwords may be forgotten, and token-based methods of identification such as passports and driver's licenses may be forged, stolen, or lost. Thus, biometric systems of identification are enjoying a renewed interest. Various types of biometric systems are being used for real-time identification. The most popular are based on face recognition and fingerprint matching, but some utilize iris and retinal scan, speech, facial thermograms, and hand geometry.

A biometric system is essentially a pattern recognition system that makes a personal identification by determining the authenticity of a specific physiological or behavioral characteristic possessed by the user. An important issue in designing a practical identification system is to determine how an individual is recognized. Depending on the context, a biometric system can be either a verification (authentication) system or an identification system.

A person's identity can be resolved in two ways: verification and identification. Verification (I am what I am, but am I whom I claim to be?) involves confirming or denying a person's claimed identity. In identification, one has to establish a person's identity (Who am I?). Each approach presents certain complexities, which could probably be solved best by selecting a certain biometric system from the following list:

- ◆ Fingerprint identification
- ◆ Hand geometry
- ◆ Speaker recognition
- ◆ Face location
- ◆ Retina scanning

Tickets

In TechTarget, tickets are used in the Kerberos authentication system as a secure method for authenticating a request for a service in a computer network. Kerberos was developed in the Athena Project at the Massachusetts Institute of Technology (MIT). If you recall your Greek mythology, Kerberos was a three-headed dog who guarded the gates of Hades. Kerberos—the technology—lets a user request an encrypted "ticket" from an authentication process that can then be used to request a particular service from a server. The user's password does not have to pass through the network. A version of Kerberos (client and server) can be downloaded from MIT, or you can buy a commercial version.

Briefly, here's how Kerberos works:

1. Suppose you want to access a server on another computer (which you can get to by sending a Telnet or similar login request). You know that this server requires a Kerberos "ticket" before it can honor your request.

2. To get your ticket, you first request authentication from the authentication server (AS). The authentication server creates a "session key" (which is also an encryption key), basing it on your password (which it can get from your username) and a random value that represents the requested service. The session key is effectively a "ticket-granting ticket."

3. You next send your ticket-granting ticket to a ticket-granting server (TGS). Although the TGS may be physically the same server as the AS, it is now performing a different service. The TGS returns the ticket that can be sent to the server for the requested service.

4. The service either rejects the ticket or accepts it and performs the service.

5. Because the ticket you received from the TGS is time-stamped, it allows you to make additional requests using the same ticket within a certain time period (typically, eight hours) without having to be reauthenticated. Making the ticket valid for a limited time period makes it less likely that someone else can use it later.

The actual process is much more complicated than the outline presented here. The user procedure may vary somewhat according to implementation.

Tokens

A token is actually a physical security device that knows something of the user, such as a certificate, personal identification number (PIN), or password, and enables authorized access to a system or network. An example of a one-time password token mechanism is RSA's SecureID.

Security tokens provide an extra level of assurance through a method known as *two-factor authentication*: The user has a PIN, which authorizes her as the owner of that particular device. The device then displays a number that uniquely identifies the user to the service, allowing her to log in. The identification number for each user is changed frequently, usually every five minutes or so.

Unlike a password, a security token is a physical object. A key fob (a small hardware device with built-in authentication mechanisms), for example, is practical and easy to carry, and thus easy for the user to protect. Even if the key fob falls into the wrong hands, it can't be used to gain access because the PIN (which only the rightful user knows) is also needed.

Custom scalability and flexibility

Another important aspect to consider when implementing a secure SAN foundation is an open customization policy or method prescribed by a computer operating system or by an application program by which a programmer's application can make requests of the operating system or another application. An advantage of this policy type is that it is extensible with application programming interfaces (APIs), which internal developers can use to create custom security solutions and new vendors can use to participate in the open optimization of security features.

Security domain zones

Several types of domain zones should be implemented for dependable security architecture. They refer to unique administration groups within which members can easily collaborate. This structure simplifies administration when, for example, you need to change privileges or add resources. The changes can be applied to the domain as a whole and also affect each individual component. A domain trust can be employed as a relationship established between two domain zones.

The recommended security domain zones, shown in Figure 4-9, for a SAN foundation include that between the host and switch (Zone A), between the administrators and the access control management systems (Zone B), between the management systems and the switch zone (Zone C), and between separate switch zones (Zone D).

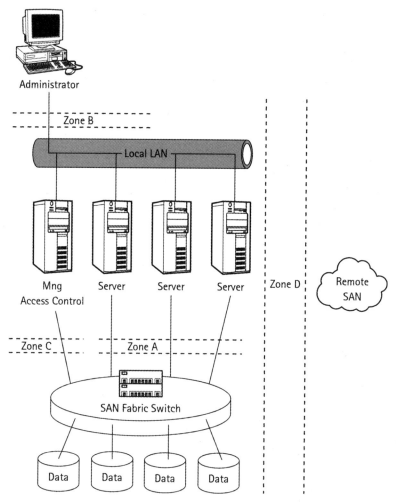

Figure 4-9: Recommended security domains

Host/switch security domain zone

Within the host/switch Zone A, communication between a host and the fabric switch should be controlled by an ACL. This can enforce a conduit of individual device ports to switch ports to secure the connections. Be sure to select a fabric OS that provides secure connection functions, such as enforcing port WWN and fabric ACL.

Administrative/management systems security domain zone

At this zone (Zone B), you should consider employing specific administrative authentication and verification to provide control over the security configurations of the SAN fabric. Your security policy should enforce a marriage between management controls and the security functions.

Management systems/switch security domain zone

Authentication management and monitoring is an important aspect of Zone C. Utilities can be employed to store and encrypt passwords as well. Private/public key encryption should be employed here from the security management systems and the switch, respectively. All data elements should be encrypted by the security management system.

Switch/switch security domain zone

At this juncture, member switches of the SAN fabric should be managed and monitored. Digital certificates and/or public key encryption should be employed during the authentication performed normally between switches. SNMP trap notifiers can be implemented as part of the switch-to-switch fabric security by authorized security managers only.

Security controls overview

According to the Brocade SIA labs (a worldwide storage leader where SANs are rigorously tested), the key components of security controls for a stable and secure SAN infrastructure include the following:

- **Fabric configuration servers:** One or more switches act as trusted devices in charge of zoning changes and other security-related functions.
- **Management access controls:** Management policies and ACLs control access to the switch from different management services.
- **Secure management communications:** Secure management communications interface to the fabric by encrypting certain data elements, such as passwords.
- **Switch connection controls:** ACLs and digital certificates within the switch authenticate new switches and ensure that they can join the fabric.
- **Device connection controls:** Port-level ACLs lock particular WWNs (world wide numbers) to specific ports.

Fabric Configuration Servers

Management access from unsecured and unauthorized sources represents a major threat to fabric security. To address this threat, *Fabric Configuration Servers* enable sensitive administrative operations to be performed only from specified, trusted switches. These designated switches are responsible for managing the configuration and security parameters of all other switches in the fabric. Any number of switches within a fabric can be designated as Fabric Configuration Servers (as specified by WWN), and the list of designated switches is known as *fabric-wide*. In this way, Fabric Configuration Servers secure the manager-to-fabric connection in-band as well as out-of-band.

Within the set of Fabric Configuration Servers is the concept of a "primary" server. Only the primary Fabric Configuration Server can initiate fabric-wide management changes. This capability helps eliminate unidentified local management requests initiated from untrusted switches.

To increase administrator access control, a fabric-wide login name and password database replaces the previous model of switch-specific login names and passwords. This facility applies the same semantics to the SNMP community strings (which constitute a password-type facility to control access to SNMP functions). Organizations can disable this facility through two options, one for SNMP community strings and the other for the standard login name database. Disabling this new security policy results in a reversion to the original policy of unique logins and community strings on each switch.

If the fabric-wide password and community string policies are enabled, any change in login name and/or password or SNMP community string is reflected on all switches in the fabric. In addition, when a new switch joins the fabric, its login/password database is changed to reflect the fabric view.

Management Access Controls

Because certain management services (such as SNMP, SES, API, and Telnet) represent a potential threat of unauthorized access, Management Access Controls restrict their access to the fabric based on policy. If enabled, these policies control access by either IP addresses or WWNs, and the policies are known fabric-wide.

Management Access Controls secure the in-band manager-to-fabric connection by controlling the HBA-to-fabric connections as well. These HBA-to-fabric controls apply to in-band access only. They can also turn off serial ports either individually or fabric-wide to limit access to trusted access points within the fabric.

Organizations can use these controls to selectively disable management access and restrict facility access to a specified set of end points. For example, an end point might be a specific IP address for SNMP, Telnet, or API access—or a specific port WWN for an HBA in a management service used for in-band methods such as SES or Management Server. In this way, Management Access Controls provide additional control beyond the secure management channels by restricting access to trusted access points within the network. These restrictions and any ACLs are known fabric-wide and are automatically installed in new switches that join the fabric. This capability helps prevent unauthorized users from manually changing fabric settings.

Secure management communications

Fibre Channel switches enable standard IP-based management communications between a switch and a manager. Certain elements of the manager-to-switch communications process, such as passwords, are encrypted to increase security.

Switch connection controls

The switch connection controls utilize PKI technology to provide the most comprehensive security solution available for SAN environments. PKI capabilities provide authentication, confidentiality, integrity, and non-repudiation as compared to other types of security solutions.

Switch connection controls enable organizations to restrict fabric connections to a designated set of switches, as identified by WWN. When a new switch is connected to a switch that is already part of the fabric, the new switch must be authenticated before it can join the fabric. Each switch has a digital certificate and a unique private key to enable secure switch-to-switch authentication.

Switch connection controls address this security need by authenticating switches and providing specifications for an authorized switch list. The digital certificate authentication process ensures that an entity professing to be a switch is, in fact, a switch, and that its WWN is correct.

Each E_Port connection between switches invokes a mutual authentication process by using digital certificates and private keys to enable a cryptographically secure multiphase authentication protocol. If the authentication process fails, the E_Port is set to the "segmented" state, logically disconnecting the two switches. This authentication process validates that a specific E_Port connects two legitimate switches, so it must be used on all E_Ports—even if many of them connect to the same pair of switches.

The authorized switch list (as specified by switch WWN) is used during fabric initialization and when a new switch attempts to join a fabric. New switches are configured with certificates and private keys at the time of manufacture. However, organizations with existing switches need to upgrade them with certificate and key information at the installed location.

Switch-to-switch operations are managed in-band, so no IP communications are required. This practice prevents users from arbitrarily adding switches to a fabric.

Device connection controls

Because access control methods deployed in today's SANs use a requestor's WWN to verify access rights, WWN spoofing is a potential threat to SAN security. For example, Brocade Secure Fabric OS addresses this vulnerability with port-level ACL controls known as device connection controls. These controls secure the server (HBA)-to-fabric connection for both normal operations and management functions.

Device connection controls enable organizations to bind a particular WWN to a specific switch port or set of ports, preventing ports in another physical location from assuming the identity of an actual WWN. This capability allows for better control over shared switch environments by allowing only a set of predefined WWNs to access particular ports in the fabric.

Security auditing using a Tiger Box

Vulnerability scanning and penetration testing are part of problem identification auditing and network defense testing against techniques used by intruders. Regularly scheduled security audits should be practiced, whether they apply to enterprise-level or smaller SAN environments. *Tiger teams* are teams of programmers or security professionals that evaluate security to expose errors or security holes. They use what's coined a *Tiger Box*, which contains tools designed to discover, scan, and in some cases penetrate security vulnerabilities.

The central element of a Tiger Box is the operating system foundation. A first-rate Tiger Box is configured in a multiple-boot configuration setting that includes *NIX and, believe it or not, Microsoft Windows operating systems. Currently, Tiger Box utilities for Microsoft's OS are not as popular as those for its *NIX counterpart, but Windows is becoming more competitive in this regard. As you know by now, UNIX is a powerful operating system originally developed at AT&T Bell Laboratories for the scientific, engineering, and academic communities. By its nature, UNIX is a multi-user, multitasking environment that is both flexible and portable; it offers electronic mail, networking, programming, text-processing, and scientific capabilities. Over the years, two major forms (with numerous vendor variants) of UNIX have evolved: AT&T UNIX System V and the University of California at Berkeley's Berkeley Software Distribution (BSD). In addition to Sun Microsystems' Solaris, it is Linux, the trendy UNIX variant, that is commonly configured on a Tiger Box. Linux offers direct control of the O/S command line, including custom code compilation for software stability and flexibility. Linux is customized, packaged, and distributed by many vendors, including the following:

- ◆ **Red Hat Linux** (www.redhat.com)
- ◆ **Slackware** (www.slackware.org)
- ◆ **Debian** (www.debian.org)
- ◆ **TurboLinux** (www.turbolinux.com)
- ◆ **Mandrake** (www.linux-mandrake.com)
- ◆ **SuSE** (www.suse.com)
- ◆ **Trinux** (www.trinux.org)
- ◆ **MkLinux** (www.mklinux.org)
- ◆ **LinuxPPC** (www.linuxppc.org)
- ◆ **SGI Linux** (http://oss.sgi.com/projects /sgilinux11)
- ◆ **Caldera OpenLinux** (www.caldera.com)
- ◆ **Corel Linux** (http://linux.corel.com)
- ◆ **Stampede Linux** (www.stampede.org)

A multiple-boot configuration makes it easy to boot different operating systems on a single Tiger Box. (Note that for simplicity, the Windows complement should be installed and configured prior to *NIX.) At the time of this writing, the Windows versions that are most stable and competent include Windows 2000/Professional/Server. The *NIX flavor regarded as most flexible and supportive is Red Hat Linux (`www.redhat.com`) version 7.3, and/or Sun Microsystems' Solaris 8 (`wwws.sun.com/software/solaris/`). The good news is that, with the exception of the Microsoft operating system, you can obtain the Linux and Solaris binaries at no charge.

Incidentally, if multiboot third-party products "rub you the wrong way," the Red Hat install-ation, among other variants, offers the option of making a boot diskette (containing a copy of the installed kernel and all modules required to boot the system). The boot diskette can also be used to load a rescue diskette. Then, when it is time to execute Windows, simply reboot the system minus the boot diskette; or when using Linux, simply reboot with the boot disk. Inex-perienced users may benefit from using a program such as BootMagic (`www.powerquest.com/products/index.html`) by PowerQuest Corporation for hassle-free, multiple boot setup with a graphical interface.

> **CROSS-REFERENCE:** Chapter 9 covers how to design a sound storage security testing plan, and for more information and detailed instructions on installing and configuring a Tiger Box, refer to Wiley Publishing's *Hack Attacks Testing* publication, or visit `www.TigerTools.net`.

Summary

This chapter begins with the following question: If DAS and NAS can handle databases and heterogeneous file sharing, respectively, what can a SAN offer? The chapter answers that question by defining a SAN and its components and by describing its operation, features, options, and the methods in which it can be connected. There is no doubt that a SAN can provide great flexibility to a company looking to centralize and consolidate data resources. Although the discussion in this chapter primarily revolves around the SAN architecture and the disk-based storage used in that architecture, SANs provide a foundation for other storage devices, including SAN-based tape backup devices.

Security relating to SANs and SAN technologies, as well as critical security issues that can affect a SAN, are also outlined. These criteria are used to create a matrix to assist in evaluating security strengths and weaknesses. This matrix can be modified to accommodate the security strengths and weaknesses of a given product, including its options.

To sum up, SANs offer flexibility, excellent capacity, reliable attachments, more secure connections, and oftentimes more options then DAS or NAS, including the flexibility to connect a NAS device to a SAN.

Chapter 5
Data Availability

One of the primary functions of the International Information Systems Security Certification Consortium, Inc. (ISC)^2 is to maintain a Common Body of Knowledge (CBK) for information security. The CBK is divided up into ten domains and contains applicable security information collected globally for Information Security (IS) professionals. One of the fundamental components of the Ten Domains of Computer Security is the C.I.A. (Confidentiality, Integrity, and Availability) triad. These components are also referred to as the "Big Three," or the "Three Tenets of InfoSec."

- ♦ **Confidentiality** refers to the prevention of the unauthorized disclosure of information.

- ♦ **Integrity** ensures that data modifications are made only by authorized personnel using authorized processes and procedures, and that data consistency is maintained both internally and externally.

- ♦ **Availability** (as it relates to information security) ensures that access to systems and data is available to authorized personnel, reliably and when needed. Any components that affect data availability (systems, network, security devices, and so on) are part of this equation.

In this chapter, we focus on data availability, components that can enhance it, and alternative methods that can make data more available. Confidentiality and integrity are addressed throughout the remaining chapters of this book.

SECURITY THOUGHT: The opposite of C.I.A. is D.A.D (Disclosure, Alteration, and Destruction).

Data Availability Defined

Without much effort, you can find many definitions of data availability. Some storage manufacturers use the term to define products and services designed to ensure data is accessible even in the event of a disaster. Other definitions follow more closely the definition of availability listed above. In terms of storage networks, the goal of data availability is to provide authorized access to the data in a timely fashion under varying circumstances. In order to accomplish this goal, you must understand the keys to data availability.

Keys to data availability

To make data highly available, each area that can affect availability must be known, understood, and accounted for. Since many factors can affect data availability, we have chosen to define the following primary key factors in making data available. Each of these key factors defines a critical area of data availability. They are used as guiding principles to help create a solid foundation to ensure that data remains highly available:

- Capacity planning
- Access methods
- Fault mitigation
- Disaster mitigation
- Duplication
- Management
- Monitoring
- Support plan
- Data protection
- Data backup window

Capacity planning

Data can only remain highly available if you have enough room for all data to co-exist. Although most storage systems and even the applications that use them can have thresholds set and alerts sent out when the thresholds have been reached or exceeded, the fact still remains that if a system runs out of storage space, bad things can happen.

Access methods

Access methods determine how data is accessed. However, each component of data access must be identified individually. These components include the end-user device; access methodology; security components, including identification, authentication, and authorization; data interface; data operation; and intended use (assuming the business need has already been defined). The choice of access method may depend on how a given application functions, who the intended users are, what the intended security is, and many other factors. The following list takes a look at some of these components, working its way backwards from the application to the end user.

- **Intended use:** The intended use is ultimately the reason for implementing an application. Suppose you own a music company, and you want to give consumers the ability to purchase music over the Internet. In this case, you have determined the end-user device access method based on the business requirement. However, this access can be allowed in a variety of ways, ranging from those that have no security to those that are highly secure.

♦ **Data operation:** Once you have a need and intended use, you must determine how this need will be addressed (type of data operation). Does the requirement call for a hierarchical, mesh, relational, or object-oriented database? Equally important, how does the database function? When users access the database, is data transferred to the end user for processing, or is it processed locally and only the results sent to the end user? This question raises a very important security (and performance) consideration, especially when data travels over wide area links.

♦ **Data interface(s):** For a given type of data or application, the data interface may be predetermined, or it may allow for multiple interfaces. An example of using multiple interfaces would be Microsoft Exchange, which can be accessed directly over a network connection, via a POP or IMAP connection, and over the Internet using a browser for Web-based front-end access. In terms of the music company that was just mentioned, prospective buyers would access the data via a Web interface, while internal users, such as accounting, purchasing, and marketing, would most likely use a different interface with greater functionality.

♦ **Identification, authentication, and authorization:** Security must always be a factor when determining the access method. The strength of the security directly impacts the availability of the data. If you give users unsecure access to data over a public connection (such as the Internet), data integrity will be compromised, and data availability will not be far behind. Data protection is covered in Chapter 6.

♦ **Access methodology:** With multiple access options from which to choose, including client/server, thin, fat, and emulation, it would be imprudent not to pick the most secure option. The access methodology greatly affects the authentication and authorization mechanisms that can be used, the type of data interfaces that may be available, and ultimately, the type of data store that may be used.

♦ **End-user device:** The end-user device (or intended user) also affects data availability. Suppose you are responsible for ensuring data availability for a major manufacturing company. You must enter orders, arriving by various means, into a database. This same database contains modules that control inventory and invoicing. The end-user devices that communicate with this database also have Internet and e-mail access, but no virus protection; or they use outdated definition signatures. As you can see, this situation is a recipe for disaster. Allowing the unprotected machines to access the database could corrupt or compromise the data. And what about the user that leaves a remote control program running on his or her machine to connect to it over the Internet?

Based on the factors in this list, it becomes apparent that the combination of the key factors to data availability determines the access method and can dramatically affect what steps must be taken to ensure data availability. Figure 5-1 illustrates a network with multiple access points.

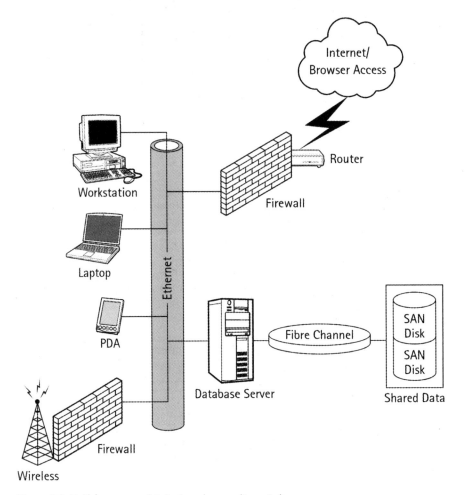

Figure 5-1: Multiple access points that require security controls

Fault mitigation

Fault mitigation refers to the process of determining what types of faults/failures cause data to become unavailable and taking steps to reduce their occurrence. Fault mitigation addresses hardware failures, data corruption, network link failures, security device failures, host failures (micro-, mini-, mainframe, and supercomputer), power failures, and the ways to ensure data availability should any of these occur.

> **CROSS-REFERENCE:** Data protection is also a component of fault mitigation that's discussed in Chapter 6.

Disaster mitigation

Disaster mitigation is the process of preparing for multiple failures or an event that can be categorized as a disaster and then taking steps to mitigate such an event. Events classified as disasters would include long-term power/communication outages, floods, fires, tornadoes, hurricanes, terrorism, and breaches causing loss of data. ISC^2 practices dictate checking even the most secure items to ensure thoroughness in the determination of disastrous events. One of the most effective ways to ensure data availability in the event of a disaster is through data replication.

> **NOTE:** The term *mitigation* is used because reducing the effects of a given disaster to zero may not be possible.

Duplication

Data duplication (or replication) refers to the many methods by which data is backed up, copied, cloned, or otherwise duplicated and used to ensure data availability. Such methods include mirroring, snapping, cloning, data replication technologies, and tape backups and are designed to address the growing business continuance concerns. These technologies are used to reduce the effects of faults, failures, disasters, and breaches that can lead to the destruction of data. Security measures for each type of data duplication must be taken into account when determining which type of data duplication will be used and ultimately how its security will be handled in order to ensure that data remains available.

Management tools

Management tools can be an integral part of ensuring data availability. Such tools can include modules to ensure network and security availability that are critically important to ensuring data availability/accessibility, specific data management tools like database consistency checking tools, indexing tools, and more complex distributed database synchronization and duplication. Storage network devices often include management tools designed to ease the implementation of many of the features available within the storage network device. These types of management tools are often one of the primary differentiators between storage network devices and can include tools to migrate data between platforms, enhance clustered solutions, and manage multiple data duplication/replication options.

Proactive monitoring/alerting

As one of the most overlooked or downplayed features within a network and storage network environment, monitoring tools provide a proactive way to learn about pre-failure and failure situations. Many failures can be avoided simply by providing redundancy within the storage framework design and by setting thresholds and monitoring those thresholds. When a device begins to slip out of the threshold boundaries—such as a disk drive spinning at 15,000 revolutions per minute (RPM)—it can be replaced before it fails completely. If the device threshold is set at 2 percent above or below and the drive RPM drops to 11,999 RPM or below, the drive may continue to operate for a period of time before actually failing. If the device is monitored and an alert is met, the device can be automatically taken out of the production pool and replaced with an online spare. Such an operation allows the drive to be replaced before it fails.

Monitoring and altering should also include all the critical components that allow data to be available, including network, application, authentication/authorization, security, and storage. We'll cover some of these, alongside intrusion detection monitors, in Chapter 9.

Support plan

To create an effective support plan, you must thoroughly understand not only the data classification, but also the level of failure and potential for further failure. In a storage system containing one or more terabytes of data with only two power supplies, you would want to replace one of the power supplies posthaste if it failed. If no provisions had been made for such an event, a replacement might not be available for more than 24 hours—a nerve-wracking situation, at best. Therefore, developing a sound support plan is critical for ensuring data availability.

> **NOTE:** One term used today to globally describe data is *metadata*. In essence, metadata defines the characteristics of data, including data availability, integrity and content, and usage and role(s).

Data protection

Data protection is as important to data availability as any of the previously mentioned tools. However, the methods to protect data are many and varied, and as such, are covered in Chapter 6 in detail.

Backup window

The backup window refers to the amount of time required to back up a given set of data. As data increases, so does the window required to back it up. Backups fall under the data protection category and, as such, secure backup technologies are discussed in Chapter 6.

With a good understanding of the keys to data availability, you can begin to see how the computing environment dramatically affects it. We now look at some secure computing components that embrace one or more of the keys to data availability.

Data availability interdomains

Four interdomains of data availability embrace the key factors that were previously mentioned. These domains ensure the availability of data across the complete spectrum of your environment at the highest level, and should be implemented accordingly.

- ♦ **System domain:** In this domain, you rely on system-specific attributes of availability such as hot plug devices, redundancy, reboot or remote reboot on failure, remote management, multithreaded operating systems, enhanced support, and uninterruptible power supplies (UPSs).

♦ **Storage domain:** In this domain, you rely on availability components of your SAN, NAS, and/or DAS. Also in this domain, you focus on RAID, hot swap drives, external storage, and backup systems, with centralized management backup and restore.

♦ **Application domain:** In this domain, you find availability components like redundant servers, application clustering, load balancing, network connection redundancy, and transparent failover.

♦ **Infrastructure domain:** This domain is responsible for continuous operation and real-time data availability by means of site mirroring.

Each of the components of the interdomains can be applied separately to your environment; however, for concrete high availability, particularly in regards to critical data-sensitive infrastructures, we recommend you pay attention to and apply all interdomains to your environment.

> **CROSS-REFERENCE:** We provide a complete cookie-cutter compendium of the complete set of interdomain security topics in Chapter 8.

Figure 5-2 shows a graphic representation of the four interdomains as part of a standard infrastructure.

Infrastructure availability

For our purposes, the term *infrastructure* includes the components that make up a computing environment, such as security, network hosts, storage, applications, and services. Therefore, the term *infrastructure availability* encompasses overall environment and individual component availability.

The most well-thought-out storage network is useless if its intended users cannot access the data it contains. There can be no doubt that the infrastructure—its design, implementation, security, and maintenance—is among the most critical factors that can determine if data is available. You should ensure that each component of the network is as available as possible.

Security

Security affects both data availability and data protection (though it can sometimes be hard to tell which it affects most). Moreover, proper (or improper) security design, implementation, maintenance, and so on directly affects each of the keys to data availability. Without security, data can still be made available, but it will probably not remain so for very long. Even where security is taken seriously, if the human equation isn't addressed, the most seemingly innocuous act can cause data availability issues.

> **SECURITY THOUGHT:** All too often, the human component of security is not properly addressed, which can lead to accidents or even social engineering breaches.

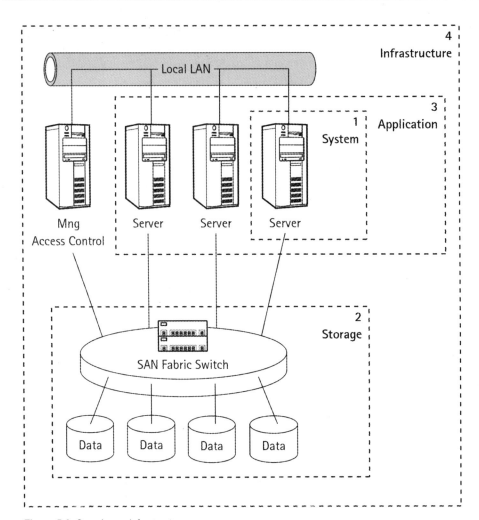

Figure 5-2: Securing an infrastructure

One of the most common nonmalicious security breaches occurs when a user shares his/her authentication information with another individual. The reasons may be harmless, but the results can be disastrous. We can recall several incidents in organizations where someone shared their network credentials with a new employee. In some areas of an organization, this might be considered a minor security infraction. However, what if the culprit was a software developer with full rights who is allowed multiple connections to an application? The implications for data availability would be grievous.

Another very real security problem arises anytime humans manually perform multiple tasks including configurations, updates, upgrades, and tests. This is where a solid security plan, including formalized change control and backup/back-out procedures, must be implemented.

Network access

Whether you are talking about wide area networks (WANs), metropolitan area networks (MANs), campus area networks (CANs), or SANs, the key word is *network*. Almost any network component, including its design, protocol selection, connection options, hosts, and implementation, can affect data availability in some way. The network must be included in the data availability equation if data is to remain highly available. Taking the network into account for data availability is accomplished using different methods depending upon the network component being evaluated. Within an organization, each area of the network must be evaluated to determine the level of availability required to reach the corporate goals, since it is not likely that complete redundancy throughout an organization will be cost-effective. Volumes and volumes of network design information are available, so we do not attempt to duplicate them here. Instead, we point out some general highlights in the following areas that can help increase data availability in your network:

- ◆ Cabling
- ◆ Hubs/switches
- ◆ Routers
- ◆ CAN/MAN/WAN links
- ◆ Internet
- ◆ Wireless p-p, broadcast, cellular infrared, satellite
- ◆ Dial-in
- ◆ Power
- ◆ Alternate access

Cabling

Know and understand cabling and cable strengths and limitations. The cabling should fit the environment and network conditions and should be the right level for the technology, topology, speed, and distances. You must evaluate the environment before you can choose the right type of cabling. If the environment is industrial, containing heavy machinery that can cause electromagnetic interference (EMF), FDDI, fiber, or Fibre Channel are wise choices. Those media are not susceptible to EMF.

Stay within the limitations of the technology, and test all cabling to ensure it passes the necessary requirements.

Provide duplicate cabling runs using separate paths to reduce the possibility of a single cable run failure.

Hubs/switches

Hubs and switches can pose single points of failure. In general, it is not cost-effective to completely duplicate every hub and switch within an organization. Perform a data availability assessment to determine what level of network availability is required for a given grouping within a company so you can decide on and justify redundancy requirements.

How a given switching technology is implemented can also greatly impact availability. Since one component of availability is timely access to the data, a properly designed—but poorly implemented—solution can have an adverse effect.

A full mesh design can pose scalability problems in a large network environment, since it requires a connection from one switch to every other switch. In very large environments, this is simply not practical. A good solution is to provide redundancy in a loop style design, providing alternative paths in the event of a failure. Figure 5-3 illustrates one possible switch redundancy method that can be scaled as needs grow.

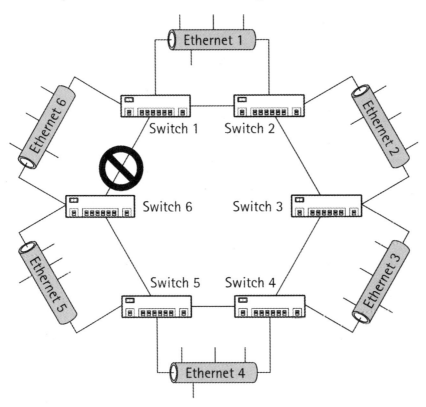

Figure 5-3: Adding availability to your switching core

As you can see, the primary communication path for Ethernet 1 to Ethernet 6 is the direct connection between Switch 1 and Switch 6. If that path became unavailable, or if Switch 1 or Switch 6 happened to fail, Ethernet 1 could still communicate to Ethernet 6 using the alternate paths.

Routers

Much like switches, routers can also pose single points of failures. The same general concepts that apply to switches also apply here. However, routers are often summation points for multiple network segments. When this is the case, the gravity of a single failure increases. If possible, provide redundancy through multiple connections. Figure 5-4 builds on the redundant switch design to incorporate redundancy for routed connections.

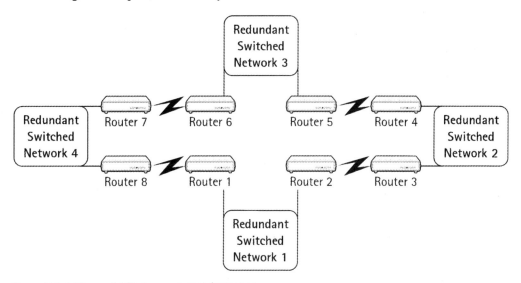

Figure 5-4: Adding availability to your router infrastructure

In much the same fashion as the redundant switched network design, a routed network can also be made redundant. If any single link or router fails in Figure 5-4, an alternate path can be used to reach a given destination. If Router 3 fails, for example, all other switched networks can still communicate to Redundant Switched Network 2 through Router 4.

CAN/MAN/WAN links

Physical considerations also make campus area, metropolitan area, and wide area network link redundancy important. More than once, utility companies, construction crews, road crews, and any number of natural disasters have caused a link to be severed. If this link provides the only connection to a given destination, no redundancy exists, and data has been centralized in another facility, then data is no longer available. To avoid this situation, employ redundant links and ensure that—whenever possible—they run through completely different channels and paths and enter a building or facility at different points.

It is also good practice to use providers that do not use the same communications networks and paths for redundancy. Having two links from the same provider or from providers that use the same network may still allow a single point of failure to occur.

Internet

During the 1960s, the U.S. Department of Defense's Advanced Research Projects Agency (ARPA, later called DARPA) began an experimental wide area network (WAN) that spanned the United States. Called ARPANET, its original goal was to enable government affiliations, educational institutions, and research laboratories to share computing resources and to collaborate via file sharing and electronic mail. It didn't take long, however, for DARPA to realize the advantages of ARPANET and the possibilities of providing these network links across the world.

By the 1970s, DARPA continued to aggressively fund and conduct research on ARPANET, to motivate the development of the framework for a community of networking technologies. The result of this framework was the Transmission Control Protocol/Internet Protocol (TCP/IP) suite. (A *protocol* is defined as a set of rules for communication over a computer network.) To increase acceptance of the use of protocols, DARPA disclosed a less expensive implementation of this project to the computing community. The University of California at Berkeley's BSD UNIX system was a primary target for this experiment. DARPA funded a company called Bolt Beranek and Newman, Inc. (BBN) to help develop the TCP/IP suite on BSD UNIX.

This new technology came about during a time when many establishments were in the process of developing local area network technologies to connect two or more computers on a common site. By January 1983, all of the computers connected on ARPANET were running the new TCP/IP suite for communications. In 1989, Conseil Européen pour la Recherche Nucléaire (CERN), Europe's high-energy physics laboratory, invented the World Wide Web (WWW). CERN's primary objective for this development was to give physicists around the globe the means to communicate more efficiently using *hypertext*. This soon developed into a language by which programmers could generate viewable pages of information called HyperText Markup Language (HTML). In February 1993, the National Center for Supercomputing Applications at the University of Illinois (NCSA) published the legendary browser, Mosaic. With this browser, users could view HTML graphically presented pages of information.

At the time, there were approximately 50 Web servers providing archives for viewable HTML. Nine months later, the number had grown to more than 500. Approximately one year later, there were more than 10,000 Web servers in 84 countries comprising the World Wide Web, all running on ARPANET's backbone, called the Internet.

Today, the Internet provides a means of collaboration for millions of hosts across the world. The current backbone infrastructure of the Internet can carry a volume well over 45 megabits per second (Mbps), about one thousand times the *bandwidth* of the original ARPANET. Today it provides communication over varying types of connections, including point-to-point, frame relay, xDSL, and broadband connectivity. Because of its widespread use, the Internet has become a very public and commercial medium, allowing global communication to occur almost seamlessly.

Multiple paths to the same destination may exist with the Internet providing a level of re-dundancy. Some companies leverage the connectivity of the Internet to provide services such as e-mail and additional connectivity and redundancy within their own organizations, using technologies like VPN. Other organizations use the Internet as an extension of their marketing and sales departments to provide customers with data and the ability to purchase their products online. For these organizations, one major component of data availability is the ability to make data available to prospective customers. In general, the way an organization uses the Internet can dramatically affect its definition of data availability.

As mentioned earlier, many companies are leveraging the connectivity of the Internet to provide additional connectivity and presence for their companies. Figure 5-5 illustrates how the Internet can and has been used to provide redundancy. By implementing secure multiple paths for communicating between locations (that is, having each router physically located at a separate office), you can accommodate availability.

Wireless technology

Wireless technology offers flexibility for the computing world. It is also true that forms of wireless (such as microwave, spectrum radio, and satellite) have been used to pass data for many years. However, the new rage in wireless is cellular data: 802.11b and even Bluetooth. Although these technologies can deliver greater mobility, they may also affect data availability if not implemented using sound security practices. In fact, security for wireless devices has fallen under great scrutiny because data can be captured using wireless packet and data analyzers. Numerous organizations have been breached through wireless and infrared devices.

> **CAUTION:** If wireless devices are necessary, implement them using sound security practices and test the security thoroughly and often. Creating a wireless DMZ with its own firewall, allowing only very specific access and using technologies like PKI and VPN, can help reduce the exposure.

Dial-in

Believe it or not, dial-in/up access is still widely used. In fact, it is commonly used for most Internet connections. In addition, using challenged dial-in access before the actual connection is granted can provide a secure means of access into a network. In order to provide timely access to data, it may be necessary to implement a remote dial-in tool with access control that performs the processing and provides only screen updates.

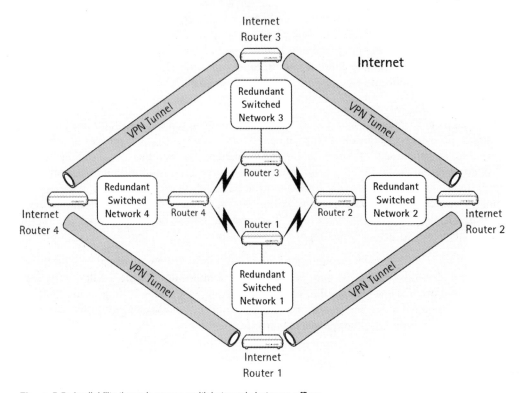

Figure 5-5: Availability through secure multiple tunnels between offices

Power

Power is an often overlooked component of data availability. Assume for a moment that redundancy has been provided throughout the network in the form of duplicate hubs, switches, routers, links, Internet connectivity, wireless options, and dial-in, but that backup power exists only for devices in the data center. If power fails and users are not in the data center, their data is not available. One way to overcome this availability obstacle is to provide backup power to critical users at their locations. Another more cost-effective method is to provide a number of user machines located in the data center that can leverage the backup power of the data center.

Think through possible power outage scenarios (both short- and long-term) and don't forget about power requirements and backup power needs from end to end. You can use ripple security logic (discussed early in Chapter 1) to help you determine end-to-end connectivity.

Alternate access

Today, users can be directly connected to the storage network instead of gaining access through another device. One way to achieve such direct access is to place the users directly on the storage network. In the case of NAS, the NAS and users can be placed on a separate segment together. When a SAN is used, SAN adapters can be placed directly into user machines to allow direct access to the SAN (assuming that the SAN you choose supports such a connection method). If all the redundancy features discussed here have been implemented for NAS or SAN, this method can provide not only great data availability, but can also reduce security risks and simultaneously provide excellent performance.

Hosts/servers

Most access to shared storage is achieved via some sort of host. The host may have directly connected storage, as is the case for DAS and NAS devices, or it may be connected to a SAN storage device. Users can only gain access to the data if the host remains available. Hosts and servers often contain multiple levels of redundancy—in the form of redundant power supplies, network interface cards, processors, memory busses, disk controllers, and disks—to help ensure their availability. In addition to a host's redundancy features, hot-swapping of these components may also be possible, allowing the host to continue operation in the event of a single failure. However, even with all these redundancy features, it is still possible for a single device to fail, causing a loss of data availability. For this reason, many manufacturers and software developers provide additional fault tolerance through standby, online, and clustering features.

Host/server standby/failover

The level of required data availability can greatly impact which method of host/server re-dundancy makes the most sense from a cost perspective. If several minutes to an hour of downtime is acceptable, then a standby, or failover, solution works just fine. Such a system is designed to take over the functions of the primary system in the event of a failure. In the case of a hot-standby device, a level of monitoring of the primary device typically occurs in order to determine that it is no longer available. When it becomes unavailable, it is automatically taken offline, and the standby device comes online. The standby device may need to be re-cycled in order to assume the responsibilities of the primary device. The combination of the recycle time and the time it takes for users to reconnect to the device determines how long the data is unavailable.

Clustering

When even a couple minutes of downtime is not acceptable, clustering is an option that pro-vides a greater level of availability. Clusters can be formed with two or more servers/nodes and can operate in an active-passive or active-active fashion.

♦ An **active-passive cluster** operates similarly to a failover server scenario in that one server performs the processing while the other remains passive. If applications are "cluster-aware" and a failure occurs in the active server, the users may notice only a temporary slowdown of processing while the application fails over to another passive server. Users will not appear to lose their connection.

♦ In an **active-active cluster**, two or more servers share the processing of the application. Users are not aware of a single-server failure. However, it's important to realize that if a cluster has only two servers, each server must be able to carry the full processing load to achieve data availability in a timely fashion. For this reason, we recommend that at least three servers participate in the cluster, as shown in Figure 5-6.

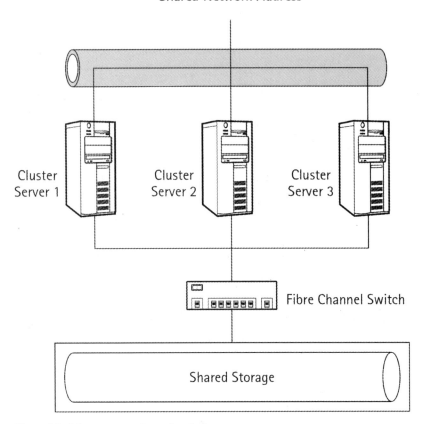

Figure 5-6: A three-server active-active cluster

Application availability

Although redundancy at the system and storage interdomains of data availability helps reduce outages, it does not offer protection in the event of a software or complete system failure. Organizations requiring increased application availability above the system and storage domains can deploy *system-level redundancy*.

While the system and storage domains focus on hardware redundancy within individual products, the application domain focuses on using software tools for monitoring applications and on coupling systems together to provide improved application availability. The software tools, or *middleware*, monitor the health of an application by detecting application hangs, data accessibility, networking dependencies, and full system failures and then performing the necessary steps to route around a failure or to get the application back in service.

Clustering can take multiple forms, but the most common provide system availability should a server go down. Leveraging industry-based standards can deliver load balancing and application failover clustering for high availability.

Load balancing cluster

Load balancing distributes user requests among multiple independent servers that are running the same application(s). Because the application is running on multiple servers, a server is always available to service the users in the event that one fails. Each server periodically sends a heartbeat message to the other servers and also listens for the heartbeat that it receives from the other servers. Load balancing assumes that a server is functioning normally as long as it participates in the normal heartbeat exchange. If other servers do not receive a heartbeat message from a load balancing cluster member after a certain period of time, then the remaining servers are automatically adjusted, the workload is redistributed, and the server is removed from the cluster. To the end user, in most cases, the client software automatically retries any failed connection, and the client experiences a delay of a few seconds before receiving a response.

Application failover cluster

Unlike a load balancing cluster, a high availability *application failover cluster* provides support for applications that require protection for dynamic data sets. Both of the servers can be active and running different applications. In the event that one of the clustered servers fails, its application and application data is transferred over to the other server. High availability clusters help to ensure that critical applications are online when needed by removing the physical server as a single point of failure. By transferring the users to a backup system, high availability clustering helps minimize the amount of downtime due to unplanned outages.

The systems in the high availability cluster are interconnected via a private LAN, and they use this LAN for a heartbeat mechanism to determine the health of each system. When a failure occurs, the effort required to restart the application can vary greatly depending on the application type and its data. When an application switches from one cluster member to another, the disruption a user experiences varies, from none at all to an extensive application restart.

Another way to maximize uptime for applications is by using cluster-aware applications, such as Microsoft Exchange and Microsoft SQL Server. *Cluster-aware applications* can perform an operation to determine if the application is responding. If it isn't, the cluster software assumes that the application is hung and the application is restarted on the same system. This process is referred to as a *local recovery*. It is much quicker to perform than a failover to a backup server and results in better application availability.

High availability clusters use technology (ranging from low-cost SCSI cluster solutions to enterprise-class solutions based on high-end storage and the operating system) that provides the flexibility to meet a variety of functionality and availability levels. .

Using the application interdomain, you can manage planned downtime effectively. You can perform both hardware and software maintenance on one server while the other provides functionality for users, enabling more flexibility for maintenance scheduling.

Application monitoring and fault prevention continues to be a primary focus for improving application availability. Ongoing improvements in application availability include speeding up the process of detection, faster restarting of application environments, and implementing proactive and corrective measures before an application experiences problems.

Services needed to help ensure maximized application availability begin with clustered application design and implementation, designed for high availability. We also recommend that organizations train their personnel on the full systems and any services prior to live implementation.

Data services

Data is a company asset, from the smallest word processor document to the most sophisticated database. Data can be classified as quantitative and qualitative; it can even be categorized by storage formats, which include fixed format and free format. In terms of storage and storage security, however, you should be most concerned about the type of data you have and, ultimately, about its overall value and data availability requirements.

User/company data

Until recently, the cost and performance implications of storing all user data on the network for very large organizations was prohibitive. However, with systems containing up to a terabyte of available storage for less than 1.5 cents per megabyte, giving a user 500MB of storage only costs a company $7.50. Even when coupled with the added administrative and maintenance costs, the benefit of having the data centrally stored, managed, and backed up, being able to retrieve lost files and documents that would otherwise take up productive time to be re-created can pay for an individual user's storage cost after just one incident.

However, security and administration of security becomes paramount. One of the risks when data is centralized and sharable is unauthorized access and disclosure of a document. If two users are given the same level of access to a document, one could logically deduce that the chance of accidentally losing that document is twice what it would be if a single individual was involved. If the number of individuals were increased to three, the loss expectancy would increase to three times that of a single user, and so on. If such a document were highly complex (for example, it's composed of multiple spreadsheets or it's a Microsoft Excel Workbook referencing other data sources), losing that document without the ability to recover it would definitely constitute a data availability failure. However, since this data was centralized, and even if only a previous tape backup of the file existed, the loss and ultimately the cost to reproduce the document can be reduced. The losses can be further reduced using tools such as cloning and snap shotting technologies.

E-mail

Another type of data that is requiring very high levels of data availability is electronic mail, or e-mail. As more and more companies grow dependent on e-mail, not just for general communications but to accept and send orders, transfer quotes, automatically notify suppliers when inventory needs to be replenished, and so on, their dependency on e-mail availability also increases.

Most e-mail systems use some form of database or database engine to provide the robust features required by businesses today. This arrangement also means that to ensure high availability, methods providing for the quick recovery of e-mail are required. Multiple copies of the data should be available, and all components that surround e-mail and can affect its availability should contain redundancy.

Databases

One of the main purposes of sharing data is to share some form of a database. The information databases can contain and the ways this information may be manipulated are virtually limitless. Database design and implementation is a topic unto itself, but it is important to understand that a database's design and implementation can greatly affect its overall availability.

Design

The design of a database and how it accesses the data can either enhance or detract from data availability. For example, if all information is contained in one large flat file database, a failure or corruption of that database may cause complete failure.

In contrast, a database that uses multiple smaller databases with limited co-dependencies may remain available for many to most functions even in the event that one or more of the databases becomes unavailable. This equates to a higher level of database availability.

Types

When it comes to storage, you most often see the following types of databases:

- **Hierarchical** databases are among the oldest databases around. They store data in records and keep track of record types. They are based on a parent/child philosophy. Hierarchical databases are still used for inventory and accounting in hospitals and government agencies . They are also commonly used in banks and insurance companies, oftentimes based on mainframe computing platforms.

- **Relational** databases are not quite as old as hierarchical databases, but they run a close second. They are based on a table design that utilizes a column and row structure, much like a spreadsheet. SQL is an example of a relational database.

♦ **Object-oriented** databases do not store data in columns and rows like a relational database; rather, they store them as persistent objects. This gives the user more flexibility in terms of how the data can be manipulated and stored. Java is a good example of an object-oriented database.

♦ **Object-relational** databases combine object-oriented and relational database types.

♦ **Distributed** databases, as the name implies, allow database functions to be broken up for processing over two or more database host machines. This setup is one of the most effective ways to mitigate the effects of a database failure by reducing the number of users affected. However, it also holds true that if all the other components of data availability are not at appropriate levels, distributing data can actually reduce data availability.

Multimedia

Although multimedia databases exist, multimedia data services can provide some unique data availability challenges. Multimedia data can take up large amounts of storage compared to other data types and often requires much greater bandwidth availability. These facts must be considered when multimedia data services are required. You can ensure data availability for multimedia data services by properly configuring a network to allow multicasting of multimedia data to reduce the bandwidth requirement and by ensuring that adequate storage exists (capacity planning).

Disk Availability

Disk availability is the root of data availability. Without disk availability, the data on the disk(s) cannot be available (copies of it can be made available, but not the actual data that resides on the disk). Computer manufacturers have constantly been designing and refining techniques to increase disk availability, such as RAID, snap, clone, replication, and virtualization technologies. The use of these technologies can go a long way toward providing high levels of data availability on the storage devices under your care.

RAID systems

RAID systems have been around for a while now and have proven valuable in mitigating DAS, NAS, and SAN device failures. RAID can be accomplished via software or hardware. It allows data to be stored across multiple disks, although how this occurs depends on the RAID level. The RAID configuration can appear as one drive to an operating system. Several levels of RAID exist, each of which provides different functionality. However, within the definition of RAID, one level, RAID 0, actually creates less availability.

♦ **RAID 0:** RAID 0 does not provide any redundancy; rather, it allows data to be striped across multiple disks, thereby enabling the disks to be combined to create a bigger logical storage space than was possible using only the capacities of each drive. This space appears as one large storage device to the host operating system. However, such a setup can seriously impact availability. When RAID 0 is used, any single drive failure will cause the entire logical storage to become unavailable. Data availability is reduced in this scenario because the chance of any single device causing all the data of that volume to become unavailable increases by a factor of the number of drives participating in the RAID 0 set. For example, if five drives are participating in a RAID 0 set, the chance that a drive failure will cause loss of that data actually increases.

♦ **RAID 1:** RAID 1 doesn't provide any additional space. Rather, it allows the data of one drive to be duplicated (mirrored) to another drive. RAID 1 is most commonly used today to provide redundancy for the operating system and configuration of host devices. An example would be mirroring the internal boot disk that contains a Linux operating system. *Mirroring* refers to the copying of data from one drive to another, but is most commonly implemented using the same disk controller. In the event of a disk drive controller failure, the system would cease to function because both drives (the primary and the mirror) would not be available. In order to address this single point of failure, disk duplexing could be implemented. *Disk duplexing* implements a second controller to which the mirror drive connects, eliminating the hard drive controller as a single point of failure.

♦ **RAID 2:** RAID 2 defines a 39-disk set, where 32 of the disks are used for data and 7 are used for parity. Parity is created using a Hamming Code for error detection. RAID 2 uses something similar to striping with parity, but it is not the same as what is used by RAID levels 3 to 7. It is implemented by splitting data at the bit level and spreading it over a number of data disks and a number of redundancy disks. The redundant bits are calculated using Hamming Codes, a form of error correcting code (ECC). Each time something is to be written to the array, these codes are calculated and written alongside the data to dedicated ECC disks; when the data is read back, these ECCs are read as well to confirm that no errors have occurred since the data was written. If a single-bit error occurs, it can be corrected "on the fly." Because of its design and expense, RAID 2 is not used in practice.

♦ **RAID 3, 4:** RAID 3 and 4 both function in similar fashion to RAID 0, but both make use of a parity drive. This parity drive allows the data to be rebuilt in the event of a single drive failure, making it not as susceptible to single drive failure issues. The primary difference between RAID 3 and RAID 4 is that RAID 3 performs its functions at a bit level, and RAID 4 performs its functions at a block level.

♦ **RAID 5:** RAID 5 is among the most popular RAID implementations today. It performs parity using interleaving, which allows the parity information to be stored across all drives rather than on a single drive. Parity information is computed, and the result is stored on the next available drive rather than on a dedicated parity drive.

♦ **RAID 6:** RAID 6 adds a second parity scheme to RAID 5 that is distributed across different drives. This level of RAID offers greater fault tolerance than RAID 5, but is not used commercially because few companies are willing to pay for the extra cost to insure against a relatively rare event—it's unusual for two drives to fail simultaneously (unless something happens that takes out the entire array, in which case RAID 6 won't help anyway).

♦ **RAID 7:** RAID 7 is also a variation of RAID 5 that provides both parity and disk path protection. Parity is protected in much the same way as RAID 6. RAID 7 uses a virtual disk methodology to provide disk path redundancy. If a path to a disk fails, the virtual disk still functions.

♦ **RAID 10:** RAID 10 combines the features of RAID 0 and RAID 1 to create a very redundant, but expensive solution because each data hard drive must also have a mirror hard drive. Therefore, a 5-disk RAID 10 set mirrored would require ten drives (five for the data and five for the mirror).

> **NOTE:** Understanding RAID is very important because devices within DAS, NAS, or a SAN can be divided up into multiple logical devices, each using a different form of RAID.

RAID can go a long way towards helping ensure that data remains available, but what happens when a drive fails? When a RAID 1–10 drive fails, the best thing to do is get the failed drive replaced as quickly as possible. Since most RAID devices today support hot swapping of drives, the failed drive simply needs to be identified, removed, and replaced while the remainder of the RAID set continues to run. Once replaced, the drive must be rebuilt. In most cases, this process happens automatically. Be sure to properly identify the failed drive—the device perceives the removal of the wrong drive as multiple drive failures, and some RAID levels can't handle this.

Another popular method of drive replacement is online hot sparing of drives. Many DAS, NAS, and SAN devices today support one or more online hot spare drives that can be automatically (logically) inserted into the position of a failed drive to protect against a second failure in the array. The original failed drive should still be replaced as quickly as possible.

RAID technologies can provide a good means of mitigating disk hardware failures. Remember to design hardware redundancy throughout your storage platforms in order to maintain high availability. Duplicate power supplies, duplicate controllers, split backplanes, RAID, and even duplicate storage cabinets using RAID are all sound methods to reduce the effects of a single failure.

Snap technology

Much of what we have discussed in this chapter is designed to provide higher levels of data availability by reducing the effects of a failure. However, other technologies can help ensure that data remains highly available. Many of these actually cross boundaries between data availability and data protection.

Overview

Some companies manufacture software-snapshot technology products that are installed on a server, while other products are implemented directly into the firmware of either a NAS or SAN product and can be used optionally. In either case, the general principle is the same: using snap technology creates a point-in-time representation of the data, where a snapshot of sorts is created.

Snap or snapshot technology has been mentioned several times throughout this book because it provides a good means of making data more available. Manufacturers implement snap technology using different methods, but they manifest certain commonalities. Unlike some of the other technologies we discuss, snapshots take a fraction of the storage space required for the original data, depending on the term (how long the snapshot will be used) of the snapshot. This characteristic of snap technology is very appealing to customers with large data requirements.

How it works

To create a snap, storage space must be available. Some manufacturers require that this space be dedicated to a specific snap, whereas others allow multiple snaps to share the same space. In either case, enough space should be available to duplicate the entire volume being snapped if the snap is going to remain for a period of time.

When a snap is created, the snap contains pointers to the original data blocks. As the data blocks are changed, the original data blocks are preserved, and the changed data is stored. The way this process occurs varies depending on manufacturers' implementations, but the general concept is the same. Because every data block in a volume can be changed, up to 100 percent of the space requirements for a volume might be used for a snap. Once every block is changed, and all the original blocks have been saved for the snap, further changes will not require any additional space requirements.

If space permits, multiple snaps are possible, but the numbers vary by manufacturer.

Uses

Snaps can be used for a number of purposes, including:

♦ **Backups:** One of the biggest problems that today's companies face is the ability to back up ever increasing data in decreasing time windows. Backing up "live data" oftentimes causes the data to be unavailable during the backup time. This is especially true for many databases and e-mail systems that must be shut down so files are not open, or require special programs to back up the open files. A snapshot can be taken and the backup can then be performed offline, leaving the database free to operate.

♦ **Rollback protection:** Snaps can be used to provide a means of rolling back to a known good point in time. For example, if a snapshot (or multiple snapshots) were taken of an e-mail system at a known good point in time, and the e-mail system became corrupt, one of the snapshots could be used to roll back to a working condition in a fraction of the time it would take to do a complete tape restore. In fact, with some snapshot tools it can be as simple as unmapping a drive letter and mapping the unmapped drive letter to the snapshot.

♦ **Development:** Snapshots could potentially be used to share real data that could be used for development or testing purposes. However, cloning is usually a better choice for this type of application.

♦ **Space conservation:** Snapshots are often used because there is not enough disk space to completely duplicate the original data. A short-term snapshot may be created only to provide a backup and then deleted until the next scheduled backup.

> **TIP:** Determining the right amount of space for a snapshot when there is not enough room to duplicate 100 percent of the original data is not an exact science. Such a decision is based on many factors, including the percentage of data changed during a period of time. However, as a rule, you should set aside a storage amount equal to a minimum of 20 percent of the original data and expire the snapshot within 24 hours.

Security issues

Security and data availability concerns can arise when using some snapshot tools. For example, if the original data blocks that were used to make the snapshot become unavailable and 100 percent of the data has not been changed, the snapshot itself will not contain 100 percent of the data; therefore, the snapshot may not be able to provide the data.

Because most snapshots are used to protect volumes, they themselves can be mounted as a volume. This means that highly classified data might be replicated several times, and may become available if not properly protected. Snapshots (and clones, as you'll see in the next section) should be treated with the same care given to the original data.

Clone technologies

Cloning is another method that can be used to create greater levels of data availability. Since one of the keys to data availability is protecting the data by ensuring that it remains available, and since cloning can provide a complete duplication of data, it too crosses the boundaries of data availability and data protection.

Overview

Earlier in this chapter, we discussed RAID 1. Cloning operates similarly to RAID 1, duplicating (mirroring) data. This process may take place through hardware or software depending on each manufacturer's implementation. The data is duplicated on disks, but options for cloning can vary by manufacturer. Generally speaking, manufacturers' implementation of cloning provides some definite benefits over RAID 1. For example:

♦ You will almost certainly be able to easily "break off" a clone and allow access to the data.

♦ One major difference between RAID 1 or operating system–level mirroring and cloning is that cloning takes place independently of the CPU on the host/server or the host/server hardware. An example would be a SAN that leverages cloning. The devices that connect to it (its hosts/servers) do not know that cloning is being performed, as it is handled by the SAN.

How it works

Unlike snapshots, which only capture a representation of the data, cloning creates a duplicate of the volume, which requires a duplication of drive space. In many implementations, a separate volume or clone space is set up to equal that of the volume to be cloned. Once created and started, all data from the original volume is duplicated on the clone volume. Clones do not happen instantly because cloning takes time to duplicate all data from one volume to another. As long as the clone remains active, data changes on the original volume are reflected (cloned) to the clone volume.

Clones can be compared to snapshots in that they may become point-in-time duplications. This happens when a clone is told to stop tracking any changes from the original volume. However, to make clones truly valid copies, applications should be shut down and the clone volume should be allowed to finish synchronizing with the original volume. Once this occurs, the clone volume can be separated from its primary volume and used for other purposes.

Uses

Once data has been cloned, it can be used for many of the same purposes as a snapshot. It also has some additional uses.

- ◆ **Backups:** Clones do not reduce the backup window as much as snapshots because of the time it may take to create and update a clone. However, as a general rule, cloning takes a fraction of the time of a complete backup. Therefore, a clone can provide an excellent means of achieving full backups in a reduced backup window.

- ◆ **Rollback protection:** Clones can provide a form of rollback protection if they are broken off from their original volume. However, if corruption occurs on the original volume and the clone volume is still active, the corruption will likely be cloned to the clone volume.

- ◆ **Development:** One of the best uses for cloning is to provide for the sharing of live data for development or testing purposes. If data is cloned, and the clone is then broken off, the cloned data can be served up to developers or testers. Instead of having developers or testers enter test data, real data can be used to simulate a "live" data environment. One added advantage is that as users are being productive (entering actual data), they are also helping the developers and testers without any additional required resources.

- ◆ **Reduced startup time:** Cloned data can be used in situations where a multilocation company opens another location. Instead of starting from scratch, cloned data may be used to create a baseline operating environment, limiting the startup time, while allowing the new location to benefit from the knowledge of the existing organization.

Security issues

Many of the security concerns that affect snapshots also affect cloning, with one major difference. If a copy of the snapshot data alone (without the original data being available) were compromised, the effects might be minimal. However, if a clone were compromised, it is a full working copy of a volume. For this reason, it is good practice to break up applications into manageable pieces and distribute them in such a fashion that losing one cloned volume would cause minimal impact.

An example of this would be breaking up tables that contain customer information and contact information into separate databases or database files that require dependency, but do not reside on the same volume.

Data replication technologies

Data replication can mean many things. Replication can be defined as the copying of information from one database to another to provide consistent data to multiple locations. It can also be defined as the process of duplicating volumes of data at remote locations. Relating to storage and storage networks, both definitions are important, but the latter is the definition that is most commonly accepted.

Overview

If cloning is like RAID 1, then data replication must be like cloning, right? Unfortunately, the answer is not that simple. With RAID 1 and cloning, data on physical or logical drives or volumes is duplicated. Data replication, on the other hand, can be used like RAID 1 or cloning, or it can be used to selectively duplicate data. This replication may occur locally, or over a CAN, MAN, or WAN. Very often, data replication is used to provide business continuance, because data can typically be replicated over long distances.

> **NOTE:** How replication is used may be based on a manufacturer's implementation of replication technology.

How it works

Data replication technology implementations vary. Some use bit- or block-style duplication technology, while others may leverage the file system of an operating system. Many file system–based technologies provide greater flexibility than the bit or block styles because they allow more granularity in the selection of which data is to be replicated.

Much like cloning, when data replication is initially implemented, it takes some time to duplicate the data (even more if the data is being changed). Once the data has been duplicated, only the changes to the data are transferred for duplication. Figure 5-7 is a very simple representation of data replication using a bit scheme.

In Figure 5-7, the original data 10110 is duplicated to the "Replicated Data Location." As changes occur, only the changes are sent—as shown by the bold digits in the lower half of the illustration (111111).

Data replication can be implemented at a hardware or software level. At the hardware level, data replication may be integrated as a feature of a NAS or SAN device and may be resident within the ROM, BIOS, Flash, or other embedded operating code. However, this integration does not necessarily mean that only bit or block data replication can occur. If the data replication operating code can read file systems, it is likely that operating code can also perform file system–based replication.

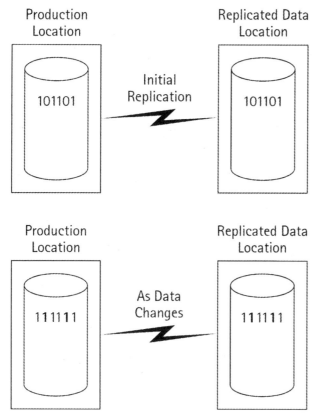

Figure 5-7: Bit scheme illustration of data replication

Data replication software can also be implemented using software designed to run on an operating system. This software may be implemented directly on the device to be replicated, or on a separate device capable of accessing either the storage or file system of the data to be replicated. File system–based data replication may also be called *asynchronous data replication*.

In addition to generic data replication, database replication products provide the ability to not only replicate, but also to synchronize replicas across an enterprise. These products allow databases to be distributed where needed to provide excellent data availability while creating duplicates that can be used as replicas.

Some data replication technologies allow changes to be stored locally and batch processed at more convenient times. Such an arrangement may effectively allow transmissions to occur when traffic is not as heavy, but it may also reduce the effects of data replication in regards to availability because a loss of the original location could cause greater amounts of non-replicated data to be lost as well.

Uses

One of the main uses of data replication today is to provide duplicate data in a different physical location than the original data. This duplicate data can be used for many purposes, such as for snapshots and clones and others that are primarily used with data replication.

♦ **Disaster mitigation:** Data replication is highly leveraged for mitigating disasters. Since data can be replicated over long distances, sites can be cities, states, or even countries apart. In the event of a disaster, and with the proper planning, the replicated data site can be used as a disaster recovery site.

♦ **Backups:** Similar to snapshots and clones, replicated data can be backed up without affecting the production network. The replica may need to be paused temporarily to ensure that changes are not occurring while the backup runs offline. This can be an effective backup centralization tool for some organizations,, especially if multiple sites use a single site for business continuance.

♦ **Rollback protection:** Data replication is not as useful for rollback protection as a snapshot or clone unless it is done in similar fashion to breaking off a clone. The reason it's not as useful is because data replication is making changes as they occur. If data corruption were to occur, the likelihood that the corruption would be replicated is high. Therefore, a combination of technologies (for example, data replication coupled with snapshots) may be the best choice to ensure both storage security and availability.

♦ **Development:** Much like a clone, replicated data can be used to provide developers with much needed real data.

♦ **Reduced startup time:** Since data replication provides for disaster mitigation, by design, it can reduce work stoppage when a disaster occurs. However, using this same philosophy to start up a new office can also decrease startup time, as was the case with cloning.

♦ **Bidirectional replication:** Another major benefit of data replication is that some of its implementations can operate bidirectionally, which means that data from one site can be replicated to another, used, and its changes replicated back. Such an arrangement allows production data to be highly available to an enterprise while allowing real-time use.

> **NOTE:** Remember, cloning and data replication differ primarily in these three ways: data replication is generally used over longer distances, replication can be bidirectional, and it can be selective.

Security issues

Believe it or not, security for data replication is often overlooked, although that may not originally be the case. Many companies start out strong, using a replica site for business continuance planning only; however, those same companies become vulnerable when they decide to get more out of the replica site and do not follow the same security processes, procedures, guidelines, and standards that the primary site follows.

As with snapshots or clones, breaking up replicated data can prove to be a sound strategy for limiting the effects of a compromise. If a company has multiple sites and databases that are distributed, replicating the data to sites that do not allow data to be matched up is a good philosophy. Breaking a database into multiple replicas and distributing them to a location that contains none of the other database components is one method.

A replica site can contain a little, some, or all of a company's data. Centralization of this magnitude must be approached with great caution. Even the slightest oversight can cause serious damage. Remember, you need to find all the security holes; the hacker only needs to find one.

Storage virtualization

One of the hottest topics on the storage circuit is *storage virtualization*. Manufacturers are implementing virtualization in different ways. Its effectiveness can be determined by where the technology fits within the storage implementation arena. The premise of virtualization is storage consolidation and real-time allocation and reallocation of storage resources. In effect, storage virtualization means that if a company maintains hundreds of devices and many terabytes of storage and the storage requirements of one host change, then more storage can be added or subtracted from that host and reallocated to another from somewhere in the virtualized storage area.

Overview

Storage virtualization works differently depending on the manufacturer's implementation, but in general, most virtualization products allow the creation of virtual pools of storage from one or more storage devices, often leveraging remote storage devices as part of the overall pool(s). For example, if a company has three SANs, and each SAN has ten terabytes, pools of storage can be created using resources from any or all of the three SANs and allocated to a specific host(s). If the storage requirements change, as is often the case, the pool(s) are changed accordingly. One such example is a new implementation where in the planning stages a specific amount of storage space is determined as necessary (some space initially, and some space for growth). If, after a period of time, it is determined that the growth will not consume the allocated space, the unused space can be reclaimed and used elsewhere.

How it works

How a given manufacturer implements storage virtualization can determine the technology method used. Although there are several methods of storage consolidation and allocation, including multihost arrays, LUN masking, redirectors, and storage domain servers, the general goal is the same—finding, combining, carving up, and publishing storage from multiple devices. To accomplish this, some manufacturers take a host approach. In other words, they create software that allows the storage of a host to be seen and used in one or more virtual pools.

Another method involves masking LUNs. Manufacturers create drivers that prevent hosts from accessing storage devices that they do not "own." The driver then assigns virtualized space to a host that now believes it owns that space. Such assignments can also keep a host from accessing nonvirtualized storage it does not own. However, the mechanics of each method of virtualization are not as important as the security issues surrounding virtualization.

Security issues

Each virtualization technology functions differently, so there is no one answer to the security questions surrounding virtualization. The pros and cons of each technology must be evaluated based on security strengths and weaknesses. For example, if LUN masking is used, a rogue server that is not using host masking may be able to access any LUN to gain access to the data causing a compromise or to cause corruption that (if other measures are not taken) can lead to data loss.

Other options, such as virtualization engines that provide storage virtualization and security, can reduce security threats by placing themselves between the host and the storage, in effect providing another level of storage security.

Outsourcing companies

Another method of making data highly available is to leverage security providers, storage solution providers, a data warehouse company, an ASP, a disaster recovery firm, or other data service firms. Such companies can offer an alternative to creating these solutions in-house, especially where resources are limited. Companies that can provide the necessary redundancy in a cost-effective and secure manner are becoming more and more popular. One of the major benefits they provide is depth of knowledge. Since they do this sort of work for other companies, they may already have a solution that suits your needs.

Outsourced services are valuable when you do not have the facilities to secure your data or make it highly available onsite. Many outsourced companies can help you determine which database and method is most efficient and secure for your needs, which storage methodology is right, how to secure your storage, and which data availability technologies will help your company's data remain highly available.

But follow these guidelines when you start looking at outsourced companies:

♦ Check their credentials, get references, talk to their clients, talk to their personnel, and understand and check certifications.

♦ Ensure that the legal responsibilities of each party (your company and the outsourcing firm) are fully understood.

♦ Understand the physical responsibilities and roles of each party.

♦ Ensure that their processes and procedures are thoroughly documented and available to you for review.

A Word about Common Data Availability Failure Points

Only when all single points of failure are eliminated can you be assured of true data availability. The most common points of failure—among those presented in this chapter—are external power systems, followed by secondary failure points in network IP address availability, switches, and other networking devices. Each of these concerns can be addressed using the previously discussed methodologies; however, consider the following strategies to deal with these common failure points:

♦ The effectiveness of availability in regards to power can be maximized by placing the passive and active masters on different power circuits, as well as placing them into different switches.

♦ In regards to IP address availability and failover, each server's actual and virtual IP should be monitored by an existing network monitoring tool so that responsible personnel can be notified if the server fails.

Summary

Throughout this chapter, we cover many methods that help ensure that data remains highly available. We outlined how the Common Body of Knowledge (CBK) defines availability as one of the critical elements for data security and how all components must be considered when creating a highly available environment. Each component fills a unique portion of the data availability puzzle. From capacity planning through data protection, the planning, design, implementation, and testing processes must ensure that data remains available.

It is not enough to ensure that data remains available; it is also critical that available data remains secure. Each component that can help make data more available must also be evaluated for its security strengths and weaknesses in order to create a highly available secure environment.

Finally, elements within the environment—such as switches, routers, power, and even environmental controls—must be included in any high availability design, as these items can either enhance or detract from data availability.

Chapter 6

Data Protection, Backup, and Recovery

Although data availability and data protection are separate topics, Information System Security Certification Consortium (ISC)[2] combines portions of each into one domain with business continuity planning (BCP) and disaster recovery planning (DRP). Ultimately, this domain is designed to reduce the effects and impact of a major disruption to normal business operations and provide guidelines for protecting data. As discussed earlier in this book, storage devices are part of the internal network framework, and the need to protect the data and devices is critical. Perimeter security is just not enough to protect against malicious users and local/remote attackers. Therefore, your security policy should hold fast to ripple security logic. You must design a storage foundation that covers access control, integrity, and privacy.

For several reasons, backup solutions fall into both the data availability and protection categories; however, most backup solutions fit best into the data protection category because they are primarily designed to allay the effects from loss of data caused by data corruption or hardware failure. Even if the necessary steps to ensure that data is available and protected have been taken, you still need to ensure that the data is not only backed up, verified, and stored in a secure fashion, but that the many issues concerning backups and security are also addressed. After all, the primary purpose of creating backups is to protect the data asset. The existence of the Enhanced Backup Solutions Initiative (EBSI) and groups like the Storage Networking Industry Association (SNIA) proves that these issues pose real challenges.

Framework for Protecting Data

Recall the four interdomains of data availability discussed in Chapter 5: system, storage, application, and infrastructure. These interdomains adopt the keys to data availability and ensure the availability of data across each domain of your environment at the highest level. At the lowest level, however, data protection begins at the storage interdomain highlighted in Figure 6-1. At this level, you should incorporate high availability and redundant components to protect the server and/or storage unit from faults.

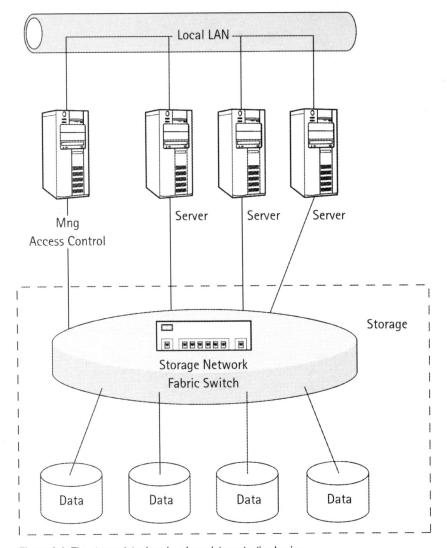

Figure 6-1: The storage interdomain, where data protection begins

Data protection adds to platform availability characteristics. It is designed to protect data residing on storage devices attached internally or externally, with the level of protection increasing though advancements in storage technology (for example, ATA, SCSI, and Fibre Channel). This interdomain introduces features designed to help eliminate single points of failure so that data is available to users, even if the storage device is in a degraded state. In order to provide continuous access to data, information must be available if any of the following software or hardware components fail or change: file, directory structure, logical disk volume, physical hard disk drive, host bus adapter or controller, enclosure management module, data bus, or pathway to data.

Redundant Array of Independent Drives (RAID) technology is frequently used to improve data availability and disk I/O performance. Different RAID levels provide different levels of availability and performance. The RAID level indicates the type of algorithm used to derive parity values and describes how the data is mapped across the multiple physical drives. Again, the most common RAID levels are 0, 1, 3, 5, and 10.

Backing up data is the most basic method of protecting data on disks. It involves copying the data from the disk to another type of portable media, such as tape. If a disk fails the data can be recovered and restored. However, data backup can be difficult and time-consuming because the amount of data and the number of storage resources increase throughout the network. Storage architectures, such as NAS and SAN, have been devised to consolidate storage resources, which can help eliminate backup traffic on the network and minimize the length of time it takes to back up data.

> **NOTE:**The ability to perform online or "live" backups, which enable data to be backed up to tape while users access information, is an important consideration when building a highly available computing environment.

Storage area networks (SANs) offer advantages over local backup, including better use of storage resources, decreased time to back up data, and lowered impact on network traffic. SANs are based on Fibre Channel (FC) technology and allow numerous RAID, tape, and other storage devices to reside on a network separate from the servers. This enables very efficient data transfer between storage arrays and tape devices without impeding the flow of traffic on the primary network. In addition, the amount of disk space assigned to a particular server can be changed, or the RAID striping algorithm can be changed, without taking down the SAN or the server.

Data can also be protected in this interdomain with the following methods:

♦ **Snapshots.** Snapshots are point-in-time data captures that help protect against accidental deletion, loss, or corruption of files, and damage from computer viruses.

♦ **Redundant data paths.** Redundant data paths help ensure availability of a data delivery path—should one path fail or become disconnected, another path will allow successful transfer of information.

♦ **Redundant controllers.** Redundant controllers help ensure the availability of a controller component—if one controller fails, the other takes over.

♦ **Database replication.** Database replication helps protect against data loss by duplicating database information to other systems, disk arrays, and so on.

♦ **Online volume expansion.** Online volume expansion enables an administrator to increase the logical disk capacity of a disk volume, while the volume remains visible and accessible to users on the network.

Networked attached secure disk

You employed and revised techniques of the network attached secure disk (NASD) system to provide a secure data protection foundation template. Later, in Chapter 8, you examine the specific secure implementations in a cookbook fashion, including outer perimeter security mechanisms. With that said, your data security methodology is based on the NASD system, and this section discusses the overview, design goals, and capabilities of the system sourced from the studies of Howard Gobioff, Garth Gibson, and Doug Tygar from Carnegie Mellon University (see Figure 6-2).

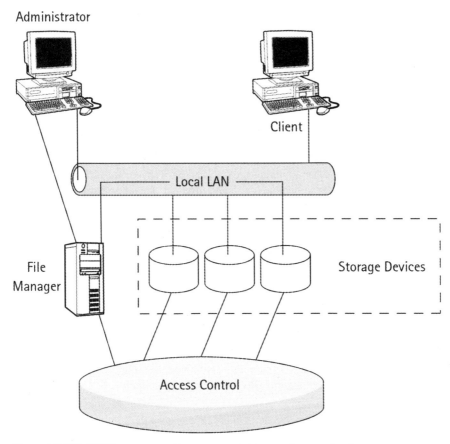

Figure 6-2: With NASD, you can provide access control to your storage network

The NASD system with a file manager makes access decisions in a scalable, secure, and efficient manner. For a file system to run securely, the policy maker (file manager) and enforcer (drive) must exchange a minimum amount of information. When a file manager grants access to a user, the file manager must communicate the user's access rights to the drive. The drive must check that the information came from the file manager and is fresh. The goal of the NASD security system is to achieve this communication in a safe, flexible, and efficient way. One approach is to have the file manager inform the drive directly of a user's rights, which the drive enforces when it later identifies the named user's requests. However, this approach requires that the drive be aware of the user's identity and have a user authentication mechanism. If the authentication mechanism is bound to the drive, an important degree of flexibility is removed from the design of the high-level file system. Additionally, the drive is forced to maintain information on a per-user basis, which requires more state than a capability system.

One alternative, which you use in NASD, is to pass access rights to the drive through a cryptographic capability. The capability allows the authentication mechanism to be removed from NASD and a decision of the file system implementor rather than being dictated by NASD. Instead of being aware of the user's identity, the drive is only aware of a user's access rights, defined by the capability arguments that describe a user's access rights, and the capability key, which proves that the user has the rights he claims to have. The keys are derived from the capability arguments and a working key associated with the partition on which the object resides.

How can the file manager efficiently and safely control access to the contents of a network attached drive? The file manager must be able to perform management functions on the drive and control client access to storage. NASD's security infrastructure is designed to perform these functions while being resistant to attacks by an adversary with full knowledge of the NASD protocol.

Since the hypothetical adversary knows your protocol, the ultimate security of the system rests on keeping the keys private through the use of key management. The NASD key management hierarchy balances flexibility of use and security. You should support key management that can take advantage of tamper-resistant hardware when it exists, and in other cases affects key management through software control.

NOTE: The National Institute of Standards and Technology (NIST) provides guidelines for key management at `http://csrc.nist.gov/encryption/kms/`. Part 1 will contain General Guidance, Part 2 will provide guidance for system and application owners for use in identifying appropriate organizational key management infrastructures, establishing organizational key management policies, and specifying organizational key management practices and plans, and Part 3 is intended to provide guidance to system administrators regarding the use of cryptographic algorithms in specific applications, select products to satisfy specific operational environments, and configure the products appropriately.

Following are the goals for designing the security for NASD:

♦ The NASD security system should explicitly separate the policy enforcement mechanism from the policy decision process so the file manager must be able to communicate policy decisions to the drive.

- The protocol should prevent unauthorized modification of client requests and capabilities, along with protecting privacy of requests if dictated by the policies of clients or file managers.
- To minimize interaction with the file manager, the drive should be able to validate client operations without direct communication with the file manager.
- To allow for low memory drive implementations, there should be no long-term state shared between drive and client. Overall state requirements of the drive should be kept at a minimum, but additional memory should enhance performance.
- The security protocol should add as little overhead as possible in terms of computation and the number and size of messages.

The heart of the NASD security system is the capability architecture governing access to NASD objects. A NASD capability is made up of the capability arguments and a capability key. The capability arguments are a tuple containing the following items:

- Drive identifier
- Partition
- Object identifier
- Region (byte range)
- Access rights
- Expiration time
- Basis key (black or gold)
- Minimum protection requirements
- Audit identifier

The capability key is a cryptographic key used by a client to bind a specific NASD request to a capability through use of a Message Authentication Code (MAC) algorithm. The MAC is a keyed hashing algorithm that uses a symmetric session key. When using this type of algorithm, the receiving application must also possess the session key to recompute the hash value so it can verify that the base data has not changed. The MAC creates a relationship between the fields of the capability, the request, and the message hash of the content (digest). If the drive generates the same MAC that was included in the request, the drive can be confident that the MAC, the capability arguments, and the request were all received without tampering.

The first four fields of the capability key identify the set of bytes for which the capability is valid. The *access rights* and *expiration time* limit the operations and time range for which the capability is valid. The lifetime of a capability cannot exceed the lifetime of the working key under which it was issued; otherwise, the validity of the capability cannot be verified. The *basis key* indicates whether this capability was issued with the black working key or the gold working key, which is used to generate the capability key. The *minimum protection* indicates a floor set of security options that the file manager requires of the client for all operations using the capability. This permits the file manager to require a higher standard of security than is required by the partition.

Finally, the *audit identifier* is a field where the file manager can associate arbitrary values with the capability key. In auditing implementations of NASD, the drive records the audit identifier in a log record for an operation performed with the capability. This allows a log analyzer to later extract this information from the logs on the drive. With the audit identifier, you can easily integrate drive security with other applications, such as transaction management (by recording a transaction ID in the audit identifier) or audit trails (by recording the user's identity in the audit identifier).

NASD requires that the file-system-specific client-file-manager protocol provide private transmission of capability keys to the clients, along with transmission of the capability arguments. You expect this to be performed as part of a directory lookup process, but it is not a requirement for NASD. The capability arguments are necessarily kept private. If an adversary can read the capability arguments, he still cannot access the object without a working key or the capability key. If an adversary modifies either the request or the response, he at best executes a Denial-of-Service attack. A client can prove it has the right to access an object by using a capability key to encrypt and/or digest a request. The capability keys are derived from the capability arguments and a working key for the partition where the object resides. When the capability arguments are given to the drive, the drive can independently compute the capability key and verify the critical parameters for an access check.

If the capability arguments and capability key don't match, the drive cannot validate the request. Since clients know neither of the working keys, clients are unable to generate a forged key. If the working key changes, then the drive is also unable to generate the expected capability key. However, in this case, the changes correspond to expected invalidations of access rights.

Security of Hash and MAC

How does the "Hash and MAC" approach affect the security of the system? MACing the concatenation of hash values is very similar to signing them with a public key, except it is much faster and does not provide the non-repudiability property associated with public key signatures. Nonrepudiation is the ability to identify users who performed certain actions, thus irrefutably countering any attempts by a user to deny responsibility.

If you assume that the basic MAC function is secure, is the MAC of hash values secure? When something is considered "secure," it is normally secure for an arbitrary input. If there were a class of inputs for which it was insecure, then the MAC function as a whole would not be secure. An adversary breaks a MAC if she can recover the key or generate a MAC value for a message that she has not seen before. Concretely, if you break "Hash and MAC" by attacking the MAC function, then you have defined a set of inputs (the concatenation of hash values) that you can use as an input to the MAC to break the original MAC.

An adversary could attack "Hash and MAC" through the message digest. "Hash and MAC" trades off some security in exchange for increased performance. An adversary can mount an offline attack (essentially computing with no information about the message being attacked) against the message digest function. With a normal MAC, an adversary could not start an attack until he was given a message to attack because the result of the key-dependent computation is essential to the attack. An adversary can apply arbitrary computational power to precompute two data blocks that generate the same digest (for example, a collision). Alternatively, an adversary who observes a series of requests and their associated message digests can attempt to find a second data block that generates the same digest as a given message block (for example, a second pre-image). The difference with having observed a series of requests or not is ultimately between the adversary being allowed to select both blocks in the collision as opposed to being given one of the blocks, which can be viewed as a challenge, and trying to find a second block that generates the same MAC. As long as NASD uses a strong message digest with a large output, the offline attack is a small risk. The best current attacks against these message digests requires a brute force search (where an encrypted message is cracked using brute force) of the input space. In order to find a second pre-image of a given message digest, an adversary expects to compute digests of, on average, 2,160 data blocks. A far simpler task, given large amounts of memory, is to find a pair of data blocks that generate the same hash by exploiting the birthday paradox; however, this attack is still expected to require 280 digest calculations.

> **NOTE:** The birthday paradox phenomenon is useful in several different areas (such as with cryptography and hashing algorithms). You can try it yourself—the next time you are at a gathering of 20 or 30 people, ask everyone for their birthdate. It is likely that two people in the group will have been born on the same day.
>
> The reason this is so surprising is because we are used to comparing our particular birthdays with others. For example, if you meet someone randomly and ask him what his birthday is, the chance both of you have the same birthday is only 1/365 (0.27%). In other words, the probability of any two individuals having the same birthday is extremely low. Even if you ask 20 people, the probability is still low—less than 5%. So, we feel like it is very rare to meet anyone with the same birthday as our own.
>
> When you put 20 people in a room, however, the difference now is that each of the 20 people is asking each of the other 19 people about their birthdays. Each individual person only has a small (less than 5%) chance of success, but each person is trying it 19 times. That increases the probability dramatically.
>
> You can calculate the exact probability in two different ways. The first way involves counting the pairs of people in the room. In a room of 20 people, there are 190 (20 × 19/2) possible pairs. Each pair has a success probability of 0.27% (1/365), and thus a failure probability of 99.726% (1 – 0.27%). If you raise the probability of failure to the 190th power, then you get: 99.726% ^ 190 = 59%.
>
> So the probability of success is 41% (100 – 59%). It turns out your friend was slightly off—you must have 23 people in the room to get 50/50 odds. If you have 42 people in the room, the probability rises to a 90% chance of two people having the same birthday!

If he can find one, an adversary can exploit a collision if one of the colliding blocks is already within the storage system and he can replace the in-system block with the out-of-system colliding block in a message exchange. An adversary can potentially tabulate a large number of digests and watch message traffic to the drive for an opportunity, but the odds of such an opportunity presenting itself is considerable.

An adversary has an easier task if he can insert one half of a collision into the storage system and then replace it with the other half. In this case, the attacker may have already written the second of the two blocks to the storage rather than swapping the blocks while they were being read. Thus, an adversary can primarily exploit a collision in a multi-tier system, such as a database system, where write operations are filtered through another host, which decides if a write should be forwarded to the storage. If a collision is found, the adversary can swap a bad data block for the forwarded data block. Because the filtering host is making a decision based on the contents of the initial write request, it is implicitly enforcing some structure on the writes it forwards on to storage. Since one half of the collision must fit the required structure of the filtering host that forwards it on, this structure improves security by constraining the set of useful collisions an adversary can theoretically generate.

Because "Hash and MAC" generates multiple independent digests that are used to create the final MAC, an adversary can parallelize an attempt to find a second pre-image of the digests. If the request is divided into r different data blocks, an adversary can attack r different values when trying to find the second pre-image of a digest. In contrast, a normal MAC algorithm has a single MAC value that can be attacked because all partially computed values are key-dependent and hidden in the MAC's internal state. Even for extremely large requests and heavily used storage devices, r is not large enough to substantially reduce the 2^{160} computations required to find a second pre-image. For example, if a client transferred a terabyte of data and the digests were generated on 8K disk blocks, then an adversary could attack 222 unique message digests. This only reduces the work factor from 2^{160} down to 2^{138}. In order for parallelism to reduce the work of finding a second pre-image down to finding a simple collision, the adversary would need to observe 2^{80} disk blocks and attack them in parallel.

Precomputing security with Hash and MAC

Precomputation can be used to improve the performance of security. However, if data is shared using different keys, perhaps one per user, precomputation requires significantly more storage space to store the different MACs or it does not benefit read requests from different users. However, it is possible to decouple MAC calculation into a keyed and an unkeyed component and explicitly delay the binding of the key to the computation. Based on existing message authentication code and message digest algorithms, this approach, called Hash and MAC, does the following:

♦ When a drive object is written, the drive precomputes a sequence of unkeyed message digests over each of the object's data blocks.

♦ For each read request, the drive generates a MAC of the concatenation of the unkeyed message digests corresponding to the requested data blocks.

Normal MAC algorithms involve the key throughout the entire computation of the message authentication code. In contrast, Hash and MAC removes the key from the per-byte calculation, only using the key in the final step of the calculation. Because the key is not involved in the per-byte calculations, the results of the per-byte calculation, a set of message digests, can be stored and used for multiple read requests to the same disk block from different clients. Additionally, since no key needs to be identified before a message digest can begin, message digest processing may be simpler for high-speed hardware than MAC processing, which must delay until the proper key is identified.

The Hash and MAC approach is very similar to encrypting or signing a message digest. However, it does not provide the nonrepudiation that a public key system provides. In this sense, it is more like a normal MAC or encrypting a message digest with a symmetric key system. In contrast to encrypting a digest, a MAC has better defined properties to protect against modification.

User/administrator-to-system security

Consider employing specific administrative authentication and verification to provide control over the security configurations. Your security policy should enforce a marriage between management controls and the security functions, and you should employ strong user identification and authentication, such as encryption and strong passwords. Some user identification and authentication methods also include biometrics, tickets, and tokens.

Password policies should be enforced and should contain circumstances such as changing passwords at least every three to six months, immediately after a password is relinquished, and/or as soon as a password has been compromised or even suspected of a compromise.

When changing passwords or when passwords expire, the new password should contain at least eight characters, of which at least two must be letters and at least one a nonletter character. Any new passwords must also differ from the old ones by at least three characters. Your password policy should follow the general password guidelines instituted by the U.S. government:

- Passwords must contain at least eight nonblank characters.
- Passwords must contain a combination of letters (preferably a mixture of upper- and lowercase letters), numbers, and at least one special character within the first seven positions.
- Passwords must contain a nonnumeric letter or symbol in the first and last positions.
- Passwords must not contain the user login name.
- Passwords must not include the user's own or a close friend's or relative's name, employee number, Social Security number, birthdate, telephone number, or any information about him or her that the user believes could be readily learned or guessed.
- Passwords must not include common words from an English dictionary or a dictionary of another language with which the user has familiarity.

♦ Passwords must not contain commonly used proper names, including the name of any fictional character or place.

♦ Passwords must not contain any simple pattern of letters or numbers such as "qwertyxx."

Biometrics

In the world of security, biometrics is the study of measurable biological characteristics. In computer security, biometrics refers to authentication techniques that rely on measurable physical characteristics that can be automatically checked. Examples include computer analysis of fingerprints or speech. Though the field is still in its infancy, many people believe that biometrics will play a critical role in the future of security. Personal computers of the future might include a fingerprint scanner, on which you would place your index finger to gain access to the machine. The computer would analyze your fingerprint to determine who you are and, based on your identity, authorize different levels of access. Access levels could include, for example, the ability to use credit card information to make electronic purchases.

Biometrics refers to the automatic identification of a person based on his/her physiological or behavioral characteristics. This method of identification is preferred over traditional methods involving passwords and PINs for various reasons: (i) the person to be identified is required to be physically present at the point-of-identification; (ii) identification based on biometric techniques obviates the need to remember a password or carry a token. With the increased use of computers as vehicles of information technology, it is necessary to restrict access to sensitive/personal data. By replacing PINs, biometric techniques can potentially prevent un-authorized access to or fraudulent use of ATMs, cellular phones, smart cards, desktop PCs, workstations, and computer networks. PINs and passwords may be forgotten, and token-based methods of identification such as passports and driver's licenses may be forged, stolen, or lost. Thus, biometric systems of identification are enjoying a renewed interest. Various types of biometric systems are being used for real-time identification, of which the most popular include:

♦ Fingerprint identification

♦ Face recognition

♦ Hand geometry

♦ Speech pattern recognition

♦ Face location/facial thermograms

♦ Iris and retina scanning

A biometric system is essentially a pattern recognition system that makes a personal identification by determining the authenticity of a specific physiological or behavioral characteristic possessed by the user. An important issue in designing a practical system is to determine how an individual is identified. Depending on the context, a biometric system can be either a verification (authentication) system or an identification system.

Verification (I am what I am, but am I whom I claim to be?) involves confirming or denying a person's claimed identity. As an identification system, one must establish a person's identity (Who am I?) to the system. Each approach presents its own complexities and could probably be solved best by a hybrid biometric system.

Tickets

Tickets are a means of authentication. In regards to Kerberos and as explained by TechTarget, tickets are used in the authentication system as a secure method for authenticating a request for a service in a computer network. Kerberos was developed in the Athena Project at the Massachusetts Institute of Technology (MIT). The name is derived from Greek mythology: Kerberos was a three-headed dog who guarded the gates of Hades. Kerberos lets a user request an encrypted "ticket" from an authentication process that can then be used to request a particular service from a server. The user's password does not have to pass through the network. You can either download a version of Kerberos (client and server) from MIT, or you can buy a commercial version.

Briefly and approximately, here's how Kerberos works:

1. Suppose you want to access a server on another computer (which you may get to by sending a Telnet or similar login request). It's a given that this server requires a Kerberos "ticket" before it honors your request.

2. To get your ticket, you first request authentication from the authentication server (AS). The authentication server creates a "session key" (which is also an encryption key), basing it on your password (which it can get from your username) and a random value that represents the requested service. The session key is effectively a "ticket-granting ticket."

3. You next send your ticket-granting ticket to a ticket-granting server (TGS). The TGS may be physically the same server as the authentication server, but it now performs a different service. The TGS returns the ticket to you, which can be sent to the server for the requested service.

4. The service either rejects the ticket or accepts it and performs the service.

5. Because the ticket you received from the TGS is time-stamped, it allows you to make additional requests using the same ticket within a certain time period (typically, eight hours) without having to be reauthenticated. Making the ticket valid for a limited time period makes it less likely that someone else can use it later.

The actual process is much more complicated. The user procedure may vary somewhat according to implementation.

Tokens

A token is a physical security device (for example, a key fob or an access card) that is preconfigured to provide something about the user, such as a certification, personal identification number (PIN), or password, which enables authorized access to a system or network. An example of a one-time password token mechanism is RSA's SecureID—two-factor authentication that is based on something you know (a password or PIN) and something you have (an authenticator)—providing a much more reliable level of user authentication than reusable passwords.

Security tokens provide an extra level of assurance through a method known as *two-factor authentication*: The user possesses a PIN, which authorizes her as the owner of that particular device; the device then displays a number that uniquely identifies the user to the service, allowing her to log in. The identification number for each user is changed frequently, usually about every five minutes.

Unlike a password, a security token is a physical object. A key fob (a small hardware device with built-in authentication mechanisms), for example, is practical and easy to carry, and thus, easy for the user to protect. Even if the key fob falls into the wrong hands, however, it can't be used to gain access because the PIN is also needed.

Data Protection by Viral Defense

A typical virus is a computer program that makes copies of itself by using a host program. The virus *requires* a host program; thus, along with executable files, the code that controls your hard disk can, and in many cases will, be infected. When a computer copies its code into one or more host programs, the viral code executes and then replicates. A virus is classified according to its specific form of malicious operation:

♦ Partition sector virus

♦ Boot sector virus

♦ File-infecting virus

♦ Polymorphic virus

♦ Multipartite virus

♦ Trojan Horse virus

♦ Worm virus

♦ Macro virus

Computer viruses that attackers spread tend to carry a *payload*—that is, a virus element that causes some kind of damage after a specified period of time. The damage can range from file corruption and data loss to hard disk obliteration. Viruses are most often distributed through e-mail attachments, pirate software distribution, and infected disk dissemination. The damage to your system caused by a virus depends on the kind of virus it is. Popular renditions include active code that can trigger an event upon opening an e-mail (as with the infamous I Love You and Donald Duck bugs).

To date, more than 69,000 viruses spread via technological means have been documented; more emerge every day via mutations or creations. Computer viruses display three distinct life stages:

- **Activation.** The point at which the computer first "catches" the virus, commonly from a trusted source.

- **Replication.** When the virus spreads, to infect as many "victims" as it can within its reach.

- **Manipulation.** When the virus begins to take effect—referred to as the *payload*. This may be determined by a date (Friday 13 or January 1) or by an event (the third reboot, or during a scheduled disk maintenance procedure).

Virus protection software is typically reactive by design, so it's difficult to achieve a complete anti-viral lockdown position. Consequently, you should look for the following three features when choosing anti-virus software for your infrastructure and local user systems:

- **Active scanning:** With active scanning, virus protection modules continuously operate in the background, scanning files when you open them. The module also protects against unauthorized file modification and warns when system file sizes have been altered. A unique companion capability in this process is Internet filtering. Upon download, files are scanned for known infections; hostile Java applets and ActiveX controls are blocked; and some even allow custom configurations to block access to specific undesirable sites.

- **Mail watching:** Mail watching is a recent critical addition to virus protection. This technique directs virus software to look for viruses as attachments to new mail that you receive. You can typically configure the daemon to clean any viruses it finds in your e-mail, or have them moved or deleted.

- **Live-definition updating:** This technique employs an automatic update process for virus signatures, which is important because new infections seem to mutate on a daily basis. Viral signatures are stored in a database that is used to protect against the thousands of computer viruses. Removal updates may be posted once or twice daily. Furthermore, live-definition update engines can automatically query your vendor for new updates, download them, and install the new database.

Backup Challenges

Even as you read this material, the amount of electronically stored data is growing. Electronic media such as e-mail, voice mail, faxing, audio and video, and much more must be accounted for. The fact that NAS and SAN devices continue to come down in price—and the fact that they are being implemented in areas that previously could not afford the hefty price tags of a SAN—confirms this fact. The increase in storage space, coupled with data centralization, means that backup solutions must also scale to NAS and SAN environments reliably, securely, and with greater speeds than ever before. For these reasons, the issues surrounding backups must be included in any sound storage implementation strategy. These issues include:

- Determining the primary requirement (backup, restore, or archive)
- Backup window
- Integrity of backup(s)
- Verification of backed-up data
- Indexing/cataloging
- Media life
- Redundancy in backup solutions
- Data replication and business continuance
- Secure backup strategy

Determining the primary purpose of the backup system

If a loss assessment has already been performed, you have a good idea how exposed you are to single and annualized data loss. In addition, before deciding which technology you should use to achieve your goal, the goal must be clearly understood. Is the primary purpose for backing up the data one, some, or all of the above points? The answer can greatly affect not only the choice of technology, but the methods used to make the selection more secure. Oftentimes, the answer is all of the above, without a complete understanding of what each point means and what potential security concerns each entails.

> **SECURITY THOUGHT:** Data security in the context of backups refers largely to ensuring that data is replicated, retained, and available (in an uncompromised fashion) for use in the event of data loss.

Backup

A *backup* creates a copy of electronic data. Such data can include an entire disk, partition, file system, or individual files, individual blocks, or even individual bits. However, in the computing world, a backup most often refers to a copy of the entire contents stored on a computer, which might include a single disk or multiple disks. Such a copy provides a means of recovering the data in the event that a failure causes the data to become unavailable.

Although backups can be performed on many types of media, to date the most commonly accepted media used to copy the contents of a computer has been magnetic tape media. Many users make the mistake of not performing backups. Other users perform backups, but do not perform them on a consistent or recurring basis. Such mistakes can be costly when only one person is involved, but even more so when multiple users are affected. Suppose data loss occurs in a company where hundreds of people enter information into a central repository. That type of exponential loss can devastate the company. In fact, most companies that experience devastating data loss and have not adequately planned for their recovery go out of business within the first or second year after the loss. That's a pretty compelling argument for implementing BCP and DRP.

Restore

In terms of electronic data, a *restore* is essentially the reverse process of a backup. In the event of a failure causing data loss, the data can be resurrected from the media to which the backup was performed.

Relating to BCP and DRP, a restore is a vehicle to retrieve data stored at a given point in time if it is lost. The restore is often accomplished using magnetic tape. In today's world, however, magnetic tape is not the only option. Other media can be used for very special backup/restore purposes, such as optical devices that are not susceptible to magnetic corruption or complete erasure due to magnetism. These types of devices also offer a longer storage life when compared to their magnetic counterparts. Some CDs have a storage shelf life rating of up to 100 years; although this brings up the issue of technology availability (will a CD be available in 100 years?).

Some organizations choose their backup philosophy based primarily on the restore process. For example, if within the operating environment user data is backed up and requests for restores are frequent (as might be the case in an environment where several spreadsheets are used/shared, modified, or accidentally deleted), a process that requires cataloging of tapes and hours to complete might not be the best choice. Such a cataloging process only adds unnecessary time to the restore process.

Remember, however, a restore is necessary in the first place because data has been lost. Therefore, the combination of method of backup, hardware, software, selection criteria, media, verification techniques, confidentiality, and media protection is critical to ensuring that data can be restored. In other words, all the components of integrity and availability as discussed in Chapter 5 apply to the backup process in order to ensure the restore process.

Archive

An archive can either be a duplicate of a backup that is created for the purpose of long-term storage, or it can refer to specific files that have not been used for a given period of time that are migrated to slower, less expensive long-term storage media. Three types of archives are generally found.

♦ When referring to an individual file or group of files, archiving is a method of storing those files in a single file. This *file-format method* often compresses the files. Once archived, the files can be extracted in the event of data loss. This method is also often used to combine multiple files into one compressed file for transmission purposes. Examples are PKZIP, WinZip, Arc, LHARC, RPM, and .tar files.

♦ The second method is often referred to as the *operating system method* and involves transferring files from faster disk drives (which are typically thought of as more expensive) to slower less-expensive media, such as floppy disks, WORM, CD-R/-RW, DVD-R/-RW, or magnetic tape. The operating system method is often accompanied by a process with associated software and hardware called Hierarchical Storage Management (HSM). One of the main advantages of an HSM-style solution is the ability to archive based on periods of nonuse of data. HSM will be discussed later in this chapter.

♦ The third method involves using an off-site solution. Many companies offer remote backup and archival systems as a service. Off-site backup and archival systems offer services that can archive data using data copy methods similar to those used for HSM, or simply by ensuring that any files that have had their archive bit set are backed up or copied to the remote site.

All three general archive definitions are listed because each plays a role in a BCP or DRP. The file-format definition is pertinent, since many backup solutions use file compression as a means of storing more data on a given media type. However, when referring to tape devices, compression can be accomplished either through the software used to create the backup or by the hardware. Therefore, backup solutions use software and/or hardware to perform the compression. Both software and hardware solutions can handle compression in different fashions. Some solutions perform file compression, while others perform compression in different fashions. For example, a tape device might perform compression by looking at streams of data in segments and by compressing each segment.

The operating system method also typically refers to tape media, but as noted, this reference does not exclude other media as options. Other media can include floppy disks, CD-R, CD-RW, magneto-optical, WORM, DVD-R, and DVD-RW, as well as system-to-system backups using available shared disk space.

In some situations, files that have been archived must be retracted or recalled. When this recall needs to happen quickly, the archive medium may be a worm jukebox, or one that can accommodate such requests. This is often part of a HSM plan.

Companies may also archive when they need to store data for long-term usage that does not change frequently or at all, such as a life insurance policy. The policy may not be changed for several years, but it must be stored and archived.

Some organizations or businesses may be legally obligated to store data for predetermined periods of time or indefinitely. In such cases, archiving data is often the best choice.

Once the need is understood and the method(s) defined, additional challenges and parameters must be addressed.

Backup window

The *backup window* is defined as the time it takes to complete a given backup. This window is determined by the combination of the size of the data to be backed up and the speed at which the backup device can handle the data. This means that the amount of data that can be placed on a given type of media in a given period of time is limited. Since data is ever-increasing, you can see how the backup window would also be taking longer. In many cases, the backup time runs into production time, especially in cases of 24-hour operations. Companies that allow purchasing of their products from anywhere in the world via the Internet, for example, would be greatly affected.

There are many ways to address the backup window, including leveraging incremental and differential backups and clones and snapshot technology. Clones and snapshot technology are discussed in detail later in this chapter.

To better understand the issues associated with the backup window, look at this simple formula, encompassing the amount of data to be backed up and the speed of the backup device if a full backup is to be performed.

```
500GB ÷ 300MB per minute = 1666.6666666666666666666666667 minutes or
27.7777777777777777777777778 hours.
```

As you can see, backing up half a terabyte using a 300MB-per-minute Digital Linear Tape (DLT) speed does not allow the backup to complete in one day, much less the allotted daily backup window,which is likely required to allow daily operations to continue. How this scenario is addressed, along with the application used to perform the backup, can dramatically impact security, as we will show throughout this chapter.

> **NOTE:** Tape devices today are capable of backing up data at a rate up to 432GB per hour, with improvements coming at a much more rapid pace than in past years.

Integrity of backup

The next issue pertaining to BCP and DRP is the integrity of the backup or archive. Ensuring integrity is often one of the most neglected components relating to backups. Because the backup window must decrease to keep up with the constant increase in data to be backed up on a regular basis, the data that is transferred to tape or other media is often not verified by comparing it against the original data or by performing a test restore on a consistent basis. Therefore, even if the BCP or DRP are outlined correctly, the verification component may not be adhered to, preventing the organization from adequately recovering from a major disruption because the data is not complete. Restoration would therefore not occur in the outlined fashion, if at all.

However, being able to restore the data is not the only component of integrity. The data must also be uncompromised. In other words, you must ensure that the backup was performed securely and that the chain of custody has not been broken.

> **NOTE:** *Chain of custody* refers to the touch (exposure) points of data backups. When transferring backups to off-site storage, you should know everyone in the chain of custody (individuals involved in the transfer, as well as anyone else that had access to the backups).

Verification of backed-up data

As you know, tape (and other magnetic) media is susceptible to magnetic interference, including complete erasure. Therefore, many organizations have employed a verification practice in an effort to reduce the chance that the integrity of a backup has been compromised. This often means performing a complete restore of data to a test or other temporary environment and validating that the data stored on the media is both complete and can/will be made available when needed. The validation process varies depending on the selected backup solution, but in general, the backed up data will need to be compared to the original data, and the chain of custody for the backup media (both storage and retrieval) will need to be in place.

Indexing and cataloging

One issue concerning many tape backup products is the ability of the product design to help the customer manage ongoing backup processes, and thereby reduce the restore process in the event of a failure. Cataloging and indexing help address the aforementioned issue. Often, the cataloging or indexing files that need to be retained and updated as backups occur are contained in only one location, usually on the device performing the backup. The fact that catalog and/or index files are stored in one location may be due to the software design or improper implementation. Because many backup implementations store the catalog or index files on the same system that is being used for the backup, if these files become unavailable due to failure or corruption, they may need to be rebuilt in order to perform a restore. This may add time to the restoration process and should be considered as part of the backup device and software selection process. Products that distribute such files or allow them to be distributed to more than one system can provide a more robust and, ultimately, faster means of restoration. However, as with any duplicated data, planning and completely understanding where this data should reside is critical to data security, as well as taking great care to ensure such files are stored and accessed in a secure fashion.

Media life

Magnetic tape, floppy drives, Zip disks, Jazz disks, and even hard drives use a surface that can be polarized, or charged, in some spots and remain nonpolarized in other spots. Using this format, data is written to the tape to create a combination and pattern/sequence of polarized and nonpolarized spots. Magnetic media devices perform this polarization in different fashions, but the basic concept is the same.

Because the media can be polarized, it can also be erased both intentionally and unintentionally. Many magnetic media devices are coated, allowing them to be polarized; however, if the coating wears off, so does the ability to be polarized. Should this type of degeneration occur on media used for restoring data, you may not be able to restore the data. This is a common problem with magnetic media but holds great significance for tape-based magnetic media in particular.

As tape-based magnetic media is forwarded and rewound, it can stretch, which may create areas on the tape that do not polarize or hold their polarization as efficiently as if the tape were new. Combine this with tape media, where the tape physically touches the magnetic heads within a tape device, and the material almost certainly wears out eventually. Tape material can also lose its polarization just sitting in storage. The combination of temperature and humidity can greatly affect the rate at which this happens.

For the above reasons, both a consistent backup validation process and a tape (and other magnetic media) end-of-useful-life-cycle program should be contained within any BCP or DRP. Many software programs today can account for such issues by reading the barcode on a tape and keeping track of its usage. This information can be used to ensure that the useful life of a given magnetic media device is not overrun.

Magneto-optical devices use a combination of magnetic and optical technologies to achieve higher density storage than their magnetic counterparts. For example, a magneto-optical device that is approximately 3.5" (similar to a 3.5" floppy) can store upwards of 100+MB. Such devices can still be damaged or erased both intentionally or unintentionally.

Unlike magnetic media, optical media is written and read by laser. It is thus not affected by magnetic interference. However, the densities (space needed) required to back up most devices today are not sufficient on CDs or DVDs due to their limited storage capacities. Therefore, tape media remains the preferred method of performing data backups because tape devices come in autoloader and library configurations.

Redundancy in backups (on-site plus off-site copies)

Because of the issues discussed previously relating to magnetic media, a BCP or DRP must include redundancy in the backup process. Although this creates another potential security risk (duplicate data must be treated using the same security precautions), the risk is greatly outweighed by the need to prevent data loss due to magnetic media failure. Therefore, it is highly recommended that backups and backup copies be performed and verified simultaneously. Although it will take additional time, if it is not possible to create duplicate backups simultaneously, perform two backups in rapid succession and verify both, or use the original backup set to create a duplicate backup set and verify them against each other. The cost of the tapes is well worth the investment should a media set become unavailable.

Either the original or a copy should be stored off-site—preferably an adequate distance away to protect the data in the event of a disaster. It is almost impossible to specify exactly where the off-site storage should take place. The location differs from environment to environment and is largely based on how accessible the data needs to be. As a general rule, however, off-site storage should be at least 25 miles away. This is an adequate distance for most disasters, yet still allows the data to be accessible in a reasonable amount of time. Note that you should periodically send data to yet another off-site storage facility that is much further away.

Each off-site data store should be evaluated for its security and storage and access practices, as well as its preparedness for disaster or a catastrophic event. Media should be couriered by a predetermined tape storage source, and only in secure fireproof containers.

> **SECURITY THOUGHT:** Numerous accounts of accidents, improper handling, and other such events that cause the loss of precious company data warrant additional security and protection measures when data is being physically transported (couriered). For an added measure of protection, place media in secure, sealed, Electro-Magnetic Interference (EMI)–resistent containers that can only be accessed by company personnel. Remember to ensure that someone in a remote location also has the access information should a catastrophic event occur.

Data replication

Data replication is an excellent method of ensuring that critical data is duplicated, but it should also be a key component of any business continuance plan (BCP) and disaster recovery plan (DRP). Data replication is generally defined as the process of data being replicated to a remote location in real time. Figure 6-3 illustrates this concept.

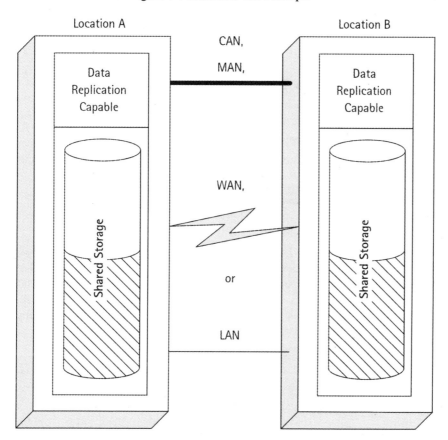

Figure 6-3: Remote data replication

In Figure 6-3, data is replicated from one location to another. This replication can occur unidirectionally or bidirectionally. In many cases, the data being replicated will reside on shared storage devices. Although this type of data replication is considered the preferred method, some organizations may not find it cost-effective. If an organization cannot afford the cost of redundant locations, links, duplicate hardware, duplicate software (where necessary), or combinations thereof, alternative solutions are available.

One such solution available today is to use an outsourcing company. Outsourcing companies specialize in storing (duplicating) your data off-site (unlike the previous solution, in which the company owns the equipment). This storage can be accomplished in different ways, but security must always be the foremost consideration. When looking to outsource, keep the following issues in mind:

- Outsourcing companies should be thoroughly investigated to ensure they leverage only the best security practices—such as those outlined in this book and the CBK.

- Ensure that the company's security practices are well-documented and available for your review.

- Leverage private circuits where possible.

- Validate the strength of the company's authentication/identity management.

- Make sure the company you choose transmits highly encrypted data using both connection encryption and file encryption.

- Evaluate and validate the outsourcing company's backup and off-site storage procedures (depending on the location of your site, it might be more cost-effective over several years for you to set up and manage the off-site storage for your own data). When a possible replication site is within 60km, fiber may be an option that can be used for connectivity, and thus the overall costs might be less versus an outsourced site that is hundreds or even thousands of mile away.

- Inspect the outsourcing company's facilities and storage hardware. Your data likely resides on a shared device like a SAN. Volumes should be separated—physically, if possible—so that even within the outsourcing company's facility, data loss is minimized should one of their devices fail.

- Inspect the physical security of the location to ensure it complies with CBK physical security standards.

- Review the company's BCP and DRP.

- Review and, if necessary, modify confidentiality agreements to fit both/all companies involved.

- Since security cannot be guaranteed 100 percent, investigate the company's willingness to share some of the financial risk. Companies that are willing to share some of the risk are often reasonably sure of their processes, procedures, and security measures. However, do not let a company's willingness to share some of the financial risk keep you from performing your due dilligence in checking them out.

If off-site outsourcing is not an option, alternatives are available. For example, you can build a system where backed-up data is restored in a remote location as a data backup validation procedure; that same remote location can be used as a recovery site. Send backups to that location, have them restored, and have the restore verified as often as possible, but whatever you do, ensure it is scheduled and tracked. Use monitoring tools to manage the health of systems, including remote devices.

If outsourcing or the other options discussed are not viable, determine which data is absolutely critical, and then use a portable disk device(s), secure transmission to another location (that is, a company owned by your company or maybe a sister company) with available storage capacity, or use other such means to back up the necessary data. These devices should be placed in secure, fireproof, EMI-resistant containers and stored off-site.

For databases that are, say, 10GB in size, you may be able to use an external Firewire or USB drive to duplicate the data. With this method, another device can be preconfigured and tested to access the data. In the event of a failure, the external drive can be connected to the preconfigured device, and operations can continue. This solution obviously works best for a relatively small amount of data (10GB), but its logic can be scaled for even greater amounts.

SECURITY THOUGHT: As you may recall from the discussion of DAS in Chapter 2, data stored on easily accessible media, such as USB or Firewire, can be easily breached. Therefore, file-encryption technologies should be used if possible.

Another method being leveraged in some environments is full-drive imaging using tools that can create a copy of an entire drive, partition, or selected files. This method can be considered a form of offline cloning because you can use it to re-create or duplicate data as needed (often called *drive imaging*). Some of these tools can leverage optical devices, including CD-R/RW and higher-capacity DVD-R/RW. Such tools may play an integral part of a comprehensive recovery plan that can greatly reduce restore times.

Some organizations have connections to service providers for any number of purposes, including new equipment configurations, mobile-office-user hot-swap programs, help-desk support, and remote assistance, as well as other services. If such connections already exist, explore leveraging them where possible, but make absolutely certain that security is sound.

Finally, the choice of backup software can also provide a measure of data replication. Many backup programs are able to perform a backup and make a copy of the backup copy simultaneously. Although this is not true data replication, it can provide an extra measure of protection against tape failure or loss.

Business continuance plan

Simply stated, the goal of a business continuance plan is to reduce the impact of failures on business operations. Think about the effects of a failure purely from a consumer perspective. When you Web surf for a new product or service, you are likely to find at least one site that doesn't respond. Do you remember the name of the site? Do you try again later? If, in fact, you return to the site when it is up and running, how confident do you feel about its ability to deliver?

In 30 percent of the cases where an Internet consumer tries to access a site for the first time and finds that it is not available, he will move on and never access the site again. In most cases, the Internet consumer will make the purchase from someone else; if he has a pleasurable experience, he will likely return to the site for future transactions. This means that an Internet company that undergoes a business failure will lose 30 percent of its customers and most of its purchases during the downtime. Furthermore, some percentage of the company's customers will convert to a competitor.

Another example of what can happen without a solid business continuance plan can be found by examining a device that is used to keep track of billing information. Imagine a device connected to a central phone switch that is used to keep track of calls in order to bill customers for their usage. If 200,000 calls per minute were placed at 2 cents per minute, an hour of downtime could cost $240,000.

```
(200,000 calls x2 cents per minute x60 minutes per hour /100( pennies
per dollar = $240,000
```

Two hundred and forty thousand dollars is an expensive proposition without a BCP or DRP. Although not every scenario is this severe, improper BC and DR planning costs companies billions in hard dollars every year. In addition to the traceable losses, intangible losses occur. For example, companies may lose consumer and employee confidence and sales due to competitors using the outage to their advantage. Each of these only compounds the financial loss.

SECURITY THOUGHT: Backups, BCPs, and DRPs are business operation insurance policies, and like insurance policies, they cost money. You would not insure a $10 item for $1,000, nor would you insure a $1000 item for only $10. Make sure you apply appropriate insurance levels for the value of the data.

Guidelines for contingency plans

Procedures known as contingency plans should be coordinated with backup and recovery events if a disaster occurs and IT systems become unavailable. Be sure your contingency plans cover the following points:

♦ Continuity of mission-critical functions

♦ Continuity of IT systems and networks

♦ Employee role adaptation to disaster responsibilities and contingency procedures

♦ Continuity procedures of third-party providers

♦ Documentation of restoration procedures for backups

Choosing a secure backup strategy

Using the information just created, you can now start an objective backup evaluation, which is prioritized by the value of the data. This is an important factor because backup solutions are often chosen with little or no quantifiable evaluation criteria, based on the unique needs of a given application that is not critical to company operation or goals and does not contain the necessary security requirements to provide adequate protection of the data.

The next step in choosing a secure backup method is to determine which type of backup provides the best protection. Tape is the leader, but as noted earlier, disk is being used more frequently. Table 6-1 explores the major strengths and weaknesses of each.

Table 6-1: Tape Versus Disk Backup

Tape Backup Strengths	*Disk Backup Strengths*
Portability	Speed (faster than tape)
Price per MB is cheaper than disk	Real-time transmission
Archival using tape barcode as an identifier	Can easily provide alternative access to data
Tape Backup Weaknesses	*Disk Backup Weaknesses*
Media lifetime (shorter than disk)	Not as portable as tapes
Speed (slower than disk)	Typically more expensive than tapes
Tape drive devices fail more frequently when compared to hard drives.	Deleted files or corruption can be replicated to disks.
Might need to restrict access during backup to allow applications to be shut down so files are not open (quiesced)	Provides another potential live or production vulnerability point, as the data can be live and therefore accessible over the network

Let's take a look at a couple of examples of how each differs. If disk replication is the primary form of backup and a user deletes a file, the file is also deleted from the replica. Likewise, if corruption occurs on the original, it is likely to be replicated in the copy.

Tape backups are a point-in-time copy of data, which means that if a user deletes a file that was backed up by tape, it is recoverable.

> **NOTE:** Options do exist to recover deleted files from many disk systems. However, if they have been deleted and erased from the disk system, the preceding disk replication scenario holds true.

Backup device hardware

Before we continue, you should understand that many different types of tape drives and tape technologies are available, including QIC, DAT 4mm, DAT 8mm, AIT, DLT II-IV, SDLT, LTO, SLR/MLR, and even devices that use VHS tapes. Most tape drives are also rated in a value/value manner. The first value is generally the capacity in uncompressed mode, whereas the second is the capacity in compressed mode. It is not the intent of this book to cover these values; however, they should be included as part of your overall tape evaluation strategy.

In addition to the types of tape technologies, there are many methods of providing the tape backup capacities needed for your growing storage requirements. Tape device configurations include single tape drive, cartridge autoloader, RAID/Arrays, and libraries.

Although they do not fall into the tape category, other devices may be used to perform backups or archives, and their strengths and weaknesses compared to each option should also be evaluated. Such devices include Zip/Jazz, CD-R/RW, DVD-R/RW, WORM, magneto-optical, and jukeboxes.

Secure backup connection methods

In your evaluation of backup devices, you should also include an evaluation of the connection method(s) available for the backup device. Most backup devices connect using the same technologies outlined in the connection sections in Chapters 2–4. Later in this chapter, Figure 6-6 shows an example of backup technology security evaluation criteria.

Backup device placement

In addition to the connection technology, the physical placement of the backup device should be considered. Some of the reasons to consider the physical placement might be obvious, while others might not. Figure 6-4 shows two placement scenarios.

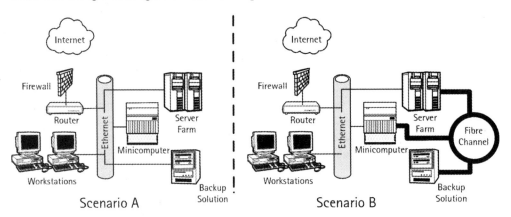

Figure 6-4: Backup device placement scenarios

In Scenario A, the tape backup device is located on the same segment as all the other devices. This setup presents both advantages and disadvantages. With the correct backup software, the tape backup device can be easily configured to back up all devices, including workstations. However, this can pose a security threat because the tape backup device is on the same segment. Additionally, depending on the speed of the network, placement on the production network can (and in many cases does) slow down the backup process.

In Scenario B, the tape backup device is located on a Fibre Channel segment that only has connections from the server farm and the minicomputer, which means that the device is probably not accessible by all the other devices on the Ethernet segment. By placing the backup device directly on the Fibre Channel segment, you gain an additional measure of security. Additionally, the performance of the backup is probably greater than on that of the production network. The trade-off is that it might not be possible to back up a workstation (or other devices) that do not have Fibre Channel connections.

Backup software

One of the most critical components of any secure backup solution is the backup software itself. Although the primary function of a backup product is to create a copy of the data of your choice, many products have functions and features that can either enhance or detract from security. The intent of this section is not to compare products, but rather to help you understand what can enhance security relating to your backup process and the reliability of the restore process when needed.

> **SECURITY THOUGHT:** In some cases unfortunately, choosing the backup software product dictates which backup hardware you can use, and vice versa. You must weigh the security strengths of each option to determine the most secure of the available options.

Choose software that implements the following protective measures to create a more secure backup environment:

- ◆ Federal Information Processing FIPS 46-3—Data Encryption Standard (DES) or higher levels of encryption for additional security defines a data encryption standard. It is a good practice to leverage encryption technologies like those used in this standard to protect sensitive government data. One such example would be FIPS-197 Advanced Encryption Standard, which can use 128, 192, or 256 bits to encrypt and decrypt data.

- ◆ Encrypted data storage allows data to be stored in encrypted format. Restoration of data requires decryption before the data can be restored.

- ◆ Encrypted file compression allows compressed data to be stored in encrypted format. Restoration of data requires decryption before the data can be restored.

- ◆ On-demand connections allow the backup software to only be connected to a given device as required. This can limit exposure due to open connections.

- ◆ The software should contain the ability to encrypt and compress catalog or index files files.

- ◆ You should look for flexibility in the storage of software maintenance files, including logs, indices, and catalog files. In other words, the software should possess the capability to store centrally or distribute such files, as well as possess the capability to store them in a format other than clear text if necessary.

◆ In addition to software cataloging and indexing, software that can leverage the reading of the barcodes on the tape cartridges themselves can also assist in cataloging, monitoring, and tracking tape usage and tape life. This can be useful, not only to keep tapes in a rotation scheme from becoming so worn that they cannot be relied upon, but also for long-term archival scenarios.

◆ Where possible, the software should support the backup hardware devices you select rather than requiring you to select products that they support.

◆ Backup software should also contain some intelligence about what is being backed up. For example, certain backup software programs understand that when an e-mail containing an attachment is sent to a group of users, only one copy of the attachment needs to be backed up. This can help conserve tape space while reducing the backup time.

File selection methods

Most tape backup products support some sort of hierarchical backup method. In general, methods such as Grandfather, Father, Son, and Towers of Hanoi are merely derivations of the three primary backup methods outlined by ISC^2 and the CBK.

Take a look at the three primary backup selection methods and the differences between each:

◆ **Full backup.** Creates a copy of all files.

◆ **Incremental backup.** Copies files with the archive bit set and resets the archive bit. These are typically only files from the current (business) day that have been changed, since the archive bit gets reset when the file is backed up.

◆ **Differential backup.** Files from the current day and each previous day that a full backup has not taken place. Since the archive bit is only reset upon a full backup, the files that need to be backed up grow as the days pass without another full backup.

The following sections provide a more detailed description of each file selection method.

Full backup

A full backup creates a copy of all the files on the selected system. The intent of a full backup is to provide a means of quickly restoring all files, including operating system files—in other words, to shorten the restore process in the event of a failure that would require rebuilding the failed system, operating system, and data files. However, a full backup can also be used to perform a partial restore of files by selecting only those files that need to be restored.

An example of a partial restore would be using a full backup to restore only a database that has become damaged or corrupt and cannot be fixed using available tools.

Incremental backup

An incremental backup copies new or changed files most often based on the status of the archive bit.

> **NOTE:** The archive bit is a bit associated with a file that, when set, denotes that the file has been changed since it was last archived.

A previous backup resets the archive bit on files. When a file is created or modified, the archive bit is set. When the next incremental backup occurs, these files are backed up, and their archive bit is reset. Incremental backups occur without regard to status of other backups and require a full backup for a complete restore of all files.

Differential backup

A differential backup backs up all files that have changed since the last full backup. This is accomplished by resetting the archive bit only when a full backup is performed. Each differential backup does not reset the archive bit; therefore files changed or created today are backed up, along with files that have been created or changed since the last full backup. This method requires a full backup to perform a complete restore of all files.

Derivatives (synthetic full)

As the backup window decreases and backup time becomes even more critical, companies are designing ways to leverage whatever backup information they can to reduce real-time backups. For example, one such innovation is referred to as a *synthetic full backup*. This procedure involves taking information from a full backup and creating another full backup using information obtained from incremental or differential backups. The backup can be created offline while the system still functions with interruption.

Failure recovery backup

Because many tape backup software programs reside on the same disk as the operating system of the device they back up, and because they generally rely on the operating system to be available for the tape device(s) to function, problems can occur when a failure affects this area. Some software packages have what is referred to as a *failure recovery backup feature*. Such programs might use a combination of floppy disks, Zip/Jazz disks, or even CD-R/RWs to create a recovery disk or disk set. This recovery disk or disk set can then be used to quickly get a failed system back to functioning status. In basic terms, the recovery disk set is able to lay down the operating system, or enough of one, so that the tape device can function and begin a restore. This process helps reduce the time to restore in the event of a failure that would affect tape backup operations.

HSM

Hierarchical Storage Management (HSM) is a method of migrating less frequently used files from typically more expensive disk media to slower, less expensive media while maintaining the ability to access the file if needed. Many HSM solutions migrate data from a disk to an optical device and then to tape. In this fashion, the more expensive disk media can be used for frequently accessed or current files. HSM is policy- or rule-based, and as such, can be configured to archive files in different fashions at different timeframes. Furthermore, HSM can be configured to ignore certain files or file types. Figure 6-5 illustrates how an HSM solution functions.

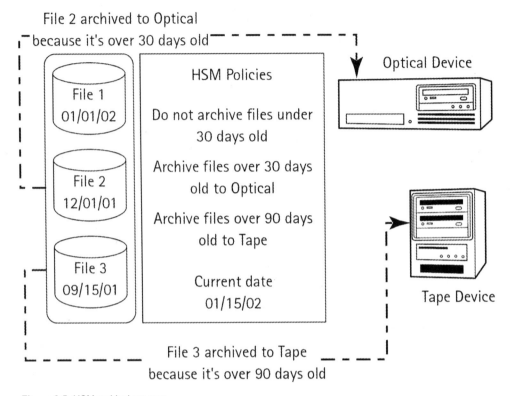

Figure 6-5: HSM archival process

In the preceding scenario, if a file that was archived to either an optical device or tape is needed, the HSM product retrieves the file and places it back onto disk, usually with a new archive date.

Although HSM is a good method of archiving infrequently used data, it is important to remember that the data must be available when needed. If the intent is to archive files for long-term storage, you must make certain that future devices can read the file format. If, for example, you wish to store data for 50+ years, it is not likely that that device you originally archive the data to will be available in 50+ years. You must ensure that archived data is migrated to newer media and validated as part of your overall archival program. The verification process also helps to ensure data is available when needed.

Leveraging clone and snapshot technologies for backups

Cloning and snapshot technologies were previously mentioned in the context of helping ensure data availability. However, as data continues to grow and backup windows continue to shrink, these technologies are finding new uses.

Many database applications must be temporarily shut down in order to perform a backup, which causes them to be unavailable. One of the great features of a clone or snapshot is that it can help reduce this timeframe dramatically. A clone can be "broken off" to allow for a backup, and a snapshot causes the data to be unavailable briefly while the database is "quiesced" to allow the creation of the snapshot. Since many snapshots can occur in seconds (even for some large data volumes), this temporary shutdown of activity might not even be noticed by users, especially if the snapshot occurs only during off-peak usage times. This effectively increases the backup window. By having a copy of the data, a backup can occur at any point in time without requiring the shutdown of live data for the purpose of the backup.

> **NOTE:** The term *quiesce* refers to placing a computer resource into a temporarily unavailable state. In terms of data, it can refer to a program, database, thread, or even an entire computer.

Snapshots are not a complete copy of data, but rather a point-in-time "snapshot" of the data. As data is changed, the original data is copied to the snapshot and then the production data is changed. For this reason, a snapshot starts out very small but can grow to the same size as the original data.

How clones and snapshots affect the backup window can be seen by comparing a backup without the benefit of a clone or snapshot to a backup that uses a cloning or snap shotting technique.

If the time to back up a current data volume is eight hours, the required downtime might also be eight hours to ensure files are not open or changed during the backup process. With cloning or snap shotting, however, the downtime might only be minutes or seconds. If this time reduction is evaluated on an annual basis, the results are dramatic, as shown in Table 6-2.

Table 6-2: Clone and Snapshot Benefits

Backup Without Cloning or Snap shotting	*Backup Using Cloning or Snap shotting*
8 hours per day	Clone break off or snap time 1 minute
365 days per year	365 days per year
Downtime = 8 x 365 or 2920 hours or 121+ days	Downtime = 1 x 365 or 365 minutes or 6.083 hours

As you can see, there's a dramatic difference—approximately 33 percent of available processing time lost when not using cloning or snap shotting versus approximately .069 percent of downtime when employing either method.

Another benefit of using clone or snapshot technology for backups is that they might eliminate the need to use open file agents.

> **SECURITY THOUGHT:** Remember that using cloning or snap shotting creates duplicate data; thus, the duplicated data must be treated with the same precautions as the original.

Open file and database agents

When backups of active data need to be performed without closing or shutting down files and databases, open file and/or database backup agents might need to be employed. In effect these agents perform the quiesce or lock function necessary to complete the backup. However, the file(s) or database(s) may be unavailable for a longer period of time when compared to a clone or snapshot.

> **SECURITY THOUGHT:** An open file or database agent could be modified to keep file(s) or database(s) locked, which can create a DoS condition.

Verification/notification options

Most backup software programs today provide a good means of verifying that the information contained on the tape is consistent with what was supposed to be backed up (integrity verification). In addition to verifying the integrity of the backup, many backup software products also have the ability to provide real-time reporting and notification of this information, via e-mail, fax, pager, and SNMP alerting. In the event of a failure, notification via alert can trigger an escalation to an administrator. The administrator can immediately intervene in the process to ensure the success of the backup and verification. Without this notification, the issue may go unnoticed and when needed, the backup might not be valid.

> **SECURITY THOUGHT:** Implementation of the various notification options can pose additional security concerns; thus, each one should be evaluated individually.

No swapping of tapes or other media if possible

Although a measure of protection can be gained by splitting backups onto multiple media, research has shown that if manual swapping of media is required, backups are not completed as often. The trade-off of security versus completeness and continuity of backups is often not worth it. In cases where manual swapping of media would be necessary you can use autoloaders, libraries, or RAID solutions to eliminate the need to manually swap media as it is being backed up. These devices allow the backup to complete and the media can be swapped when it is more convenient to do so.

If manual swapping of media is a must, consider a process that limits the number of times per week that media must be manually swapped. For example, if a CD-R/RW or DVD-R/RW is being used to create backups, the use of a full/incremental backup philosophy can help to ensure that backup of changed data occurs.

Media availability

Certain types of failures may require that media be available in order to restore a service. For this reason, media should also be considered part of the backup process. It should be archived in accordance with licensing laws and stored in different locations to limit its exposure. Many companies that have replication sites store backups of their media in a third location. They assume that if that location is the site of a disaster, the company can recopy the media and restore it. If another location becomes unavailable and the media is needed, it can be obtained from the third location.

Choosing a secure backup solution

Choosing a secure backup solution can be a daunting task. With the myriad of available hardware and software options and hardware and software providers, making a choice is difficult at best. The following matrix should help you select a solution based primarily on security concerns. In an effort to make the evaluation thorough while maintaining a good measure of consistency, some categories must be excluded from a given evaluation section. These have been blocked out on the matrix. Each product should be evaluated using this matrix, and its score noted. The best solution comprises the most secure technology in each category. In the event that the most secure technology cannot interoperate all selected components, the most secure combination that can interoperate should be used. Figure 6-6 contains the matrix with nonpertinent areas blocked out.

Data Recovery

Simply put, data recovery is the ability to re-create data in the event that the usable (often referred to as production) data becomes unavailable either permanently or temporarily. Data can become unavailable for many reasons, including disasters, faults, failures, or loss/destruction. You can protect your data by using sound backup methodologies, but it is also necessary to understand and plan the steps that must be taken if these situations occur. Proper planning is the key, and thinking through the hurdles that can hinder recovery is also essential.

Disaster recovery

Any good disaster recovery plan (DRP) should account for the health and well-being of people. In their effort to ensure that data is safe, companies often forget how certain DR decisions affect personnel.

Disasters fall into two main categories (natural and man-made) but can come in many forms, including long-term loss of power, fire, flood, tornado, hurricane, earthquake, and terrorism. Whatever the disaster, one or more facilities, campuses, cities, or perhaps even regions could become unavailable temporarily or for a long period of time. Therefore, disaster recovery includes much more than just ensuring that data is replicated. A good DRP must account for all the factors that ensure a company's vitality in the event of a disaster (this is a topic unto itself, so it will not be covered in its entirety here).

BACKUP TECHNOLOGY SECURITY EVALUATION CRITERIA

	A=Acceptance	B=Breachable	C=CISS Compliance	D=Common Knowledgebase	E=Connection	F=Data Protection	G=Framing/Protocol	H=Hardware Fault Tolerance Exposure	I=Optional Security Measures	J=Physical Security Issues	K=Special Config Software Issues	Total	Average
HARDWARE CONNECTION METHOD													
FC-AL												0	
FC-Fabric												0	
HiPPI Parallel												0	
HiPPI Serial												0	
SSA												0	
SSA Fiber												0	
Ethernet												0	
iSCSI												0	
FC-IP												0	
USB												0	
Firewire												0	
IDE/ATA												0	
SCSI												0	
HARDWARE DEVICE (Tape/Disk/Other)													
Single												0	
Autoloader												0	
Library												0	
RAID													
Zip/Jazz													
CD-R/RW													
DVD-R/RW													
Worm													
Magneto Optical												0	
SOFTWARE FEATURES													
FIPS+Authentication												0	
Encrypted Storage												0	
Encrypted Compression												0	
Encrypted Index/Catalog												0	
On-Demand Connect												0	
Barcode Capable												0	
Device Support												0	
Intelligence												0	
File Selection												0	
Recovery Features												0	
Notification Options												0	

Sorted Alphabetically — For each category, the scale is 1–5; however, the numbers mean different things.

A	Acceptance:	1=Widely accepted thru 5=Not accepted
B	Breachable:	1=Easily breached thru 5=Very hard to breach
C	CISS Compliance:	1=Not compliant thru 5=100% compliant
D	Common Knowledgebase:	1=General knowledge thru 5=Uncommon
E	Connection:	1=Very common thru 5=Proprietary/Uncommon
F	Data Protection:	1=No protection thru 5=Highly protected
G	Framing/Protocol:	1=Standard/Very common thru 5=Proprietary/Very uncommon
H	Hardware Fault Tolerance Exposure:	1=Highly fault-tolerant thru 5=No fault tolerance
I	Optional Security Measures:	1=No security measures thru 5=Highly secure
J	Physical Security Issues:	1=Any physical access thru 5=Fully CISS-compliant
K	Special Configuration Software Issues:	1=Not available thru 5=Multiple levels of protection

Figure 6-6: Backup technology security evaluation criteria

However, disaster recovery planning must include sound strategies, processes, procedures, validation points, and maintenance points to ensure data is protected and available in the event of a disaster. As with most other security plans, disasters should be categorized. Disasters that don't cause a facility shutdown might allow the recovery process to occur more rapidly than disasters that do, but it may also be true that getting the same facility back to a functional condition would take more time than it would to activate a Disaster Recovery (DR) site. Whatever the case, disaster recovery and data recovery must be a component of a BCP and DRP. Fault mitigation and recovery packets aid in the recovery process by reducing the time it takes to recover a failed system to an operation state. Fault mitigation and recovery packets are discussed later in this chapter.

> **SECURITY THOUGHT:** Except in grave situations (for example, when national security is compromised), the preservation of data should never be more important than personnel safety.

Organizing data

To create any sound business continuance plan or disaster recovery plan (which is essential to a sound data recovery plan), you need to understand and organize the data to be protected. This involves understanding what type of data is used, as well as the value of that data, by using the formulas outlined by the Common Body of Knowledge (CBK). These formulas, which are described in the following sections, include determining both quantitative and qualitative values for the data.

Single loss expectancy

Single loss expectancy (SLE) helps you determine the anticipated loss that would occur from a single event. It comprises an exposure factor (EF) and an asset value (AV) and is computed using the following formula:

```
SLE = EF x AV
```

The exposure factor is a percentage assigned to the failure. Therefore, if a failure caused a 50 percent exposure and the asset was valued at $100,000, the single loss expectancy would be $50,000.

Annualized loss expectancy

The annualized loss expectancy (ALE) is simply the number of times within a given year that the SLE is expected to occur. Therefore, the formula to compute ALE is:

```
ALE = SLE x Frequency
```

Frequency can be a fraction or whole number typically represented in decimal format. Using the previous example, if such an event were only expected to happen once every 2 years, the formula would be SLE ($50,000) × Frequency (.5) = $25,000.

Frequency may be a small number, as would be the case if ALE were being evaluated based on nuclear holocaust or a higher number as might be represented by a virus attack.

NOTE: The frequency value .5 was chosen for this example because it represents an event that occurs once every 2 years. A frequency value of 1 would indicate that the event occurred once a year.

Once a good understanding of the value of the data has been reached and the loss expectancies have been calculated, the data should be categorized by:

- **Value:** Determine the value using both the quantitative and qualitative formulas.

- **Business usage:** Determine the data's business use. For example, is the data used for research, marketing, sales e-mail, and so on?

- **Storage requirements:** Discover how much storage is currently being used by each data component (data and the application that uses the data in most instances) and how much growth is anticipated.

- **Data type:** For example, if the application is a database, is it flat, relational, object-oriented, and so on? If it's an audio file, what format is it in?

- **File types:** What type of data is it: database, CAD/CAM files, graphics, audio, video text, executables, and so on?

- **General composition:** How is the data composed? Is it centrally located, or is it stored in multiple locations? Is it live data or a duplicate, as can be the case with data replication, clones, and snapshots?

- **Application type:** What type of application is it (graphical (CAD/CAM), e-mail, database)?

- **Access method:** Is the data accessed directly by a client or is it client-server-based? Is the data accessed locally, remotely, or through another process? By what types of devices and users is it accessed?

- **Response requirements:** How available does the data need to be? For example, a customer service representative might need the ability to search for a customer ticket and bring up information within a few seconds to provide the level of support (service levels) necessary to achieve the goals of a support contract, whereas a program that automatically compares information and generates reports might only need to be run once a day, and its processing time (within reason) might not matter. Therefore, it can process overnight.

After these items have been outlined, use them to build the requirements for the backup solution.

Using recovery packets for fault and failure mitigation

As part of the BCP or DRP, ways to reduce the impact of faults or failures should be planned for. Besides those mentioned previously, additional measures can be taken to either mitigate or otherwise limit the effects of a fault or failure.

SECURITY THOUGHT: No potential fault or failure should be dismissed without consideration, no matter how remote the possibility of its occurrence. Accounting for and evaluating each possibility can help to ensure thoroughness of your security and recovery plan.

Many of the faults or failures occur on single devices, and many can easily be fixed by replacing a single component without affecting the data. But suppose a hard drive controller becomes defective and corrupts or erases data. RAID levels do not help in this case because the controller has erased both the configuration information and data, including the operating system. Since the controller is integrated, the system board needs to be replaced, and since the system board contains the configuration information for the machine, the machine has to be reconfigured. This could be accomplished manually from documentation (assuming the configuration was documented).

However, most manufacturers provide the ability to back up the hardware configuration electronically. If this were a common practice, the configuration file would exist, and the time to return the device back to service would be reduced. That type of logic can be extended to the creation of a *recovery packet*.

A recovery packet is designed to reduce the time it would otherwise take to return a failed device to production status, and the contents of the recovery packet depend greatly on the available tools. As a general rule, however, the packet should include:

- Hardware configuration instructions (printed and electronic if possible)
- Hardware configuration software as appropriate
- An operating system image using imaging tools or backup tools if possible
- A data restoration option (tape backup or other device used to perform the backup)
- Media retrieval instructions as needed to include operating system, applications, and backup media
- Necessary contact information and escalation instructions

Much of this information can be stored electronically, but remember to ensure a means of readily accessing it in the event of a failure, as it primarily functions to reduce restoration time in the event of a failure.

> **NOTE:** In the unlikely event that data cannot be recovered, consider sending the backup media (hard disk, tape, CD, and so on) to a data recovery company. This does not guarantee recovery and can be an expensive proposition from both a time and cost perspective, but if the data is otherwise unrecoverable, the company may be able to help.

Loss mitigation

Data loss occurs when active (live or production data) becomes permanently unavailable for use. If mirroring or cloning were used as an example, and data loss or corruption occurred at the primary data location, it is possible that both copies of the active data would be erased, corrupt, or otherwise unusable.

Undoubtedly, one of the most important steps you can take to ensure that data can be recovered is proper and adequate data availability planning. However, implementing a sound backup plan does not ensure that the recovery plan will be effective and timely unless recovery options and the recovery plan have been addressed and are tested on a recurring basis.

With the technology advancements that have been made to date, you can use another method to recover from potential data loss or corruption without having to perform a restore. Using a clone (previously broken off) or a snapshot, data can be rolled back quickly—in many cases, as quickly as disk drive assignments can be changed.

Practical example

Company XYZ is using snapshot technology to provide a rollback plan for their e-mail platform. Their data resides on a SAN. Snapshots are scheduled to occur once every 2 hours during normal business hours. At 2:00 p.m., e-mail quits working. At 2:15 p.m., the company discovers that the e-mail store has become corrupt. SAN administrators decide to roll back to the last snapshot, which was at 12:00 p.m. They change drive assignments from the production volume to the snapshot and test the snapshot containing the e-mail database from 12:00 p.m to 2:30 p.m. The snapshot from 12:00 p.m. is not corrupt and functions normally.

The company operates without incident for the remainder of the day and that evening performs a complete backup using the snapshot. The company restores to the original volume and changes the necessary drive assignment back to the original condition.

The net result is up to 2.5 hours of lost e-mail versus a full day of lost e-mail and the associated longer interruption if the company were only using tape backup.

Rollback planning

A solid plan must be designed if you want data to be rolled back effectively using clone or snapshot technology. This rollback plan design varies based on the value and critical nature of the data. In the preceding example, Company XYZ determined that e-mail was critical enough to scale the rollback plan in 2-hour increments throughout the business day. In other environments, this might be too frequent or not frequent enough. Performing a data evaluation can help determine the correct requirements for a given environment.

Secure recovery methods

Failures come in many different forms. Proper planning can help reduce the possibility that failure occurs. However, even with the best security, planning, processes, procedures, monitoring, backups, maintenance, and so on, failures can still occur. The speed at which recovery can take place is directly related to both the planning and investment you take towards mitigating a failure. Choosing to use secure backup methods also means understanding what might be required in the event that a restore is needed. Consider the following scenarios.

Restore problem scenario 1

Suppose that your company invests a great deal of money into performing a business continuance/disaster recovery assessment and creating a BCP and DRP. The plans, as outlined, require that data replication and spare equipment be housed in or near the replication site. However, in an effort to limit the costs, no equipment is housed near the replica site. In the event of a disaster, this would definitely hinder the ability to restore services to an operational status within the timeframes outlined in the BCP and DRP. Therefore, the exposure outlined in the plans increases.

Restore problem scenario 2

A multilocation company has implemented bidirectional (two-way) data replication between two of their locations. Since data replication is being performed at both sites, the company decides to back up only one of the sites with tape. One day, the location with the tape backup becomes unavailable and, in the process, corrupts the data. The corrupt data is replicated to and corrupts data at the second location. The first location contains a hardware failure that can not be readily fixed. Since only one location contained tape backup(s)—with the express purpose of performing a restore from that tape backup—and that location is down, the second site must acquire the necessary equipment and tapes to replicate the affected tape backup at the second site, causing increased overall downtime.

Restore problem scenario 3

One of the most common problems occurs when verification of backed-up information is not performed on a consistent basis, or its success is not verified. As tape media begins to wear out, it loses its ability to be polarized. When this happens, data may appear to have been backed up, but due to the tape wear, the information is not valid. Because the backup window has decreased, one of the first items many companies turn off is the verification process. This can be a serious mistake. Verification should be considered an absolute necessity and should not be compromised. If the backup window is becoming too long, pursue other options to increase the backup window, such as cloning, snap shotting, or other software and/or hardware that can accomplish the backup and verification in the allotted backup window.

Restore problem scenario 4

Your company uses a highly secure, highly encrypted backup solution. You have experienced a failure that requires a restore, but the encryption codes and keys are not available. Provisions to acquire these in the event of a failure have not been accounted for. The restoration process cannot begin until you receive the codes and keys.

In this scenario, access to the encryption codes and keys should be defined in the security and the disaster recovery plans. Codes and keys may be kept in a locking device like a safe. If this is the case, access methods to the safe, along with who is authorized to gain access, should also be documented in each plan.

Restore problem scenario 5

A power outage has just caused your data to become corrupt, and a restore is needed. However, your backup power only accounts for the system—not the tape backup/restore device(s). The restore cannot happen until some form of power is restored.

Some of these scenarios may seem far-reaching, but you may be surprised at how often similar horror stories still take place. The moral of the story is to make sure your BCP and DRP are well-thought-out, thorough, and constantly being evaluated and revised as new scenarios are discovered.

Testing the restoration plan

Many organizations spend a great deal of time designing and implementing sound data protection schemes, only to fall short in the testing category. In many organizations, technologists get caught up in firefighting mode when issues occur. Although this approach may be necessary to address the most serious aspects of the situation, it often leads to the lack of performance of other less immediate tasks. This lack of performance is often the case when the testing plan calls for performing test restores and validation of data backups. Unfortunately, not performing these tests can cause much more exposure to data loss in an organization than the immediate issue.

To ensure that validation testing does not become a secondary consideration in daily operations, it should be formally scheduled and tracked, and the test's results should be validated. Periodic audits of the test's completeness should also be performed by management and executive staff as appropriate.

Finally, any decision not to perform such testing individually or in whole should be well documented. It should present a rationale for the decision, as well as appropriate authorization.

Proper disposal of data

Another often overlooked component of backup data security is proper disposal of data when it is no longer needed. Data and media disposal should be a documented component of any sound security program. Destruction should also be witnessed to ensure that your data doesn't fall into the wrong hands. Different types of media require different data erasure and destruction methods.

Tape media

One of the most effective methods of erasing or deleting data on a tape is to use a *degaussing tool*. A degaussing tool is an electro-magnetic device capable of creating strong Electro-Magnetic Interference (EMI). This EMI is used to change the polarized state of tapes, effectively erasing the data on the tape.

If a degaussing tool is not available, many of today's tape drives can both erase and reformat tapes. This can be used as an initial means of erasing data that is no longer needed. Overwriting tapes with new information can achieve the same goal.

Finally, when a tape's life appears to be completed, use a combination of degaussing and tape destruction to ensure data cannot be compromised. One method of destruction includes removing the tape from its cartridge or spindle and shredding it.

> **NOTE:** Choose and follow environmentally sound destruction procedures as appropriate.

Magnetic diskette media

Magnetic diskette media is media that is removable. Floppy disks are still the most common form. Deleting files is not an effective method of erasing sensitive data, as the data could (and most likely does) still exist and be recovered. Degaussing tools can also be effective for diskette media. Additionally, you can find certain software programs that will completely erase data stored on diskettes.

Optical media

Since optical disks are not susceptible to EMI, using a degaussing tool does not destroy the data. If the device is considered a write-once, read-many device, as is the case with WORM and CD-Rs, the best method to ensure that data is not compromised is to completely destroy the media itself. If the media is re-writable, software programs exist to completely erase the data.

Magnetic disk media (hard drives)

Because hard disk drives are sealed, they are often neglected during the data disposal process. Certain software tools can ensure that data is erased from hard drives. If such tools are not available, some diagnostic programs that perform read/write tests can completely erase data on a drive by replacing data with patterns of 1s and 0s.

> **NOTE:** Where possible, erase sensitive data from drives in a pre-failure or failed condition using the methods described above before allowing them to be returned to the servicer. In the case of failed drives, try using a strong degaussing tool if no other means exist. If the data is sensitive enough, open and destroy the media within the drive to ensure it cannot be recovered. This means you physically break the device using a safe method, such as a compactor. However, you are not able to return it for any credit once destroyed, which means you will probably have to purchase the replacement outright.

Summary

For several reasons, backup solutions fall into both the data availability and protection categories; however most "backup" solutions fit best into the data protection category, because they are primarily designed to allay the effects from loss of data caused by data corruption or hardware failure. Recall that the four interdomains of data availability and protection ensure the redundancy of data and access control across each domain of your environment at the highest level. Data protection adds to platform availability characteristics. In order to provide continuous access to data, information must be available if any of the following software or hardware components fail or change: file, directory structure, logical disk volume, physical hard disk drive, host bus adapter or controller, enclosure management module, data bus, or pathway to data.

Backing up data is the most basic method of protecting data on disks. If a disk fails, the data can be recovered and restored. However, data backup can be difficult and time-consuming, as the amount of data and the number of storage resources increase throughout the network. Storage area networks (SANs) offer advantages over local backup, including better use of storage resources, decreased time to back up data, and lowered impact on network traffic. Remember that whenever you have multiple copies of data, each must be appropriately secure.

Throughout this chapter, the many facets of data protection are discussed. You explore a framework for protecting data using the storage interdomain, adhering to the keys to data availability. Methods of protecting data are discussed, including snapshots, redundant data paths, redundant controllers, database replication, online volume expansion, NASD, user/administrator access control—including biometrics, tokens, and tickets—and encryption. You also examine a foundation for implementing your own data protection security policy and discuss data backup and restoration.

Business continuity planning and disaster recovery planning require that data be protected and uncompromised when it is most needed. This involves much more than just purchasing a tape backup device and software. It means creating a secure and reliable backup program within your environment that accounts for, tests, and validates the backed-up or archived information. Ultimately, the success or failure of your secure data backup program determines whether the data is available and uncompromised when needed.

Chapter 7

Selecting a Secure Storage Solution

Until now, this book has covered many topics that affect the overall strength of security when centralized storage is used. As you choose and put together your storage system, each component—from the choice of connections to the methods and software used to back up centralized storage—must be scrutinized individually and collectively to create a secure centralized storage environment. This chapter combines the different components discussed thus far and integrates them with business needs (usage), cost, data classification categories, protocol selection and restrictions, architectures, management tools, fault-tolerance selections, data protection methods, and the steps for utilizing the selection tool.

> **SECURITY THOUGHT:** Sacrificing thoroughness in favor of speed of implementation is one of the most common, yet most avoidable, security failures.

The Approach

A multiple-matrix-style approach is used for several reasons. Primarily, experience shows that many people use only those tools (or sections of tools) that they feel are important. However, each of the included matrices is pertinent and therefore recommended for use in the calculations to select a secure storage solution. It is also worth noting that without a solid understanding of business reasons, business justifications, capabilities, capacities and usage scenarios (including sizing), the security of each cannot be adequately planned, implemented, and tested. With that said, you should begin with a needs analysis and then compile design requirements from the infrastructure selection guidelines.

Infrastructure Needs Analysis

This analysis is important because it helps you recognize the existing network, document current applications, protocols, topology, number of users, and business issues, and then assess the health of the existing network and its ability to support growing storage needs. Before you select and design a storage network, this analysis enables you to identify the following characteristics:

♦ Access restrictions and bottlenecks

♦ Potential problems casued by storage growth

♦ Systems that must be incorporated into the design

♦ Business constraints

> **NOTE:** You can download spreadsheet templates for all of the sections in this chapter at `www.wiley.com/compbooks/chirillo` and `www.TigerTools.net` or `www.InfoTress.com`.

I. Applications

Create a spreadsheet and list current and/or required network applications and associated number of users and hosts for each network, as shown in the following table. Use the Notes section for information relevant to the type of application, scalability concerns, and/or business strategies.

Application	# of Users	# of Hosts	Notes
Oracle v.x	75	4	Transaction processing database. Plan to scale to 150 users and 7 hosts.

II. Protocols

Approximately 30 years ago, networking protocols were developed so that individual stations could be connected to form a LAN. This group of computers and other devices, dispersed over a relatively limited area and connected by a communications link, enabled any station to interact with any other on the network. These networks allowed stations to share resources, such as laser printers and large hard disks.

Create a spreadsheet and list the current and/or required network protocols and associated number of users and hosts for each network, as shown in the following table. Use the Notes sections for information relevant to the type of protocol, scalability concerns, and business strategies.

Protocol	# of Users	# of Hosts	Notes
Session Initiation Protocol (SIP)	125	15	Application layer protocol for interactive video and voice.

III. Topology map

Create a topology map of the current network using any third-party modeling suites such as Microsoft Visio. Be sure to accurately label each segment, including speed, addresses, and names and addresses of internetworking devices and server hosts. In addition, document any notes that are relevant to issues such as scalability concerns and business directions. See Figure 7-1 for an example.

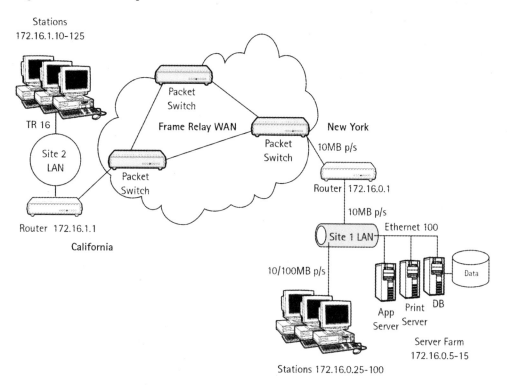

Figure 7-1: A sample network topology map

IV. Network analysis

A *network analyzer* (also called a *protocol analyzer*) decodes the various protocol layers in a recorded frame and presents them as readable abbreviations or summaries, detailing which layer is involved (Physical, Data Link, and so forth) and which function each byte or byte content serves. Most network analyzers can perform many of the following functions:

◆ Filtering traffic that meets certain criteria so that, for example, all traffic to and from a particular device can be captured

- ◆ Time-stamping captured data
- ◆ Presenting protocol layers in an easily readable form
- ◆ Generating frames and transmitting them onto the network
- ◆ Incorporating an "expert" system in which the analyzer uses a set of rules, combined with information about the network configuration and operation, to diagnose and solve, or offer potential solutions to, network problems

Using a protocol analyzer or sniffer product, perform a local network analysis to identify segment bottlenecks in the current network. The network analysis report should contain any congestion and traffic issues that must be addressed and remedied before and/or during the implementation of any storage networks. This infrastructure audit should include the following report types:

- ◆ **User problem report.** This report includes issues such as slow boot times, file/print difficulty, low bandwidth availability, and spontaneous connection terminations.
- ◆ **Composition of traffic by protocol family.** This chart is shown as a percentage breakdown by protocol in Figure 7-2; utilized by the network during the capture period. Each frame or a packet of transmitted information is categorized into protocol families. If more than one protocol applies, a frame is categorized according to the highest protocol analyzed. Thus, for example, a TCP/IP frame encapsulated within Frame Relay would be categorized because TCPand all the bytes in the frame would be counted as part of the TCP/IP percentage.

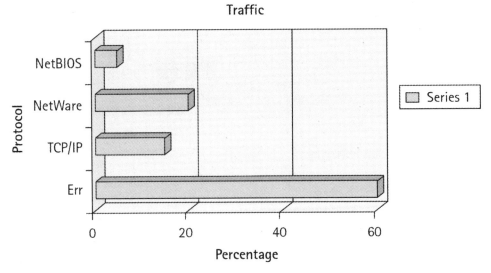

Figure 7-2: Composition of traffic chart

♦ **Network segments/stations versus symptoms.** This report breaks down the network stations and symptoms found—specifically, the network stations discovered, including the number of errors or symptoms per each station (see Figure 7-3). Some possible symptoms that might be detected are:

- *Frame freeze* indicates a hung application or inoperative station.

- *File retransmission* indicates that an entire file or a subset of a file has been retransmitted generally due to an application that is not using the network efficiently.

- *Low throughput* is calculated based on the average throughput during file transfers.

- *Redirect host* indicates that stations are receiving an ICMP "redirect message," meaning a router or gateway may have sent the message to inform stations that a better route exists or that one is not available.

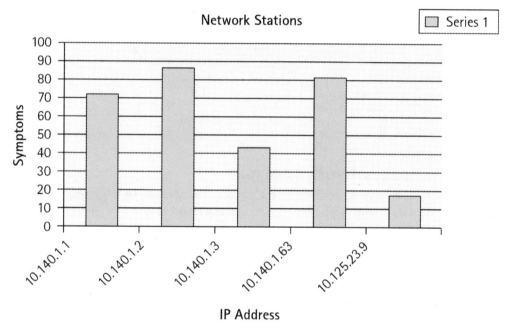

Figure 7-3: Network segments and their symptoms chart

♦ **Bandwidth utilization.** This report indicates the total bandwidth utilized via stations during the analysis session (see Figure 7-4). From this data, recommendations can be made to increase throughput and productivity.

NOTE: Configure the monitoring tool for average network utilization statistics at least every hour to determine the peak usage hours.

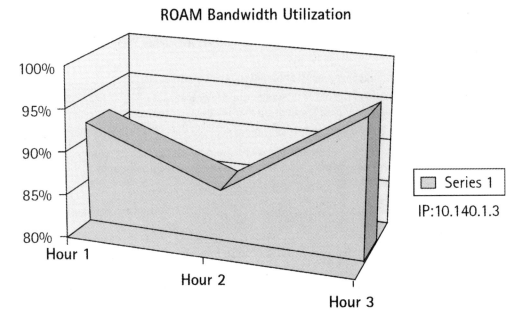

Figure 7-4: Bandwidth utilization by hour

V. Wide area network analysis

Using a protocol analyzer or sniffer product, perform a WAN analysis to identify bottlenecks in the current wide area network (WAN). The analysis report should contain the following report types:

- **Internetworking equipment discovery.** This is an inventory of current internetworking hardware, including switches, routers, firewalls, and proxies.

- **Alarms and thresholds.** This function should track all HTTP, FTP, POP3, SMTP, and NNTP traffic, as well as custom-defined site access information, in real time. Other monitored access information includes, in summary form, network load, number and frequency of each user's access, and rejected attempts.

- **Alarm/event logging.** These reports include excerpts from the actual log files during the analysis session.

VI. Network availability and performance

Obtain more thorough statistics from clients in regards to network performance. Document downtime as the mean time between failure (MTBF) and break it down in the following manner:

- ♦ Cost by department for a network outage (per hour)
- ♦ Cost to the company for a network outage (per hour)

Use the Notes field to document the cause of the outage.

	Downtime Occurrence	*Downtime Duration*	*MTBF*	*Notes*
Company				
Network Segment				

VII. Network reliability and utilization

Summarize the wide and local area network analyses with the following monitored output:

- ♦ Total number of frames to compute average frame size
- ♦ Total number of CRC errors
- ♦ Total number of MAC-layer errors (collisions, Token Ring soft errors, FDDI ring ops, and so on)
- ♦ Total number of broadcasts/multicast frames
- ♦ Network utilization for each hour in peak and average states

There are several average rates you need to calculate. You should become familiar with the following formulas:

- ♦ For the average frame size, divide the total number of megabytes (MB) by the total number of frames.
- ♦ To calculate the average network utilization, add each hourly average (utilization by hour for each segment/number of segments) and divide by the number of hourly averages.
- ♦ For the peak network utilization, record the highest hourly average.

The rate calculations are more complex. Your concern here is the amount of errors or broadcasts compared to the amount of normal traffic or average utilization.

- ♦ To calculate the CRC error rate, divide the total number of CRCs by the total amount of megabytes.
- ♦ For the MAC-layer error rate, divide the total number of MAC-layer errors by the total number of frames.
- ♦ For the broadcasts/multicasts rate, divide the total number of broadcasts/multicasts by the total number of frames.

	Average Frame Size	CRC Error Rate	MAC-Layer Error Rate	Broadcast/ Multicast Rate	Average Utilization	Peak Utilization
Network Segment						

Next, summarize total protocol bandwidth on each segment using the following report types:

♦ **Relative usage.** Protocol bandwidth compared to the total bandwidth and shown as a percentage

♦ **Absolute usage.** Protocol bandwidth compared to segment capacity (for example, 100 Mbps Ethernet)

	Relative Usage	Absolute Usage
IP	For example, 50%	For example, 75 Mbps
IPX		
NetBIOS		
SNA		

VIII. Business strategies

Summarize any potential business strategies that affect the current and future infrastructure. Include items such as:

♦ Corporate structure

♦ Information flow prioritization

♦ Mission-critical data and/or operations

♦ Policies

♦ Technical expertise

♦ Internal politics

IX. Network healthiness

Document any network health issues. Based on knowledge gained from Cisco Systems, Inc., specifically CCDP, CCNA, and CCNP certifications, a healthy network—whether it be a SAN or NAS/DAS storage network—complies with the following maximum allowable capacity issues:

♦ No shared Ethernet segments are saturated (40 percent network utilization).

♦ No shared Token Ring segments are saturated (70 percent network utilization).

♦ No WAN links are saturated (70 percent network utilization).

♦ The response time is generally less than 100 milliseconds (1/10 of a second).

- No segments have more than 20 percent broadcasts/multicasts.

- No segments have more than one CRC error per million bytes of data.

- On the Ethernet segments, less than 0.1 percent of the packets are collisions.

- On the Token Ring segments, less than 0.1 percent of the packets are soft errors not related to ring insertion.

- On the FDDI segments, there has been no more than one ring operation per hour not related to ring insertion.

- Routers are not over-utilized (5-minute CPU utilization under 75 percent).

- The number of output queue drops has not exceeded more than about 100 in an hour on any router.

- The number of input queue drops has not exceeded more than about 50 in an hour on any router.

- The number of buffer misses has not exceeded more than about 25 in an hour on any router.

- The number of ignored packets has not exceeded more than about 10 in an hour on any interface on a router.

Infrastructure Selection Guidelines

Based on CCNP certification and training from Cisco Systems, Inc., the guidelines in this section should be used when making infrastructure selections for new storage network requirements. Be sure to follow these guidelines for your protocol, client, and service design decisions.

Protocol design guidelines

A protocol is basically a set of rules for communication over a computer network. The process of configuring network protocols and services with interfaces for network communications is termed binding. Microsoft's official definition states that binding is the connection made between a network card, protocol(s), and the service(s) installed. On a Windows NT or 2000 system, to view the current protocol(s), services, and bindings, and to add new configurations, proceed to the Control Panel in Start/Settings/Control Panel and double-click the Network icon to start the network administration program. To view the protocol bindings of the current network interface card, click the Protocols tab of the network administration program. There you see the protocol(s) bound to the network adapter as configured during the setup process. From here you can add, remove, view, change, or update protocols and their settings. When making a protocol selection, use Table 7-1 for your design. It defines the amount of traffic overhead associated with most common protocols.

Table 7-1: Protocol Traffic Overhead

Protocol	Notes	Total Bytes
Ethernet	Preamble = 8 bytes, header = 14 bytes, CRC = 4 bytes, interframe gap (IFG) = 12 bytes	38
802.3 with 802.2	Preamble = 8 bytes, header = 14 bytes, LLC = 3 or 4 bytes, SNAP (if present) = 5 bytes, CRC = 4 bytes, IFG = 12 bytes for 10 Mbps or 1.2 bytes for 100 Mbps	46
802.5 with 802.2	Starting delimiter = 1 byte, header = 14 bytes, LLC = 3 or 4 bytes, SNAP (if present) = 5 bytes, CRC = 4 bytes, ending delimiter = 1 byte, frame status = 1 byte	29
FDDI with 802.2	Preamble = 8 bytes, starting delimiter = 1 byte, header = 13 bytes, LLC = 3 or 4 bytes, SNAP (if present) = 5 bytes, CRC = 4 bytes, ending delimiter and frame status = about 2 bytes	36
HDLC	Flags = 2 bytes, addresses = 2 bytes, control = 1 or 2 bytes, CRC = 4 bytes	10
IP	With no options	20
TCP	With no options	20
IPX	Does not include NCP	30
DDP	Phase 2 (long "extended" header)	13

Workstation client design guidelines for NetWare

NetWare is a network operating system (NOS) that provides transparent remote file access and numerous other distributed network services, including printer sharing and support for various applications such as electronic mail transfer and database access. NetWare runs on virtually any type of computer system, from PCs to minicomputers to mainframes. Following is a brief description and summary of the principal communications protocols that support NetWare's client-server architecture. A remote procedure call occurs when the local computer program running on the client sends a procedure call to the remote server. The server then executes the remote procedure call and returns the requested information to the local client.

The NetWare suite of protocols supports several media-access (Layer 2) protocols, including Ethernet/IEEE 802.3, Token Ring/IEEE 802.5, Fiber Distributed Data Interface (FDDI), and Point-to-Point Protocol (PPP).

Internetwork Packet Exchange

Internetwork Packet Exchange (IPX) is the original NetWare Network layer (Layer 3) protocol used to route packets through an internetwork. IPX is a connectionless datagram-based network protocol. IPX is the Internet Protocol, or IP, found in TCP/IP networks. IPX utilizes the services of a dynamic distance vector-routing protocol known as Routing Information Protocol (RIP), or the Netware Link-State Protocol (NLSP).

IPX RIP sends routing updates every 60 seconds. To make best-path routing decisions, IPX RIP uses a "tick" as the metric, which is the delay expected when using a particular length. One tick is 1/18th of a second. In cases where two route paths have an equal tick count, IPX RIP uses the hop count as its secondary priority in decision making. It is important to understand that IPX's RIP is *not* compatible with RIP implementations used in other networking environments.

No different than other network addressing schemes, a Novell IPX network address must be unique. The IPX network addresses are represented in hexadecimal format and consist of two parts:

1. A network number (32-bit length)
2. A node number (typically a MAC address—a 48-bit length)

IPX's use of the MAC address for the node number enables the system to send nodes to predict what MAC address to use on a data link. However, because the host portion of an IP network address has no correlation to the MAC address, IP nodes must utilize Address Resolution Protocol (ARP) to determine the destination MAC address.

IPX encapsulation types

NetWare IPX supports multiple encapsulation schemes on a single router interface; however, multiple network numbers must be assigned. Encapsulation is the process of packaging upper-layer protocol information and data into a frame.

NetWare supports the following four encapsulation schemes:

♦ **Novell Proprietary.** Also called "802.3 raw" or Novell Ethernet 802.3, Novell Proprietary serves as the default encapsulation scheme. It includes an Institute of Electrical and Electronic Engineers (IEEE) 802.3 Length field, but not an IEEE 802.2 (LLC) header. The IPX header immediately follows the 802.3 Length field.

♦ **802.3.** Also called Novell 802.2, 802.3 is the standard IEEE 802.3 frame format.

♦ **Ethernet Version 2.** Also called Ethernet-II or ARPA, Ethernet Version 2 includes the standard Ethernet Version 2 header, which consists of Destination and Source Address fields followed by an EtherType field.

♦ **SNAP.** Also called Ethernet SNAP, SNAP extends the IEEE 802.2 header by providing a type code similar to that defined in the Ethernet Version 2 specification.

Service Advertisement Protocol

The Service Advertisement Protocol (SAP) is an IPX protocol through which network resources, such as file servers and print servers, advertise their addresses and the services they provide. Advertisements are sent via an SAP message every 60 seconds. Particular services are identified by a hexadecimal number, which is called the *SAP identifier* (for example, 4 = file server and 7 = print server).

An SAP operation begins when routers listen to SAPs and build a table of all known services along with their network address. Routers can then send their SAP table every 60 seconds. Novell clients send a query requesting a particular file, printer, or service. The local router responds to the query with the network address of the requested service, and the client can then contact the service directly.

SAP is found throughout NetWare 3.11 and earlier networks, but is utilized less frequently in NetWare 4.0 networks because workstations locate services by consulting a NetWare Directory Services (NDS) Server. SAP, however, is still required in NetWare 4.0 networks for workstations when they boot up to locate an NDS server.

Sequenced Packet Exchange

The Sequenced Packet Exchange (SPX) protocol is the most common NetWare transport protocol at Layer 4 of the OSI model. SPX resides atop IPX in the NetWare Protocol Suite. SPX is a reliable, connection-oriented protocol that supplements the datagram service provided by the IPX, NetWare's Network layer (Layer 3) protocol.

AppleTalk

AppleTalk was designed in the early 1980s in conjunction with the Macintosh computer. It was developed as a client-server, or *distributed*, network system. Through AppleTalk, users share network resources, such as files and printers, with other users. Computers supplying these network resources are called *servers*. AppleTalk identifies several network entities. The most common is a *node*. Simply stated, a node is any device connected to an AppleTalk network.

The most common nodes are Macintosh computers and laser printers, but many other types of computers are also capable of AppleTalk communication, including IBM PCs, DEC VAX, and numerous other types of workstations. A router maintains a node on each connected network. To avoid confusion, these are referred to as *ports*. The next entity defined by AppleTalk is the *network*. An AppleTalk network is simply a single logical cable. Lastly, an AppleTalk *zone* is a logical group of one or more (possibly noncontiguous) networks.

The original implementation of AppleTalk is called Phase I and was originally designed for local workgroups. With the proliferation of over 1.5 million Macintoshes in the first five years of the product's life, Apple found that some larger corporations were exceeding the "built-in" limitations of AppleTalk Phase I. They then created AppleTalk Phase II, which extends the number of nodes in an internetwork to over 16 million and the number of zones to 255. With AppleTalk Phase II, Apple also enhanced AppleTalk's routing capabilities.

TCP/IP Transport and Network layers

As you know by now, the protocol generally accepted for standardizing overall computer communications is the seven-layer set of hardware and software guidelines called the Open Systems Interconnection (OSI) model. At the Transport layer of the OSI model, you find TCP and UDP. This layer, if you recall, is responsible for reliable, connection-oriented communication between nodes and for providing transparent data transfer from the higher levels, with error recovery. At the Network layer of the OSI model, routing protocols and logical network addressing operate. An example of such a protocol is the Internet Protocol (IP), part of the TCP/IP suite.

TCP

IP has many weaknesses, one of which is unreliable packet delivery. In other words, packets may be dropped due to transmission errors, bad routes, and/or throughput degradation. The Transmission Control Protocol (TCP) helps reconcile these issues by providing reliable, stream-oriented connections. In fact, TCP/IP is predominantly based on TCP functionality, which is based on IP, to make up the TCP/IP suite. These features describe a connection-oriented process of communication.

Many components result in TCP's reliable service delivery, including:

♦ **Streams.** Data is systematized and transferred as a stream of bits, organized into 8-bit octets or bytes. As these bits are received, they are passed on in the same manner.

♦ **Buffer flow control.** As data is passed in streams, protocol software may divide the stream to fill specific buffer sizes. TCP manages this process and assures avoidance of a buffer overflow. During this process, fast-sending stations may be stopped periodically to keep up with slow-receiving stations.

♦ **Virtual circuits.** When one station requests communication with another, both stations inform their application programs and agree to communicate. If the link or communications between these stations fail, both stations are made aware of the breakdown and inform their respective software applications. In this case, a coordinated retry is attempted.

♦ **Full-duplex connectivity.** Stream transfer occurs in both directions, simultaneously, to reduce overall network traffic.

Sequencing and windowing

TCP organizes and counts bytes in the data stream using a 32-bit sequence number. Every TCP packet contains a starting sequence number (first byte) and an acknowledgment number (last byte). A concept known as a *sliding window* is implemented to make stream transmissions more efficient. The sliding window uses bandwidth more effectively because it allows the transmission of multiple packets before an acknowledgment is required.

For example, suppose a sender has bytes to send in sequence (1 to 8) to a receiving station with a window size of 4. The sending station places the first 4 bytes in a window and sends them, then waits for an acknowledgment (ACK = 5). This acknowledgment specifies that the first 4 bytes were received. Assuming its window size is still 4 and that it is also waiting for the next byte (byte 5), the sending station moves the sliding window 4 bytes to the right, then sends bytes 5 to 8. Upon receiving these bytes, the receiving station sends an acknowledgment (ACK = 9), indicating it is waiting for byte 9. And the process continues.

At any point, the receiver may indicate a window size of 0, in which case the sender does not send any more bytes until the window size is greater than 0. Typically, a buffer overflow may cause this particular situation.

TCP packet format

Because it is important to differentiate between "captured" packets—whether they are TCP, UDP, ARP, and so on—the parts of the TCP packet format should be identified. The specific components are defined in the following list.

- **The source port** specifies the port at which the source processes send and receive TCP services.
- **The destination port** specifies the port at which the destination processes send and receive TCP services.
- **The sequence number** specifies the first byte of data or a reserved sequence number for a future process.
- **The acknowledgment number** is the sequence number of the very next byte of data the sender should receive.
- **The data offset** is the number of 32-bit words in the header.
- **The flags** control information, such as SYN, ACK, and FIN bits, for connection establishment and termination.
- **The window size** is the sender's receive window or available buffer space.
- **The checksum** specifies any damage to the header that occurred during transmission.
- **The urgent pointer** is the optional first urgent byte in a packet, which indicates the end of urgent data.
- **The options** are TCP options, such as the maximum TCP segment size.
- **The data** is upper-layer information.

Ports, endpoints, and connection establishment

TCP enables simultaneous communication between different application programs on a single machine. In regards to station-to-station communication, TCP uses port numbers to distinguish each of the receiving station's destinations. A pair of *endpoints* identifies the connection between the two stations. Colloquially, these endpoints are defined as the connection between the two stations' applications as they communicate; they are defined by TCP as a pair of integers in this format: (host, port). The *host* is the station's IP address, and the *port* is the TCP port number on that station. An example of a station's endpoint is:

The host address	The port
192.168.0.1	:1011

An example of two stations' endpoints during communication is:

Station 1	Station 2
192.168.0.2:1022	192.168.0.51:26

This technology is very important in TCP, as it allows simultaneous communications by assigning separate ports for each station connection. When a connection is established between two nodes during a TCP session, a *three-way handshake* is used. This process starts with a one-node TCP request by a SYN/ACK bit, and the second node TCP response with a SYN/ACK bit. At this point, communication between the two nodes will proceed. When there is no more data to send, a TCP node may send a FIN bit, indicating a close control signal. At this intersection, both nodes close simultaneously.

UDP

The User Datagram Protocol (UDP) operates in a connectionless fashion; that is, it provides the same unreliable datagram delivery service as IP. Unlike TCP, UDP does not send SYN/ACK bits to assure delivery and reliability of transmissions. Moreover, UDP does not include flow control or error recovery functionality. Consequently, UDP messages can be lost, duplicated, or arrive in the wrong order. And because UDP contains smaller headers, it expends less network throughput than TCP and can thus arrive faster than the receiving station can process them.

UDP is typically utilized where higher-layer protocols provide necessary error recovery and flow control. Popular server daemons that employ UDP include Network File System (NFS), Simple Network Management Protocol (SMTP), Trivial File Transfer Protocol (TFTP), and Domain Name System (DNS), to name a few.

UDP formatting, encapsulation, and header snapshots

UDP messages are called *user datagrams*. These datagrams are encapsulated in IP, including the UDP header and data, as it travels across the Internet. Basically, UDP adds a header to the data sent by a user and passes the datagram along to IP. The IP layer then adds a header to what it receives from UDP. Finally, the Network Interface layer inserts the datagram in a frame before sending it from one machine to another.

As just mentioned, UDP messages contain smaller headers and consume fewer overheads than TCP. The UDP datagram format and its components are defined in the following list:

- ♦ **Source/destination port.** A 16-bit UDP port number used for datagram processing
- ♦ **Message length.** Specifies the number of octets in the UDP datagram
- ♦ **Checksum.** An optional field to verify datagram delivery
- ♦ **Data.** The information handed down to the TCP protocol, including upper-layer headers

Multiplexing, demultiplexing, and port connections

UDP provides *multiplexing* (a method that enables multiple signals to be transmitted concurrently into an input stream, across a single physical channel) and *demultiplexing* (the actual separation of the streams that have been multiplexed into a common stream back into multiple output streams) between protocol and application software.

Multiplexing and demultiplexing, as they pertain to UDP, transpire through ports. Each station application must negotiate a port number before sending a UDP datagram. When UDP is on the receiving side of a datagram, it checks the header (destination port field) to determine whether it matches one of the station's ports currently in use. If the port is in use by a so-called listening application, the transmission proceeds; if the port is not in use, an ICMP error message is generated, and the datagram is discarded.

IP

The Internet Protocol (IP) part of the TCP/IP suite is a four-layer model. IP is designed to interconnect networks to form an Internet to pass data back and forth. IP contains addressing and control information that enables *packets* to be routed through this Internet. A packet is defined as a logical grouping of information, which includes a header containing control information and, usually, user data. The equipment—routers—that encounter these packets strip off and examine the *headers* that contain the sensitive routing information. These headers are modified and reformulated as a packet to be passed along.

One of the IP's primary functions is to provide a permanent-connection (termed *connectionless*), unreliable, best-effort delivery of *datagrams* through an internetwork. We know that datagrams can be described as a logical grouping of information sent as a Network layer unit over a communications medium. IP datagrams are the primary information units in the Internet. Another of IP's principal responsibilities is the fragmentation and reassembly of datagrams to support links with different transmission sizes.

During an analysis session, or *sniffer capture*, it is necessary to differentiate between types of packet captures. The following describes the IP packet and the 14 fields therein:

♦ **Version.** The IP version currently used

♦ **IP header length.** The datagram header length in 32-bit words

♦ **Type-of-Service (ToS).** How the upper-layer protocol (the layer immediately above, such as transport protocols like TCP and UDP) intends to handle the current datagram and assign a level of importance

♦ **Total length.** The length, in bytes, of the entire IP packet

♦ **Identification.** An integer used to help piece together datagram fragments

♦ **Flag.** A 3-bit field, where the first bit specifies whether the packet can be fragmented. The second bit indicates whether the packet is the last fragment in a series. The final bit is not used.

- ♦ **Fragment offset.** The location of the fragment's data, relative to the opening data in the original datagram. This allows for proper reconstruction of the original datagram.
- ♦ **Time-to-Live (TTL).** A counter that decrements to zero to keep packets from endlessly looping. At the zero mark, the packet is dropped.
- ♦ **Protocol.** Indicates the upper-layer protocol receiving the incoming packets
- ♦ **Header checksum.** Ensures the integrity of the IP header
- ♦ **Source address/destination address.** The sending and receiving nodes (station, server, and/or router)
- ♦ **Options.** Typically, contains security options
- ♦ **Data.** Upper-layer information

Initialization constraints

When workstations initialize, the packet generation, especially on large networks, can cause a heavy load on the network. The following tables illustrate the packet initializations for the most common workstation types.

Table 7-2 shows the packets that a Novell NetWare client sends when it boots. The approximate packet size is also shown. In addition to the packet size, add the Data Link layer overhead, such as 802.3 with 802.2, 802.5 with 802.2, or FDDI with 802.2. Network layer and Transport layer overhead are already incorporated in these examples. Depending on the version of NetWare, the packets might be slightly different than the ones shown here.

Table 7-2: NetWare Client Initialization

Packet	Source	Destination	Packet Size in Bytes	Number of Packets	Total Bytes
GetNearestServer	Client	Broadcast	34	1	34
GetNearestServer response	Server or router	Client	66	Depends on number of servers	66 per server
Find network number	Client	Broadcast	40	1	40
Find network number response	Router	Client	40	1	40
Create connection	Client	Server	37	1	37
Create connection response	Server	Client	38	1	38
Negotiate buffer size	Client	Server	39	1	39

Packet	Source	Destination	Packet Size in Bytes	Number of Packets	Total Bytes
Negotiate buffer size response	Server	Client	40	1	40
Log out old connections	Client	Server	37	1	37
Log out response	Server	Client	38	1	38
Get server's clock	Client	Server	37	1	37
Get server's clock response	Server	Client	38	1	38
Download login.exe requests	Client	Server	50	Hundreds, depending on buffer size	Depends on number of packets
Download login.exe responses	Server	Client	Depends on buffer size	Hundreds, depending on buffer size	Depends on number of packets
Login	Client	Server	37	1	37
Login response	Server	Client	38	1	38

Table 7-3 shows the packets that an AppleTalk station sends when it boots. The approximate packet size is also shown. On top of the packet size, add Data Link–layer overhead. Depending on the version of Macintosh system software, the packets might be slightly different than the ones shown here.

Table 7-3: AppleTalk Client Initialization

Packet	Source	Destination	Packet Size in Bytes	Number of Packets	Total Bytes
AARP for ID	Client	Multicast	28	10	280
ZIPGetNetInfo	Client	Multicast	15	1	15
GetNetInfo response	Router(s)	Client	About 44	All routers respond	44 if one router
NBP broadcast request to check uniqueness of name	Client	Router	About 65	3	195
NBP forward request	Router	Other routers	About 65	3	195

Packet	Source	Destination	Packet Size in Bytes	Number of Packets	Total Bytes
NBP lookup	Router	Multicast	About 65	3	195
If Chooser started:					
GetZoneList	Client	Router	12	1	12
GetZoneList reply	Router	Client	Depends on number and names of zones	1	Depends on packet sizes
NBP broadcast request for servers in zone	Client	Router	About 65	Once a second if Chooser still open; decays after 45 seconds	About 3,000 if Chooser closed after 45 seconds
NBP forward request	Router	Other routers	About 65	Same	Same
NBP lookup	Router	Multicast	About 65	Same	Same
NBP reply	Server(s)	Client	About 65	Depends on number of servers	Depends
ASP open session and AFP login	Client	Server	Depends	4	About 130
ASP and AFP replies	Server	Client	Depends	2	About 90

Table 7-4 shows the packets that a NetBIOS station sends when it boots. The approximate packet size is also shown. On top of the packet size, add Data Link–layer overhead. Depending on the version of NetBIOS, the packets might be slightly different than the ones shown here.

Table 7-4: NetBIOS Client Initialization

Packet	Source	Destination	Packet Size in Bytes	Number of Packets	Total Bytes
Check name (make sure own name is unique)	Client	Broadcast	44	6	264
Find name for each server	Client	Broadcast	44	Depends on number of servers	44 if 1 server

Packet	Source	Destination	Packet Size in Bytes	Number of Packets	Total Bytes
Find name response	Server(s)	Client	44	Depends on number of servers	44 if 1 server
Session initialize for each server	Client	Server	14	Depends on number of servers	14 if 1 server
Session confirm	Server	Client	14	Depends on number of servers	14 if 1 server

Table 7-5 shows the packets that a traditional TCP/IP station sends when it boots. In this case, "traditional" means that the station is not running the DHCP. The approximate packet size is also shown. On top of the packet size, add Data Link–layer overhead. Depending on the implementation of TCP/IP, the packets might be slightly different than the ones shown here.

Table 7-5: TCP/IP Client Initialization

Packet	Source	Destination	Packet Size in Bytes	Number of Packets	Total Bytes
ARP to make sure its own address is unique (optional)	Client	Broadcast	28	1	28
ARP for any servers	Client	Broadcast	28	Depends on number of servers	Depends on number of servers
ARP for router	Client	Broadcast	28	1	28
ARP response	Server(s) or router	Client	28	1	28

Table 7-6 shows the packets that a TCP/IP station running DHCP sends when it boots. Although a DHCP client sends more packets when initializing, DHCP is still recommended. The benefits of dynamic configuration far outweigh the disadvantages of the extra traffic and extra broadcast packets. (The client and server use broadcast packets until they verify each other's IP addresses.) The approximate packet size is also shown. On top of the packet size, add Data Link–layer overhead. Depending on the implementation of DHCP, the packets might be slightly different than the ones shown here.

Table 7-6: DHCP Client Initialization

Packet	Source	Destination	Packet Size in Bytes	Number of Packets	Total Bytes
DHCP discover	Client	Broadcast	576	Once every few seconds until client hears from a DHCP server	Depends on number of packets
DHCP offer	Server	Broadcast	328	1	328
DHCP request	Client	Broadcast	576	1	576
DHCP ACK	Server	Broadcast	328	1	328
ARP to make sure its own address is unique	Client	Broadcast	28	3	84
ARP for client	Server	Broadcast	28	1	1
ARP response	Client	Server	28	1	28
DHCP request	Client	Server	576	1	576
DHCP ACK	Server	Client	328	1	328

Topology design guidelines

Topologies, such as Ethernet, make up the networking infrastructure that connects stations to LANs, LANs to wide area networks (WANs), and WANs to Internets. A local area network (LAN) protocol uses a bus or star topology, supporting data transfer rates of 10 Mbps. The first Ethernet, Ethernet DIX, was named after the companies that proposed it: Digital, Intel, and Xerox. During this time, the Institute of Electrical and Electronics Engineers (IEEE) had been working on Ethernet standardization, which became known as Project 802. Upon its success, the Ethernet plan evolved into the IEEE 802.3 standard. Based on carrier sensing, as originally developed by Robert Metcalfe, David Boggs, and their team of engineers, Ethernet became a major player in communications media, competing head-to-head with IBM's proposed Token Ring, or IEEE 802.5.

When a station on an Ethernet network is ready to transmit, it must first listen for transmissions on the channel. If another station is transmitting, it is said to be "producing activity." This activity, or transmission, is called a *carrier*. In a nutshell, this is how Ethernet became known as the *carrier-sensing communication medium*. With multiple stations all sensing carriers on an Ethernet network, this mechanism was called *Carrier Sense with Multiple Access*, or *CSMA*.

If a carrier is detected, the station waits for a pre-programmed minuscule timeframe (9.6 microseconds), after the last frame passes, before transmitting its own frame. When two stations transmit simultaneously, a *fused signal bombardment*—otherwise known as a *collision*—occurs. Ethernet stations detect collisions to minimize problems. This capability was added to CSMA to become *Carrier Sense with Multiple Access and Collision Detection,* or *CSMA/CD.*

Stations involved in a collision immediately abort their transmissions. The first station to detect the collision sends an alert to all stations. At this point, all stations execute a random collision timer to force a delay before attempting to transmit their frames. This timing-delay mechanism is termed the *back-off algorithm.* If multiple collisions are detected, the random delay timer is doubled.

Ethernet design, cabling, and adapters

Ethernet comes in various flavors. The actual physical arrangement of nodes in a structure is termed the *network topology.* Ethernet topology examples include bus, star, and point-to-point.

- A **bus** is a linear LAN where a station's transmissions are propagated and viewed by all stations.

- A **star** is a structure wherein endpoints are connected to a common central switch or hub by direct links.

- In the **point-to-point** topology, the physical connection and communication passes from one station to another.

Ethernet options also come in many variations, some of which are defined in the following list:

- **Ethernet, 10Base5.** Ethernet with thick coaxial (coax) wire uses cable type RG-08. Connectivity from the NIC travels through a transceiver cable to an external transceiver and finally through the thick coax cable. Due to signal degradation, a segment is limited to fewer than 500 meters, with a maximum of 100 stations per segment of 1,024 stations total.

- **10Base2.** Thin-wire Ethernet, or *thinnet*, uses cable type RG-58. With 10Base2, the transceiver functionality is processed in the NIC. BNC T connectors link the cable to the NIC. As with every media type, due to signal degradation, a thinnet segment is limited to fewer than 185 meters, with a maximum of 30 stations per segment of 1,024 stations total.

- **10BaseT.** Unshielded twisted-pair (UTP) wire uses cable type RJ-45 for 10BaseT specifications. Twisted-pair Ethernet broke away from the electric shielding of coaxial cable, using conventional unshielded copper wire. Using the star topology, each station is connected via RJ-45 with UTP wire to a unique port in a hub or switch. The hub simulates the signals on the Ethernet cable. Due to signal degradation, the cable between a station and a hub is limited to fewer than 100 meters.

Using that overview of Ethernet design and cabling as a foundation, you can begin to understand the underlying Ethernet addressing and formatting models. Every station in an Ethernet network has a unique 48-bit address bound to each NIC. These addresses not only specify a unique, single station, but also provide for transmission on an Ethernet network to three types of addresses:

♦ **Unicast address.** Transmission destination to a single station

♦ **Multicast address.** Transmission destination to a subset or group of stations

♦ **Broadcast address.** Transmission destination to all stations

The Ethernet frame is of variable length, which is to say that no frame is smaller than 64 octets or larger than 1,518 octets. Each frame consists of a preamble, a destination address, a source address, the frame type, frame data, and cyclic redundancy check (CRC) fields. These fields are defined as follows:

♦ **The preamble** aids in the synchronization between sender and receiver(s).

♦ **The destination address** is the address of the receiving station.

♦ **The source address** is the address of the sending station.

♦ **The frame type** specifies the type of data in the frame to determine which protocol software module should be used for processing.

♦ **The frame data** indicates the data carried in the frame based on the type latent in the Frame Type field.

♦ **The cyclic redundancy check (CRC)** helps detect transmission errors. The sending station computes a frame value before transmission. Upon frame retrieval, the receiving station must compute the same value based on a complete, successful transmission.

Congestion problems

As a result of ongoing technological advances and the advent of complex, bandwidth-intensive applications, network congestion continues to increase dramatically. In a snowball effect, we create more complex applications as more bandwidth becomes available, which in turn causes greater congestion. Concomitantly, network response time decreases, which of course lowers productivity.

Benefits and guidelines of Fast Ethernet

Using the same foundation and cabling as Ethernet, Fast Ethernet operates at 100 Mbps and is designed to handle high-bandwidth network requirements. The benefits of 100BaseT Fast Ethernet include the following:

♦ High performance due to high bandwidth at 100 Mbps

♦ You can use existing cabling and most network equipment, with easy updating from 10 Mbps to 100 Mbps by adding Fast Ethernet hubs and/or switches, and 100 Mbps network interface cards (NICs).

♦ Fast Ethernet is based on Ethernet specifications.

To accommodate bandwidth-intensive applications and network expansion, the Fast Ethernet Alliance (composed of 3Com Corporation, DAVID Systems, Digital Equipment Corporation, Grand Junction Networks, Inc., Intel Corporation, National Semiconductor, Sun Microsystems, and Synoptics Communications) was formed to promote 100 Mbps technology.

To understand the difference in transmission speed between 10BaseT and 100BaseT, take a look at the following formula:

Station-to-Hub Diameter (meters) = 25,000 / Transmission Rate (Mbps)

Here are some examples of that formula in use:

For a 10 Mbps 10BaseT Ethernet network:

Diameter (meters) = 25,000 / 10 (Mbps)

Diameter = 2,500 meters

For a 100 Mbps 100BaseT Fast Ethernet network:

Diameter (meters) = 25,000 / 100 (Mbps)

Diameter = 250 meters

From these equations, it can be deduced that 100 Mbps Fast Ethernet requires a station-to-hub diameter, in meters, that is one-tenth that of 10 Mbps Ethernet. This speed-versus-distance ratio in Fast Ethernet allows for a tenfold scale increase in maximum transmitted bits. Other prerequisites for Fast Ethernet include 100 Mbps station NICs, Fast Ethernet hub or switch, and Category 5 UTP (data grade) wire.

Benefits and guidelines of Gigabit Ethernet

At 1 Gbps, Gigabit Ethernet offers 100 times the performance over Fast Ethernet. The new Gigabit Ethernet Alliance and the IEEE 802.3 specify an easy migration from Fast Ethernet to Gigabit Ethernet, without changing network protocols, server operating systems, or applications. Three Gigabit Ethernet standards have been employed, with the following specifications:

♦ **1000BaseCX** operates at 1,000 Mbps in half-duplex mode (2,000 Mbps in full-duplex mode), over 25 meters, or 82 feet.

♦ **1000BaseSX** operates at 1,000 Mbps in half-duplex mode up to 316 meters, or 1,036 feet, and 2,000 Mbps in full-duplex mode up to 550 meters, or 1,804 feet.

♦ **1000BaseLX** operates at 1,000 Mbps in half-duplex mode up to 316 meters, or 1,036 feet, and 2,000 Mbps in full-duplex mode up to 5,000 meters, or 16,404 feet.

Scalability constraints

In regards to the most common topology, namely Ethernet, the most significant design rule is that the round-trip propagation delay in one collision domain must not exceed 512 bit times, which is a requirement for collision detection to work correctly. This rule means that the maximum round-trip delay for 10 Mbps Ethernet is 51.2 microseconds. The maximum round-trip delay for 100 Mbps Ethernet is only 5.12 microseconds because the bit time on 100 Mbps Ethernet is 0.01 microseconds as opposed to 0.1 microseconds on 10 Mbps Ethernet. See Table 7-7 for 802.3 scalability constraints.

Table 7-7: Scalability Constraints for IEEE 802.3

	10Base5	*10Base2*	*10BaseT*	*100BaseT*
Topology	Bus	Bus	Star	Star
Max. Segment Length (Meters)	500	185	100 from hub to station	100 from hub to station
Max. Number of Attachments per Segment	100	30	2 (hub and station or hub-hub)	2 (hub and station or hub-hub)
Max. Collision Domain	2,500 meters of 5 segments and 4 repeaters; only 3 segments can be populated.	2,500 meters of 5 segments and 4 repeaters; only 3 segments can be populated.	2,500 meters of 5 segments and 4 repeaters; only 3 segments can be populated.	See next discussion.

To make 100 Mbps Ethernet work, one confronts more severe distance limitations than those required for 10 Mbps Ethernet. The general rule is that a 100 Mbps Ethernet has a maximum diameter of 205 meters when UTP cabling is used, whereas 10 Mbps Ethernet has a maximum diameter of 2,500 meters. See Table 7-8 for 10 Mbps Fiber/Ethernet scalability constraints.

Table 7-8: Scalability Constraints for 10 Mbps Fiber Ethernet

	10BaseFP	*10BaseFB*	*10BaseFL*	*Old FOIRL*	*New FOIRL*
Topology	Passive star	Backbone or repeater fiber system	Link	Link	Link or star
Allows DTE (End-Node) Connections?	Yes	No	No	No	Yes

	10BaseFP	*10BaseFB*	*10BaseFL*	*Old FOIRL*	*New FOIRL*
Max. Segment Length (Meters)	500	2,000	1,000 or 2,000	1000	1,000
Allows Cascaded Repeaters?	No	Yes	No	No	Yes
Max. Collision Domain in Meters	2,500	2,500	2,500	2,500	2,500

The original specification for running Ethernet on fiber cable was called the Fiber-Optic Inter-Repeater Link (FOIRL) specification. 10BaseF is based on the FOIRL specification, which includes 10BaseFP, 10BaseFB, 10BaseFL, and a revised FOIRL standard. The FOIRL differs from the old one in that it allows DTE (end-node) connections, rather than just repeaters.

As in 10 Mbps Ethernet, the overriding design rule for 100 Mbps Ethernet is that the round-trip collision delay must not exceed 512 bit times. However, the bit time on 100 Mbps Ethernet is 0.01 microseconds as opposed to 0.1 microseconds on 10 Mbps Ethernet. This means that the maximum round-trip delay for 100 Mbps Ethernet is 5.12 microseconds, as opposed to the more lenient 51.2 microseconds in 10 Mbps Ethernet.

To make 100 Mbps Ethernet work, distance limitations are imposed. The limitations depend on the type of repeaters that are used. In the IEEE 100BaseT specification, two types of repeaters are defined:

♦ Class I repeaters have a latency of 0.7 microseconds or less. Only one repeater hop is allowed.

♦ Class II repeaters have a latency of 0.46 microseconds or less. One or two repeater hops are allowed.

Table 7-9 shows the maximum size of collision domains, depending on the type of repeater(s).

Table 7-9: Maximum Collision Domains for 100BaseT

	Copper	*Mixed Copper and Multimode Fiber*	*Multimode Fiber*
DTE-DTE (or Switch-Switch)	100 meters	N/A	412 meters (2,000 if full duplex)
One Class I Repeater	200 meters	260 meters	272 meters
One Class II Repeater	200 meters	308 meters	320 meters
Two Class II Repeaters	205 meters	216 meters	228 meters

To check a path to make sure the path delay value (PDV) does not exceed 512 bit times, add up the following delays:

- ♦ All link segment delays
- ♦ All repeater delays
- ♦ Delay Time (DTE)
- ♦ A safety margin (0 to 5 bit times)

Use the following steps to calculate the PDV:

1. Determine the delay for each link segment (link segment delay value, or LSDV), including interrepeater links, using the following formula. (Multiply by 2 so that it's a round-trip delay):

   LSDV = 2 × segment length × cable delay for this segment

   For end-node segments, the segment length is the cable length between the physical (PHY) interface at the repeater and the PHY interface at the DTE. Use your two farthest DTEs for a worst-case calculation. For interrepeater links, the segment length is the cable length between the repeater PHY interfaces.

   Cable delay is the delay specified by the manufacturer if available. When actual cable lengths or propagation delays are not known, use the delay in bit times as specified in Table 7-10. Cable delay must be specified in bit times per meter (bt/m). Table 7-10 can be used to convert values specified relative to the speed of light (c) or nanoseconds per meter (ns/m) to bt/m.

2. Sum together the LSDVs for all segments in the path.

3. Determine the delay for each repeater in the path. If model-specific data is not available from the manufacturer, determine the class of repeater (I or II) and use the data in the table.

4. MII cables for 100BaseT should not exceed 0.5 meters each. When evaluating system topology, MII cable lengths need not be accounted for separately. Delays attributable to the MII are incorporated into DTE and repeater delays.

5. Use the DTE delay value shown in Table 7-10 unless your equipment manufacturer defines a different value.

6. Decide on an appropriate safety margin between 0 and 5 bit times. Five bit times is a safe value.

7. Insert the values obtained in the calculations described in the following formula for calculating the path delay value (PDV):

   - PDV = link delays + repeater delays + DTE delay + safety margin
   - If the PDV is less than 512, the path is qualified in terms of worst-case delay.

Table 7-10 shows round-trip delay in bit times for standard cables and maximum round-trip delay in bit times for DTEs, repeaters, and maximum-length cables.

Table 7-10: Network Component Delays

Component	Round-Trip Delay in Bit Times per Meter	Maximum Round-Trip Delay in Bit Times
Two TX/FX DTEs	N/A	100
Two T4 DTEs	N/A	138
One T4 DTE and one TX/FX DTE	N/A	127
Cat 3 cable segment	1.14	114 (100 meters)
Cat 4 cable segment	1.14	114 (100 meters)
Cat 5 cable segment	1.112	111.2 (100 meters)
STP cable segment	1.112	111.2 (100 meters)
Fiber optic cable segment	1.0	412 (412 meters)
Class I repeater	N/A	140
Class II repeater with all ports TX or FX	N/A	92
Class II repeater with any port T4	N/A	67

Source: IEEE 802.3 u—1995, "Media Access Control (MAC) Parameters, Physical Layer, Medium Attachment Units, and Repeater for 100 Mb/s Operation, Type 100BASE-T."

Some cable manufacturers specify propagation delays relative to the speed of light (c) or in nanoseconds per meter (ns/m). To convert to bit times per meter (bt/m), use Table 7-11.

Table 7-11: Conversion for Cable Delays

Speed Relative to c	ns/m	BT/m
0.4	8.34	0.834
0.5	6.67	0.667
0.51	6.54	0.654
0.52	6.41	0.641
0.53	6.29	0.629
0.54	6.18	0.618
0.55	6.06	0.606
0.56	5.96	0.596
0.57	5.85	0.585

Speed Relative to c	ns/m	BT/m
0.58	5.75	0.575
0.5852	5.70	0.570
0.59	5.65	0.565
0.6	5.56	0.556
0.61	5.47	0.547
0.62	5.38	0.538
0.63	5.29	0.529
0.64	5.21	0.521
0.65	5.13	0.513
0.654	5.10	0.510
0.66	5.05	0.505
0.666	5.01	0.501
0.67	4.98	0.498
0.68	4.91	0.491
0.69	4.83	0.483
0.7	4.77	0.477
0.8	4.17	0.417
0.9	3.71	0.371

Source: IEEE 802.3 u—1995, "Media Access Control (MAC) Parameters, Physical Layer, Medium Attachment Units, and Repeater for 100 Mb/s Operation, Type 100BASE-T."

Table 7-12 lists some scalability concerns when designing Token Ring segments. You should see the IBM Token Ring planning guides for more information on the maximum segment sizes and maximum diameter of a network.

Table 7-12: Scalability Constraints for Token Ring

	IBM Token Ring	IEEE 802.5
Topology	Star	Not specified
Max. Segment Length (Meters)	Depends on type of cable, number of Multistation Access Units (MAUs), and so on	Depends on type of cable, number of MAUs, and so on

	IBM Token Ring	IEEE 802.5
Max. Number of Attachments per Segment	260 for STP, 72 for UTP	250
Max. Network Diameter	Depends on type of cable, number of MAUs, and so on	Depends on type of cable, number of MAUs, and so on

FDDI does not actually specify the maximum segment length or network diameter. It specifies the amount of allowed power loss, which works out to the approximate distances shown in Table 7-13.

Table 7-13: Scalability Constraints for FDDI

	Multimode Fiber	Single-Mode Fiber	UTP
Topology	Dual ring, tree of concentrators, and others	Dual ring, tree of concentrators, and others	Star
Max. Segment Length	2km between stations	60km between stations	100 meters from hub to station
Max. Number of Attachments per Segment	1,000 (500 dual-attached stations)	1,000 (500 dual-attached stations)	2 (hub and station or hub-to-hub)
Max. Network Diameter	200km	200km	200km

Routing protocol guidelines

Before determining what routers need to effectively route, it's important to understand what routers actually do. Routers have both a routing and a switching function and both operate as relay devices to forward packet data. The switching function forwards frames (much like a "switch"), but it only does so after the first frame goes through the routing process. The routing process examines the frame to determine the logical address (IP or IPX, for example). Once the logical address is determined, it is compared against the known routes in the routing table. If there is a match (for example, the destination network is known), the frame is then modified to incorporate the new next-hop-MAC address and is switched to the outbound interface.

Routers make forwarding decisions based on logical addresses, unlike switches which forward frames based on the MAC (or hardware) address. Routers can only make these decisions if they can determine routing paths and least-cost metrics, such as hop count, bandwidth, and delay. In an internetwork where there is more than one path to a given network, the goal should be obvious—to send the packet via the most efficient path.

Suppose you live in the suburbs and need to get downtown during rush hour. Rush hour is *dynamic*. In other words, at any given time during rush hour, the "metrics" may be different.

Along the way, an accident may cause traffic to be backed up, while at other times, traffic may flow freely. Routers can also make decisions based on "traffic patterns." In a network that has redundant links, for example, when one link is congested routers can reroute traffic to a less congested link. Think for a moment about times when you've been stuck in traffic and decided to get off the freeway to take another route. Routing works in a similar fashion. Also consider that you would not have left the freeway if there were no other paths and you did not know of another path to the destination. A router uses similar logic.

- ♦ **Type of traffic?** The router must be able to support the protocol for the type of traffic/routing. Three of the most common network protocols are IP, IPX, and AppleTalk.

- ♦ **Known Address?** Does the router know the address? In many cases, the router does not know the exact address, but rather that if it falls within a specified range, it needs to be routed to a specific interface.

- ♦ **Interface?** When the routing table contains entries for the destination address (or network), where should the packet be directed (next hop)? Once an address is compared to the routing table, and the best path is determined, it is forwarded to the associated interface.

Take the U.S. Postal service as an example. If I decide to send a package from Los Angeles to Chicago, the postal service must be able to:

1. Accommodate the type of package (standard letter, overnight package, oversized package).

2. Verify the address. This is just like looking up the destination address in the routing table. Where should I forward this package? For example, to get to Chicago, I may have to go through the Denver hub; therefore, Denver is the next hop.

3. Place the package on the transport to Denver and then forward to Los Angeles.

As you can see, the router does not know every path the package needs to take, but rather where to forward the package to get it closer to its destination. Of course, all of this activity utilizes bandwidth. Consult Table 7-14 when calculating bandwidth used by routing protocols.

Table 7-14: Routing Protocol Bandwidth

Routing Protocol	Default Update Timer (Seconds)	Route Entry Size (Bytes)	Network and Update Overhead (Bytes)	Routes per Packet
IP RIP	30	20	32	25
IP IGRP	90	14	32	104
AppleTalk RTMP	10	6	17	97
IPX SAP	60	64	32	7
IPX RIP	60	8	32	50

Routing Protocol	Default Update Timer (Seconds)	Route Entry Size (Bytes)	Network and Update Overhead (Bytes)	Routes per Packet
DECnet IV	40	4	18	368
Vines VRTP	90	8	30	104
XNS	30	20	40	25

In some network designs, more than one IP routing protocol is configured. If a router has more than two routes to a destination, the route with the lowest administrative distance is placed in the routing table. Table 7-15 shows the default administrative distances for IP routes learned from different sources.

Table 7-15: Administrative Distances for IP Routes

IP Route	Administrative Distance
Connected interface	0
Static route using a connected interface	0
Static route using an IP address	1
Enhanced IGRP summary route	5
External BGP route	20
Internal enhanced IGRP route	90
IGRP route	100
OSPF route	110
IS-IS route	115
RIP route	120
EGP route	140
External Enhanced IGRP route	170
Internal BGP route	200
Route of unknown origin	255

Every network must send routing update information. How this is accomplished is determined primarily by the routing protocol used. *Convergence* is the time it takes for the network to become synchronized or to update when the network topology changes. This can occur at periodic intervals or when changes in the network topology are detected. Each protocol handles convergence differently. Packets may not be reliably routed to all destinations until convergence takes place. Convergence is a critical design constraint for some applications. For example, convergence is critical when a time-sensitive protocol such as SNA is transported in IP.

Convergence depends on timers, network diameter and complexity, frequency of routing protocol updates, and the features of the routing protocol. In general, Enhanced IGRP and the link-state protocols converge faster than distance vector protocols. Convergence has two components. The first is the time it takes to detect the link failure. The second is the time to determine a new route.

Table 7-16 indicates the time required by the interface to detect a link failure and the action taken by the routing protocols.

Table 7-16: Time to Detect Link Failure

Serial Lines	Immediate if Carrier Detect (CD) lead drops. Otherwise, between two and three keepalive times. Keepalive timer is 10 seconds by default.
Token Ring or FDDI	Almost immediate due to beacon protocol
Ethernet	Between two and three keepalive times. Keepalive timer is 10 seconds by default. Immediate if caused by local or transceiver failure.

Key Requirements of a Scalable Network

As a network professional, it is your responsibility to ensure that the networks you design are not only functional, but scalable as well. Since many new networks start out relatively small and grow as the business grows, the initial design determines how effectively a network scales. In addition to new networks, the vast array of networks already in existence can benefit from application of this methodology as well. It's the network that starts out small (and is not well-designed) that poses the most challenges when it is scaled for growth or changes in technology.

Reliability and availability

Reliability and *availability* (redundancy) are key requirements of any design. When deciding how critical reliability and availability are to a given environment, the nature of the environment and business must be taken into account. For example, if access *must* be available 24×7×365, reliability and redundancy are critical design factors. Conversely, if downtime is not a major concern, reliability and availability concerns are relatively minimal. As a general rule, the core layer needs to be highly reliable and available, primarily due to the number of users/services that are affected if the system is not available. In many companies, a failure at the core layer affects large portions or all of their business. Protocols like Open Shortest Path First (OSPF) and Enhanced Interior Gateway Routing Protocol (EIGRP) scale well, use multiple metrics, and converge quickly, because they maintain network topology information—this allows them to send and receive topology changes rather than complete routing tables. This also reduces convergence time associated with network changes.

> **NOTE:** When designing redundancy, ensure there are no single points of failure. For example, if you have a critical business application that needs to be available 24×7×365, make sure all components associated with making that application available are redundant. We can't count the number of times customers have gone through considerable cost to ensure availability, only to find out later that one component of the network (a single switch in a closet, for example) was not connected to an Uninterruptible Power Supply (UPS).

Responsiveness

Responsiveness requires an understanding of latency. *Latency*, simply put, is the combined end-to-end travel time for a packet. Therefore, responsiveness requires an understanding of the attributes and factors that affect latency. During the design phase, care should be taken to reduce latency whenever possible. As with many of the design parameters, responsiveness (or what is considered acceptable responsiveness) is directly affected by both the infrastructure layer and the environment. For example, in a hospital environment, which may need to transmit/view real-time emergency images to a "specialist," responsiveness (or reducing latency) becomes very important. On the other hand, if the images need not be transmitted/viewed in real time, latency may not be as critical a factor.

Responsiveness can be affected by many factors, including latency, bandwidth, distance, routing protocols, and equipment. Once again, protocols like OSPF and EIGRP are good choices. As previously stated, OSPF and EIGRP maintain topology information within the router, making multiple path selection/alternative path selection possible and thus allowing for both redundancy and load balancing. Redundant links (both dial backup and lower cost online) can be integrated and configured to add bandwidth during peak usage. Segmenting, grouping, and reducing hops can all help reduce latency and thus increase responsiveness.

Efficiency

Efficiency means reducing and/or eliminating all unnecessary traffic. This reduction can be enterprise-wide or at local levels. The ultimate goal of efficiency is to preserve available/ usable bandwidth. The following methods can be used to help control or reduce bandwidth consumption:

- Access lists can be used to "permit" or "deny" traffic. This traffic may be protocol-specific, port-specific, routing updates, and broadcasts.

- Route summarization can reduce the entries in routing tables that can reduce routing update information. Incremental routing updates can also reduce bandwidth usage by reducing the frequency of routing updates.

- Dial-on-Demand Routing (DDR) can be used to selectively initiate connections based on "interesting traffic." It can be initiated on items like traffic type (TCP port, for example), address or address range (IP address/range), as well as many other options. When the interesting traffic is complete, the connection can be dropped. By only using bill-by-usage lines when necessary, the costs can be greatly reduced. This can be coupled with snapshot routing—which allows the use of dynamic routing protocols —to cut down the overhead of routing protocol updates on DDR lines.

♦ Switched access using frame relay or X.25 can allow for global connectivity. Compression over WAN links can also reduce bandwidth utilization. This can be accomplished using header and data compression.

Adaptability

Adaptability, as it refers to designing and building a scalable network, is the ability to anticipate change, as well as implement features that allow the network to "adapt to changes." Providing support for multiple protocols (both routable and nonroutable) is essential, as there are very few "heterogeneous" network environments, including balancing the requirements of each protocol within the network, as well as creating island networks as appropriate. For example, EIGRP supports IP, IPX, and AppleTalk. Route redistribution is another key adaptability feature because it allows one or multiple routing protocols to learn routes from another routing protocol.

Accessibility and security

Accessibility and security effectively define who has access to what and at what level. Access lists (as defined earlier) can be used to "permit" or "deny" traffic. This traffic may be protocol-specific or port-specific, and include routing updates and broadcasts. Authentication protocols can also be implemented to assist in controlling access to resources (for example, PAP and CHAP using PPP). Accessibility and security can be accomplished using dedicated and switched WAN support. This can include digital links, as well as frame relay, X.25, ATM, and SMDS. Exterior Protocol support is another component of accessibility and security—for example, EGP (Exterior Gateway Protocol) and BGP (Border Gateway Protocol).

Tackling the Most Common LAN Problems

Understanding isolation techniques in troubleshooting common TCP/IP problems requires that one has a solid understanding of the TCP/IP Internet Suite, general knowledge of how it works, and some knowledge of how it relates to the OSI model. This type of knowledge and information can be gained rather easily through books or technology-related Web sites.

Some of the major points on the suite are:

♦ Seven layers of the OSI model

♦ IP packet format

♦ IP addressing and subnetting

♦ Internet routing

♦ TCP packet format

♦ Domain name systems

This list is not exhaustive, but it comprises the primary topics—those that will give you a basic level of knowledge and help you apply common problem-isolation techniques to solve network problems. Once the foundational knowledge is present, you are ready to start applying diagnostic tools and techniques to solve common TCP/IP problems, including where Windows NT/95 clients and servers exist on the same network. Regardless, the most common issues and resolutions are addressed in the following outline.

TCP/IP problems and troubleshooting techniques

The Internet Protocol Suite, of which the Transmission Control Protocol (TCP) and the Internet Protocol (IP) are the two best-known protocols, came about with the goal of heterogeneous connectivity in mind. Successful network communication is critical, whether utilizing the Internet or a WAN, or within the confines of a local area network.

Some of the more common symptoms of TCP/IP LAN problems include the following:

- ◆ Difficulty establishing a connection between a client and its server or between two separate networks
- ◆ Random disconnections once a connection is established
- ◆ The inability to find hosts, services, and Web sites when attempting to link to them
- ◆ Stalled downloads

TCP/IP is the software package that governs all Internet communication. A corrupted TCP/IP stack is a fairly common problem under Windows 95/98 and Windows NT. In many cases, the problem can be resolved by a quick re-installation of the TCP/IP software. However, problems can occur (such as those listed above) that do not result from a corrupted TCP/IP stack. Following are proven problem-isolation techniques to resolve common TCP/IP problems and the suggested application of diagnostic tools to solve network problems that include systems running TCP/IP with Windows NT/95 clients and servers.

Using router diagnostic commands

Cisco routers provide numerous integrated commands to help you monitor and troubleshoot your internetwork. The following sections describe the basic use of these commands:

- ◆ **The show commands** help monitor installation behavior and normal network behavior, as well as isolate problem areas.
- ◆ **The debug commands** assist in the isolation of protocol and configuration problems.
- ◆ **The ping commands** help determine connectivity between devices on your network.
- ◆ **The trace commands** provide a method of determining the route by which packets reach their destination from one device to another.

Diagnostic commands

Two common tools for troubleshooting IP problems are actually found within the TCP/IP Protocol Suite: ping and traceroute. On some UNIX platforms, you may need to install a traceroute package, but in a Windows NT/95 network environment, these two tools are typically, by default, inherent to the operating system and ready to use.

Ping

Ping is a tool that uses the IP ICMP (Internet Control Message Protocol) echo request and echo reply messages to inquire and determine whether communications exist between the host and a remote system. In essence, ping is verifying that an IP packet is able to reach the destination system and return to the originating IP address.

The ping returns two pieces of information:

♦ Confirmation and verification that an IP packet can be sent to the destination and can be returned to the originator.

♦ The RTT, or "round-trip time" (typically in milliseconds). The RTT value returned is valuable only as a comparative reference. The RTT depends on many variables, such as the hardware on which the systems are running, software configurations, and other unique elements of the particular systems involved.

Following are some sample ping options from a command prompt or terminal:

```
ping [-t] [-a] [-n count] [-l size] [-f] [-I TTL] [-v TOS] [-r count] [-s count] [-j
host-list]   [-k host-list] [-w timeout]  destination-list
```

The following list defines these options:

-t	Ping the specified host until stopped. To see statistics and continue, type Control+Break; to stop, type Control+C.
-a	Resolve addresses to hostnames
-n count	Number of echo requests to send
-l size	Send buffer size
-f	Set Don't Fragment flag in packet
-i TTL	Time to Live
-v TOS	Type of Service
-r count	Record route for count hops
-s count	Time-stamp for count hops
-j host-list	Loose source route along host list
-k host-list	Strict source route along host list
-w timeout	Timeout in milliseconds to wait for each reply

Remember, firewalls and even routers can be configured in such a way as to *not* allow devices to be pinged, yet still allow other types of IP traffic. This should be kept in mind, because a ping failure between two devices can be mistakenly interpreted as nonexistent IP connectivity.

If the ping fails, another tool that can be used to help isolate the problem is traceroute. It is important to note that if the ping returns with an unusual RTT, traceroute should be used as well. It is also possible to vary the size of the ICMP echo payload to test problems related to maximum transfer unit (MTU) size.

Traceroute or tracert

The traceroute utility sends out one of two requests: either an ICMP echo request (Windows environment) or UDP (User Datagram Protocol) messages. These requests include gradually increasing IP TTL (Time to Live) values to the destination to investigate the path by which an IP packet transverses the network. Each router along the path decrements the TTL on the packet by at least 1 before it forwards the packet to the next router. Essentially, this makes the TTL a hop counter—when the TTL reaches 0, the router then sends an ICMP Time Exceeded message to the source system.

Traceroute or tracert determine the route by sending the first echo packet with a TTL value of 1 and then incrementing the TTL value by 1 on each subsequent transmission until the destination system responds or the maximum TTL has been reached. The actual route is then determined by examining the ICMP Time Exceeded messages sent back by intermediate routers. It should be pointed out, however, that some routers drop packets with expired TTL values and are not determinable by traceroute.

Following are some sample tracert options from a command prompt or terminal:

```
tracert [-d] [-h maximum_hops] [-j computer-list] [-w timeout] target_name
```

Following is an explanation of what these options do:

-d	Specifies not to resolve addresses to computer names
-h maximum_hops	Specifies maximum number of hops to search for target
-j computer-list	Specifies loose source route along computer list
-w timeout	Waits the number of milliseconds specified by timeout for each reply
target_name	Name of the target computer

Other tools, like *packet debuggers,* are available. They are often provided with routers and provided by the router manufacturer. It should be noted that this type of debugging can be bothersome and can cause a router to become inoperative until it is reset. Packet debugging should be used only with great care and by highly experienced engineers.

Additionally, *network analyzers* are tools that can be used for analyzing and decoding network problems. Network analyzers are typically applications that capture and analyze network packets. The analyzers gather information about data passing through your network and decode the analyzed data. A good network analyzer should include full decoding of the most commonly used networking protocols.

Since TCP/IP does not store information regarding route paths in its packets, it is possible that a functional path exists from one source to a destination, but *not* in the opposite direction. In some cases, therefore, it may be necessary to perform problem-isolation and troubleshooting techniques along an IP path in both directions.

Additional techniques and suggestions

When a TCP/IP connectivity problem exists or is suspected, you must first distinguish the two systems or at least identify suspected source and destination components. Once this is done, test to confirm that the problem or symptom is actually exhibited between the two systems when trying to connect or communicate between the two devices. Possible problems include, but are not limited to:

♦ A Physical layer issue somewhere along the path

♦ A first-hop Layer 3 connectivity issue in the local LAN segment

♦ A Layer 3 IP connectivity issue somewhere along the packet's path

♦ DNS or name resolution issues

A suggestion would include trying to ping from the source to the destination device by IP address. If the ping fails, you may have a local connectivity problem.

Local connectivity issues

This section covers some basic techniques to identify problems within LAN segments or to the "next-hop" router. The most common LAN segment problems are:

♦ Configuration problems

♦ DHCP or BOOTP problems

First identify the IP configuration of the source device. On Windows 95 or 98, use `winipcfg.exe`. On Windows 2000, XP, or NT, use `ipconfig.exe`. Look specifically for the IP address and subnet mask. On Windows 9x or Windows 2000 platforms, the default gateway address should also be displayed.

If no IP address is configured, verify that this node receives its IP address from BOOTP or DHCP. Otherwise, an IP address should be configured for this interface. If no address exists, configure one. If the source is configured to receive an IP address via DHCP or BOOTP and is not receiving one, make sure that the BOOTP (IP) helper address is configured on the router interface facing the source device.

If the destination is on the same subnet as the source, try pinging the destination by IP address. If the destination is on a different subnet, then try pinging the default gateway or appropriate next hop obtained from the routing table (if available). If the ping fails, double-check the configuration of the next-hop router to see if the subnet and mask match the source's configuration.

Sometimes, the problem might be duplicate IP addressing, which is a relatively easy problem to identify. Simply disconnect the suspected device from the LAN, or shut down the suspected interface and then try pinging the device from another device on that same LAN segment. If the ping is successful, another device on that LAN segment is using the IP address.

You may also experience problems at the Physical layer. In this case, first check configurations to make sure that all cables are connected to the appropriate ports and that all cross-connects are properly patched to the correct location using the appropriate cable and method. Verify that all switch or hub ports are set in the correct VLAN or collision domain and have appropriate options set for spanning tree and other considerations.

Next, check your cable connections. Verify that the proper cable is being used. If this is a direct connection between two end systems (for example, a PC and a router) or between two switches, a special crossover cable may be required. Verify that the cable from the source interface is properly connected and in good condition. If you doubt that the connection is good, reseat the cable and ensure that the connection is secure. Try replacing the cable with a known working cable. If this cable connects to a wall jack, use a cable tester to ensure that the jack is properly wired. Also, check any transceiver in use to ensure that it is the correct type, properly connected, and properly configured. If replacing the cable does not resolve the problem, try replacing the transceiver with one that's not being used. The primary goal here is to confirm that the proper cables and connectors are being utilized and are in working order, and also to ensure that all connectors are correct and seated properly.

You can also check the interface configuration and verify that the interface on the device is configured properly and is not shut down. Check to ensure that all associated ports are enabled and configured correctly. Also check port speed and duplex mode.

Check the network interface as well. If the interface has indicator lights that do not show a valid connection, power off the device and reseat the interface card.

Try to ping from the source to the destination device by name. If the ping is not successful, you may be experiencing a Domain Name Server problem. An IP address can successfully ping, but it is still possible for the DNS name resolution to fail.

Another approach is to ping the destination by name and look for an error message indicating that the name could not be resolved. If the name does not successfully resolve, determine which name server you are using. On Windows 95 or 98, use `winipcfg.exe`, and on Windows 2000 or NT, use `ipconfig.exe`. Next, try to resolve names within your own domain. Then try to resolve at least two domain names outside of your own domain.

If you cannot resolve names from all domains except that of the destination, you may have a problem with the DNS for the destination host. If you cannot resolve names within your own domain or a large number of external domains, the problem may lie with the local DNS (or your host could be using the wrong domain server).

If you can ping the destination by both name and address, you probably have an upper-layer problem.

Even though there may be IP connectivity between a source and a destination, problems may still exist for specific upper-layer protocols, such as FTP, HTTP, Telnet, and others. These protocols ride on top of the basic IP transport but are subject to protocol-specific problems relating to packet filters and firewalls. If you can confirm that IP connectivity does success-fully function between the two systems, the issue must reside at the Application layer.

Investigate the following issues for upper-layer problems:

♦ A packet filter or firewall issue might have arisen for the specific protocol, data connection, or return traffic.

♦ The specific service at the server could be down.

♦ An authentication problem may have occurred.

♦ There could be a version incompatibility with the client and server software.

General IP troubleshooting suggestions

This section approaches the process of troubleshooting TCP/IP connectivity issues with the assumption that you can have access to the client (or source) but not access to the server (or destination). If the problem is determined to be a server issue, contact the server administrator. If you are the server administrator, you can apply the troubleshooting process in reverse (server to client) to further troubleshoot connectivity issues. For the specifics of trouble-shooting server-side IP services, consult the manual or Web page for the software or service running on the server.

Because TCP/IP does not store path information in its packets, a packet can have a working path from the source to the destination (or vice versa) but no working path in the opposite direction. For this reason, you may need to perform all troubleshooting steps in both directions along an IP path to determine the cause of a connectivity problem.

To efficiently troubleshoot a TCP/IP connectivity problem, you must identify a single pair of source and destination devices that are exhibiting the connectivity problem. When you've selected the two devices, test to make sure that the problem is actually occurring between these two devices. Possible problems include:

♦ A Physical layer issue somewhere along the path

♦ A first-hop Layer 3 connectivity issue, in the local LAN segment

- A Layer 3 IP connectivity issue somewhere along the packet's path
- A name resolution issue

Here's where to start:

1. Try to ping from the source to the destination device by IP address. If the ping fails, verify that you are using the correct address, and try the ping again. If the ping still fails, go to the next section, "Troubleshooting local connectivity problems." Otherwise, proceed to Step 2.

2. Try to ping from the source to the destination device by name. If the ping fails, verify that the name is correctly spelled and that it refers to the destination device, and then try the ping again.

3. If you can ping the destination by both name and address, you are likely experiencing an upper-layer problem.

Troubleshooting local connectivity problems

This section describes how to troubleshoot local connectivity problems on LAN segments, such as Ethernet or Token Ring. Going through the methodology in this chapter will help determine and resolve problems involving moving packets on the local LAN segment or to the next-hop router. If the problem is determined to be past the local LAN segment, then you should refer to the section "Troubleshooting IP connectivity and routing problems" later in this chapter.

Possible problems may relate to:

- Configuration
- DHCP or BOOTP
- The Physical layer
- Duplicate IP address

Check for configuration problems

To start troubleshooting, display and examine the IP configuration of the source device. The way to determine this information varies greatly from platform to platform. If you are uncertain how to display this information, consult the manual for the device or operating system. Refer to the following examples:

- On a Cisco router, use `show ip interface` and `show running-config`.
- On Windows 95 or 98, use `winipcfg.exe`.
- On Windows 2000 or NT, use `ipconfig.exe`.
- On a UNIX platform, use `ifconfig`.

Examine the configuration, looking specifically for the IP address and subnet mask. On Windows 9x or Windows 2000 platforms, the default gateway address should also be displayed. If no IP address is configured, verify that this node receives its IP address from BOOTP or DHCP. Otherwise, an IP address should be statically configured for this interface. Configure an address if one is not present. If the source is configured to receive an IP address via DHCP or BOOTP and is not receiving one, make sure that the BOOTP (IP) helper address is configured on the router interface facing the source device.

If the incorrect IP address, subnet mask, or default gateway is configured, verify that this node receives its IP address from BOOTP or DHCP, and then contact the DHCP or BOOTP administrator. Ask the administrator to troubleshoot the DHCP or BOOTP server's configuration. If the address is statically configured, configure the correct address.

Check for local connectivity

If the destination is on the same subnet as the source, try pinging the destination by IP address. If the destination is on a different subnet, then try pinging the default gateway or appropriate next hop obtained from the routing table. If the ping fails, double-check the configuration of the next-hop router to see if the subnet and mask match the source's configuration.

If the configuration is correct, check that the source or next-hop router is capable of pinging any other device on the local LAN segment. If you cannot ping the next-hop address, and if the next-hop address is an HSRP virtual address, try pinging one of the next-hop router's actual IP addresses. If the actual address works but the virtual address does not, you may be experiencing an HSRP issue. Failure to communicate with some or all devices on the LAN segment could indicate a physical connectivity problem, a switch or bridge misconfiguration, or a duplicate IP address.

Ruling out duplicate IP addresses

To rule out a duplicate IP address, you can disconnect the suspect device from the LAN or shut down the suspect interface and then try pinging the device from another device on that same LAN segment. If the ping is successful, another device on that LAN segment is using the IP address. You can determine the MAC address of the conflicting device by looking at the ARP table on the device that issued the ping. If, at this point, you still do not have local connectivity for either the source or the next-hop router, proceed to the next section.

Troubleshooting physical connectivity problems

This section describes how to troubleshoot Layer 1 and 2 physical connectivity issues on LANs, such as Ethernet or Token Ring. Even though it may seem logical to first troubleshoot at the Physical layer, problems can generally be found more quickly by first troubleshooting at Layer 3 and then working backward when a physical problem is found or suspected.

Problems can occur when:

- Configuration is incorrect.
- Cable is faulty or improperly connected.
- Wiring closet cross-connect is faulty or improperly connected.
- Hardware (interface or port) is faulty.
- Interface has too much traffic.

Rule out a configuration problem

Check to make sure that all cables are connected to the appropriate ports. Make sure that all cross-connects are properly patched to the correct location using the appropriate cable and method. Verify that all switch or hub ports are set in the correct VLAN or collision domain and have appropriate options set for spanning tree and other considerations.

Check cable connections

Verify that the proper cable is being used. If the connection is a direct connection between two end systems (for example, a PC and a router) or between two switches, a special crossover cable may be required. Verify that the cable from the source interface is properly connected and in good condition. If you doubt that the connection is good, reseat the cable and ensure that the connection is secure. Try replacing the cable with a known working cable. If this cable connects to a wall jack, use a cable tester to ensure that the jack is properly wired. Also, check any transceiver in use to ensure that it is the correct type and is properly connected and configured. If replacing the cable does not resolve the problem, try replacing the transceiver if one is being used.

Check the configuration

Verify that the interface on the device is configured properly and is not shut down. If the device is connected to a hub or switch, verify that the port on the hub or switch is configured properly and is not shut down. Check both speed and duplex.

Check the network interface

Most interfaces or NICs have indicator lights that show a valid connection; often, this light is called the *link light*. The interface may also have lights to indicate whether traffic is being sent (TX) or received (RX). If the interface has indicator lights that do not show a valid connection, power off the device and reseat the interface card.

Troubleshooting IP connectivity and routing problems

When troubleshooting IP connectivity problems across large networks, it always helps to have a network diagram handy so that you can understand the path that the traffic should take and compare it to the path that it is actually taking.

When IP packets are routed across a network, problems can potentially occur at every hop between the source and the destination; therefore, the logical troubleshooting methodology is to test connectivity at each hop to determine where it is broken.

The following issues could be the problem:

♦ A router may not have a route to the source or destination.

♦ The network might have a routing loop or other routing-protocol-related problem.

♦ A physical connectivity problem might have occurred.

♦ A resource problem on one router might be prohibiting proper router operation. This could possibly be caused by lack of memory, lack of buffers, or lack of CPU.

♦ A configuration problem might have occurred on a router.

♦ A software problem might have occurred on a router.

♦ A packet filter or firewall might be preventing traffic from passing for an IP address or protocol.

♦ An MTU mismatch problem might have occurred.

The most thorough way to find a problem is, obviously, to start at the next hop away from the source and work your way one hop at a time toward the destination, exploring all possible paths along the way. You would then test basic IP connectivity and possibly protocol connectivity from each router forward. In some cases, this is the only method available; however, the process can generally be shortened by first performing a traceroute from the source to the destination to determine the first problematic hop. If the traceroute method does not provide an answer, you will have to fall back on the longer method.

When you have found a starting point, connect to that router via telnet or console, and verify that it is capable of pinging the source and the destination. When doing this, keep in mind that the router sources the ping packet from the interface closest to the ping target. In some cases, you may want to use an extended ping to specify a source interface because the ping target may not know how to get to the default source address; this is common on interfaces configured with private addressing.

What's next?

Now that we've classified the current infrastructure components, detailed the network specifications, and ruled out common problems and conflicts with the troubleshooting guidelines, it's time to make selections using the criteria from the selection matrix in the next section.

Please note that although cost is almost always a consideration, we do not use cost in any of the storage network evaluation criteria. The logic is to find what fits best, and then scale back from there based on cost. However, ensure you do not jeopardize security in this process without properly documenting the risk.

Storage Solution Component Matrix

It quickly becomes apparent that many factors must be considered when selecting a secure storage solution. In addition to the matrices, found on the companion Web site and already presented, pertinent areas of the following components are included in the selection process.

- ◆ Capacity planning (sizing)
- ◆ Need/use
- ◆ Hardware platforms
- ◆ Operating systems
- ◆ Applications
- ◆ Architecture (file systems, protocols, and topology)
- ◆ Data classification categories (sensitivity)
- ◆ Fault tolerance (failure avoidance)
- ◆ Performance tuning/Quality of Service (QoS)
- ◆ Storage software requirements/data availability
- ◆ Data protection
- ◆ Choosing a security infrastructure (NASD, Zoning, Security Domain Zones, and so on)

The selection matrix here is designed to help you determine which type of solution or solutions best fit the requirements entered into the evaluation criteria matrix. This matrix is not meant to include every possible scenario; rather, you should view it as a solid foundation on which to build your evaluation criteria.

Each of the areas in the matrix has been previously discussed, with the exception of data classification. Data classification is a critical component for ensuring that data security is appropriate.

CROSS-REFERENCE: For more on data classification, see Chapter 8.

Environment

The matrix is divided into 14 parts and contains two worksheets. The first worksheet contains pertinent environment questions with the ability to select requirements. The second worksheet summarizes the selections. The first component of the first worksheet, shown in Figure 7-5, is a validation that the work outlined earlier in this chapter has been performed and the target network is capable of supporting storage centralization/consolidation.

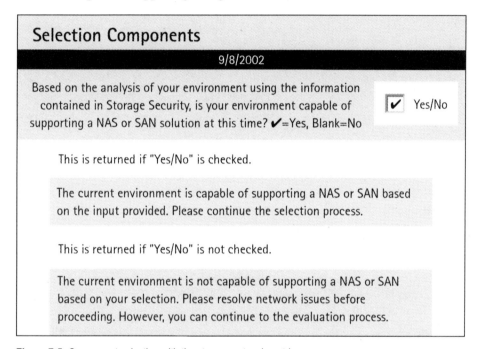

Selection Components

9/8/2002

Based on the analysis of your environment using the information contained in Storage Security, is your environment capable of supporting a NAS or SAN solution at this time? ✔=Yes, Blank=No   ✔ Yes/No

This is returned if "Yes/No" is checked.

The current environment is capable of supporting a NAS or SAN based on the input provided. Please continue the selection process.

This is returned if "Yes/No" is not checked.

The current environment is not capable of supporting a NAS or SAN based on your selection. Please resolve network issues before proceeding. However, you can continue to the evaluation process.

Figure 7-5: Component selection with the storage network matrix

Before moving on, it is important to note that the matrix is designed to be simple. It uses a simple requirement scheme that allows the user to select only those components that are required. Simply check the box if a given item is required in the environment, and the summary builds itself based on your selections. Once all the selections have been made and the summary is complete, you can print out the results of the summary. Figure 7-6 illustrates a needs-versus-use list.

Note that multiple requirements are selected in Figure 7-6. Only one priority rating of (5) exists (for Storage Consolidation), and only one priority rating of (1) exists (for API Interface). This means that out of the requirements, Storage Consolidation is the most important and API Interface is the least important. The rest of the priorities are somewhere in between.

	Need/Use	R
7.	Server consolidation (is server consolidation a requirement)?	✔
8.	Storage consolidation (is storage consolidation a requirement)?	✔
9.	Increase backup window (is addressing an extended backup window a requirement)?	✔
10.	Multihardware platform support (is multiplatform support a requirement)?	✔
11.	Clustering (is clustering a requirement for storage consolidation)?	✔
12.	Multiplatform development (is file sharing between platforms a requirement)?	✔
13.	File sharing (is over-the-network file sharing a requirement)?	✔
14.	Web services (will Web services be attached to the central storage device)?	
15.	API interface (is near-line storage in addition to centralized storage a requirement)?	✔
16.	Data replication (is data replication and or tape library support a requirement)?	✔
17.	Business continuance (excluding general fault tolerance, are higher levels of data availability a requirement)?	✔

Figure 7-6: Selecting service requirements is easy with the selection matrix

Capacity

The next worksheet "Capacity in Megabytes," shown in Figure 7-7, is a simple way to determine how much storage is required for those systems that use the central storage device (NAS or SAN). This worksheet calculation is not a total of all systems, but only those that use the central storage system rather than the current method. Remember to use megabytes as the baseline (for example, you would convert 1GB to 1,000MB). Therefore, 500GB is equal to $500 \times 1,000$MB, or 500,000MB.

In this example, 2.75TB of total space is available, but you are only using 1.25TB. Growth is not a driving factor, since the environment contains enough storage space to accommodate the estimated growth. However, 12 systems of the total 53 will run out of storage space sometime within the first 2 years. This may necessitate adding drives or further review of centralizing storage.

> **NOTE:** It is not uncommon to have less than 50 percent used space when multiple hosts and volumes are considered.

Need/use and hardware platform

In most cases, storage centralization doesn't occur unless there's a reason for it. Current devices, for example, may have reached their capacity limits.

		Capacity in Megabytes	
1.		Drives (add up the capacity of all drives being considered for centralization).	27500000.00
2.		Volumes (add up all the volumes and provide a volume count).	63
3.		Minus required for operating systems (how much internal space will be used for operating systems)?	88000.00
4.		Used (what's the total drive space actually in use)?	1250000.00
5.		Estimated growth (what is the current 2-year data-growth-rate estimate above what is currently in use in MB)?	1000000.00
6.		Are there any devices that are (or will be in the next year) out of disk space? If so place the number here, or 0 for none.	12

Based on your input above, the summary worksheet returns this.

Storage Space Requirements

The storage space requirements for the next two years = 2162 GB

You currently have 2750 GB Total available and 45.4545454545455% of your available space is currently being used.

Storage should be consolidated because one or more systems are low on space.

Figure 7-7: The capacity worksheet

The following two sections of the matrix (Need/Use and Hardware Platform) help you determine which type of storage is needed—DAS, NAS, SAN, or even *near-line storage* (also called *Content Addressed Storage*, or *CAS*). Figure 7-8 illustrates the Need/Use section.

Operating systems

With the possible exception of not being able to find any support for a specific network operating system (NOS), the choice of storage technology (DAS, NAS, or SAN) may not depend as much on the operating system as on other factors. However, the NOS(s) that is used may tip the scales in one direction or another, and the choice of which (manufacturer's) solution to implement will almost certainly be affected. For example if you use only one network operating system, and it is Microsoft Windows 2000, there are many options to choose from. However, if multiple operating systems, such as OpenVMS and Novell, are the products, the options are more limited. Selecting and prioritizing each assists in the evaluation process. Figure 7-9 illustrates the selection process and one possible result.

	Need/Use	R
7.	Server consolidation (is server consolidation a requirement)?	✔
8.	Storage consolidation (is storage consolidation a requirement)?	✔
9.	Increase backup window (is addressing an extended backup window a requirement)?	✔
10.	Multihardware platform support (is multiplatform support a requirement)?	✔
11.	Clustering (is clustering a requirement for storage consolidation)?	✔
12.	Multiplatform development (is file sharing between platforms a requirement)?	✔
13.	File sharing (is over-the-network file sharing a requirement)?	✔
14.	Web services (will Web services be attached to the central storage device)?	☐
15.	API interface (is near-line storage in addition to centralized storage a requirement)?	✔
16.	Data replication (is data replication and/or tape library support a requirement)?	✔
17.	Business continuance (excluding general fault tolerance, are higher levels of data availability a requirement)?	✔

	Hardware Platform (direct usage)	R
18.	Intel (if the environment contains Intel platforms that will be connected to central storage, list Intel as required).	✔
19.	Apple (if there are Apple platforms that will be connected to the central storage, list Apple as required).	☐
20.	RISC (if there are RISC platforms that will be connected to central storage, list RISC as required).	☐
21.	Alpha (if there are Alpha platforms that will be connected to central storage, list Alpha as a required).	✔
22.	Mini (mini platforms include such devices as AS/400, VAX, and HP9000).	☐
23.	Mainframe (mainframes that must connect to central storage).	☐
24.	Supercomputer (it is likely that a supercomputer may drive the storage initiative in many instances).	☐

Based on your input above, the summary worksheet returns this.

Storage Type Requirements
Based on the current data, Network Attached Storage and a Storage Area Network should be used. In addition to the above listed requirements, some benefit may be derived from near-line storage.

Figure 7-8: The Need/Use worksheet versus the Hardware Platform (direct usage) worksheet

Network/Mini/Mainframe Operating System	R
25.	Microsoft (Windows NT, 2000).	✔
26.	Novell (NetWare 4.x through 6.x).	✔
27.	Unix (is direct attachment to central storage device needed)?	☐
28.	Linux (does a Linux device require attachment to the central storage device)?	✔
29.	Mac OS (specific versions and compatibility must also be checked here).	✔
30.	VMS (if Virtual Memory System/OpenVMS is used, it needs to connect to the central storage).	☐
31.	OS/400 (OS/400 as well as other midrange operating systems do not connect to all central storage devices).	☐
32.	OS/390 (OS/390 and other mainframe operating systems).	☐

Based on your input above, the summary worksheet returns this.

Technology Requirements

The NOS(s) used in the environment = Microsoft, Novell, Linux, Mac-OS.

Ensure the tape backup software is compliant with the above selections.

Figure 7-9: The operating system worksheet

In Figure 7-9, you can see that four network operating systems are in use. The summary worksheet displays both the NOSs and also ensures that the backup software is capable of handling them.

The operating systems of the workstations themselves are not likely to determine the storage technology used unless they need to share files directly between multiple workstation operating systems. This is addressed in the Needs/Use section. However, it is important to know which operating systems are used for security backup and data protection issues. Figure 7-10 illustrates a sample output.

Note that as you continue to fill out the "Selection Criteria" worksheet, you are building a summary document that will help you evaluate the effectiveness of a given solution. Figure 7-10 shows that, in addition to the NOS selections made earlier, you now have the correct information from the workstation OS section.

The remaining areas in the "Storage Selection Criteria" worksheets are:

♦ Applications

♦ Architecture (file systems, protocols, topology)

♦ Data classification categories (sensitivity)

♦ Fault tolerance (failure avoidance)

- ◆ Performance tuning/Quality of Service (QoS)
- ◆ Storage software requirements/data availability
- ◆ Data protection
- ◆ Choosing a security infrastructure (NASD, zoning, security domain zones, and so on)

	Workstation Operating System	R
33.	Microsoft (Windows 95, 98, ME, NT, 2000, XP)	✔
34.	Unix (there are many versions; the key here is if the devices require direct attachment to the central storage).	
35.	Linux (much like Unix the key here is if the devices require direct attachment to the central storage).	✔
36.	Mac OS (is direct attachment to the central storage device required)?	

Based on your input above, the summary worksheet returns this.

Technology Requirements

The NOS(s) used in the environment = Microsoft, Novell, Linux, Mac-OS.

Ensure the tape backup software is compliant with the above selections.

The Workstations Operating systems in the environment = Microsoft, Linux.

Multiple workstation operating systems exist—ensure proper classification and storage measures are taken.

Figure 7-10: Operating system selection worksheet

If you have not already done so, obtain a copy of the matrix from the companion Web site, and familiarize yourself with the remaining contents. Fill it out in its entirety to determine the important criteria for your environment.

Once you have determined which storage solution(s) is/are best for your environment, go to the evaluation matrices listed in the individual chapters (also downloadable from www.wiley.com/compbooks/chirillo and www.TigerTools.net or www.InfoTress.com) and complete them to determine which overall solution is best for your environment.

> **SECURITY THOUGHT:** If you have data that is considered "CONFIDENTIAL" or "TOP SECRET," we highly recommend enlisting the services of a competent data security company.

Summary

This chapter helps you recognize the existing network, document current applications, protocols, topology, number of users, and business issues, and then assess the health of the existing network and its ability to support growing storage needs. Experience shows that many people use only those tools (or sections of tools) that they feel are important, for this reason a multiple worksheet matrix is recommended for your criteria selection. We believe that each of the additional matrices are important and are therefore used in the ultimate calculations to select a secure storage solution. But first you should start with a needs analysis and then compile design requirements from the infrastructure selection guidelines in this chapter.

When evaluating storage solutions, it is very important that all factors affecting both the selection and security be evaluated. Using combinations of your own evaluation materials and the tools shown here, you can ensure that the selection process is thorough and well documented. The results from the tool can be provided to your prospective centralized storage and security team/vendors to ensure their compliancy to your criteria. The spreadsheet tool presented in this book will be continually updated based on feedback from readers and will be available at www.wiley.com/compbooks/chirillo and www.TigerTools.net or www.InfoTress.com.

Chapter 8

Designing and Implementing a Sound Data (NAS/SAN) Security Program

By now, you should have a good handle on which centralized storage technology or technologies are right for your environment. The next step is to secure the technology using *ripple security logic*.

In medieval times, the castle was protected at all costs. The site was chosen very carefully, often on high ground with a strategic view. The land surrounding the castle had to be fertile, providing water, food, and other necessities. The castle was made of the finest and hardest earthen and rock materials available, and the walls were built high and thick. Atop the walls were guards, archers, and other protective tools—such as boiling oils—designed to defend the castle at the point of attack. The entrance was guarded and protected by a gate. A moat surrounded the castle, and a drawbridge covered the gate, providing an extra level of protection for the entrance. Nonetheless, many a castle could be broken into if it was attacked using the right methods, tactics, tools, and forces.

With that said, kings and queens began to seek additional measures to protect their castles and provide advanced warning so the castle could be better prepared to mount its defense in the event of an attack. Such measures included posting garrisons strategically outside the castle walls, as well as sending out scouts and spies.

Alliances between neighboring lands were formed and strategic messages were sent via scroll or parchment tightly rolled, sealed with wax—which was stamped with the emblem of the sender—and encased for transport. The messenger was often escorted by guards to ensure that the message reached its intended recipient. However, even with these measures in place, messages fell into the wrong hands, were destroyed, or simply never delivered. Again, the kings and queens (along with their trusted advisors) sought new means of protecting the castle . . . and so on and so on.

Many parallels can be drawn between protecting a castle and protecting your centralized data. In fact, if you look deep into the design used to protect a castle, you see logic that is similar to ripple security logic: Kings and queens started implementing fortification in the center of the castle and then expanded this protection outward. Protecting your centralized data can be accomplished in much the same fashion. Furthermore, just as the medieval landscape was always changing, forcing new methods of fortification, the technological landscape is always changing.

SECURITY THOUGHT: Security threats and issues are constantly changing. Constant and ongoing attention must be paid, or the castle may be overtaken.

In this chapter you see how ripple security logic can be used to help ensure the sound design and implementation of a security program, with an eye on each type of storage technology. Ripple security logic is a two-way street, which means that each concentric circle must be viewed as both cascading outward and cascading inward, and its effects must be evaluated based on legitimate and illegitimate use, as well as co-dependencies. For example, two SAN devices may exist in the same environment; when a ripple hits the second SAN, what potential effect can it have when viewed from both directions on the second SAN? Does the first SAN have any effect on the second and vice versa? Do they communicate with each other? If so, how, and can the security of one SAN have a positive or negative effect on the other SAN?

Designing the Plan

At this stage, the need for central storage has already been defined, the criteria outlined, and the centralized storage technology or technologies have been identified. A DAS, NAS, or SAN approach—or a combination of all three—will be used. The specific technology evaluation(s) for each have been completed, and the appropriate components chosen.

The next step is to design and implement a security plan for your centralized data. Although this plan should be part of the overall security program, protecting the data is important enough to warrant a separate security protection design. At its base, the plan should include physical and logical security and safety precautions.

Some of the physical precautions you should take have already been discussed throughout several chapters of this book. At a minimum, they should include:

- A site survey
- Controlling physical access to the device (for example, a locked cabinet)
- Containment in a secure room (preferably using identity management to gain entry)
- Power and connection protection (so that connections can't accidentally be disconnected, for example)
- Safety (proper fire prevention for data center)
- Facility access control as required

Administrative controls should include protocol standards, contingency plans, internal security audit procedures, authentication and authorization for data access, intrusion response documentation, specialized personnel, and training.

Technical controls should provide data integrity, confidentiality, and availability, with a tree of rights and permissions, and user access control with audit and trail logs. Finally, be sure to include security policies, procedures, and guidelines in your design plan.

> **NOTE:** The following storage security steps can also be performed for existing installations.

Common storage security steps

When designing a sound data (DAS/NAS/SAN) security program, you must take both common (well known physical and procedural) steps and technology-specific steps. The common steps can be combined in one section of the plan to eliminate redundancy. However, these common steps apply to each device both collectively and individually.

- Classification categories for the data must be identified.
- Combine data classification categories.
- Categorize the data types.
- Define legal obligations for data.
- Work out from the center.
- Define encryption strategy.
- Define connection strategy.
- Separate/segment storage use.
- Define configuration identity management.
- Protocol selection must be performed for the chosen storage technology.
- Device firewall(s), location, and use must be identified.
- Choose operating system access and method.
- Access control methods must be outlined.
- A comprehensive security checklist must be created.
- An enterprise security plan must be created.
- Intrusion detection options and implementation scenarios must be defined.
- Incident response planning must take place.
- Design review must be accomplished by the security team.
- Training of all appropriate personnel must be outlined and performed.
- A testing program must be created, formalized, and implemented.
- Depict how classifying data and selecting a storage network technology by data classification can be good for security, data availability, and data protection (in selecting a secure storage solution).

Step 1. Classification categories

We recommend using five primary data classification categories. These are a combination of public- and military-style categories. It's important to understand that it is not the application(s) being classified, but the data produced and how the application handles the data. For example is the data encrypted by default or does it transmit data in clear text? It is possible to produce a public document, as well as a private document, in a word processor. Handling of such classifications is the goal. Here's a breakdown of what the classifications mean:

- **Public.** Public data is available to the general public, or—if disclosed to the public—it at least does not affect the organization in a negative way.

- **Sensitive.** Sensitive data should be protected from disclosure or unauthorized modification. Such data is not for public eyes, but it is not considered private or confidential.

- **Private.** The unauthorized disclosure of private data could adversely affect a company, its business, or employees. Personnel information containing employee names, home addresses, and phone numbers is an example of such data. Disclosure could result in both legal action against the company and loss of consumer/customer confidence.

- **Confidential.** Confidential data is generally considered the highest classification within a company. If this information were compromised (disclosed, altered, and so on), an organization could experience severe consequences, such as its dissolution. Some examples of data that may fall into this category include prototypes and designs, new product development information, and contract negotiations.

- **Top Secret.** Although the top secret category is most often used in the military security scheme, it can be used to provide an extra level of data security even in the private sector. The definition of top secret for military purposes is that if it is disclosed, it can cause grave damage to national security. A private organization could modify this definition to provide a level of security designated only for a specific purpose. For example a top secret communicaton in a corporation might be correspondence between the president and CEO exclusively.

The category in which data is placed often depends on the organization's primary business. For example, employee information within a placement agency may be considered classified.

> **NOTE:** Military classifications are used in military organizations: unclassified, sensitive but unclassified, confidential, secret, and top secret. Definitions of these categories can be found by searching for "u.s. military security classifications" on your favorite search engine.

Step 2. Combine data classifications

Once the data has been classified, combine similar data classifications together. Each data classification should have its own associated security policy, and data should not be in more than one classification category. If during the classification process data appears in two classification categories, use the highest classification.

Step 3. Categorize the data

In addition to classifying the data, application categories should be defined and separately classified if all the data produced from an application falls into one category. The key here is to understand the nature of the data and where the data is needed. Some examples of data categories are:

♦ Engineering applications used only for prototypes

♦ Databases containing only one classification of data

♦ Identity management stores

♦ E-mail used to communicate both internally and externally

NOTE: Add additional application categories as needed, but make sure common definitions are consistently used.

Step 4. Define legal obligations for data

Define both the potential legal repercussions and legal obligations the company can face in the event of data loss or corruption, unauthorized access, unauthorized disclosure, and the many other security issues discussed throughout this book. Equally important is knowing what constitutes illegal activities both within the company and from an outside source that can be used against the company, as well as what the company responsibilities and legal obligations are. The best recommendation here is to do your homework, and consult legal counsel that specializes in data security law/litigation.

Step 5. Work out from the center

Ripple security logic is predicated on starting from the center and working out, and you should start as microscopic as possible. For example, many people start their ripple security logic evaluation from the disk, but it is possible to start from a file, block, bit, or even electron. Your evaluation starting point will vary depending on your environment.

Also use this logic to ensure that there are no other known or unknown connections to the device.

Step 6. Define encryption strategy

Encryption is the process of converting plain text into cipher text using cryptographic techniques. Effectively, the data is "scrambled" into an illegible form. The recipient with the appropriate decipher code/key is able to unscramble the message, allowing it to be read. Encryption can be accomplished at varying levels.

♦ **Block.** Disk and block encryption can provide an extra measure of protection against unauthorized access. Additionally, this type of encryption helps reduce the possibility that an in-house hacker could carry out data. If the data is encrypted on the disk or at the block level, the hacker would not only need access to equipment similar to that being used, but also the encryption technology used along with the appropriate key(s).

♦ **Files.** File-level encryption is also a common method used to secure file data. One good use for file-level encryption is to add an extra measure of protection when a NAS solution is employed.

♦ **Databases.** In addition to the abovementioned encryption technologies, specific encryption techniques exist for databases. These encryption programs protect the database from unauthorized viewing and can be used in conjunction with or separate from other encryption mechanisms.

♦ **E-mail.** Many people assume that their e-mail is secure. Unfortunately, this is seldom the case. Much electronic mail is still sent in unsecured formats. Many companies spend hundreds to millions of dollars protecting their perimeter, only to have some of that protection negated by not using encrypted e-mail.

We can recall the owner of a services company who stated to all of his employees, "Don't send anything over e-mail that you wouldn't want to see on the front page of a local or national newspaper." The statement has merit, but it should also be followed up with the implementation of appropriate security technology. Any e-mail transmission that would cause such a problem should at a minimum also be encrypted.

Step 7. Define a connection/technology strategy

Once a technology was selected (DAS, NAS, or SAN), you should have returned to the individual technology worksheets to choose which components of that technology provided the best security. The technology worksheets may have dictated both the technology (HiPPI, SCSI, and so on) and the connection strategy. However, the worksheet may have revealed that two technologies have the same score. When this is the case, you must decide which is more important: security or another factor (for example, performance or cost). Additionally, you may be presented with multiple connection options. For example, if a SAN were chosen and Fiber Channel was the selected topology, should the host devices connect directly to the SAN or should a switch or switches be used? If switching is used, how should it be configured?

Step 8. Separate/segment storage use

To help create a more secure environment, centralized storage can be segmented. This segmentation divides up the data and reduces the effects of a single loss. However, much like distributed storage, security of each data division must be accounted for in the security plan. The following bulleted items outline the methods for segmentation:

♦ **Physical division.** Even with DAS, NAS, and SAN devices, it is possible to break up connections physically (separate device access). In the case of NAS, the device may only reside on one small network segment that does not allow outside access. For a SAN, it is possible to physically break up connections using separate/multiple controllers in both the SAN device and the host device(s).

♦ **Logical division.** Most storage network devices have the ability to "carve up" the storage, creating logical devices that appear to be separate physical devices (most often represented as Logical Unit Numbers—LUNs) to hosts. This is currently the most commonly used method of dividing up shared storage, and when configured properly, it provides a good measure of protection. Where possible, mask LUNs to all devices that do not need access, and allow access from only required devices.

♦ **Logically segmenting.** In addition to the aforementioned methods, it is also possible (and from a security perspective preferable) to segment communications to devices. In the case of NAS devices, the creation of another network or implementing VLANs to create separate segments can provide an additional measure of protection by requiring routing to allow communication to other networks. Separate firewalls and IDS can be used here as well. For Fibre Channel networks, both Hard and Soft zoning can be used in a similar fashion to VLAN/VPN communications, allowing only certain hosts to communicate with certain storage components.

Step 9. Define configuration identity management

Configuration identity management is the process of ensuring that persons making configuration changes are not just authenticated, but that they are uniquely identified. The following list defines configuration control and authentication control/identity management.

♦ **Configuration control.** Configuration control has already been mentioned a few times. Improper or accidental misconfigurations are among the easiest ways to lose data, yet configuration control is often one of the most neglected from a security perspective. In most instances, there are devices that have the ability to control the configuration and management of centralized storage. These devices may also have the ability to provide multiple levels of administrative control based on user profiles, much like access rights. However, the device is in the data center and only data center personnel can access it; therefore, only the basic configuration is used, which can be a very dangerous situation.

♦ **Authentication control/identity management.** Once proper configuration control practices are in place, how can you ensure that the person performing configuration changes is who he says he is? This process uses the *something you know and something you have* method of authentication. A password addresses the *something you know* portion of the equation because it is known, but the problem with password-only authentication is that a password can be shared, guessed, or cracked. However, it is more difficult to thwart the *something you have* portion of the equation (especially if it's a part of your body, like your thumbprint). Authentication is a prime area for a biometric solution.

SECURITY THOUGHT: Remote control and remote administration are excellent tools to help reduce administrative overhead. However, do not forget them in the overall security scheme. For example, if biometric authentication is required at the central storage device, don't allow password-only protection to the same device using remote control, as it defeats the purpose of your security.

Step 10. Protocol selection

Select only the protocol(s) necessary for operation, and disable all unnecessary protocols. If more than one protocol can be used to accomplish the goal, choose the most secure. For example, if both IP and IPX are used within an environment and no outside access to the centralized data (from the Internet or other external sources) is needed, using IPX only can provide an additional measure of security against unauthorized access from external devices.

Step 11. Device firewalls

It's a good idea to add additional firewalls, which can be used to provide enhanced security and access control to central storage solutions. For performance reasons, make sure the traffic patterns are understood and the firewall device can handle the traffic. If central security measures are used (for example, RADIUS), keeping the storage device firewall separate creates another administration point but also provides another separate security measure.

> **SECURITY THOUGHT:** When separate security measures are used, it is critical that they adhere to appropriate security standards, or they can become a liability.

Step 12. Choose operating system access

Let's face it: the primary purpose of storage (centralized or otherwise) is to allow data to be read and written. This access is usually provided by some form of connected device, like a NAS operating system (in the case of a NAS, the operating system is often integrated), network operating system, mini- or mainframe operating system, and so on. Each one of these connected operating systems introduces yet another potential for breach. It is also true that more exploits exist for certain operating systems than for others. A security case can be made for choosing the operating system with the least exploits, vulnerabilities, and viruses.

In the real world, there are cases where choosing the operating system with the least exploits is not plausible, as the solution that fits the environment may specify the operating system. Knowledge is power, tools rule, control is a must, and you should expect to spend money. If you have to use a predefined operating system, get the best means to protect it.

Step 13. Access control

In the military, access is granted only when there is a "need to know" and when the appropriate clearance has been met. If both of these criteria are not met, access is not granted.

In the corporate world, the same military-style logic can be used. One approach includes creating a matrix with data classifications, possible access entities, and conditions under which access will be granted. Two such methods are listed within the CBK. The first is the Take-Grant model, and the second is the Bell-LaPadula model.

The Take-Grant model

This model specifies the rights a user/process can transfer to or take from an object. The term *object* can refer to any administered item that users or processes can transfer to or take from. However, it typically refers to files, disks, printers/print servers, databases, and the like. In the case of a database, several Take-Grant rules are most likely assigned based on the need for access to specific database functions and data. For example, if a database contains both human resources and payroll information, a payroll clerk may only need access to the employee name, address, phone number, and specific payroll information, but not to any associated personnel-related information.

Often, a grid is created for the Take-Grant model, specifying the resource and the associated access needs of users/processes. Table 8-1 illustrates a sample matrix.

Table 8-1: Take-Grant Matrix

Users	File1	File2	Payroll	Human Resources	General Ledger
Billy Bob	Read	Read/Write	Execute	Poll	Admin
Jane Doe	Read	Read/Write	Poll	Poll	Poll
John Doe	Read/Write	Read/Write	Admin	Admin	None
John Smith	Read	Admin	Execute	Execute	Execute
Kyra Smith	None	Read	Poll	Execute	Execute
Tom Thumb	Admin	Read	None	None	None

The Bell-LaPadula model

This model addresses the special needs of the Department of Defense's security policies ("unclassified" through "top secret") and issues concerned with ensuring confidentiality. However, it does not address the availability or integrity of the protected material. For most purposes, the Take-Grant model works, but you can fully review the Bell-LaPadula model if necessary.

In addition to choosing the right security model, choosing the right security administration process is very important. In some instances, distributed security management (with central policy control) is a good practice. You don't want to put all your eggs into one basket. If a single failure or breach occurs, it may not affect any other area. Conversely, if central policies are not adhered to, it could affect the entire organization.

Central security policy management and central security control/authentication can be accomplished using many different tools. Remote Authentication Dial-In User Service (RADIUS) and Terminal Access Controller Access Control System (TACACS) are two methods used to administer security on multiple devices from a central point. Although this can provide a consistent administration point, be sure to have a backup plan if the central security control/authentication fails.

Whatever the device, security definitions and access control policies should be applied both globally and to each individual device. As noted earlier, strong passwords should be used. The minimum recommendation is 8 characters using alphabetical, numeric, and special codes—randomly generated. The best method of password protection is to memorize your password and never publish or document it. If the password is documented, appropriate access control, encryption, and password protection should be applied.

The bottom line is to create an access control grid or matrix and formalize the access control procedure. Use the appropriate security method, with either distributed or centralized security.

Step 14. Select an appropriate secure backup

Using the criteria from Chapter 6 on data protection, backup, and recovery, select the appropriate protection measures for your solution. For example, if a NAS solution is used, select a backup solution capable of handling the protocol that NAS is using, and ensure that the appropriate backup security criteria is applied.

Step 15. Create a comprehensive security checklist

Security checklists for each device (not just the central storage device) should be created and used based on the type of device. For example, many companies use a Windows 2000 security checklist for Windows 2000 and a UNIX security checklist for UNIX. The same holds true for a DAS, NAS, and/or SAN setup. However, unlike the abovementioned operating systems, DAS, NAS, and SAN security checklists may not be as readily available because some of the technology is still in its developing stages. We recommend creating a security checklist based on your environment using ripple security logic. This checklist includes all devices.

If connectivity to the central storage device traverses a switch, router, and firewall, each (and every) device should be accounted for on the security checklist. For example if an NT server, a Linux server, a switch, and a router are connected, each device should be added to the security checklist, and each device's strengths and weaknesses should be listed.

> **SECURITY THOUGHT:** Multiple access points to a given device are often overlooked. Remote administration, dial-in, and other access points must be accounted for and protected.

Step 16. Enterprise security plan

The central storage security plan should be built in conjunction with enterprise policies, but once it has been completed, the plan should be reviewed against such policies. In many instances, the enterprise security policies need to be updated to accommodate the needs of the central storage security program. However, once completed, the central storage security program should become an integral part of the overall enterprise security plan.

Step 17. Intrusion detection

Once data is centralized, intrusion detection systems should be required. The best protection measures are useless without proactive checking for unauthorized, suspicious, malicious, or other nonapproved use.

Set up IDS, firewall, and other monitoring devices to proactively monitor such activities and to send notifications and alerts to the appropriate personnel and devices.

Step 18. Incident response planning

All the features of this wonderful technology can become severely limited if you don't have a plan to address issues as they arise. It's here that incident response comes into play. You have gone through the process of charting, mapping, plotting, planning, documenting, and researching, but what happens when unplanned activity occurs?

An incident response plan should be descriptive, categorized, and formal. This is yet another area where a matrix or grid could be helpful. However, since an unplanned activity (for example, a breach) is, by nature, unexpected, ensure the categories cover an event such as a breach. By assigning priority levels to each unplanned activity, the method to deal with them can be outlined in the incident response plan. For example:

♦ Undefined errors—TOP PRIORITY

♦ Breach (for example, unauthorized access)—TOP PRIORITY

♦ Spoofed address—HIGH PRIORITY

♦ Port scan—HIGH PRIORITY

♦ Blocked access—PRIORITY

♦ Authorized access—NORMAL

Each priority and its associated action should be defined. Be very descriptive, as there could be legal implications as might be the case for a breach in the financial industry. Some examples of how to prioritize, which will vary by environment, are:

♦ **TOP PRIORITY.** Disable *all* access; assess the breach, notify appropriate personnel (CEO, president, and so on.), collect all logs, ensure logs are archived for long-term access, and follow additional business-/company-specific processes.

♦ **HIGH PRIORITY.** Research the issue, notify appropriate personnel (managers, directors, and others on the notification list), archive logs, make recommendations, and follow business-/company-specific processes.

Incident planning should be a complete process unto itself. For now, know that it is an integral part of any successful security plan.

Step 19. Training
Don't forget about training. New plans, processes, procedures, and programs require that personnel be trained.

Step 20. Design review
Once the design is complete, it should be reviewed thoroughly to ensure it is accurate and complete. If the plan has been created by a third party, have the plan reviewed by another competent party (personnel within the company perhaps). Document everything, including the policies, procedures, references, and resources.

Step 21. Testing
Testing the design and implementation is one of the most critical components of any security program. Because testing is so critical, and because there are many potential vulnerabilities to

test for, testing is covered in the following chapter. For now, it is important to note that each component of the security program should be thoroughly tested.

> **SECURITY THOUGHT:** Think like a hacker—try to access it, steal it, break it, corrupt it, deny a service, or perform other unauthorized functions.

Implementing the Plan

Now that you have decided which central storage technology to use and you have identified the major steps to help you secure that storage, you must build a plan.

To illustrate how to build a plan, let's take a look at three fictitious companies: SJBCware, a software development company; SlickBC Insurance; and KCMessaging. Each company will be used in a different case study depicting a unique technology scenario. The steps are modified to apply to each scenario.

NAS case study

Synopsis/Diagram: SJBCware designs software applications that run on Personal Digital Assistants (PDAs), handhelds, notebooks, desktops, and servers. They support Windows, Linux, *NIX, MAC, and remote connectivity (thin-client) solutions. SJBCware also develops six applications: Two are custom Web site services, two are electronic file-storage applications, and two are business image-scanning applications. The Web sites are pre-populated with industry-researched and -obtained information that the customer can add to or modify; the other application is used or populated by the clients when they purchase the application. The average file size is 36K, and only the development team needs access to the NAS.

The members of each of the development areas needs read/write access to their development application, and since the three products integrate with each other, each application group member needs read access to the other two groups' information.

E-mail is hosted by a third party on the Internet. Since the development team needs to access e-mail and perform research on the Internet, they also need outbound Internet access using the company's Internet connection. The development team also tests direct network connections and wireless technologies.

SJBCware is booming, and the data requirements have grown exponentially and are expected to continue to do so. The company currently needs 1TB of storage capable of sharing file data between each of these platforms that can be accessed using any of the above listed scenarios. Figure 8-1 illustrates the current environment.

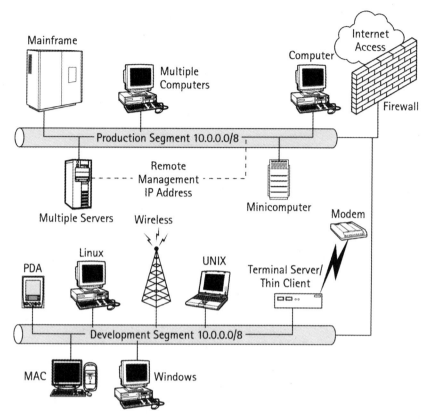

Figure 8-1: SJBCware current environment

Using the matrices available at www.wiley.com/compbooks/chirillo, www.Tiger-Tools.net, or www.InfoTRESS.com, you can determine that this company is most likely to select a NAS solution to address their needs. They can use CIFS and HTTP as the communication protocol.

Without performing any additional security analysis, the company might purchase the NAS, implement it, and continue to go about their business. Figure 8-2 shows what this might look like.

As you can see, the only real change to the environment is that the NAS device is connected, and every device on the network can access it. But that's not the only risk present here.

If you use the steps to build a security program as listed above in conjunction with ripple security logic, you can see what needs to happen to make this environment more secure.

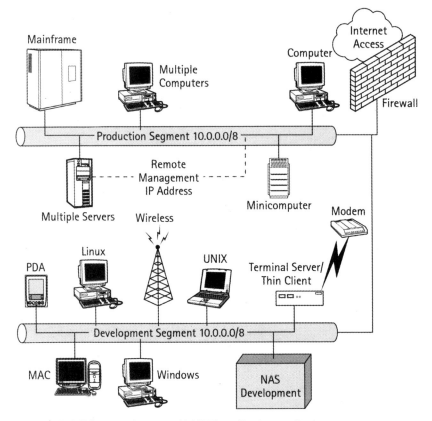

Figure 8-2: SJBCware environment with NAS but without a security plan

Step 1. Classify the data

The company uses the standard corporate definitions of public, sensitive, private, and confidential data, as listed earlier in the chapter.

Step 2. Combine data classifications

For business reasons, the company has determined that the following classifications apply to each of the application categories.

- Web—Classified
- File—Private
- Scanning—Private

NOTE: If the company produced six applications, the application or data could be classified differently. Therefore you could have more than one classification based on the application.

Step 3. Categorize the data

The data is primarily new SJBCware application development. However, since software development is the business of this company, it should be considered and treated like production (active/live) data is in many other organizations. The data categories here are:

♦ **Development.** All development applications

♦ **Production.** All production applications

♦ **Web.** Web applications

♦ **File.** File and scanning applications

Step 4. Define legal obligations for data

Legal obligations have been defined in conjunction with SJBCware legal counsel. Externally, each product has been appropriately addressed for customer-related obligations. Internally (relating to the products being developed), the company is responsible for protecting its intellectual properties and ensuring that development information is not compromised.

Step 5. Work out from the center

If you begin to work out from the center using the NAS device as the point of reference, you find that:

♦ The NAS device cannot perform block-level encryption.

♦ The NAS device can perform file-level encryption.

♦ The device can be logically partitioned but cannot be physically segmented.

♦ Only one connection from the network to the NAS device is used.

♦ The network is flat (that is, one segment/subnet).

♦ Terminal services, including dial-in access, are directly connected.

♦ Laptop and other portable devices are allowed on the network.

♦ Wireless connectivity is provided to the network.

♦ Multiple operating systems are used.

♦ Internet access is provided to the network.

♦ Mini- and mainframe computers are on the production network.

Step 6. Define encryption strategy

File-level encryption is a feature of the NAS device and should be enabled. Additionally, to better secure the Web access connectivity, SSL and PKI should be used. This encryption strategy can be set up directly or by using a Web security device. The best recommendation is to use a device that specializes in such security.

SJBCware's applications also provide the ability to encrypt files directly within the application using PKI, and the third-party e-mail provider has options for encrypting e-mail that needs to be leveraged.

Step 7. Define connection/technology strategy

The NAS device should have only one connection to the network using Ethernet unless redundancy is required.

Step 8. Separate/segment storage use

To protect the NAS from unauthorized access, and since only the development team needs access to the NAS, a separate segment should be created (physically using a router or logically using a switch and layer-3 switching or a router).

It is further recommended that the segment be upgraded to at least 1GB Ethernet to provide a high-speed connection for the required backup.

The NAS device is a single unit, and the storage can be partitioned logically but not physically. Therefore, confidential data is stored on one partition using the highest levels of file encryption, and the private data is stored on another logical partition.

Step 9. Define configuration identity management

Since NAS is going to be used and since data exists on the NAS that is confidential, SJBCware has decided to use biometric technology as an identity management process for configuration of the NAS device. Implement the biometric technology first. For example, if thumbprint technology is to be used, implement it before configuring the NAS device for use. This helps ensure that the identity management technology works with the NAS device as required.

Step 10. Protocol selection

In this scenario, the protocol selection was easy, since SJBCware specified that CIFS and HTTP must be used due to the applications they develop.

Step 11. Device firewalls

It has been determined that the development team should be segmented onto their own network in an effort to reduce security risks. In addition to this measure, it is possible to provide a separate firewall on this segment to provide even more security. Since the development team only needs to access e-mail and the Internet (outside of the NAS), this firewall can be used to block all incoming traffic and to allow only outbound e-mail and Internet traffic.

Step 12. Choose operating system access

The NAS selected uses an embedded proprietary operating system. SJBCware has contracted with the embedded proprietary operating system company to ensure that it automatically receives updates and patches, as well as notification of any new exploits and vulnerabilities as they are found.

Step 13. Access control

It has been determined that each application group needs read/write access to their application files and read access to the other two group's files. The Take-Grant matrix shown in Table 8-2 would apply.

Table 8-2: Access Control Take-Grant Matrix

Users	Web Applications	File Applications	Scanning Applications
Web developers	Read/Write	Read	Read
File developers	Read	Read/Write	Read
Scanning developers	Read	Read	Read/Write
Administrators	Admin	Admin	Admin

Step 14. Select an appropriate secure backup

Because a NAS is used and CIFS and HTTP are the protocols, the selected backup must support CIFS. The files accessed by HTTP can also be accessed and backed up using CIFS. At a minimum, the secure backup solution should be able to accommodate the encryption used, up to 1TB over Ethernet. A tape library capable of 1GB Ethernet was selected.

Step 15. Create a comprehensive security checklist

Combine all the items discussed so far into a security checklist or multiple security checklists as appropriate. In this example, separate security checklists should be used for:

♦ Internet access risks/security measures
  • One-way-only traffic from development

♦ Wireless access risks/security measures
  • Separate segment
  • VPN only
  • Separate firewall
  • DHCP disabled

♦ Dial-in access risks/security measures
  • Can it be disabled?
  • Keyfab

♦ *NIX operating system vulnerabilities/viruses/backdoors/Trojans/DoS
♦ Windows vulnerabilities/viruses/backdoors/Trojans/DoS
♦ MAC operating system vulnerabilities/viruses/backdoors/Trojans/DoS
♦ NAS operating system vulnerabilities/viruses/backdoors/Trojans/DoS

- ◆ Segment security issues (VLAN or physical)
- ◆ Segment firewall type, installation, known vulnerabilities/viruses/backdoors/ Trojans/DoS
- ◆ Existing security issues that could affect the NAS installation
- ◆ Address the issues with the implementation, not issues that do not pertain to the implementation.

> **NOTE:** A security checklist/instructions exist for many of the operating systems in existence today. Searching both the Internet and the manufacturers' Web sites is a good start.

Step 16. Enterprise security plan

Compare your findings with the enterprise security plan. Address any discrepancies. If the enterprise security plan did not account for your findings, ensure they are brought up and that the enterprise security plan is modified appropriately.

If your findings do not need to be incorporated into the enterprise security plan, document the findings and the reasons for not updating the plan. For example, the production network uses remote management. You would note this and list it as a potential risk to the production network but not to your development network.

As part of this step, you would also validate items such as virus protection and compliancy to the enterprise plan, including the appropriate devices—PDAs, tablet PCs, notebooks, work-stations, servers, and so on.

Step 17. Intrusion detection

Intrusion detection was implemented to watch both in front of the development firewall and behind. Do not confuse the block with a single device. The block can represent a single device or multiple redundant devices. Notice that an intrusion detection system (IDS) was not set up on the production segment. If you were responsible for overall security, you would have included IDS on the production segment as well.

Ensure appropriate monitoring is enabled to enhance the IDS solution. Servers, firewalls, and many other devices can watch traffic for suspicious activity. It is also possible to set up a packet-capture device using promiscuous mode to watch traffic.

Step 18. Incident/response planning

In the case of this fictitious company, the incident response definitions are very simple.

- ◆ **Suspicious/malicious activity** is defined as an unsuccessful attempt to gain unauthorized information and includes port scans, Trojan probes, spoofing, spamming attempts, relaying attempts, data modification attempts, and the like.
- ◆ **Breach** is defined as any successful attempt to gain unauthorized access; to deny a service or services; to view, modify, or destroy data; or any other successful use of company assets for unauthorized purposes.

SJBCware decides that in the case of suspicious or malicious activity, no services should be shut down. Immediate investigative action should begin to determine the five Ws (who, what, where, when, and why).

- ♦ Who was the offender? (Can you obtain an address, name, or any other identifier?)
- ♦ What were they after? (What was the nature of the activity: port scan, spam, or something else?)
- ♦ Where are they from? (Can their location be determined? Are they inside or outside?)
- ♦ When did this occur? (Once or more than once?)
- ♦ Why did this occur? (Was the activity random or targeted?)

In the case of a breach, all services are temporarily shut down to the development network to determine the extent of the breach. A report is filed with the appropriate state and federal agencies, and an investigation begins immediately. Once the nature of the breach has been determined, any services that could not and will not be affected by the breach may be returned to service. When there is confidence that the breach has been protected against, the service can be returned to an active status. However, the investigation continues as needed. All logs are archived permanently for future reference.

Appropriate notifications occur depending on the classification of the data. If the data is confidential, notification up to and including the CEO should occur. For private and sensitive data, the escalation extends up to the CTO, and for public data up to the Director of IT.

Once the five Ws have been determined, you should follow up with one big "H." How do you keep this from happening again? If the act was successfully blocked, great, but don't let your guard down. Was there any evidence in the event that can lead you to further strengthen your defenses? Remember, security is dynamic, not static.

Step 19. Training

Both users and technical personnel should be trained on the new technology/technologies. Users should be taught how to access the system, any restrictions or requirements involved in accessing data, and what to do if they suspect either suspicious or malicious activity or a breach.

IT personnel should be trained to fully understand both the technology and security aspects of the new environment, including processes, procedures, response requirements, responsibilities, and notification requirements.

Step 20. Design review

Whew! That's a lot for just a simple NAS, but you're not done yet. After you complete all of the preceding steps, you should perform a formal review of the plan. Compare your plan with the enterprise plan requirements again. Consult a qualified outside security service firm to validate your plan. Modify the plan as necessary.

Once the review is complete and all modifications have been made, the implementation plan is as simple as listing the order in which you address each of the necessary steps.

Step 21. Testing

All your work could be for naught if you neglect the testing phase. The testing plan should be comprehensive, dynamic, and flexible. Testing is a topic unto itself, and as such, it is addressed in the following chapter.

> **NOTE:** One benefit of using ripple security logic is that you often catch other security risks that already exist within an environment.

Once the implementation is complete, your new NAS environment—based on the preceding assessments—should look similar to that shown in Figure 8-3.

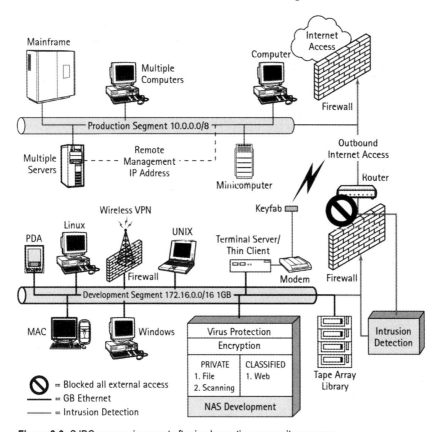

Figure 8-3: SJBCware environment after implementing a security program

SAN case study

Synopsis/Diagram: One of the problems with using a cookbook-style approach is that not all steps apply in every situation. This holds true when designing a sound security program for storage networks.

This case study uses a series of evaluative questions to help you decide which steps should be used and which may not be necessary. Then the specific steps are listed, just as they were in the discussion of the NAS case study.

SlickBC is a company in the insurance business that has several servers. Each server runs the same application but uses a different database for different types of insurance. One server handles automobile insurance, one handles life insurance, and another handles property insurance. Automobile policies are assigned a private classification, while life insurance policies fall into the confidential category. Some property insurance policies also fall into the confidential category.

The company that manufactures the database software that SlickBC uses has developed a package that can be clustered and can share one overall database that leverages single customer names for multiple insurance types or that can leverage one customer database between multiple servers while still keeping separate databases for each line of business. The NOS is Novell's NetWare, and the database application runs on top of the NOS. Each server is also operating as a Web server, allowing customers to access and change their customer information or view their policies. The database has the ability to provide database-specific encryption technology.

SlickBC has decided to upgrade to the new package, but has elected to keep each server separate and not part of a cluster. Furthermore, each server continues to serve only one business segment (auto, life, or property). They leverage a single customer database but continue to keep their policy information separate. Each business unit has Internet access through a central router and firewall. Figure 8-4 illustrates the current environment.

The company uses both standard corporate security categories and military categories because they insure properties for both the military and commercial entities. To prepare for the future each database used can be assigned both a corporate and a military classification up to confidential as appropriate. Legal obligations were previously outlined, defined, and accepted.

SlickBC employees can access the SlickBC databases only during the hours of 7 a.m. and 7 p.m. central standard time (CST). Using the selection tools, it was determined that a SAN would be the best solution. The solution has only been tested on Fibre Channel technology, and SlickBC does not have the luxury of spending any additional time or money to test other options. Therefore, the solution is a SAN using Fibre Channel. Each server should be separately connected to the SAN fabric using a single HBA (no redundancy or load balancing).

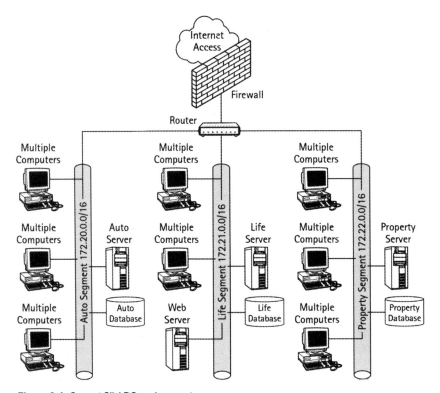

Figure 8-4: Current SlickBC environment

The database was developed with military specifications in mind, and as such, it can allow both the commercial and military data to coexist in a given policy database without compromising the data. Since SlickBC has a security program in place they may make the same mistake many other companies make by not being thorough in their assessment of their security program needs. At a minimum SlickBC should ask themselves the following questions:

Questions

Question 1: Does the data need to be classified, combined, and categorized (Steps 1–3)?

Question 2: Is Step 4 required?

Question 3: Is it necessary to go through Step 5 in this scenario?

Question 4: Since you're not changing the data, do you need to define an encryption strategy?

Question 5: Do you need to define a connection technology/strategy?

Question 6: Can and should you separate/segment the storage?

Question 7: Is identity management required here?

Question 8: What protocol should be used?

Question 9: Should separate device firewalls be used?

Question 10: What operating system should you choose, or is Step 12 even required? (Remember, this question refers to the storage device OS.)

Question 11: Does access control need to be defined?

Question 12: The amount of data has not changed. Is there a need to look at backups?

Question 13: Do you have to create/build a complete security checklist?

Question 14: Does the enterprise security plan need to be revised?

Question 15: You didn't have IDS before, but do you need it now?

Question 16: If your data isn't changing, do you need an incident response plan?

Question 17: You know how to use your application; can you skip the training step?

Question 18: It doesn't seem like you've been able to skip many of the steps. Can you skip the design review?

Question 19: You know you'll need testing, but do you need to change the testing process?

Providing a secure SAN foundation

Much like the NAS case study, in order to provide a secure SAN foundation, you must build a sound SAN security program. In order to build this security program, you must understand how the steps can be altered or changed depending on the environment, differing data needs/requirements, and different storage selections. The following steps account for SlickBC's environment and the choice of a SAN for their storage needs.

Step 1. Classification categories

SlickBC is somewhat unique in that it uses both the standard corporate definitions as well as the military definitions. Thus, the highest security classification takes precedence. Typically, the data element would carry only one classification, based on its status as corporate or military. Within the insurance organization, it would be best to classify the data element using only one data classification scheme (corporate or military) even if the policy is on a building owned by a corporation but used by the military. If you ever experience a situation where both a corporate and military classification need to be assigned, security should be based on the highest/most restrictive classification.

Step 2. Combine data classifications

As depicted in the previous case study, it may be necessary to assign data elements—within a given application—multiple classifications. When this is the case, the application must use the highest classification when evaluating its security. In this scenario, the following data element classifications exist:

- **Auto database.** Private (corporate)
- **Life insurance database.** Classified (corporate)
- **Property database.** Private (corporate)
- **Military information in any of the databases.** Confidential (military)

Notice that the classifications have not been combined. It is likely that the military data would use the same database engine but would be contained in a separate database unless the database had the ability to segment and protect the data.

> **NOTE:** The military has very specific requirements relating to data classifications. If you intend to work with the military on security issues, you must fully understand these requirements.

Step 3. Categorize the data

The data requires long-term storage and is primarily of the same style (policies); however, the application that stores the data is a database. This database generates policies as separate files for long-term archival. Therefore, the data categories are:

- **Database.** Policy database
- **File.** Files for long-term archival

Step 4. Define legal obligations for data

Legal obligations are a paramount concern in this example due to the nature of some of the property policies. In such situations, a company should ensure its policies have been submitted to all appropriate parties, and accepted by all appropriate parties including outside entities such as the company that provides SlickBC's databases. The ramifications of a breach should be clearly understood by both parties and predefined mitigation and incident response factors should be mutually agreed on.

Externally, once the submission/acceptance process has been accomplished, each product and each data element must be outlined to ensure it has been appropriately addressed by legal obligations, and that all obligations are both understood and accounted for by all external parties.

Internally, the application should also be verified against (or made compliant) to the highest security rating that would be applied to any individual data element.

Step 5. Work out from the center

As discussed in the first case study, it is important to start at the smallest element and work out from there. In this case, it is important to be aware of individual data file elements, since any one of them can be assigned a separate data classification. For this reason, if you begin at the center and work out, using the SAN device as the point of reference, you find that:

- The SAN device must be able to support block-level encryption.

- The SAN device must be able to support file-level encryption.

- The device can be both physically and logically partitioned, allowing each database to be physically separated onto centrally contained but physically divided storage.

- Multiple connections from server devices are required, but only the customer database information is shared. Within the database itself, certain customer information may need to be hidden. From a connection standpoint—even though the solution has only been tested on Fibre Channel—it may be wise to check the solution on another technology, such as HiPPI.

- The current network is segmented using the IP protocol into three separate segments. A SAN will be used, but depending on which connection technology is selected, the physical media devices may vary. For example, if HiPPI is selected, the physical controllers and other connectivity devices also vary. If Fibre Channel SCSI is selected, again the devices used vary. For your purposes, Fibre Channel SCSI did end up being selected.

- Remote control applications are not used; however, Internet access is allowed, and the potential vulnerabilities caused by this type of outside access must be accounted for and protected against.

- Each network (172.16.20.x, 172.16.21.x, and 172.16.22.x) contains both servers and workstations for a given division.

- No wireless connectivity is provided to the network.

- Novell NetWare is installed on each server, and each server runs a separate instance of the database package.

- Outbound Internet access is provided from the workstations to the Internet, and inbound Internet access is provided to each server so that customers can view their own policy data and change pertinent customer information.

- No mini- and mainframe computers are on the production network.

- VLANs are not used, but physical segmentation is.

Step 6. Define encryption strategy

Because each type of data can be assigned varying levels of security classification, as well as more than one classification (commercial or government), block-, file-, and database-level encryption is a requirement. Also, e-mail is not mentioned in the previous scenario. The question, "What is the current e-mail platform—if any?" should be asked and answered. If e-mail exists, e-mail encryption should be included.

- **Block.** The selected SAN solution must be able to perform disk and block encryption. Security is the greatest concern here, so performance implications are secondary (within reason). Enabling disk- and block-level encryption makes it more difficult for a "would be" hacker to obtain data.

- **Files.** File-level encryption is employed and will use varying levels of cryptography based on the classification of the data. Some links to samples are listed in Appendix B.

- **Databases.** The database application is able to provide different levels of encryption per database. The customer database only contains standard customer information, such as name, phone number, address (not insured property address), and contact information. Each of the individual databases contains policy-specific information. Therefore, the customer database should be encrypted, and the internal users and the Web servers able to decrypt the information. The remaining databases are separately encrypted using different algorithms, to help ensure that only those that can decrypt them have access to the information. The Web servers will not be able to decrypt any of the specific databases (Auto, Live, or Property).

- **E-mail.** E-mail is an external service, and the company hosting the e-mail provides encryption. It is SlickBC's responsibility to ensure that the third-party hosting company complies with their policies. One of the keys here is to ensure that the e-mail host not only complies, but can demonstrate compliancy. This should be accounted for in the security policies.

Step 7. Define a connection/technology strategy

Because the application has only been tested on Fiber Channel technology, and SlickBC has elected not to be a test site for other technologies, it has been determined that Fiber Channel should be used. Since all three business units need access to the customer database, SlickBC must use a Fibre Switch (multiple if redundancy is needed) and connect both the servers and the storage to the switch.

In addition, the Web servers must be connected to the SAN fabric to allow it to communicate with the customer database. Finally, in regards to the Web server, if the SAN has the ability to support both direct connection and switched connections as totally separate channels, it is wise to connect the Web server directly. This limits the possibility that a misconfiguration of the switch could allow access to other zones.

Step 8. Separate/segment storage use

To help create a more secure environment, centralized storage can be segmented. This segmentation divides up the data and reduces the effects of a single loss. However, much like distributed storage, security of each data division must be accounted for in the security plan. The following bulleted items outline the methods for segmentation:

- **Physical division.** Each data store has been configured to be physically separate within the central storage device. This means that storage for each database uses its own storage controller(s).

    Since a specialized Web server security device should be used, the Web server was removed (physically separated) from the 172.21.x.x network and placed on its own network. This allowed the Web server and the Web security device to reside only on a single segment. It has been placed on its own network to physically break up connections using separate/multiple controllers in both the SAN device and the host device(s).

- **Logical division.** Because the SAN has been configured as a separate storage device, there is no current need to logically divide the storage.

♦ **Logically segmenting.** As each device connects to the switch(es), zoning needs to be used. It is also important that only required devices can see a data store. Therefore, LUN masking should also be used. All servers and the Web server should have access to the customer database information, but each business unit should only have access to their database respectively. Four zones would likely be created in this scenario.

Step 9. Define configuration identity management

SlickBC does business with both the military and private industry. Since the military is involved, configuration control and identity management requirements are greater than those outlined in the NAS case study.

♦ **Configuration control.** For the current scenario, because the SAN is divided physically, there should be four controllers. Each controller allows configuration of its storage space. The recommendation here is to have only one level of configuration control and one level of monitoring control. Both configuration and monitoring control must be treated as the same security classification as the highest classification of data to be stored on the device.

♦ **Authentication control/identity management.** Because the data is classified up to confidential, identity management (in our opinion) is absolutely required here; in fact, we recommend two levels of biometric control (face and retinal recognition identity management, for example, could be implemented).

Step 10. Protocol selection

Fiber Channel was selected for use in this environment. You do not need to specify or select a protocol for the storage device. The network is IP, and all other protocols have been disabled.

Step 11. Device firewalls

Each server has direct connections to the storage device for the customer database and for its specific database using Fibre Channel. Each server also resides on its own TCP/IP network, which is connected to a common router. The router can be configured to keep the segments from communicating directly with each other internally. Still, the best recommendation is to add a second level of firewall support for two primary reasons:

♦ Configuration errors on one device may be caught by the second level.

♦ The second firewall set makes it more difficult for an attacker to gather good information.

SECURITY THOUGHT: The second-level firewall support does not need to be three separate devices; it can be another single device with the ability to have three separate segments.

Step 12. Choose operating system access

The operating system has been determined by the application, and the access is from both client workstations and customers via the Web. Search for specific NOS vulnerabilities. Since the Web server is effectively a separate network and device allowing only access to the customer data, it is also possible to search for the most secure Web server available that is supported by a SAN solution even though the Web server will be protected by a Web server security device.

Step 13. Access control

Because SlickBC does business with the military, it must conform to the Bell-LaPadula security method. An access control scheme has been developed utilizing the Bell-LaPadula method, defining the users' login and access privileges, as shown in Table 8-3.

Table 8-3: Bell-LaPadula Access Control Matrix

Users	Clearance	Need to Know	Access	Via Web	Internal	Overall
Customer	Confidential	Yes	Own info	Own info	None	Own info
Internal user	Confidential	Yes	Own department	None	Per function	Per function
Administrator customer Database	Confidential	No	Config only	None	Config only	Config only
Administrator auto Database	Confidential	No	Config only	None	Config only	Config only
Administrator life Database	Confidential	No	Config only	None	Config only	Config only
Administrator property Database	Confidential	No	Config only	None	Config only	Config only

Configuration only = No data access
Per function = Only specified policy information for which they are responsible
Own info = Only information for which they have clearance and the need to know—specific to that customer
Own department = Only information for that given department

In short, a user is allowed access to her information only if she has a need to know. The exception here is SlickBC employees. They must be able to access information for the accounts they are charged with. Therefore, they have a need to know for those customer accounts assigned to them within their department. This type of matrix can be taken several layers deeper.

This is a very simple example of a Bell-LaPadula access control matrix. Other components can make it more complex, but this should give you an idea how it differs from a Take-Grant-style matrix.

Step 14. Select an appropriate secure backup

Backups can pose some unique challenges in this case study. Should commercial and military data coexist? The easy answer is no, but it is not the only answer. If the database uses sufficient security mechanisms and is compliant with the military guidelines, then data may be able to coexist (since it is confidential, not secret or top secret). The database was developed for the military and can therefore accommodate this scenario. Still, the backup should provide adequate security and encryption, and restores should be able to be selective using secure methods without compromising the data. For example, if the database needs to be restored, the restore must be able to be accomplished without viewing the data because the person responsible for the restore will probably not have a need to know for the data contents.

Do not make the mistake of requiring identity management on the SAN device but not on the backup/restore device.

Step 15. Create a comprehensive security checklist

Use ripple security logic to create the security checklist. Start from the smallest element and work out. Start with the data element (block, file, disk, connections, and so on). Evaluate the ripple both physically and logically. Multiple encryption methods are to be used, so ensure they exist and are properly configured.

In this case study, the NOS is NetWare. Although the Web server operating system was not defined in the case study, one of the initial security checklist items should be ensuring that it was defined using the appropriate standards.

Once the Web server operating system is defined, the security checklist should be revised using best practice methods of securing the NOS and Web server products along with ripple security logic. Both Fibre Channel and Ethernet connectivity are in use for this scenario. The Fibre Channel connectivity uses both direct connect and a switch. The security checklist should ensure that zones and LUNs are designed, created, and configured properly and that LUN masking is used. The security checklist should also ensure that direct connections do not have the ability to see to any other database.

The Ethernet segments must be verified to be physically segmented rather than being segmented through VLANs. Routes must be very specific, and we recommend using static routing versus dynamic. Although this may cause more initial and ongoing administration, it helps ensure that there are no learned routes that were not accounted for.

Since the environment is IP, firewall options and allowed communications should be specifically mapped out, specifying both the source and destination communications allowed and the specific services/ports allowed.

No VPN was specified; therefore, only authenticated customers are allowed Web access and only to their customer database information.

The Web server security device must be configured to allow only secure connections to the Web server and from the client. At a minimum, we recommend using a combination of both public and private certificates for authentication.

No other outside access is identified in this scenario.

Ensure subsecurity checklists exist for each device, not just the central storage device.

Step 16. Enterprise security plan

Review the storage security plan against the overall enterprise security plan, and vice versa. This often helps identify errors and omissions in both plans. Once both plans have been verified as comprehensive and complete, integrate the storage security plan into the enterprise security plan.

In the SAN case study, no outside access, except to the Internet, exists. The enterprise plan should also reflect this. If outside access exists, it must be reflected in both plans. If the plans aren't revised accordingly, the access must be removed.

Step 17. Intrusion detection

In this scenario, IDS would be a requirement. Much like firewalls, multiple intrusion detection devices are recommended, and this is why the IDS solution is shown as a block rather than a single device. In this scenario, only one block is shown, but it can represent multiple IDS devices. Individual devices could be placed on each segment.

Step 18. Incident response planning

Due to the presence of military data classifications, some additional requirements relating to incident response planning must be met to accommodate for both the private and military classifications. The following items outline both requirements:

- **Suspicious/malicious activity.** Defined as an unsuccessful attempt to gain unauthorized access or information, suspicious or malicious activity includes port scans, Trojan probes, spoofing, spamming attempts, relaying attempts, data modification attempts, unsuccessful login attempts, and the like.

- **Breach.** A breach is defined as any successful attempt to gain unauthorized access, to deny a service or services, to view, modify, or destroy data, or to otherwise successfully use company assets for unauthorized purposes.

Due to the presence of confidential information, any suspicious/malicious activity should result in immediate action, up to and including shutdown of all services if appropriate. Immediate investigative action should begin to determine the five Ws (Who, What, Where, When, and Why).

- Who was the offender? (Can you obtain an address, name, or any other identifier?)

- What were they after? (What was the nature of the activity: port scan, spam, or something else?)

♦ Where are they attacking from? (Can their location be determined? Are they inside or outside?)

♦ When did this occur? (Once or more than once?)

♦ Why did this occur? (Was the activity random or targeted?)

If the activity was malicious, necessitating the shutdown of services (as in a password crack attempt), then an immediate evaluation should be performed in conjunction with the five Ws to determine what is required before services can be restored.

A report is filed with the appropriate agencies, and an immediate investigation begins. No services will be restored until it is determined safe to do so.

When there is confidence that the breach has been protected against, the service can be returned to an active status. However, the investigation should continue as needed. All logs are archived permanently for future reference.

Appropriate notifications occur depending on the classification of the data. At a minimum, the incident data is communicated to the appropriate parties. As with corporate-only incidents, the five Ws need to be answered, but the military often requires some other questions to be answered, including what was the extent of the incident, did a full compromise occur, and what is the current status of the investigation.

After the appropriate measures have been taken, restore any service(s) that have not already been restored.

Step 19. Training

With the new application, users can still see the same information they saw before, and since the database application allows users of a specific department to only see records for those customers with a policy from that department, the data does not appear any different to the user. However, if a customer has multiple policies, only one group may be able to change the customer information (other than the customers themselves). Therefore, some training may be required.

From an IT perspective, much training is needed on the new equipment, configuration, authentication/identity management controls, configuration options, backups, Web services, additional firewalls, intrusion detection, and for the Web security device.

Step 20. Design review

Design review for this environment is likely to be a joint effort. Corporate customers and the military will both want to ensure that the plan is accurate and complete. Each may even elect to have their own third-party reviewer evaluate the design, and completion of the review may require agreement from each due to the data requirements. Although each third party may be difficult to pull together and get agreement on, it's a good thing. The more reviewers you have, the more encompassing and complete your security plan will be.

Step 21. Testing

The military maintains specific testing requirements that must be met. Make sure you are completely aware of these requirements early on in the process. See Chapter 9 for testing information.

> **SECURITY THOUGHT:** Military classifications pose some unique challenges. For example since they use a two-fold security method that requires both the proper security clearance and a need to know, applications may not be developed to accommodate this method. Make sure you fully understand the unique security challenges and obtain the appropriate information and certifications if you intend to work with the military.

As a result of your planning effort, if you follow the recommendations outlined in the preceding steps, your new SAN design should look similar to the one in Figure 8-5.

Figure 8-5 shows a SAN with four storage segments and four zones. Each server is allowed to access Zone 1 for the customer database information. Each server is also allowed access to a second zone containing its core data. However, without going through and documenting each of the steps necessary to build a security program, what is not apparent is that each zone color code also corresponds to a specific type of database encryption. Additionally, intrusion detection was implemented to check for suspicious or malicious activity both before and after the firewall. If any remote management connections existed, they were removed from the devices connecting directly to the SAN for security reasons.

Answers

In the beginning of the SAN case study several questions were listed that should be asked even if a security program was already in place at SlickBC. The answers to these questions are listed below.

Answer 1: Yes. Since the data is being reconfigured, it should be reclassified, combined, and recategorized. For example, the customer database is more critical to all operations now; therefore, it might be reclassified. Also, if these steps were not performed initially, now is the time to do it.

Answer 2: If Step 4 was previously defined, theoretically it should not have to be redefined. You are not changing the data, only how the data functions.

Answer 3: Absolutely. In fact, this scenario requires it. Since the technology is changing, it is important to redefine the security program—especially because the databases are now centralized and potentially more accessible and vulnerable. Perform this step, even if it's only to determine how much internal exposure there is with the technology change.

Answer 4: This step should not be skipped. It may not be necessary to define an encryption strategy, as it may have already been done, but it may be necessary to ensure that the encryption strategy is still valid and can be implemented.

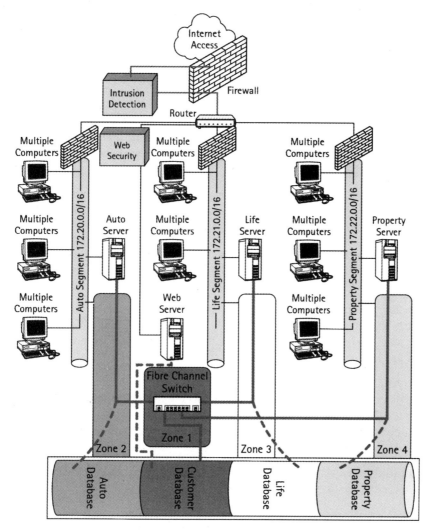

Figure 8-5: SlickBC SAN environment after building a security program

Answer 5: In this case, the connection technology was determined for us based on case study criteria; therefore you can skip this step (with the possible exception of evaluating specific products).

Answer 6: In the scenario given, separating/segmenting the storage is a requirement. Looking at how the business operates, each business unit or line of business was functioning independently from a data perspective. They are now using a common customer database, but they should not be able to see or change policy information for the other business units. In this case, zoning and LUN masking are good options.

Answer 7: Although identity management is not required, whenever you have central management and configuration of multiple data sources, our recommendation is to use identity management.

Answer 8: Fibre Channel was selected as the topology, therefore you need not choose a specific protocol.

Answer 9: As of this writing, we are not aware of any Fibre Channel–specific firewall products. However, we believe that devices of this nature are forthcoming. For now, using a solid zoning and LUN masking scheme is appropriate. It is possible to physically segment a SAN, but it is not necessary for this scenario.

Answer 10: It was determined that a SAN using Fibre Channel was needed. Beyond that, there was no specification. Therefore, it is important not to skip this step. Choose the storage operating system using the SAN-specific evaluation worksheet.

Answer 11: Absolutely! You are allowing users to share data that they were not sharing before. Certain users may now only have rights to read customer data but not modify it. Therefore, a new access control matrix should be defined.

Answer 12: Although the amount of data hasn't changed, the makeup and layout has. For this reason, the backups should be addressed. Additionally, new backups are possible since Fibre Channel is being used that can dramatically decrease the backup window and provide greater security and data protection.

Answer 13: Yes. As a general rule, the security checklist should be completely revised using ripple security logic each time a new device is added. This ensures all devices that could affect security get captured. Remember, ripple security logic uses both an inward out and an outward in look. There will be crossover, but that's okay as long as all devices and access points are accounted for.

Answer 14: Most likely. At a minimum, the enterprise security plan should be reviewed against the new security checklist and SAN requirements to ensure compliancy.

Answer 15: Remember: you are in the process of putting your data into a central location. Even though IDS was not in the environment before, it highly recommended for this environment.

Answer 16: If you have an incident response plan, it should most definitely be reviewed and revised. The data layout is no longer the same. The customer data is exponentially more critical now.

Answer 17: It may be possible to skip this step for the end users if the functions of the application remain the same. However, it is critical to ensure that IT personnel are trained on the new technology, processes, procedures, and incident response plans.

Answer 18: Skipping the design review is not recommended in any situation. Although it can always be revisited, it should be viewed as the last chance to catch security issues.

Answer 19: When new technology is introduced into your environment, the potential for new vulnerabilities greatly increases. Your testing program should reflect these changes. We recommend revisiting the testing program anytime significant change occurs in the environment. However, since the term "significant" means different things to different people, you should define what it means in your organization.

iSCSI case study

There can be no doubt that iSCSI has emerged as a viable alternative to its comparatively expensive counterpart, Fibre Channel. It is also true that iSCSI will become an increasingly common way to link servers and storage area networks over the wide area, with IPsec and SRP providing security, as well as other security options that may be on the horizon.

Simply put, iSCSI allows block transfers to occur over IP networks. Its primary appeal is that it allows existing infrastructure and technology to be used rather than purchasing less familiar, more expensive equipment such as Fibre Channel. It allows servers (and other devices) to access high volumes of storage using standard Ethernet cards. Since Ethernet technology is so widely accepted and understood, it can also be a comfortable option. Additional devices, such as tape drives that can leverage the iSCSI protocol, can allow iSCSI networks to be created much like storage area networks. Since iSCSI is an IP protocol, it also has the potential to provide mirroring and data replication over long distances at reduced costs.

Synopsis/Diagram: KCMessaging is a startup Internet-based messaging company that wants to specialize in allowing smaller companies to set up mail servers using KCMessaging shared storage, or to replicate mail stores over Internet lines. They are in the formative stages of their design. They have already decided to implement redundant Internet connections using BGP. A management machine will reside on each segment. The internal IP addresses and ports can be translated to external IP addresses and ports. KCMessaging has not yet decided on a storage solution, but they realize that whatever solution they choose will need to be IP-based and perform block transfers.

Figure 8-6 shows KCMessaging's current design without a storage solution.

Because KCMessaging is serving IP storage over the Internet at long distances, they have elected to utilize iSCSI as a solution. They have selected SCSI storage devices that are capable of failing over SCSI connections. This will allow them to very quickly remap an internal IP address and port from a failed iSCSI device or segment to an already existing external IP address and port.

Remote servers will connect to an assigned IP address and port. All data is to be considered confidential. Recently, KCMessaging developed an add-in product for mail servers that encrypts all IP block transfers.

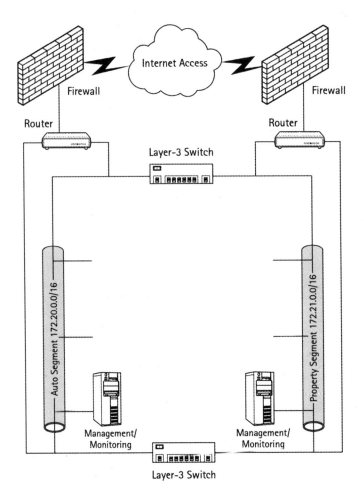

Figure 8-6: KCMessaging current environment

Using the already outlined steps, let's see what's required for this environment:

Step 1. Classify the data

KCMessaging uses the standard corporate definitions of public, sensitive, private, and confidential.

Step 2. Combine data classifications

For business reasons, the company has determined that the security of the application and all data should be considered confidential, and that security will be based on this classification.

Step 3. Categorize the data

The data transferred will be block data over IP consisting of mail/messaging collaboration and scheduling and form flow. It is all considered to be production data.

Step 4. Define legal obligations for data

Because the data is transferred over the Internet, it has been determined that KCMessaging cannot be held responsible for security of the data if the customer does not use their custom encryption. If the customer elects to use the custom encryption, KCMessaging has agreed to ensure loss up to a prespecified amount. This is incorporated into the contracts that KCMessaging will use. Additionally, KCMessaging's legal counsel has included other appropriate legal terms into these contracts.

Step 5. Work out from the center

The current scenario is definitely not for the faint of heart. The fact is, KCMessaging will be engaging in Internet business, transferring customer data at potentially high volumes. Appropriate amounts of money should be invested to ensure high levels of security (remember, 100 percent is not realistic) and capacity.

Just like the other scenarios, you need to start from the center and work out.

- Block-level encryption is available for use from KCMessaging.
- File-level encryption is the customer's responsibility.
- Devices should be logically segmented.
- Dual connections will be made, but only one will be mapped at a time.
- Dual Ethernet segments exist with redundant connectivity.
- Dual layer-3 switches exist.
- VLANs exist (layer-3 switches with different segments).
- Dual routers exist.
- Dual firewalls exist.
- Dual management/monitoring systems exist.
- Redundant Internet access is provided to the network.
- Redundant iSCSI connections are required.

Step 6. Define encryption strategy

Block-level encryption can be provided by KCMessaging. Additional levels of encryption—including file, mail, and database (as required)—are the customer's responsibility.

Step 7. Define connection/technology strategy

Several connection strategies must be addressed:

♦ **SCSI storage to iSCSI device.** Since iSCSI was chosen for the solution, the physical connection to the SCSI storage device should use SCSI. Additionally, KCMessaging has chosen to use Ultra-3 SCSI.

♦ **iSCSI device.** The iSCSI device should connect directly to the already designed Ethernet network using 1GB technology.

♦ **IP block connections.** Connections between customer devices and KCMessaging storage must be literally specified. This means that the customer IP address/port(s) and the KCMessaging IP address/port(s) are the only ones allowed to communicate with each other. This will be accomplished via the firewalls and routers. Additional connection security can be gained by specifying the MAC address of the mail host in addition to specifying the IP address.

> **NOTE:** When using the MAC address, if the Network Interface Card (NIC) is replaced, the new MAC address should be used.

Although it may be possible with some products to use an administered MAC address, it is highly recommended that you don't do this. If you can modify the MAC, it stands to reason a hacker might be able to as well.

The switches are configured for VLANs, and communication and filtering is provided because layer-3 switches are used.

Step 8. Separate/segment storage use

As in the previous two case studies you need to ensure your design provides appropriate levels of separation and segmentation. The following items outline the recommendations for this environment:

♦ **Physical division.** The network is segmented and running Gigabit Ethernet with redundant connections, but only one connection is active at a given point in time.

♦ **Logical division.** In this case study, you are mapping at a port level. Only certain externally available IP addresses and ports can communicate with internal IP addresses and ports because you have mapped internal IP address/port(s) to external IP address/port(s).

The storage on the SCSI device itself is logically partitioned on a per-customer basis. Partitions are not shared among customers.

Step 9. Define configuration identity management

Because iSCSI storage is going to be used, and since confidential data exists on the SCSI storage device, KCMessaging has decided to investigate voice recognition to allow local authentication from a remote location.

Step 10. Protocol selection

In this case study, the protocol selection was made easy as KCMessaging's offering is using iSCSI. This means that the IP protocol is used to transfer the block-style data. The management/monitoring devices use only standard IP; SNMP is not used.

Step 11. Device firewalls

The only devices on the network other than the shared storage are the management/monitoring devices. Therefore, the firewalls in this scenario should be adequate. However, adding a second-level firewall can help reduce risks due to errors in configurations. Another option here would be to implement dual firewalls to provide dual levels of protection.

In this scenario, you don't want users to be able to have VPN access to the inside network. You do know, however, that a VPN tunnel can provide extra protection. If you want to provide VPN access to the user and still protect the backside network, you could allow VPN access into the frontside firewall, while blocking access to the backside network with an additional router or firewall. The VPN tunnel would be created to a network between the first- and second-level firewalls using address translation from the backside network to the "in-between" network just described. This VPN design using dual firewalls somewhat resembles DMZ logic.

Step 12. Choose operating system access

The iSCSI device selected uses an embedded proprietary operating system. KCMessaging has contracted with the company to ensure it automatically receives updates and patches, as well as notification of any new exploits and vulnerabilities as they are found. They have also requested and received all known vulnerabilities and issues.

Step 13. Access control

One of the unique items about KCMessaging's solution is that it really doesn't require much direct access control administration. Access control remains the responsibility of the customer. KCMessaging does need to ensure that only the specified device can have access to the storage, though.

Step 14. Select an appropriate secure backup

In this scenario, you can require the customer to be responsible for his backup, or you can provide a backup solution for him. The provided backup solution would need to be an internal backup device that is allowed to see and therefore back up each SCSI storage device connected to an iSCSI device. Because this device has access to all storage, it should also use identity management (voice recognition at a minimum) as previously defined.

Step 15. Create a comprehensive security checklist

Much like you did in the other scenarios, use ripple security logic to create the security checklist. Start from the smallest element and work out. Start with the data element (block, file, disk, connections, and so on). Evaluate the ripple both physically and logically. Ensure each device is investigated for vulnerabilities. This includes switches, routers, firewalls, iSCSI devices, SCSI disk devices, and even the KCMessaging encryption program.

Ensure configuration options are thoroughly understood. Only one IP address/port or port range should map to an outside IP address/port or port range.

Since layer-3 switches are used, filtering and traffic shaping may be an option.

Since the environment is IP, firewall options and allowed communications should be specifically mapped out, specifying both the source and destination communications allowed, and the specific services/ports allowed.

Although no VPN was specified, an option to use VPN was discussed. If this option is to be used, ensure that the originator of the VPN tunnel is specific (remember, this is a mail server, and it should not be mobile).

Only allow remote administration if a remote biometric solution can be implemented.

Ensure that subsecurity checklists exist for each device, including proprietary or embedded operating systems.

Don't forget to include virus protection for your devices and remind your customers to use virus protection when setting them up.

Step 16. Enterprise security plan

Since KCMessaging is a startup company, it is likely that this security program may become the enterprise security plan. In the absence of an enterprise security plan, it's recommended that you have two known security entities validate the plan. Review the recommendations of both and compare their findings against yours. Incorporate the pertinent findings, and revise the plan as appropriate.

In this case study, it would also be wise for KCMessaging to be able to address their customers' security needs as they pertain to using KCMessaging's service. This would require KCMessaging to build a separate security program for each customer that signed up for their messaging and security service.

Step 17. Intrusion detection

In every scenario, intrusion detection has been discussed. If you are using multiple firewalls, monitoring devices and IDS devices, use them all. Sometimes, symptoms found by a non–IDS device can alert you to something that IDS did not pick up on, especially when it comes from within.

Since there are two Internet connections, you have placed two IDS blocks to ensure IDS is covered on both links.

Step 18. Incident response planning

When you are dealing with someone else's data, the incident/response plan must be jointly understood and agreed upon. The company using this service most likely has its own security program in place. For this case study, all data is considered to be confidential. In the event of any unauthorized activity, the situation must first be assessed. You can't simply shut off the service (since it's not your data). If warranted by the situation, the service (and possibly all services) will be shut down, and you will begin to work the five Ws.

Notification and communication parameters must be defined. You would have a general outline, but it is very probable that each customer's notification requirements will differ. The best advice is to plan for the highest level of notifications using previously mentioned scenarios and reduce from there as appropriate.

Step 19. Training

In this scenario, training takes on a new meaning. Not only will you have to train your personnel for the security and nuances of the environment, but the customer will also have to be trained to properly use and secure the service for their environment. During the training, such items as valid use, settings, connections, virus protection, and incident planning and response parameters should be addressed.

Step 20. Design review

Even if two (or more) security companies review the plan, perform a final review. In this case study, it is likely that the storage security plan will be the basis for the enterprise security plan (although there are many missing pieces for an enterprise security plan). During the review, note all exceptions and make final changes.

Step 21. Testing

Set up a sound testing program using information from the following chapter. KCMessaging may elect to perform their own tests as they deem necessary, but since this is a service being offered to multiple customers, our recommendation is to allow two external companies to perform any audits and tests. Using a third party (or more than one third party) to perform the testing is a good practice, because it lends credibility to the service.

Once the implementation is complete, the new iSCSI environment, based on the preceding assessments, should look similar to the setup shown in Figure 8-7.

Final notes on SAN security

For the Fibre Channel fabric, the T11 Security Study Group has been developing protocol standards. A proposal to securely authenticate Fibre Switches among each other calls for the use of the Switched Link Authentication Protocol (SLAP), which ensures that only authorized switches can participate in a Fibre Channel network. With SLAP, each switch has its own digital certificate. SLAP uses digital certificates to authenticate the e-ports on the switches. Although current switches do not have this capability, it will be forthcoming.

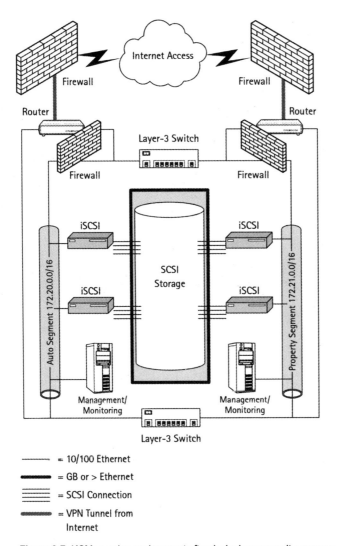

Figure 8-7: KCMessaging environment after designing a security program

For Fibre Channel storage networks, Secure Link Authentication Protocol will ensure that all switches in the fabric are properly authenticated.

Throughout this chapter and the case studies, we focused on the primary steps for creating a sound storage security program. In creating your security checklist, review the steps to determine what specific component items should be on your security checklist. Once you feel you have a comprehensive checklist that fits within your enterprise security plan, have it validated.

Finally, review the plan often to ensure it is still valid. Schedule review dates and make sure they occur. New vulnerabilities continue to be discovered.

Summary

Throughout this chapter, you learned about the importance of creating a sound data security program using a step approach. Each step is important, but collectively they are vital. Definitions, explanations, and examples were provided for each of the steps. The steps were then applied during the first case study. Next, using a second case study that included questions and answers, we illustrated when steps can and can't be omitted. Based on the results of the questions and answers, we explained what the result of the case study might look like. In the third (iSCSI) case study we showed how components of iSCSI can be similar to NAS and how other components of iSCSI may be similar to SAN.

It is important to remember that each step carries a specific importance for security reasons, and the collection of the steps ultimately ensures that data is secured. Thus, it is absolutely necessary to be very formal and thorough in designing and implementing a sound data (DAS/NAS/SAN) security program.

Finally, we noted that testing is an integral part of any sound security program, so much so that it is covered in its own chapter. See you there.

Chapter 9
Testing and Monitoring

Now that you've designed and implemented a secure storage solution, what remains—on the security side—is the implementation of a proactive auditing strategy. The International Information Systems Security Certification Consortium's Common Body of Knowledge (CBK) domains mandate problem identification auditing as testing against techniques used by intruders. Why? Consider the latest Computer Security Institute/FBI computer crime survey that reported that 90 percent of respondents claimed they detected a security breach in the past year. Financial losses totaled nearly a half-billion dollars, and that just reflects statistics from about 220 respondents. As a result, regularly scheduled local and remote security testing and monitoring are a fundamental part of an effective defense policy. In this chapter, you survey the details of a general testing cookbook you can customize for your storage system infrastructure.

Let's start with the general design and implementation of a testing system, common usages in which you test the most common threats to storage networks, and then follow up with the most common exploits and their countermeasures.

> **CROSS-REFERENCE:** For more comprehensive coverage and straightforward steps on local and remote security auditing, we recommend you read *Hack Attacks Testing* by Wiley Publishing.

Building a Testing System

Start by looking at the minimum hardware requirements for a standard testing system fitting for storage network auditing. Although these requirements typically depend on the intended usage of the system, you can make approximate calculations for a general scenario. The recommended minimum system requirements include the following:

- ♦ **Processor(s):** Pentium III+
- ♦ **RAM:** 256+ MB
- ♦ **HDD:** 20+ GB
- ♦ **Video:** Support for at least 1024 × 768 resolution at 16K colors
- ♦ **Network:** Dual NICs, at least one of which supports passive or promiscuous mode
- ♦ **Other:** Three-button mouse, CD-ROM, and floppy disk drive

The best recommendation for the software operating system foundation is UNIX: Sun Micro-systems' Solaris v.8+ and/or Linux, the trendy UNIX variant. Linux offers direct control of the O/S command line, including custom code compilation for software stability and flexibility. Linux is customized, packaged, and distributed by many vendors. For your purposes, you should use Red Hat Linux v.7.3+ (www.redhat.com). Other alternatives are:

♦ Slackware (www.slackware.org)

♦ Debian (www.debian.org)

♦ TurboLinux (www.turbolinux.com)

♦ Mandrake (www.linux-mandrake.com)

♦ SuSE (www.suse.com)

♦ Trinux (www.trinux.org)

♦ MkLinux (www.mklinux.org)

♦ LinuxPPC (www.linuxppc.org)

♦ SGI Linux (http://oss.sgi.com/projects /sgilinux11)

♦ Caldera OpenLinux (www.caldera.com)

♦ Corel Linux (http://linux.corel.com)

♦ Stampede Linux (www.stampede.org)

Recently, a new operating system has entered the equation: Apple's Mac OS X. If you choose OS X, you need to adhere to the following minimum requirements:

♦ **Hardware compatibility:** Mac OS X requires a Power Mac G3, G4, G4 Cube; iMac; PowerBook G3, G4; or iBook computer with a CD-ROM or DVD drive. Mac OS X does not support the original PowerBook G3 or processor upgrade cards. Verify your hardware is supported from the following list:

  • **Power Mac G4:** Power Mac G4 with PCI Graphics, Macintosh Server G4, Power Mac G4 Cube, Power Mac G4 with AGP Graphics, Power Mac G4 with 5-Slot, Power Mac G4 with Quicksilver

  • **iMac:** iMac (Bondi Blue), iMac (5 Flavors), iMac DV, iMac/iMac DV+/DV SE (slot loading), iMac Fall Colors, iMac (CD-RW), iMac (CD-RW July 2001)

  • **PowerBook:** PowerBook G3 Series, PowerBook G3 (USB), PowerBook G3 (USB & Firewire), PowerBook G4 (except original PowerBook G3)

  • **iBook:** iBook, iBook SE, iBook (Firewire), iBook SE (Firewire), iBook (Dual USB 2001)

  • **Power Mac G3:** Power Macintosh G3 (All-In-One, Desktop, Mini-Tower, Server), Power Macintosh G3 (Blue and White), (processor upgrade cards not supported)

♦ **RAM:** 128+MB

♦ **HDD:** 5+GB free space (from the Finder, open your startup disk and look at the top of the Disk window or any of its Folder windows to see the amount of available disk space)

Quick Sun Solaris configuration

If you choose Solaris as your primary testing operating system, follow the steps in this section as standard installation guidelines. To accommodate the predominant number of Solaris consumers—Intel Architecture (IA) users—we focus on the Intel installation and configuration in 44 steps; however, SPARC and Intel installs are very similar.

> **NOTE:** We recommend having minimum hard drive space of at least 10,000MB (10GB) including 512MB for SWAP space.

Step 1. Power up the system with the Solaris 8 installation CD-ROM. After setup initializes, you get the following message:

```
SunOS Secondary Boot version 3.00
Solaris Intel Platform Edition Booting System
Running Configuration Assistant ...
```

Configuration Assistant

Step 2. When the Solaris Device Configuration Assistant screen is displayed, press F2 to continue and you'll see the following Bus Enumeration message:

```
Determining bus types and gathering hardware configuration data...
```

Step 3. When setup has finished scanning and the Identified Devices screen is displayed, press F2 to continue.

Drivers

Step 4. The next screen displays driver information, followed by the Boot Solaris screen. On this screen, select CD and press F2 to continue.

Boot Parameters screen

Step 5. At this point, a running driver screen is displayed, followed by the Boot Parameters screen:

```
<<< Current Boot Parameters >>>
Boot path: /pci@0,0/pci-ide@7,1/ide@1/sd@0,0:a
Boot args: kernel/unix
                    <<< Starting Installation >>>
SunOS Release 5.8 Version Generic 32-bit
Copyright 1983-2000 Sun Microsystems, Inc.  All rights reserved.
Configuring /dev and /devices
Using RPC Bootparams for network configuration information.
Solaris Web Start 3.0 installer
English has been selected as the language in which to perform the
install.
Starting the Web Start 3.0 Solaris installer
Solaris installer is searching the system's hard disks for a
location to place the Solaris installer software.
```

```
No suitable Solaris fdisk partition was found.
Solaris Installer needs to create a Solaris fdisk partition
on your root disk, c0d0, that is at least 395 MB.
WARNING: All information on the disk will be lost.
May the Solaris Installer create a Solaris fdisk [y,n,?]
At the prompt, type y and then press Enter.
```

Partitioning

Step 6. The next screen displays the cylinder breakdown as shown here (note this hard disk already has a DOS partition):

```
Total disk size is 972 cylinders
            Cylinder size is 4032 (512 byte) blocks
                                            Cylinders
Partition   Status    Type          Start   End   Length   %
=========   ======    ============  =====   ===   ======   ===
1                     DOS12         0       7     8        1
SELECT ONE OF THE FOLLOWING:
   1. Create a partition
   2. Specify the active partition
   3. Delete a partition
   4. Exit (update disk configuration and exit)
   5. Cancel (exit without updating disk configuration)
Enter Selection:
At the prompt, type 1 and then press Enter.
```

Step 7. From the following partition selection prompt, type **A** and press Enter:

```
Select the partition type to create:
   1=SOLARIS    2=UNIX        3=PCIXOS    4=Other
   5=DOS12      6=DOS16       7=DOSEXT    8=DOSBIG
   A=x86 Boot  B=Diagnostic  0=Exit?
```

Step 8. Enter the percentage of disk to use for this partition and press Enter. Alternatively, you can type **C** to specify the size in cylinders (9–12 cylinders is recommended minimally).

Step 9. The next screen displays the following:

```
Should this become the active partition? If yes, it will be activated
each time the computer is reset or turned on.
Please type "y" or "n".
At the prompt, type y and then press Enter.
```

Step 10. The next screen displays the following:

```
Partition 2 is now the active partition.
SELECT ONE OF THE FOLLOWING:
   1. Create a partition
   2. Specify the active partition
```

```
   3. Delete a partition
   4. Exit (update disk configuration and exit)
   At the prompt, type 1 to create another partition and then press
Enter.
```

Step 11. From the following partition selection prompt, type **1** and press Enter to create a SOLARIS partition:

```
Select the partition type to create:
   1=SOLARIS    2=UNIX         3=PCIXOS     4=Other
   5=DOS12      6=DOS16        7=DOSEXT     8=DOSBIG
   A=x86 Boot   B=Diagnostic   0=Exit?
```

Step 12. Enter the percentage of disk to use for the main OS partition and press Enter. Then make the partition active by typing **Y** and then pressing Enter at the prompt.

Step 13. At this point, you should see the partition schedule similar to what's shown here:

```
Total disk size is 972 cylinders
            Cylinder size is 4032 (512 byte) blocks
                                         Cylinders
Partition   Status    Type           Start   End   Length    %
=========   ======    ============   =====   ===   ======   ===
1                     DOS12          0       7     8         1
2           Active    x86 Boot       8       16    9         1
3                     Solaris        17      969   953       98
SELECT ONE OF THE FOLLOWING:
   1. Create a partition
   2. Specify the active partition
   3. Delete a partition
   4. Exit (update disk configuration and exit)
   5. Cancel (exit without updating disk configuration)
Enter Selection:
At the prompt, type 4 and then press Enter.
```

Step 14. At this time from the following prompt, type **N** and press Enter:

```
No suitable Solaris fdisk partition was found.
Solaris Installer needs to create a Solaris fdisk partition
on your root disk, c0d0, that is at least 395 MB.
WARNING: All information on the disk will be lost.
May the Solaris Installer create a Solaris fdisk [y,n,?]
```

Step 15. Next, you should see the following message:

```
Please choose another installation option, see the Solaris Install
Documentation for more details.
To restart the installation, run /sbin/cd0_install.
At the system prompt, type /sbin/cd0_install and then press Enter.
```

Step 16. The next message reads:

```
The default root disk is /dev/dsk/c0d0.
The Solaris installer needs to format /dev/dsk/c0d0 to install Solaris.
WARNING: ALL INFORMATION ON THE DISK WILL BE ERASED!
Do you want to format /dev/dsk/c0d0?  [y,n,?,q]
At the prompt, type y and then press Enter.
```

Step 17. The next message reads:

```
NOTE: The swap size cannot be changed during filesystem layout. Enter a
swap partition size between 384MB and 1865MB, default = 512MB [?]
Press Enter to accept the 512MB default swap partition.
```

Step 18. The next message reads:

```
The Installer prefers that the swap slice is at the beginning of the
disk. This will allow the most flexible filesystem partitioning later in
the installation.
Can the swap slice start at the beginning of the disk  [y,n,?,q]
At the prompt, type y and then press Enter.
```

Step 19. The next message reads:

```
The Solaris installer will use disk slice, /dev/dsk/c0d0s1. After files
are copied, the system will automatically reboot, and installation will
continue.
Please Wait...
Copying mini-root to local disk....done.
Copying platform specific files....done.
Preparing to reboot and continue installation.
Need to reboot to continue the installation
Please remove the boot media (floppy or cdrom) and press Enter
Note: If the boot media is cdrom, you must wait for the system to reset
in order to eject.
Press Enter to continue.
```

Step 20. At the system reset, eject the installation CD-ROM. The next message reads:

```
SunOS - Intel Platform Edition   Primary Boot Subsystem, vsn 2.0
Current Disk Partition Information
Part#   Status   Type     Start       Length
=================================================
1                DOS12    63          32193
2       Active   X86 BOOT 32256       36288
3                SOLARIS  68544       3842496
4                <unused>
```

Select the partition you wish to boot. At that point, the screen refreshes and displays the following message:

```
SunOS Secondary Boot version 3.00
        Solaris Intel Platform Edition Booting System
```

```
Running Configuration Assistant...
Autobooting from bootpath /pci@0,0/pci-ide@7,1/ata@1/cmdk@0,0:b
If the system hardware has changed, or to boot from a different device,
interrupt the autoboot process by pressing ESC.
Initializing system
Please wait...
                <<< Current Boot Parameters >>>
Boot path: /pci@0,0/pci-ide@7,1/ata@1/cmdk@0,0:b
Boot args:
Type    b [file-name] [boot-flags] <ENTER>      to boot with options
or      i <ENTER>                               to enter boot
interpreter
or      <ENTER>                                 to boot with defaults
                <<< timeout in 5 seconds >>>
Select (b)oot or (i)nterpreter:
SunOS Release 5.8 Version Generic 32-bit
Copyright 1983-2000 Sun Microsystems, Inc.  All rights reserved.
Configuring /dev and /devices
Using RPC Bootparams for network configuration information.
```

The Solaris Installation Program screen is now displayed. Press F2 to continue.

Preinstallation

Step 21. The Introduction screen is displayed. Press F2 to continue.

Step 22. The View and Edit Window System Configuration screen is displayed. Select No changes Test/Save and Exit, and then press F2 to continue.

Step 23. The Window System Configuration Test screen is displayed. Press F2 to continue.

Step 24. Verify that the colors shown on the palette are displayed accurately, and then click Yes.

Web Start

Step 25. On the Web Start Welcome screen, click Next to continue.

Step 26. On the Network Connectivity screen, select Networked and click Next to continue.

Step 27. On the DHCP screen, select No and click Next to continue.

Step 28. On the Hostname screen, enter the hostname of your system and click Next to continue.

Step 29. On the IP Address screen, enter the IP address of your system and click Next to continue.

Step 30. On the Netmask screen, enter the Netmask of your system's IP address and click Next to continue.

Step 31. On the IPv6 screen, select whether or not to use IPv6 and click Next to continue.

Step 32. On the Name Service screen, select the type of service you want to use (NIS+, NIS, or DNS) and click Next to continue. For the purposes of this general installation guide, select DNS.

Step 33. On the Domain Name screen, enter your domain name and click Next to continue.

Step 34. On the Name Server dialog screen, select a name server and click Next to continue.

Step 35. On the DNS Server Address screen, enter the primary and optional secondary server IP addresses and click Next to continue. You may be prompted to enter optional domain names to search when a query is made. Click Next to continue.

Step 36. On the Time Zone screen sequence, select to specify your current location, then enter the current time and date, and click Next to continue.

Step 37. On the Root Password screen, type and confirm the administrative or superuser password and click Next to continue.

Step 38. On the Proxy Server screen, select and configure your optional proxy server settings and click Next to continue.

Step 39. On the Confirm Information screen, verify your configuration settings and click Confirm to continue.

Installing the O/S

Step 40. On the Welcome to Solaris screen, click Next to continue.

Step 41. On the Insert CD screen, insert the CD labeled Solaris 8 Software 1 of 2 Intel Platform Edition and click OK to continue.

Step 42. On the Select Type of Install screen, select the Default Install option and click Next to continue.

Step 43. On the Ready to Install screen, click Install Now to continue.

Installation completion

An installation status screen is displayed with the name of each package being installed in brackets above the top progress bar. The status of the entire installation is shown on the bottom progress bar. When the installation is complete, click Next to acknowledge the installation summary completion. At that point, you can select to install any additional or third-party software, or simply click Exit and then Reboot Now and you're finished.

CROSS-REFERENCE: For administration procedures, visit `http://docs.sun.com` on the Internet.

Quick Red Hat Linux configuration

If you choose Linux—Red Hat Linux v.7.3 or v.8 for the purposes here—as your primary testing operating system, follow the steps in this section as standard installation guidelines. This section is a general discussion on installing Red Hat Linux version 7.3 or v.8 in 19 quick steps. Power up the system with the Red Hat Linux Boot disk and choose the CD-ROM option from the boot loader screen and select OK. Optionally, you can boot directly from the CD-ROM if your system's setup specifies the primary boot process starting with the CD-ROM. Next, follow these steps:

NOTE: We recommend a minimum hard drive space of at least 5,000MB (5GB).

Welcome
Step 1. After setup locates your CD-ROM drive and installs specific drivers for it, the Welcome screen is displayed, with some additional help in the left panel. Click Next to begin the installation.

Language selection
Step 2. Select the appropriate language—in this case, English—and click Next.

Keyboard configuration
Step 3. Click to select the keyboard model and layout that most closely matches yours. By default, Dead Keys are enabled. Use these to create special characters with multiple key-strokes, or select Disable dead keys to opt otherwise. Click Next to continue.

Mouse configuration
Step 4. Click to select the mouse configuration that most closely matches yours. If your mouse is not listed, select one of the generic types and port (if prompted). Click Emulate 3 Buttons to use a two-button mouse as one with three buttons. In this case, the third button would be emu-lated by pressing both the right and left buttons of your two-button mouse simultaneously. Click Next to continue.

Install options
Step 5. Click to select your installation method—either Workstation, Server, Laptop, Custom, or Upgrade. It's best to choose Custom so that you may have the most flexibility. Click Next to continue.

Disk partitioning
Step 6. As you know, partitioning is a method to divide storage space into sections that oper-ate as separate disk drives. This is especially useful for multiple-boot configurations. Click to choose automatic partitioning or manual partitioning using Disk Druid or fdisk. Click Next to continue.

CROSS-REFERENCE: If you choose to manually partition the drive space (for example, using fdisk), visit `www.RedHat.com/docs/manuals/linux/RHL-7.3-Manual/install-guide/s1-diskpartfdisk.html` for details and instructions.

Network configuration

Step 7. Click to enter the IP address of your Tiger Box, the Netmask, Network, Broadcast addresses, domain name, and Gateway and DNS addresses. Click Next to continue.

Step 8. Red Hat offers additional security for your system with a firewalling daemon. Click Next to continue.

CROSS-REFERENCE: For more information on the firewall option, visit `www.RedHat.com/docs/manuals/linux/RHL-7.3-Manual/install-guide/s1-firewall-config.html`.

Language support

Step 9. Click to use more than one language on your Linux system. Click Next to continue.

Time zone

Step 10. Click to select your physical location or specify your time zone's offset from Coordinated Universal Time (UTC), which automatically selects your physical location. Click Next to continue.

Account configuration

Step 11. Click to enter the root or administrative password and then click to confirm the password in the appropriate fields. Additionally, you can create a user account by clicking Add and then entering the user's name, full name, password, password confirmation, and then clicking OK. Click Next to continue.

Authentication

Step 12. You can choose from the following authentication options shown on the Official Red Hat Linux x86 Installation Guide screen:

- **Enable MD5 passwords.** This option allows a long password to be used (up to 256 characters), instead of the standard eight characters or less.

- **Enable shadow passwords.** This option provides a secure method for retaining passwords. The passwords are stored in `/etc/shadow`, which can only be read by root.

- **Enable NIS.** This option allows you to run a group of computers in the same Network Information Service domain with a common password and group file. You can choose from the following options:
  - **NIS domain.** This option allows you to specify the domain or group of computers your system belongs to.
  - **Use broadcast to find NIS server.** This option allows you to broadcast a message to your local area network to find an available NIS server.

- **NIS server.** This option causes your computer to use a specific NIS server, rather than broadcasting a message to the local area network asking for any available server to host your system.

♦ **Enable LDAP.** This option tells your computer to use LDAP for some or all authentication. LDAP consolidates certain types of information within your organization. For example, all of the different lists of users within your organization can be merged into one LDAP directory. For more information about LDAP, refer to "Lightweight Directory Access Protocol (LDAP)" in the Official Red Hat Linux Reference Guide. You can choose from the following options:

  - **LDAP server.** This option allows you to access a specified server (by providing an IP address) running the LDAP protocol.

  - **LDAP Base DN.** This option allows you to look up user information by its Distinguished Name (DN).

  - **Use TLS (Transport Layer Security) lookups.** This option allows LDAP to send encrypted usernames and passwords to an LDAP server before authentication.

♦ **Enable Kerberos.** Kerberos is a secure system for providing network authentication services. For more information about Kerberos, see "Using Kerberos 5 on Red Hat Linux" in the Official Red Hat Linux Reference Guide. There are three options to choose from here:

  - **Realm.** This option allows you to access a network that uses Kerberos, composed of one or a few servers (also known as KDCs) and a potentially large number of clients.

  - **KDC.** This option allows you access to the Key Distribution Center (KDC), a machine that issues Kerberos tickets (sometimes called a Ticket Granting Server, or TGS).

  - **Admin Server.** This option allows you to access a server running kadmind.

♦ **Enable SMB authentication.** This option sets up Pluggable Authentication Module (PAM) to use an SMB server to authenticate users. You must supply two pieces of information here:

  - **SMB server.** This option indicates which SMB server your workstation should connect to for authentication.

  - **SMB workgroup.** This option indicates which workgroup the configured SMB servers are in.

Click Next to continue.

Package selection

Step 13. Click to select the application groups you wish to have installed on the system. We recommend selecting everything (at the end of the component list) to install all packages included with Red Hat Linux. Click Next to continue.

X configuration

Step 14. One of the most popular features of Linux is the X-Windows package—a Windows-like GUI for the Linux operating system. The install program attempts to probe your video hardware, and if the results are not accurate, you can simply click to select the correct settings. Click Next to continue.

Installation

Step 15. The next screen prepares you for the installation of the Red Hat Linux operating system. To cancel the installation, simply reboot your system, or click Next to continue. From here, your partitions will be written and the selected packages will be installed. When this process is complete, click Next to continue.

Step 16. At this point, to boot your new Linux operating system from a floppy boot disk, insert a blank formatted diskette and click Next; otherwise, click to select the Skip Boot Disk Creation checkbox before clicking Next.

Monitor configuration

Step 17. Click to select the closest match to your monitor hardware from the list. Click Next to continue.

Step 18. Continue by customizing your graphics configuration. Click Next to continue.

Installation completion

Step 19. Congratulations! The Red Hat Linux v.7.3 or v.8 installation is now complete. You are required to remove any media (for example, floppies or CD-ROMs) and reboot the system. If you choose to start Linux via floppy boot disk, insert the disk first.

Quick Apple Mac OS X/Jaguar configuration

If you are using a Mac and choose OS X as your primary testing operating system, follow the steps in this section as standard installation/upgrade guidelines. Power on your system, insert the Mac OS X CD into your CD-ROM drive, and follow these steps:

Welcome screen

Step 1. Double-click "Install Mac OS X."

License agreement

Step 2. Browse through the Read Me and license screens.

Step 3. Select the disk on which you'd like to install Mac OS X.

Installing the kernel

Step 4. Click the Install button. The first time your Mac starts up with your new system software, the Mac OS X Setup Assistant takes you through the steps necessary to set up your user account, e-mail settings, network configuration, and iTools account. When you finish, you're ready to start using Mac OS X.

Upgrading to OS X option (optional)

Power on your system and follow these steps:

Welcome screen

Step 1. Insert the Mac OS X (10.1) CD into your CD-ROM.

Installing kernel updates

Step 2. Double-click "Install Mac OS X." With this upgrade, you'll be pleased to know that all of your original settings are preserved and protected. After your Mac restarts, you see your familiar desktop, improved by the new features included in Mac OS X version 10.1.

Installing Developer Tools

Later in this chapter, you'll install and configure security analysis tools such as vulnerability scanners that require a compiler. The easiest solution for this dilemma is to install Apple's Developer Tools. Major features of these tools include the gcc3 compiler, Project Builder 2.0 with support for a highly configurable multiwindow user interface, and AppleScript Studio 1.1.

Downloading the software

Once you access the Internet, open your Web browser and follow these steps:

Step 1. Browse to `www.apple.com/developer` and click Log In.

Step 2. On the next screen, click Join ADC Now to become a free online member of the Apple Developer Connection.

Terms and conditions

Step 3. Scroll down and read all of the terms and conditions, and then click the Agree button to continue.

Sign-up form

Step 4. Click to fill in the following information in the appropriate fields:

```
Provide your name and email address.
Choose an Apple ID (account name). If you have an Apple ID, please do
not create an additional account.
Choose a password.
```

Step 5. Click to fill in clues for a forgotten password by entering your birth date and inputting a unique question and answer that only you would know. Click Continue when you finish.

Account profile

Step 6. Click to enter account profile specifics, including:

```
Shipping Address
Job Title / Department  Company / Organization / Employer
Phone Numbers
Type of Developer:*
Independent Software Vendor (ISV)
Independent Hardware Vendor (IHV)
Consultant/System Integrator
In-House/Corporate
Value-Added Reseller (VAR)
Hobbyist
Student
Other

Student Information (Required for student developers only)
```

When you finish, click Save.

The software

Next, simply click Download Software from the left menu and then Mac OS X from the submenu to display the Developer Tools options in the main frame of your browser. Click Download from the most current MacBinary of the Developer Tools, and your system should start downloading the file to your desktop.

Finally, after completing the download, click the DevTools file to install the package. When the installation is complete, you must restart your system before moving on to the next section.

Quick auditing software configuration

Several good auditing packages, tools, and utilities are available for use on Windows and *NIX-based testing systems. Some of the most popular in random order include:

- Nmap (www.insecure.org)
- TigerSuite (www.tigertools.net)
- Nessus (www.nessus.org)
- Netcat (www.atstake.com/research/tools/index.html)
- Tcpdump (www.tcpdump.org)
- Snort (www.snort.org)
- Saint (www.wwdsi.com/saint)
- Ethereal (www.ethereal.com)
- Whisker (www.wiretrip.net/rfp/p/doc.asp?id=21&iface=2)
- Internet Security Scanner (www.iss.net)
- Abacus Portsentry (www.psionic.com/products/portsentry.html)
- DSniff (http://naughty.monkey.org/~dugsong/dsniff)
- Tripwire (www.tripwire.com)

- CyberCop Scanner (www.pgp.com/asp_set/products/tns/ccscanner_intro.asp)
- Hping2 (`www.hping.org`)
- SARA (`www.arc.com/sara`)
- Sniffit (`http://reptile.rug.ac.be/~coder/sniffit/sniffit.html`)
- SATAN (`www.fish.com/satan`)
- IPFilter (`http://coombs.anu.edu.au/ipfilter`)
- iptables/netfilter/ipchains/ipfwadm (`http://netfilter.kernelnotes.org`)
- Firewalk (`www.packetfactory.net/Projects/Firewalk`)
- Strobe (`www.insecure.org/nmap/index.html#other`)
- L0pht Crack (`www.atstake.com/research/lc3`)
- John The Ripper (`www.openwall.com/john`)
- Hunt (`http://lin.fsid.cvut.cz/~kra/index.html#HUNT`)
- Ntop (`www.ntop.org`)
- NAT (NetBIOS Auditing Tool) (www.tux.org/pub/security/secnet/tools/nat10/)
- Sam Spade (`http://samspade.org/t`)
- NFR (`www.nfr.com`)
- logcheck (`www.psionic.com/products/logsentry.html`)
- Ngrep (`www.packetfactory.net/Projects/ngrep`)
- Cheops (`www.marko.net/cheops`)
- Vetescan (`www.self-evident.com`)
- Retina (`www.eeye.com/html/Products/Retina.html`)
- Cerberus Internet Scanner (`www.cerberus-infosec.co.uk/cis.shtml`)
- Swatch (`www.oit.ucsb.edu/~eta/swatch`)
- Nemesis (`http://jeff.wwti.com/nemesis`)
- LSOF (`ftp://vic.cc.purdue.edu/pub/tools/unix/lsof`)
- Lids (`www.lids.org`)
- IPTraf (`http://cebu.mozcom.com/riker/iptraf`)
- IPLog (`http://ojnk.sourceforge.net`)
- Fragrouter (http://packetstorm.widexs.nl/UNIX/IDS/nidsbench/nidsbench.html)
- Queso (`www.apostols.org/projectz/queso`)

Based on an extensive comparative analysis, we recommend adding the thorough and versatile Nessus (`www.nessus.org`) suite along with Nmap (`www.insecure.org`) to your local and remote security auditing software arsenal on your *NIX/OS X–based testing system.

Moving forward, you should begin with Nmap, given that it can and will be used by Nessus during your audits.

Installing Nmap

After downloading or copying the Nmap archive file (in this case, `nmap-2.54BETA34.tgz`) to a directory on your hard drive, follow these steps for Linux systems:

Step 1. Open a terminal session, and change directories to the partition or directory where you placed the program file.

Step 2. The file probably contains the `.tgz` extension and must be uncompressed by using the `gzip` command. Type `gzip -d nmap-2.54BETA34.tgz`.

Step 3. The installation file will be uncompressed, and the `.tgz` will be removed, leaving only `nmap-2.54BETA34.tar`. Extract this tar archive by issuing the following tar command: `tar xvf nmap-2.54BETA34.tar`.

Step 4. The program files are extracted and copied to an `nmap-2.54BETA34` directory. Change directories to the new directory by typing `cd nmap-2.54BETA34`.

Step 5. You need to configure the software by issuing the command `./configure`.

> **NOTE:** You need to have root privileges to complete the installation. If you log in with a user account, simply issue the `su` command and enter the root password to grant these privileges.

Step 6. Build and install the package by issuing the `make` command, shown here:

```
# make all
```

> **NOTE:** Advanced users can optionally edit the makefile with `vi Makefile`.

The RPM Package Manager is a powerful command-line-driven automated management system capable of installing, uninstalling, verifying, querying, and updating software packages.

To install the X86/RPM version, use the following syntax:

```
rpm -vhU http://download.insecure.org/nmap/dist/nmap-2.53-1.i386.rpm
rpm -vhU http://download.insecure.org/nmap/dist/nmap-frontend-0.2.53-1.i386.rpm
```

Installing Nessus

After downloading the latest stable release of Nessus, you should have four compressed archives similar to these:

- nessus-libraries-1.2.1.tar.gz
- libnasl-1.2.1.tar.gz

◆ nessus-core.1.2.1.tar.gz

◆ nessus-plugins.1.2.1.tar.gz

Copy these files to a directory on your hard drive, and follow these steps:

Manual installation

Step 1. Open a terminal session and change directories to the partition or directory where you placed the `nessus-libraries-x.x.x.tar.gz` file.

Step 2. Uncompress the file by using the `gzip` command; type `gzip -d nessus-libraries-x.x.x.tar.gz`.

Step 3. The installation file will be uncompressed and the `.gz` will be removed, leaving only `nessus-libraries-x.x.x.tar`. Extract this tar archive by issuing the following `tar` command: `tar xvf nessus-libraries-x.x.x.tar`.

Step 4. The program files are extracted and copied to a `nessus-libraries-x.x.x` directory. Change directories to the new directory by typing `cd nessus-libraries-x.x.x`.

Step 5. You need to configure the software by issuing the command `./configure`.

> **NOTE:** If you installed an older version of Nessus in the past, you should run `./uninstall-nessus` as root first. This script removes the old libraries and binaries left by the older version but keeps your configuration untouched.

Step 6. As root, build and install the package by issuing the `make` command.

Step 7. Perform the previous steps for each of the four files in this order:

1. Installing `libraries`
2. Installing `libnasl`
3. Installing `nessus-core`
4. Installing `nessus-plugins`

Automatic installation

Nessus Security Scanner can also be downloaded as a single installer from `www.nessus.org/download.html`. The file should be `nessus-installer.sh`. Simply download and copy the file to your home directory, open a terminal, change to your home directory, and at the terminal prompt, type:

```
sh nessus-installer.sh
```

Configuring Nessus Security Scanner

After installing the scanner, you need to perform two additional steps before starting the server and client for usage, including creating a certificate (using `/usr/local/sbin/nessus-mkcert`) and adding a user (using `/usr/local/sbin/nessus-adduser`).

Follow these steps:

Step 1. Change directories to the new Nessus installation directory by typing `cd /usr/local/sbin`.

Step 2. Create a nessusd certificate by executing `./nessus-mkcert`.

Step 3. Add a nessusd user by executing `./nessus-adduser`.

Starting the server daemon

You should be ready to start the server daemon, `nessusd`, which is located in `/usr/local/sbin`. In that directory, at the terminal prompt, type `./nessusd -D` for standard activation.

Additional notes for Linux and Solaris users

If you are using Linux, make sure that `/usr/local/lib` is in `/etc/ld.so.conf`, and then type `ldconfig`.

Solaris users must execute the following:

```
export LD_LIBRARY_PATH=$LD_LIBRARY_PATH:/usr/local/lib
```

Additionally, if you do not want the client to use GTK (if your system lacks X11, for instance), then you can compile a stripped-down version of the client that works on the command line. To do this, add the `--disable-gtk` option to configure while building `nessus-core`:

1. `cd nessus-core`
2. `./configure --disable-gtk`
3. `make`
4. `make install`

Using Your Testing System

Be sure to implement a regularly scheduled local and remote auditing program. A bimonthly agenda is best; however, some large networks have audits performed as often as once per week remotely and every other week for local scans, as mandated by their policies.

For the purposes here, the flexible Nessus scanner has been chosen to perform your local vulnerability analyses. Use the Nessus client located in the `/usr/local/bin/` directory as `nessus`. To start the client GUI, type `./nessus` at the terminal prompt in that directory, or use these command-line options:

Common options:

```
nessus [-vnh] [-c .rcfile] [-V] [-T <format>]
```

Batch-mode scan:

```
nessus -q <host> <port> <user> <pass> <targets-file> <result-file>
```

List sessions:

```
nessus -s -q <host> <port> <user> <pass>
```

Restore session:

```
nessus -R <sessionid> -q <host> <port> <user> <pass> <result-file>
```

- ◆ v: shows version number
- ◆ h: shows this help
- ◆ n: No pixmaps
- ◆ T: Output format: 'nbe', 'html', 'html_graph', 'text', 'xml', 'old-xml', 'tex', or 'nsr'
- ◆ V: make the batch mode display status messages to the screen

The batch mode (-q) arguments are:

- ◆ host: nessusd host
- ◆ port: nessusd host port
- ◆ user: username
- ◆ pass: password
- ◆ targets: file containing the list of targets
- ◆ result: name of the file where Nessus will store the results

If you're using the GUI, configuring a scan is easy with the Nessus client. First and foremost, you must log into nessusd. To do so, enter the server host, your login name and password, and then click Log in.

Plugins

The plugins represent the security checks that the scanner will test against your target(s) (see Figure 9-1). Click to select the specific types of plugins you want to test against. Be careful with some of the Denial of Service checks, as they could potentially crash a target.

Some plugins require additional arguments, such as the type of port scan to perform or what pop account to use for a pop2 overflow check, and so on. To configure plugin preferences, click the Prefs tab on the top of the client GUI and click to specify these options.

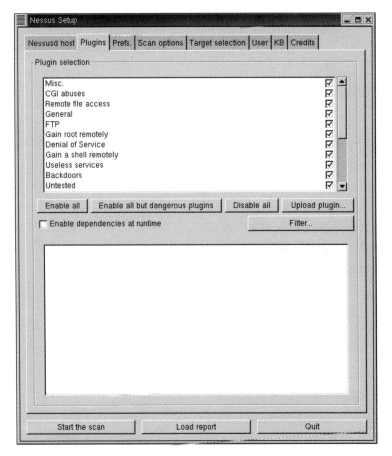

Figure 9-1: Making a plugin selection with the Nessus GUI

Scan options

The next step is to configure the scan options for a vulnerability assessment, as shown in Figure 9-2. Click the Scan Options tab on the top of the client GUI and then click to select your personal preferences (for example, which port scanner to use, such as Nmap).

Target configuration

The following steps can be used to configure and execute a vulnerability scan using Nessus. The first part involves configuring your target with the simple interface, and the second part is simply starting your scan.

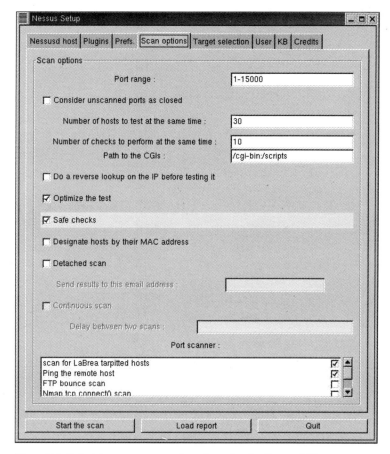

Figure 9-2: Optimizing a pre-scan configuration using the Nessus GUI

Step 1. Click the Target Selection tab on the top of the client GUI (see Figure 9-3).

Step 2. Click to enter your target host(s). As an example from Nessus, you can use the following formats:

- ♦ A single IP address (192.168.1.11)
- ♦ A range of IP addresses (192.168.1.11-48)
- ♦ A range of IP addresses in CIDR notation (192.168.1.1/29)
- ♦ A hostname in Fully Qualified Domain Name notation (www.targetdomain.com)
- ♦ A hostname (STORAGE1)
- ♦ Any combination of the aforementioned forms separated by a comma

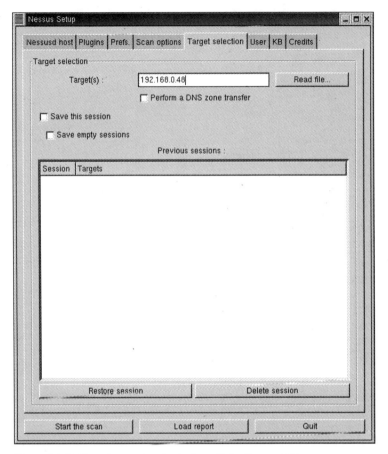

Figure 9-3: Making a to-scan target selection with the Nessus GUI

Step 3. Click "Start the scan" to begin the vulnerability assessment.

NOTE: For advanced custom configuration options, including *How to write a security test in C* and *How to write a security test in NASL*, refer to these papers at `www.wiley.com/compbooks/chirillo`, `www.TigerTools.net`, or `www.InfoTress.com`.

Reporting

The reporting function in Nessus (shown in Figure 9-4) is very simple to use. After a scan is complete, you can view the results in a GUI (tree format) or save the report to a file. You can generate the report to a file in many different formats, including:

- NSR format
- HTML format
- ASCII text
- LaTeX format

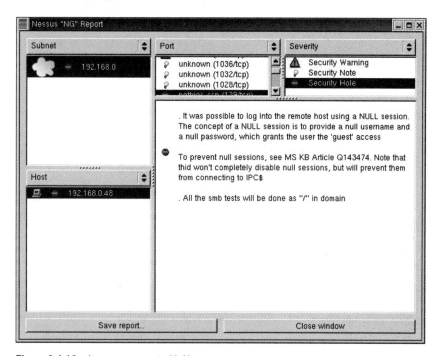

Figure 9-4: Viewing a scan report with Nessus

Auditing the most common vulnerabilities to storage networks

Be sure to specifically audit the most commonly targeted areas for intruders. Our research shows that these include host systems, WAN links, local segments and zones, management points, and archives.

Host systems

Host systems refer to host or Web servers that cross-reference storage media for database compilations. If these systems are compromised by an intruder, the connected storage network and the stored data would most likely be vulnerable to intrusion and/or data theft.

WAN links

Traffic containing storage data over WANs and/or the Internet is typically vulnerable to data theft and modification, TCP session hijacking, and spoofing attacks. Attackers typically use IP and DNS spoofing to take over the identity of a trusted host to subvert security and attain trust-ful communication with a target host. Using IP spoofing to breach security and gain access to the network, an intruder first disables, then masquerades as, a trusted host. The result is that a target station resumes communication with the attacker, as messages seem to be coming from a trustworthy port. Understanding the core inner workings of IP spoofing requires extensive knowledge of the IP, the TCP, and the SYN-ACK process.

To engage in IP spoofing, an intruder must first discover an IP address of a trusted port, then modify his or her packet headers so that it appears that the illegitimate packets are actually coming from that port. Of course, to pose as a trusted host, the machine must be disabled along the way. Because most internetworking operating system software does not control the source address field in packet headers, the source address is vulnerable to being spoofed. The attack-er then predicts the target TCP sequences and, subsequently, participates in the trusted com-munications. The most common, and likewise deviant, types of IP spoofing techniques include:

- Packet interception and modification between two hosts
- Packet and/or route redirection from a target to the attacker
- Target host response prediction and control
- TCP SYN flooding variations

Local segment and zones

Be sure to audit and monitor for unauthorized servers or switches attempting to legitimately attach to a Fibre Channel network with open ports. This includes the storage infrastructure (discussed in Chapter 4) between the host and switch, administrators and the access control management systems, the management systems and the switch zone, and separate switch zones. Be sure to use plugins or modules that test the access controls, access control lists, and encryption mechanisms.

Management points

Administrative systems, management ports, and SNMP devices may be vulnerable to attacks launched by intruders against the storage networks, especially with Denial-of-Service (DoS) attacks, insertion of viruses, and the execution of Trojan horses inside the storage network. Be sure to target these during your local audits and monitor the services and ports they use.

DoS attacks can bring networks to a screeching halt with the flooding of useless traffic. Flood-ing, generally speaking, involves the SYN-ACK (three-way) handshake, where a connection is established between two nodes during a TCP session for unambiguous synchronization of both ends of the connection. This process allows both sides to agree upon a number sequencing method for tracking bytes within the communication streams back and forth. Basically, the first node requests communication by sending a packet with a sequence number and SYN bit. The second node responds with an acknowledgment (ACK) that contains the sequence number plus one, and its own sequence number back to the first node. At this point, the first node responds, and communication between the two nodes proceeds. When there is no more data to send, a TCP node may send a FIN bit, indicating a close control signal. At this intersection, both nodes close simultaneously. In the case of a form of SYN flooding, the source IP address in the packet is "spoofed," or replaced with an address that is not in use on the Internet (it belongs to another computer). An attacker sends numerous TCP SYNs to tie up as many resources as possible on the target computer. Upon receiving the connection request, the target computer allocates resources to handle and track this new communication session, then responds with a SYN-ACK. In this case, the response is sent to the spoofed or nonexistent IP address. As a result, no response is received by the SYN-ACK; therefore, a default-configured Windows NT server retransmits the SYN-ACK five times, doubling the time-out value after each retransmission. The initial time-out value is 3 seconds, so retries are attempted at 3, 6, 12, 24, and 48 seconds. After the last retransmission, 96 seconds are allowed to pass before the computer gives up waiting to receive a response and thus reallocates the resources that were set aside earlier. The total elapsed time during which resources are unavailable equates to approximately 189 seconds.

Viruses are a form of passive penetration—passive because the attacker isn't waiting on the other end of the connection. They're used to wreak havoc. In this passive context, a virus is a computer program that makes copies of itself by using a host program. This means the virus *requires* a host program; thus, along with executable files, the code that controls your hard disk can, and in many cases will, be infected. When a computer copies its code into one or more host programs, the viral code executes and then replicates.

Typically, computer viruses that hackers spread carry a *payload*—that is, damage that results after a specified period of time. The damage can range from file corruption, data loss, or even hard disk obliteration. Viruses are most often distributed through e-mail attachments, pirate software distribution, and infected floppy disk dissemination.

The damage to your system caused by a virus depends on what kind of virus it is. Popular renditions include active code that can trigger an event upon opening an e-mail (such as in the infamous I Love You and Donald Duck "bugs"). Traditionally, there are three distinct stages in the life of a virus: activation, replication, and manipulation.

- ◆ **Activation.** The point at which the computer initially "catches" the virus, commonly from a trusted source.

- ◆ **Replication.** The stage during which the virus infects as many sources as it can reach.

- ◆ **Manipulation.** The point at which the payload of the virus begins to take effect, such as a certain date (for example, Friday 13 or January 1), or an event (for example, the third reboot or scheduled disk maintenance procedure).

A virus is classified according to its form of malicious operation:

- Partition sector virus
- Boot sector virus
- File-infecting virus
- Polymorphic virus
- Multipartite virus
- Trojan horse virus
- Worm virus
- Macro virus

When a virus acts as a Trojan, on the other hand, it can be defined as a malicious, security-breaking program that is typically disguised as something useful, such as a utility program, joke, or game download. Trojans are often used to integrate a backdoor, or "hole," in a system's security countenance.

Simple Network Management Protocol

In a nutshell, the Simple Network Management Protocol (SNMP) directs network device management and monitoring and typically utilizes ports 161 and 162. SNMP operation consists of messages, called *protocol data units* (PDUs), that are sent to different parts of a network. SNMP devices are called *agents*. These components store information about themselves in *management information bases* (MIBs) and return this data to the SNMP requesters. UDP port 162 is specified as the port that notification receivers should listen to for SNMP notification messages. For all intents and purposes, this port is used to send and receive SNMP event reports. The interactive communication governed by these ports makes them juicy targets for probing and reconfiguration, so be sure to audit them extensively.

Archives

Archives and data warehouses retain data and information backups over time, and time and again, they are overlooked. They should be audited and monitored, since they may be exposed to theft, modification, and/or deletion.

Other general storage-related insecurities

You know that perimeter security is simply not enough to protect against malicious users and local/remote attackers; therefore, some other common *critical* inherited security risks to audit include:

- **Unauthorized access.** Local users and remote attackers access classified data.
- **Unauthenticated access.** Unprivileged users access privileged data.
- **Unprotected administrator access.** This is caused by unencrypted local and remote authentication.
- **Idle host scanning and spoofing.** Advanced discovery and/or local trusted systems masquerade to retrieve sensitive information and/or compromise security.

- **Vulnerable delivery channel access points.** This includes exposed zones, islands, and remote networks.

- **Data hijacking and sniffing.** This targets exposed data links and vulnerable operating systems.

Firewalls and Intrusion Detection System Software

One of the most common available tools that can be used to warn of suspicious, malicious, or other unidentified traffic is the firewall. Many firewall products have the ability to log such activity. These logs are often accompanied by altering and notification software and options that can be configured to alert/notify you when such conditions are met. Unfortunately, too many companies do not fully implement these features.

Even if the firewall can track some of this activity, it is not a replacement for a good intrusion detection system (IDS). An IDS is a unit that inspects all inbound and outbound activity, specifically to identify any suspicious patterns. As far as the IDS knows, suspicious activity could mean an attack from an intruder trying to compromise a system within the network. With that said, IDS can be a useful addition to your perimeter and internal intrusion monitoring strategy.

An IDS should be used to supplement your current firewalling systems and access control systems by providing intrusion notification. What's more, an intrusion detection system often recognizes attacks that pass through your firewall, especially those from within the internal network.

> **TIP:** Intrusion detection systems should be configured so that they don't rely on scans coming from a single IP, but on the connection attempts to closed ports per time. In addition, IDS should be programmed to detect distributed port scans.

Be sure to check Appendix B for links and information on IDS devices and services.

Network monitors

Network monitors continuously track packets crossing a network, providing an accurate picture of network activity at any moment, or a historical record of network activity over a period of time. They do not decode the contents of frames. Monitors are useful for baselining, in which the activity on a network is sampled over a period of time to establish a normal performance profile, or baseline.

Monitors collect information such as packet sizes, the number of packets, error packets, overall usage of a connection, the number of hosts and their MAC addresses, and details about communications between hosts and other devices. This data can be used to create profiles of LAN traffic, as well as to assist in locating traffic overloads, planning for network expansion, detecting intruders, establishing baseline performance, and distributing traffic more efficiently.

Custom detection with TigerGuard IDS

TigerGuard IDS (`www.tigertools.net/ids`), shown in Figure 9-5, is a custom port blocker and watcher in an IDS-style kernel to use at your discretion. It is an advanced version of TigerWatch and can incorporate protection from most known and unknown Trojan services. The program allows you to add custom ports to the protection policy. You can also create, load, and save custom policy lists for future retrieval. In its current compilation, the daemon records, blocks, and alerts of remote hack attacks in conjunction with the policies you create. To start you off in the right direction, you can preload standard and default policy lists. By default, TigerWatch accepts up to 500 custom policies.

TigerGuard takes the mystery out of port security and monitoring. It has been designed based on the simple philosophy that if the port is in use and guarded, it cannot be exploited. There is also a companion Intrusion Sniffer and a Port Session Sniffer, with which you can secretly capture incoming TCP or UDP intrusion information.

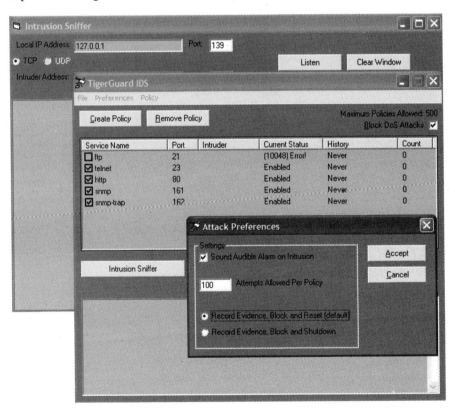

Figure 9-5: Using TigerGuard as a custom IDS

> **NOTE:** To avoid jurisdiction conflict, be sure to release port control from TigerGuard before gathering intrusion evidence with either sniffer. For all practical purposes, the Intrusion Sniffer captures all traffic per single attacker, while the Port Session Sniffer logs all traffic from multiple attackers.

The software source can be customized for your storage network's IDS monitoring and is provided in Microsoft Visual Basic v.6 format, containing four forms, two modules, and one class module. If VB rubs you the wrong way, check www.TigerTools.net for TigerGuard IDS ports to C++ and Delphi. The current release is available at www.wiley.com/comp-books/chirillo.

Forms

Forms contain the code for the main module, intrusion notification, sniffer, and policy generation utilities. Figure 9-6 illustrates the main form (frmMain) for TigerGuard.

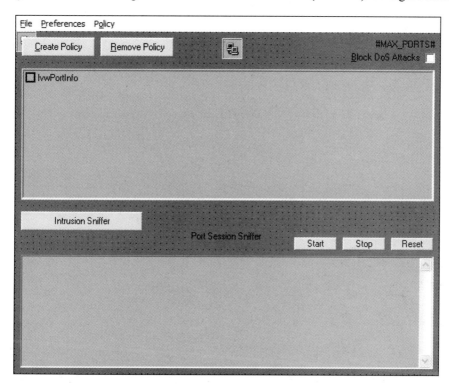

Figure 9-6: TigerGuard main form in VB

```
Dim DaemonPort As String
Dim RxData As String
Dim RMN As String
Dim RIP As String
```

```
Private Sub cmdAddPort_Click()
If lvwPortInfo.ListItems.Count >= MAX_PORTS Then
    MsgBox "You can only add " & MAX_PORTS & " policies!",
vbExclamation, "Error!"
End If
    frmPolicy.Show 1
End Sub

Private Sub Command1_Click()
frmSniffer.Show
End Sub

Private Sub mnuAddPolicy_Click()
If lvwPortInfo.ListItems.Count >= MAX_PORTS Then
    MsgBox "You can only add " & MAX_PORTS & " policies!",
vbExclamation, "Error!"
End If
    frmPolicy.Show 1
End Sub

Private Sub cmdRemove_Click()
If lvwPortInfo.ListItems.Count <> 0 Then
    lvwPortInfo.ListItems.Remove (lvwPortInfo.SelectedItem.Index)
End If
End Sub

Private Sub mnuRemovePolicy_Click()
If lvwPortInfo.ListItems.Count <> 0 Then
    lvwPortInfo.ListItems.Remove (lvwPortInfo.SelectedItem.Index)
End If
End Sub

Private Sub Form_Load()
If DOESINIEXIST = False Then
    MsgBox "The TigerGuard.INI file is missing. Please reload the
applcation.", vbExclamation, "Error"
    Unload Me
    End
End If
LoadINISettings
RefreshDisplay
End Sub

Public Sub RefreshDisplay()
lblMaxPorts = "Maximum Policies Allowed: " & MAX_PORTS
With lvwPortInfo
    .ColumnHeaders(1).Width = 2000
    .ColumnHeaders(2).Width = 700
```

```
      .ColumnHeaders(3).Width = 1400
      .ColumnHeaders(5).Width = 1700
      .ColumnHeaders(6).Width = 800
End With
End Sub


Private Sub Form_QueryUnload(Cancel As Integer, UnloadMode As Integer)
If UnloadMode = 0 Then
End If
End Sub


Private Sub Form_Unload(Cancel As Integer)
If lvwPortInfo.ListItems.Count = 0 Then
Else
For i = 1 To lvwPortInfo.ListItems.Count
    If lvwPortInfo.ListItems(i).Checked = True Then
        sckData(i).Close
        Unload sckData(i)
    End If
Next i
End If
End Sub


Private Sub lvwPortInfo_Click()
    Dim intCurrIndex As Integer
    If lvwPortInfo.ListItems.Count = 0 Then Exit Sub
    intCurrIndex = lvwPortInfo.SelectedItem.Index + 1
End Sub


Private Sub lvwPortInfo_ItemCheck(ByVal Item As MSComctlLib.ListItem)
    Dim intCurrIndex As Integer
    intCurrIndex = Item.Index
    If Item.Checked = True Then
        Load sckData(intCurrIndex)
        sckData(intCurrIndex).LocalPort = Item.SubItems(1)
        On Error GoTo err
        sckData(intCurrIndex).listen
        Item.SubItems(3) = "Enabled"
    Else
        sckData(intCurrIndex).Close
        Unload sckData(intCurrIndex)
        Item.SubItems(3) = "Disabled"
    End If
Exit Sub
err:
    lvwPortInfo.ListItems(intCurrIndex).SubItems(3) = "(" & err.Number & _
") Error!"
    lvwPortInfo.ListItems(intCurrIndex).Checked = False
    sckData(intCurrIndex).Close
```

```
        Unload sckData(intCurrIndex)
End Sub

Private Sub mnuAboutDownload_Click()
    ShellExecute Me.hwnd, "open", UPDATE_ADDRESS, "", "", 1
End Sub

Private Sub mnuAboutWebsite_Click()
    ShellExecute Me.hwnd, "open", WEBSITE_ADDRESS, "", "", 1
End Sub

Private Sub mnuFileExit_Click()
Unload Me
End
End Sub

Private Sub mnuFileLoadList_Click()
    Dim CDLG As New CommonDialog
    Dim strFilename As String
    CDLG.Filter = "Policy List Files (*.lst)|*.lst" & Chr(0)
    strFilename = CDLG.GetFileOpenName
    If Trim(strFilename) = Chr(0) Then Exit Sub
    LoadPortList strFilename
    ValidateList
End Sub

Sub ValidateList()
Dim strTmpText1 As String
Dim strTmpText2 As String
If lvwPortInfo.ListItems.Count <> 0 Then
If lvwPortInfo.ListItems.Count >= MAX_PORTS Then
    GoTo bad_list
Else
    For i = 1 To lvwPortInfo.ListItems.Count
        strTmpText1 = lvwPortInfo.ListItems(i).SubItems(1)
            For x = i + 1 To lvwPortInfo.ListItems.Count
                If lvwPortInfo.ListItems(x).SubItems(1) = strTmpText1
Then
                    GoTo bad_list
                End If
            Next x
    Next i
End If
End If
Exit Sub
bad_list:
    MsgBox "Policy List Corruption." & CR & CR & "This file cannot be
loaded!", vbExclamation, "Error!"
    lvwPortInfo.ListItems.Clear
```

```
End Sub

Private Sub mnuFileOptions_Click()
frmNotify.Show 1
End Sub

Private Sub mnuFileSaveList_Click()
If lvwPortInfo.ListItems.Count <> 0 Then
    Dim CDLG As New CommonDialog
    Dim strFilename As String
    CDLG.Filter = "Policy List Files (*.lst)|*.lst" & Chr(0)
    strFilename = CDLG.GetFileSaveName
    If Trim(strFilename) = Chr(0) Then Exit Sub
    If Right(strFilename, 4) <> ".lst" Then
        strFilename = strFilename & ".lst"
    End If
    SavePortList strFilename
End If
End Sub

Sub SavePortList(strFilename As String)
Dim TmpVal As PORTENTRY
If Dir(strFilename) <> "" Then
    If MsgBox("Overwrite " & strFilename & "?", vbExclamation +
vbOKCancel, "Confirm") = vbOK Then
        Kill strFilename
    Else
        Exit Sub
    End If
End If
For i = 1 To lvwPortInfo.ListItems.Count
TmpVal.PORTNAME = lvwPortInfo.ListItems(i).Text
TmpVal.PORTNUMBER = lvwPortInfo.ListItems(i).SubItems(1)
Open strFilename For Random As #1 Len = Len(TmpVal)
    If LOF(1) = 0 Then
        Put #1, 1, TmpVal
    Else
        Put #1, LOF(1) / Len(TmpVal) + 1, TmpVal
    End If
Close #1
Next i
End Sub

Sub LoadPortList(strFilename As String)
Dim TmpVal As PORTENTRY
lvwPortInfo.ListItems.Clear
Open strFilename For Random As #1 Len = Len(TmpVal)
For i = 1 To LOF(1) / Len(TmpVal)
    Get #1, i, TmpVal
```

```
        lvwPortInfo.ListItems.Add , , Trim(TmpVal.PORTNAME)
    With
frmMain.lvwPortInfo.ListItems(frmMain.lvwPortInfo.ListItems.Count)
        .SubItems(1) = Trim(TmpVal.PORTNUMBER)
        .SubItems(3) = "Disabled"
        .SubItems(4) = "Never"
        .SubItems(5) = "0"
    End With
Next i
Close #1
End Sub


Private Sub sckData_ConnectionRequest(Index As Integer, ByVal requestID
As Long)
Dim intIndex As Integer
intIndex = Index
If chkAntiFlood.Value = vbChecked Then
    If lvwPortInfo.ListItems(intIndex).SubItems(5) = ANTI_FLOOD_COUNT
Then
        Select Case ANTI_FLOOD_ACTION
            Case 1
                GoTo listen
            Case 2
                sckData(intIndex).Close
                lvwPortInfo.ListItems(intIndex).SubItems(3) = "Denial of
Service Warning!"
            Case Else
        End Select
    End If
End If
sckData(intIndex).Close
sckData(intIndex).Accept requestID
If BEEPONCONNECT = "1" Then
    Beep
End If
lvwPortInfo.ListItems(intIndex).SubItems(2) =
sckData(intIndex).RemoteHostIP
lvwPortInfo.ListItems(intIndex).SubItems(3) = "Connecting!"
lvwPortInfo.ListItems(intIndex).SubItems(4) = Format$(Time, "h:m:s") & "
" & Format$(Date, "dd/mm/yyyy")
lvwPortInfo.ListItems(intIndex).SubItems(5) =
lvwPortInfo.ListItems(Index).SubItems(5) + 1
listen:
sckData(intIndex).Close
On Error GoTo err
sckData(intIndex).listen
lvwPortInfo.ListItems(intIndex).SubItems(3) = "Enabled"
Exit Sub
err:
```

```
    lvwPortInfo.ListItems(intIndex).SubItems(3) = "Error!"
    lvwPortInfo.ListItems(intIndex).Checked = False
End Sub


Private Sub lstn_Click()
wsk.Close
DaemonPort = InputBox$("Please enter the Port to monitor:")
If DaemonPort = "" Then Exit Sub
For i = 1 To Len(DaemonPort)
    If Asc(Right$(DaemonPort, i)) < 48 Or Asc(Right$(DaemonPort, i)) >
57 Then
        MsgBox "Please enter in a valid Port number."
        DaemonPort = ""
        Exit Sub
    End If
Next i
wsk.LocalPort = DaemonPort
wsk.listen
Text1.Text = Text1.Text & "Your IP: " & wsk.LocalIP & " Daemon Port: " &
DaemonPort & vbCrLf
End Sub


Private Sub Rset_Click()
wsk.Close
wsk.listen
Text1.Text = Text1.Text & "Daemon Reset" & vbCrLf
End Sub


Private Sub stp_Click()
wsk.Close
Text1.Text = Text1.Text & "Daemon Stoped Listening." & vbCrLf
End Sub


Private Sub Text1_Change()
Text1.SelStart = Len(Text1.Text)
If Len(Text1.Text) > 47775 Then
    Text1.Text = ""
End If
End Sub


Private Sub wsk_Close()
wsk.Close
wsk.listen
Text1.Text = Text1.Text & "Remote Intruder Logged Off, Daemon Reset." &
vbCrLf
End Sub


Private Sub wsk_ConnectionRequest(ByVal requestID As Long)
If wsk.State <> sckClosed Then wsk.Close
```

```
wsk.Accept requestID
RMN = DNS.AddressToName(wsk.RemoteHostIP)
RIP = wsk.RemoteHostIP
Label1.Caption = RMN
RMN = Label1.Caption
Text1.Text = Text1.Text & "Remote Intruder Logged On: " & RMN & "(" &
RIP & ")" & vbCrLf
End Sub


Private Sub wsk_DataArrival(ByVal bytesTotal As Long)
wsk.GetData RxData
Text1.Text = Text1.Text & RxData
End Sub


Private Sub wsk_Error(ByVal Number As Integer, Description As String,
ByVal Scode As Long, ByVal Source As String, ByVal HelpFile As String,
ByVal HelpContext As Long, CancelDisplay As Boolean)
wsk.Close
If DaemonPort <> "" Then
    wsk.LocalPort = DaemonPort
    wsk.listen
End If
Text1.Text = Text1.Text & "Winsock Error: " & Number & ": " &
Description & vbCrLf
Text1.Text = Text1.Text & "Daemon was reset." & vbCrLf
End Sub
```

Figure 9-7 illustrates the notification form (frmNotify) from which you can control alarm and incident response action.

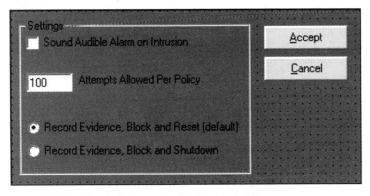

Figure 9-7: TigerGuard alerting and notification form in VB

```
Private Sub chkBeep_Click()
Dim strINIFILE As String
strINIFILE = APPPATH & INIFILE
    If chkBeep.Value = vbChecked Then
        WriteINI strINIFILE, "GENERAL", "BEEP", "1"
    Else
        WriteINI strINIFILE, "GENERAL", "BEEP", "0"
    End If
End Sub

Private Sub cmdCancel_Click()
    Unload Me
End Sub

Private Sub cmdOk_Click()
    ANTI_FLOOD_COUNT = txtConnectTimes
    SaveINISettings
    Unload Me
End Sub

Private Sub Form_Load()
Me.Icon = frmMain.Icon
txtConnectTimes = ANTI_FLOOD_COUNT
Select Case ANTI_FLOOD_ACTION
    Case 1
        optResetPort.Value = True
    Case 2
        optShutPort.Value = True
    Case Else
End Select
End Sub

Private Sub optResetPort_Click()
    ANTI_FLOOD_ACTION = 1
End Sub

Private Sub optShutPort_Click()
    ANTI_FLOOD_ACTION = 2
End Sub
```

Figure 9-8 represents the internal policy creation form (frmPolicy) used to assign access control to ports and their services.

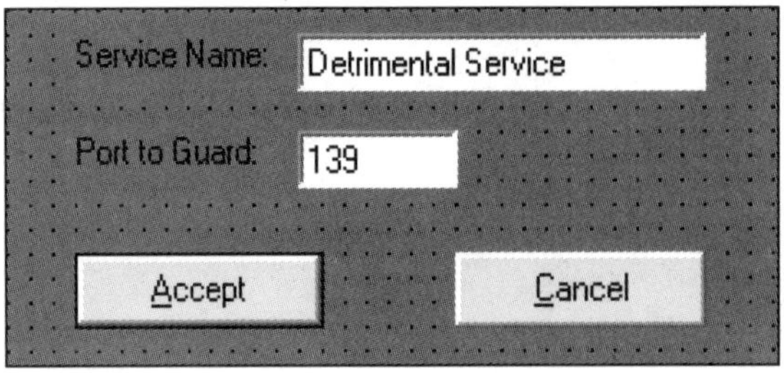

Figure 9-8: TigerGuard policy creation form in VB

```
Private Sub Cancel_Click()
Unload Me
End Sub

Private Sub cmdOk_Click()
If txtPortNumber <> "" Then
    If IsNumeric(txtPortNumber) = True Then
        If txtPortNumber >= 1 Then
            If PortExists = False Then
                If txtPortName = "" Then
                    frmMain.lvwPortInfo.ListItems.Add , ,
txtPortNumber
                Else
                    frmMain.lvwPortInfo.ListItems.Add , ,
txtPortName
                End If
            With
frmMain.lvwPortInfo.ListItems(frmMain.lvwPortInfo.ListItems.Count)
                    .SubItems(1) = txtPortNumber
                    .SubItems(3) = "Disabled"
                    .SubItems(4) = "Never"
                    .SubItems(5) = "0"
            End With
            Else
                Exit Sub
            End If
        Else
            GoTo bad_port
        End If
    Else
        GoTo bad_port
    End If
Else
    GoTo bad_port
End If
Unload Me
```

```
Exit Sub
bad_port:
   MsgBox "You must enter a valid port number to continue!",
vbExclamation, "Error!"
End Sub

Function PortExists() As Boolean
Dim i As Integer
For i = 1 To frmMain.lvwPortInfo.ListItems.Count
   If frmMain.lvwPortInfo.ListItems(i).SubItems(1) = txtPortNumber Then
       MsgBox "That port is already guarded!", vbExclamation, "Error!"
       PortExists = True
       Exit Function
   End If
Next i
PortExists = False
End Function

Private Sub Form_Load()
Me.Icon = frmMain.Icon
End Sub

Private Sub txtPortName_GotFocus()
txtPortName.SelStart = 0
txtPortName.SelLength = Len(txtPortName)
End Sub

Private Sub txtPortNumber_GotFocus()
txtPortNumber.SelStart = 0
txtPortNumber.SelLength = Len(txtPortNumber)
End Sub
```

Figure 9-9 contains the form associated with the intrusion sniffer (frmSniffer). The sniffer
supports both UDP and TCP conversations.

```
Private Sub cmdListen_Click()
Select Case cmdListen.Caption
Case Is = "Listen"
  If opTCP.Value Then
    Inet.Protocol = sckTCPProtocol
    Inet2.Protocol = sckTCPProtocol
    Inet.LocalPort = CInt(txtLocalPort.Text)
    Inet.RemoteHost = txtRemoteIP.Text
    Inet.RemotePort = CInt(txtRemotePort.Text)
    txtLocalPort.Enabled = False
    txtRemoteIP.Enabled = False
    txtRemotePort.Enabled = False
    cmdListen.Caption = "Reset"
```

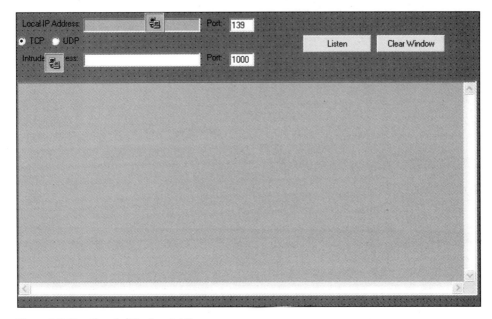

Figure 9-9: TigerGuard sniffer form in VB

```
    Inet.Close
    Inet.listen
    log "I>Capturing TCP traffic on " & Inet.LocalIP & ":" &
Inet.LocalPort
  Else
    Inet.Close
    Inet2.Close
    Inet.Protocol = sckUDPProtocol
    Inet2.Protocol = sckUDPProtocol
    Inet.LocalPort = CInt(txtLocalPort.Text)
    Inet2.RemoteHost = txtRemoteIP.Text
    Inet2.RemotePort = CInt(txtRemotePort.Text)
    txtLocalPort.Enabled = False
    txtRemoteIP.Enabled = False
    txtRemotePort.Enabled = False
    cmdListen.Caption = "Reset"
    Inet.Bind CInt(txtLocalPort.Text)
    log "I>Capturing UDP traffic on " & Inet.LocalIP & ":" &
Inet.LocalPort
  End If
Case Is = "Reset"
  Inet.Close
  txtLocalPort.Enabled = True
  txtRemoteIP.Enabled = True
  txtRemotePort.Enabled = True
```

```
  cmdListen.Caption = "Listen"
End Select
End Sub

Private Sub Command1_Click()
txtLog.Text = ""
End Sub

Private Sub Form_Load()
txtLocalIP.Text = Inet.LocalIP
End Sub

Private Sub Form_Resize()
If Not Me.WindowState = vbMinimized Then
  txtLog.Width = Me.ScaleWidth
  txtLog.Height = Me.Height - 850
End If
End Sub

Private Sub Inet_Close()
log "I>INET EVENT: CLOSED CONNECTION"
Inet2.Close
cmdListen_Click
cmdListen_Click
End Sub

Private Sub Inet_Connect()
log "I>INET EVENT: CONNECT"
End Sub

Private Sub Inet_ConnectionRequest(ByVal requestID As Long)
log "I>INET EVENT: CONNECTION REQUEST [ " & requestID & " ]"
If Inet.State <> sckClosed Then Inet.Close
log "I>CONNECTING 0 TO " & txtRemoteIP.Text & ":" &
CInt(txtRemotePort.Text)
Inet2.Close
Inet2.Connect txtRemoteIP.Text, CInt(txtRemotePort.Text)
Do Until Inet2.State = sckConnected
  DoEvents
Loop
Inet.Accept requestID
End Sub

Private Sub Inet_DataArrival(ByVal bytesTotal As Long)
Dim sData As String
Dim bData() As Byte
If opTCP.Value Then
  Inet.PeekData sData, vbString
  Inet.GetData bData(), vbArray + vbByte
```

```
    Inet2.SendData bData()
Else
  Inet.GetData sData
  Inet2.SendData sData
End If
log "I>" & sData
Exit Sub
erred:
Inet.Close
Inet2.Close
cmdListen_Click
cmdListen_Click
End Sub

Private Sub Inet_Error(ByVal Number As Integer, Description As String,
ByVal Scode As Long, ByVal Source As String, ByVal HelpFile As String,
ByVal HelpContext As Long, CancelDisplay As Boolean)
log "I>INET ERROR: " & Number & " = " & Description
End Sub

Public Sub log(Text As String)
On Error GoTo erred
txtLog.Text = txtLog.Text & Text & vbCrLf
txtLog.SelStart = Len(txtLog.Text)
Exit Sub
erred:
txtLog.Text = ""
txtLog.Text = txtLog.Text & Text & vbCrLf
txtLog.SelStart = Len(txtLog.Text)
End Sub

Private Sub Inet2_Close()
log "0>INET EVENT: CLOSED CONNECTION"
Inet.Close
cmdListen_Click
cmdListen_Click
End Sub

Private Sub Inet2_DataArrival(ByVal bytesTotal As Long)
On Error GoTo erred
Dim sData As String
Dim bData2() As Byte
If opTCP.Value Then
  Inet2.PeekData sData, vbString
  Inet2.GetData bData2(), vbArray + vbByte
  Inet.SendData bData2()
Else
  Inet2.GetData sData
  Inet.SendData sData
```

```
End If
log "O>" & sData
Exit Sub
erred:
Inet.Close
Inet2.Close
cmdListen_Click
cmdListen_Click
End Sub

Private Sub Inet2_Error(ByVal Number As Integer, Description As String,
ByVal Scode As Long, ByVal Source As String, ByVal HelpFile As String,
ByVal HelpContext As Long, CancelDisplay As Boolean)
log "O>INET ERROR: " & Number & " = " & Description
End Sub

Private Sub txtLocalPort_Change()
txtRemotePort.Text = txtLocalPort.Text
End Sub
```

Modules

Modules include the global functions, initialization file constants, and kernel standards for the suite. Following is the modGeneral module.

```
Public Declare Function ShellExecute Lib "shell32.dll" Alias
"ShellExecuteA" (ByVal hwnd As Long, ByVal lpOperation As String, ByVal
lpFile As String, ByVal lpParameters As String, ByVal lpDirectory As
String, ByVal nShowCmd As Long) As Long
Public Const INIFILE = "TIGERGUARD.INI"
Public Const CR = vbCrLf
Public MAX_PORTS As Integer
Public ANTI_FLOOD_COUNT As Integer
Public ANTI_FLOOD_ACTION As Integer
Public BEEPONCONNECT As String * 1
Public Type PORTENTRY
    PORTNAME As String * 255
    PORTNUMBER As Long
End Type

Public Function APPPATH() As String
If Right(App.Path, 1) <> "\" Then
    APPPATH = App.Path & "\"
Else
    APPPATH = App.Path
End If
End Function

Public Function DOESINIEXIST() As Boolean
If Dir(APPPATH & INIFILE) = "" Then
```

```
        DOESINIEXIST = False
Else
        DOESINIEXIST = True
End If
End Function


Public Sub LoadINISettings()
Dim strTempVal As String
strTempVal = ReadINI(APPPATH & INIFILE, "GENERAL", "MAXPORTS")
If strTempVal <> "" Then
    If IsNumeric(strTempVal) = True Then
        If strTempVal >= 1 Then
            MAX_PORTS = strTempVal
            GoTo INIVAL2
        Else
            GoTo bad_max_port
        End If
        GoTo bad_max_port
    End If
    GoTo bad_max_port
End If
INIVAL2:
strTempVal = ReadINI(APPPATH & INIFILE, "GENERAL", "ANTIFLOODCOUNT")
If strTempVal <> "" Then
    If IsNumeric(strTempVal) = True Then
        If strTempVal >= 1 Then
            ANTI_FLOOD_COUNT = strTempVal
            GoTo INIVAL3
        Else
            GoTo bad_flood_count
        End If
        GoTo bad_flood_count
    End If
    GoTo bad_flood_count
End If
INIVAL3:
strTempVal = ReadINI(APPPATH & INIFILE, "GENERAL", "ANTIFLOODACTION")
If strTempVal <> "" Then
    If IsNumeric(strTempVal) = True Then
        If strTempVal >= 1 Then
            ANTI_FLOOD_ACTION = strTempVal
            Exit Sub
        Else
            GoTo bad_flood_count
        End If
        GoTo bad_flood_count
    End If
    GoTo bad_flood_count
End If
```

```
BEEPONCONNECT = ReadINI(APPPATH & INIFILE, "GENERAL", "BEEP")
Exit Sub
bad_max_port:
    MsgBox "Invalid Maximum Policies entry in INI file. Please re-
install." & CR & CR & "Using Default of 40", vbExclamation, "Error!"
    MAX_PORTS = 40
    Exit Sub
bad_flood_count:
    MsgBox "Invalid Denial of Service in INI file. Please re-install." &
CR & CR & "Using Default of 100", vbExclamation, "Error!"
    ANTI_FLOOD_COUNT = 100
    Exit Sub
bad_flood_action:
    MsgBox "Invalid Denial of Service entry in INI file. Please re-
install." & CR & CR & "Using default (Reset Port)", vbExclamation,
"Error!"
    ANTI_FLOOD_ACTION = 1
    Exit Sub
End Sub

Public Sub SaveINISettings()
Dim strINIFILE As String
Dim strTmpVal As String
strINIFILE = APPPATH & INIFILE
strTmpVal = MAX_PORTS
WriteINI strINIFILE, "GENERAL", "MAXPORTS", strTmpVal
strTmpVal = ANTI_FLOOD_ACTION
WriteINI strINIFILE, "GENERAL", "AntiFloodAction", strTmpVal
strTmpVal = ANTI_FLOOD_COUNT
WriteINI strINIFILE, "GENERAL", "AntiFloodCount", strTmpVal
If frmMain.chkAntiFlood.Value = vbChecked Then
    WriteINI strINIFILE, "GENERAL", "AntiFloodEnable", "1"
Else
    WriteINI strINIFILE, "GENERAL", "AntiFloodEnable", "0"
End If
End Sub
```

Following is the modINI_Access module.

```
Declare Function WritePrivateProfileString Lib "kernel32" Alias
"WritePrivateProfileStringA" (ByVal lpApplicationName As String, ByVal
lpKeyName As Any, ByVal lpString As Any, ByVal lpFileName As String) As
Long
Declare Function GetPrivateProfileString Lib "kernel32" Alias
"GetPrivateProfileStringA" (ByVal lpApplicationName As String, ByVal
lpKeyName As Any, ByVal lpDefault As String, ByVal lpReturnedString As
String, ByVal nSize As Long, ByVal lpFileName As String) As Long
Public Ret As String
```

```
Public Sub WriteINI(Filename As String, Section As String, Key As
String, Text As String)
WritePrivateProfileString Section, Key, Text, Filename
End Sub

Public Function ReadINI(Filename As String, Section As String, Key As
String)
Ret = Space$(255)
RetLen = GetPrivateProfileString(Section, Key, "", Ret, Len(Ret),
Filename)
Ret = Left$(Ret, RetLen)
ReadINI = Ret
End Function
```

Following is the CommonDialog (Class Module) module.

```
Private Declare Function GetSaveFileName Lib "comdlg32.dll" Alias
"GetSaveFileNameA" (pOpenfilename As OPENFILENAME) As Long
Private Declare Function GetOpenFileName Lib "comdlg32.dll" Alias
"GetOpenFileNameA" (pOpenfilename As OPENFILENAME) As Long
Private Filename As OPENFILENAME
Private Type OPENFILENAME
        lStructSize As Long
        hwndOwner As Long
        hInstance As Long
        lpstrFilter As String
        lpstrCustomFilter As String
        nMaxCustFilter As Long
        nFilterIndex As Long
        lpstrFile As String
        nMaxFile As Long
        lpstrFileTitle As String
        nMaxFileTitle As Long
        lpstrInitialDir As String
        lpstrTitle As String
        flags As Long
        nFileOffset As Integer
        nFileExtension As Integer
        lpstrDefExt As String
        lCustData As Long
        lpfnHook As Long
        lpTemplateName As String
End Type

Public Property Let DefaultExtension(Extention As String)
    Filename.lpstrDefExt = Extention
End Property

Public Property Get DefaultExtension() As String
```

```
        DefaultExtension = Filename.lpstrDefExt
End Property

Public Property Let ObjectOwner(Objet As Object)
    Filename.hwndOwner = Objet.hwnd
End Property

Public Property Let Filter(CustomFilter As String)
    Dim intCount As Integer
    Filename.lpstrFilter = ""
    For intCount = 1 To Len(CustomFilter)
        If Mid(CustomFilter, intCount, 1) = "|" Then
Filename.lpstrFilter = Filename.lpstrFilter + Chr(0) Else
Filename.lpstrFilter = Filename.lpstrFilter + Mid(CustomFilter,
intCount, 1)
    Next intCount
    Filename.lpstrFilter = Filename.lpstrFilter + Chr(0)
End Property

Public Property Let WindowTitle(Title As String)
    Filename.lpstrTitle = Title
End Property

Public Property Get WindowTitle() As String
    WindowTitle = Filename.lpstrTitle
End Property

Public Property Let InitialDirectory(InitDir As String)
    Filename.lpstrInitialDir = InitDir
End Property

Public Property Let DefaultFilename(strFilename As String)
    Filename.lpstrFileTitle = strFilename
End Property

Public Property Get DefaultFilename() As String
    DefaultFilename = Filename.lpstrFileTitle
End Property

Public Property Get InitialDirectory() As String
    InitialDirectory = Filename.lpstrInitialDir
End Property

Public Function GetFileOpenName(Optional Multiselect As Boolean = False)
As String
    Filename.hInstance = App.hInstance
    Filename.hwndOwner = hwnd
    Filename.lpstrFile = Chr(0) & Space(259)
    Filename.lpstrFileTitle = Filename.lpstrFileTitle
```

```
    Filename.nMaxFile = 260
    If Multiselect Then Filename.flags = &H80000 Or &H4 Or &H200 Else
Filename.flags = &H80000 Or &H4
    Filename.lStructSize = Len(Filename)
    GetOpenFileName Filename
    GetFileOpenName = Filename.lpstrFile
End Function

Public Function GetFileSaveName() As String
    Filename.hInstance = App.hInstance
    Filename.hwndOwner = hwnd
    Filename.lpstrFile = Chr(0) & Space(259)
    Filename.nMaxFile = 260
    Filename.flags = &H80000 Or &H4
    Filename.lStructSize = Len(Filename)
    GetSaveFileName Filename
    GetFileSaveName = Filename.lpstrFile
End Function

Public Function Count() As Integer
    Dim intCount As Integer
    For intCount = 1 To Trim(Len(Filename.lpstrFile))
        If Mid(Trim(Filename.lpstrFile), intCount, 1) = Chr(0) Then
Count = Count + 1
    Next intCount
    Count = Count - 2
    If Count < 1 Then Count = Count + 1
End Function

Public Function GetMultiFilename(Filenumber As Integer) As String
    Dim intCount As Integer
    Dim intOne As Integer
    Dim intFile As Integer
    Dim intNext As Integer
    intOne = InStr(1, Trim(Filename.lpstrFile), Chr(0))
    intFile = 1
    For intCount = 1 To Filenumber
        intFile = InStr(intFile + 1, Trim(Filename.lpstrFile), Chr(0))
    Next intCount
    intNext = InStr(intFile + 1, Trim(Filename.lpstrFile), Chr(0))
    GetMultiFilename = IIf(Right(Mid(Trim(Filename.lpstrFile), 1, intOne
- 1), 1) = "\", Mid(Trim(Filename.lpstrFile), 1, intOne - 1),
Mid(Trim(Filename.lpstrFile), 1, intOne - 1) + "\") +
Mid(Trim(Filename.lpstrFile), intFile + 1, intNext - intFile - 1)
    If Right(GetMultiFilename, 1) = "\" Then GetMultiFilename =
Left(GetMultiFilename, Len(GetMultiFilename) - 1)
End Function
```

What's Next

You've now built a testing system to perform security audits both locally and remotely—especially targeting the most exploited areas of your storage network—and then looked at ways to monitor potential intrusions. So what's next?

In addition to the recommended solutions in this chapter, we strongly advise a regularly scheduled third-party remote security examination. The analysis should be designed to map out and audit IP filters, firewalls, routers, and other obstacles, and probe for weaknesses using these module types:

- Network Discovery
- Port scanning
- FTP
- HTTP
- Web CGI
- BackDoor
- Mail-POP/SMTP
- Network File System (NFS)
- Protocol spoofing
- Data hijacking
- Flooding
- Packet stress, malformed
- Firewalls, filters, and proxies
- Remote services
- SMB/NetBIOS
- DNS, NIS, and bind
- Intrusion detection systems
- Password guessing, brute-force, cracking
- Denial-of-Service (DoS) attacks

In addition, a patch implementation schedule is recommended to keep you abreast of future vulnerabilities and advisories—every month. If you do not have the resources to implement such a system, you should at the very least receive these notices via e-mail. You can subscribe to the TigerTools.net monthly newsletter for FREE at this Web site: www.TigerTools.net/monthly.htm.

Finally, be sure to check the companion Web sites to this text for additional material, papers, informative articles, tools, matrices, and spreadsheets: `www.wiley.com/compbooks/chirillo`, `www.TigerTools.net`, and `www.InfoTress.com`.

Review

Throughout the course of this book, we discussed the general differences between DAS, NAS, and SAN and applied general terms to each in an effort to create baseline comprehension. You were introduced to the term *ripple security logic* and its union with the Ten Domains of Computer Security and layered security.

You learned about the differences DAS, NAS, and SAN technologies can have on overall security and evaluated each of them using basic criteria from forms and schemes that can be built upon to encompass all of your technology assessment criteria. You have also been given some valuable product information and matrixes for your security toolkit and specific guidelines to build a secure foundation—whether it be a natural or hybrid storage infrastructure.

You looked at keys to infrastructure, application, data availability, and storage security, including capacity planning, access methods, fault mitigation, disaster mitigation, duplication, management, monitoring, support, and data protection. We gave you a road map to help you recognize your existing network, document current applications, protocols, topology, number of users, and business issues, and then assess the health of the existing network and its ability to support growing storage needs with a needs analysis.

With all the information provided, critical steps were identified to build a sound storage security program using both common criteria and solution-specific criteria. Using these steps and ripple security logic, you learned how two different case study environments could be made more secure by taking an inward-out and outward-in look from each device.

Finally, you were taken step by step through general procedures for building a testing system to perform security audits against your storage networks—both locally and remotely—targeting the most exploited areas. Different ways to monitor intrusions were then discussed.

Remember, the landscape of security is ever-changing—you must adapt with it. New and more dangerous hacks, vulnerabilities, viruses, Trojans, DoS attacks, and other exploits continue to pop up just when you think you've got everything under control. It is important to continually keep abreast of new security methods. Using a sound philosophy like ripple security logic can go a long way toward ensuring that goal.

Appendix A
What's on the Web Site

The companion Web site to this book contains supplementary materials, papers, tools, and matrix spreadsheets. You'll find it by pointing your browser to `www.wiley.com/compbooks/chirillo`.

Matrices

A technology security matrix can be used to evaluate each DAS, NAS, and SAN technology. You can download our own compilation matrices from the companion Web site and modify them to suit your environment. We recommend using this outside of the performance evaluation criteria to gain a good understanding of which technology makes the most sense from a security perspective. Because the components of a certain technology may not apply across technology boundaries, the scope of the technology security matrix should be limited to the type of technology being evaluated. It is also important to understand components of the data to be protected.

We've also designed a selection matrix to help you determine which type of solution or solutions best fit your storage requirements as they are entered into the matrix. This matrix can also be downloaded from the companion Web site. Note that it is not meant to encompass every possible scenario; rather, it should be viewed as a solid foundation on which to build your own evaluation criteria.

> **NOTE:** The matrix spreadsheets require Microsoft Excel with macros enabled. For more information on macros and safety measures, visit `http://search.office.microsoft.com/result.aspx?qu=macro`.

Advanced Custom Auditing

The companion Web site contains two documents: *How to write a security test in C* and *How to write a security test in NASL*. These documents provide advanced instructions for customizing security audits with the Nessus vulnerability scanner.

TigerGuard IDS Software and Other Devices

TigerGuard IDS is a custom port blocker and watcher in an IDS-style kernel to use at your discretion. The source can be customized for your storage network's IDS monitoring, and is available from the companion Web site (`www.wiley.com/compbooks/chirillo`), `www.TigerTools.net/ids`, or `www.InfoTRESS.com`.

> **NOTE:** The TigerGuard IDS source code is provided in Microsoft Visual Basic v.6 format, containing four forms, two modules, and one class module. Check `www.TigerTools.net/ids` for future ports to C++ and Delphi.

Other IDS devices and services

The companion Web site contains links for other IDS devices and services, including a repository of the following most popular systems: AAFID, ACME!, ADS, AFJ, AID, AIMS, ALERT-PLUS, ALVA, APA, ARMD, ARMOR, ASAX, ASIM, AudES, BlackICE, Bro, Centrax, CERN-NSM, Cisco Secure IDS, CMDS, ComputerWatch, CSM, CyberCop Monitor, CyberTrace, DEC, DIDS, Discovery, DPEM, Dragon, DRISC, EASEL, EMERALD, ERIDS, ESSENSE, eTrust ID, FW-1 specific NID, GASSATA, GrIDS, Haystack, HAXOR, Hummer, Hyperview, IDA(1), IDA(2), IDA(3), IDEAS, IDES, IDIOT, ID-Trak, Inspect, INTOUCH INSA, ISM, ISOA, ITA, JiNao, KSE, KSM, MIDAS, MIDS, NADIR, NAURS, NetProwler, NetStalker, NetSTAT, NFR, NID, NIDAR, NIDES, NIDX, NSM, PDAT, PRéCis, Proxy-Stalker, POLYCENTER Security ID, RealSecure, RETISS, RID, SecureNet PRO, Secure-Switch, SHADOW, SIDS, Snort, Stake Out, Stalker, TIM, Tivoli Cross-Site for Security, T-sight, UNICORN, USTAT, VisionIDS, WebStalker, and W&S.

Appendix B
Useful Resources

This appendix contains a current repository of useful resources for all things storage-related. The information outlined here is subject to change without notice and is provided "as is" without warranty of any kind. We do not endorse the products, services, or resources listed, and product names mentioned herein may be trademarks and/or registered trademarks of their respective companies. In this appendix, you'll find resources and contact information for access control and management; encryption; firewalling; intrusion detection systems, software, and services; magazines and news, search engines, storage network software, virus control, and storage network white papers.

Access Control and Management

Company	Product	Web Site/Contact E-Mail
Aladdin Knowledge Systems	ASE	sales@aks.com
Anyware Technology	EverLink Suite, ver. 1.03	sales@anywaretechnology.com
Archsoft, Ltd.	S to Infinity	sales@opens.com
Ascend Communications	Access Control	info@ascend.com
Aventail Corporation	Aventail VPN	info@aventail.com
AXENT Technologies	Defender	info@axent.com
	Enterprise Resource Manager	info@axent.com
	PCShield	info@axent.com
	Web Defender	info@axent.com
Baltimore Technologies	PKI=PLUS	info@baltimore.ie
	UniCERT	info@baltimore.ie
BorderWare Technologies	SafeWord Solutions	info@borderware.com

Company	Product	Web Site/Contact E-Mail
BrainTree Security Software, Inc.	IntraSecure	info@bti.com
Cisco Systems	PIX Firewall	cs-rep@cisco.com
CKS	CKS MyNet	lab@cksna.com
Communication Devices	MultiGuard	info@commdevices.com
	PC-Token, WinGuard	info@commdevices.com
	UnGuard	info@commdevices.com
Cryptocard	RB-1 Token	info@cryptocard.com
	ST-1 Soft Token	info@cryptocard.com
CyberSafe	TrustBroker Client	info@cybersafe.com
	TrustBroker Security SDK	info@cybersafe.com
	TrustBroker Web Agent	info@cybersafe.com
e.g. Software	AlertTrack	sales@webtrends.com
	SmartPass	sales@webtrends.com
enCommerce, Inc.	getAccess	sales@encommerce.com
Ensure Technologies	XyLoc	info@ensuretech.com
FirstAccess	FirstAccess Authentication Suite	info@access-1.com
	FirstAccess Enterprise	info@access-1.com
Frontier Technologies	E-Lock e-Cert	info@frontiertech.com
Gradient Technologies	NetCrusader	info@gradient.com
HIS Software AG, Switzerland	Proxima Single-Sign-On	sales@hissoft.ch
IC Engineering	Modem Security Enforcer	Info@ICEngineering.com
Internet Dynamics	Conclave	sales@interdyn.com
Intrusion Detection	Kane Security Analyst	info@intrusion.com
	Kane Security Monitor	info@intrusion.com
JSA Technologies, Inc.	JSA/Proxy	info@jsatech.com
Knozall Systems	FileAuditor	sales@knozall.com

Company	Product	Web Site/Contact E-Mail
LeeMah DataCom	InfoKey and InfoCard II	info@leemah.com
	SafeConnect	info@leemah.com
	TraqNet 2000 Series	info@leemah.com
	TraqNet 8000 SafeAccess Server	info@leemah.com
MEMCO Software	SeOS (Security for Open Systems)	info@memco.com
Microsystems Software	Cyber Patrol	info@microsys.com
Milkyway Network	SecurIT ACCESS	sales@milkyway.com
NeTegrity	SiteMinder	sales@netegrity.com
NetPartners Internet Solutions	WebSENSE Internet Screening System	sales@netpart.com
Network General	CyberCopVisibility	sales@ngc.com
Network Information Technology	UniShield for UNIX/Windows NT	sales@nit.com
Network-1 Software & Technology, Inc.	Access/Plus for NT— Server Version	sales@network-1.com
ON Technology Corp.	ON Guard Address Translation	info@on.com
Paralon Technologies	PathKey Remote Access Server	info@paralon.com
Raptor Systems (a division of AXENT Technologies)	EagleMobile	info@raptor.com
	EagleMobile Pro	info@raptor.com
SAC Technologies	SACcat	tdorner@sacman.com
	SACman	tdorner@sacman.com
SAGUS Security	Defensor Client	info@sagus-security.com
	Defensor Mainframe	info@sagus-security.com
	Defensor Server	info@sagus-security.com
Schumann Security Software	Security Administration Manager (SAM)	info@schumannsoftware.com

Company	Product	Web Site/Contact E-Mail
SECANT Network Technologies	CellCase45—Encryption hardware for ATM networks	info@secantnet.com
	CellCase155—Multimode Encryption hardware for ATM networks	info@secantnet.com
	CellCase155—Single Mode Encryption hardware for ATM networks	info@secantnet.com
Security Dynamics Technologies	ACE/Server 3.0	webmaster@securitydynamics.com
	ACE/Server Access Manager	webmaster@securitydynamics.com
Shiva Corp.	Shiva Access Manager	sales@shiva.com
Snare Networks	SnareNet VPN	info@snare.com
Sun Microsystems	Sun Security Manager	tony.lo@corp.sun.com
tummy.com, Ltd.	radiusContext	info@tummy.com
Unisys	Single Port Security	ssdnct@mv.unisys.com
V-ONE Corporation	SmartGate	sales@v-one.com
	SmartWall	sales@v-one.com
VASCO Data Security	Digipass 300 Authentication Token	info@vasco.com
Veritas	Authorize	vx-sales@veritas.com

Encryption

Company	Product	Web Site/Contact E-Mail
Absolute Software	CompuTrace	info@absolute.com
Advanced Encryption Technology	AccessDenied Disk Encryption with Smartcard	sales@aeti.com
Anyware Technology	EverLink Suite, version 1.03	sales@anywaretechnology.com
Archsoft, Ltd.	S to Infinity	sales@opens.com

Company	*Product*	*Web Site/Contact E-Mail*
AXENT Technologies	PCShield	info@axent.com
Baltimore Technologies	CST	info@baltimore.ie
	CST for Visual Basic	info@baltimore.ie
	J/CRYPTO v.2.0	info@baltimore.ie
	J/SSL	info@baltimore.ie
	MailSecure	info@baltimore.ie
	Secure Messaging Toolkit	info@baltimore.ie
	UniCERT	info@baltimore.ie
	Websecure	info@baltimore.ie
Celotek Corporation	CellCase Cryptographic Systems	info@celotek.com
Cettlan, Inc.	PortMarshal Encryption System	info@cettlan.com
	PortMarshal EncryptorPak	info@cettlan.com
Cylink Corp.	Cylink ATM Encryptor	info@cylink.com
	Cylink Frame Encryptor	info@cylink.com
	Cylink Link Encryptor	info@cylink.com
	NetHawk	info@cylink.com
	Privacy Manager	info@cylink.com
Digital Link Corporation	Semaphore NEU-HSST	info@dl.com
	Semaphore NEU-ST	info@dl.com
EMD Worldwide	EMD Armor 97	sales@emdent.com
	EMD Disk Armor NT	sales@emdent.com
	EMD Encryptor	sales@emdent.com
	EMD Mail Armor	sales@emdent.com
Entrust Technologies	Entrust	entrust@entrust.com
	Entrust/ICE	entrust@entrust.com
	Entrust/Solo	entrust@entrust.com

Company	Product	Web Site/Contact E-Mail
Gradient Technologies	NetCrusader	info@gradient.com
InfoExpress	VTCP/Secure	sales@infoexpress.com
Information Resource Engineering, Inc.	SafeNet/VPN	info@ire.com
Internet Devices	Fort Knox Policy Router	info@internetdevices.com
Isolation Systems	InfoCrypt Enterprise	sales@isolation.com
	InfoCrypt Solo	sales@isolation.com
McAfee	NetCrypto	support@mcafee.com
	PC Crypto	support@mcafee.com
Milkyway Network Corp.	SecurIT ACCESS	sales@milkyway.com
nCipher, Inc.	nFast	sales@ncipher.com
O'Reilly Software	Java Cryptography	software@oreilly.com
ODS Networks	CryptoCom VPN	info@ods.com
Osicom Technologies	FPX4802/DES FRAME RELAY ENCRYPTOR	info@osicom.com
Paralon Technologies	PathKey Domain Series	info@paralon.com
	PathKey DS-Client/PCS	info@paralon.com
	PathKey Series	info@paralon.com
PC Guardian	Encryption Plus for CD-ROMs	pcg@pcguardianmail.com
	Encryption Plus for E-Mail	pcg@pcguardianmail.com
	Encryption Plus for Hard Disks/ Notebooks/PCs	pcg@pcguardianmail.com
	Encryption Plus for Zip Drives	pcg@pcguardianmail.com
	Encryption Plus Lite	pcg@pcguardianmail.com
Pearl Software, Inc.	Private-I—E-Mail Encryption	judyfh@pearlsw.com
Radguard	CryptoWall	info@radguard.com

Company	Product	Web Site/Contact E-Mail
	NetCryptor	info@radguard.com
Rainbow Technologies Internet Security Group	CryptoSwift	cryptoswift@rainbow.com
	CryptoSwift/EN	cryptoswift@rainbow.com
SAGUS Security	Defensor Gateway	info@sagus-security.com
SECANT Network Technologies	CellCase45— Encryption hardware for ATM networks	info@secantnet.com
	CellCase155— Multimode Encryption hardware for ATM networks	info@secantnet.com
	CellCase155—Single Mode Encryption hardware for ATM networks	info@secantnet.com
Security Dynamics Technologies	RSA SecurPC 2.0	webmaster@securitydynamics.com
Signal 9 Solutions	ConSeal Tunnel	sales@signal9.com
Snare Networks Corp.	SnareNet, SnareNet Gold	info@snare.com
Sun Microsystems	Sunscreen Skip	tony.lo@corp.sun.com
Symantec Corporation	Norton Your Eyes Only	webmaster@symantec.com
V-ONE Corporation	SmartPass	sales@v-one.com
Veritas	Authenticate	vx-sales@veritas.com

Firewalling

Company	Product	Web Site/Contact E-Mail
AbirNet	SessionWall-3	sales@abirnet.com
Advanced Computer Research	Secure4U	info@acrmain.com
Altavista Software	Altavista Firewall 97	altavista-sales@altavista.digital.com
ANS Communications	InterLock	info@ans.net

Company	Product	Web Site/Contact E-Mail
Ascend Communications	Secure Access Firewall	info@ascend.com
Atlantic Systems Group	Turnstyle Firewall	sales@asg.unb.ca
ATronics International (ATI)	Internet Anywhere	tony@atronics.com
AXENT Technologies	Raptor Firewall	info@axent.com
BorderWare Technologies	BorderWare Firewall Server	info@borderware.com
	Secure Computing Firewall	info@borderware.com
	SecureZone	info@borderware.com
Check Point Software Technologies	Check Point FireWall-1	info@checkpoint.com
Cisco Systems	PIX Firewall	cs-rep@cisco.com
Computer Associates	eTrust Firewall	info@ca.com
CyberGuard Corporation	CyberGuard Firewall	info@cyberguard.com
Elron Software	CommandView Internet Manager	rzamagni@elronsoftware.com
eSafe Technologies	ViruSafe FireWall	sales@us.esafe.com
Finjan, Inc.	SurfinGate	info@finjan.com
Fortress Technologies	NetFortress He@tSeeker Pro	info@fortresstech.com
Galea Network Security	Avertis	info@galea.com
GearSource	Guardian Firewall	sales@gearsource.com
Global Internet Software Group	Centri Bronze	info@gi.net
	Centri Silver	info@gi.net
HIS Software AG, Switzerland	CheckPoint FireWall-1	sales@hissoft.ch
IC Engineering	Modem Security Enforcer	Info@ICEngineering.Com
Innosoft International	Innosoft LDAP Proxy Server (ILPS)	sales@innosoft.com
Interlink Computer Sciences	NetLOCK	info@interlink.com

Company	Product	Web Site/Contact E-Mail
International Transware	InterTalk MP	sales@transware.com
Internet Devices	Fort Knox Policy Router	info@internetdevices.com
Internet Dynamics	Conclave	sales@interdyn.com
Isolation Systems, Ltd.	InfoCrypt Enterprise	info@isolation.com
J. River, Inc.	ICE.Block	info@jriver.com
Lanoptics, Inc.	Guardian	sales@lanoptics.com
Legato	Legato Cluster Firewall	insidesales@legato.com
Livermore Software	Portus Secure Firewall	portusinfo@lsli.com
McAfee	PC Firewall	support@mcafee.com
	WebWall	support@mcafee.com
Micro Computer	Inetix	info@mcsdallas.com
Microtest, Inc.	WebEtc, WebEtc Pro	sales@microtest.com
Milkyway Network Corp.	SecurIT Firewall	sales@milkyway.com
NEC	PrivateNet Secure Firewall Server	nteachout@nectech.com
NetcPlus Internet Solutions	@Work-BrowseGate Proxy Server	iant@netcplus.com
Netguard, Ltd.	Guardian	info@ntguard.com
NetScreen Technologies	NetScreen 10	info@netscreen.com
	NetScreen 100	info@netscreen.com
Network-1 Software & Technology, Inc.	FireWall/Plus	sales@network-1.com
	FireWall/Plus for NT—Enterprise	sales@network-1.com
	FireWall/Plus for NT—Server Version	sales@network-1.com
ON Technology Corporation	ON Guard Firewall	info@on.com
Radguard	CryptoSystem	info@radguard.com
	PyroWall	info@radguard.com

Company	Product	Web Site/Contact E-Mail
Raptor Systems (A Division of AXENT Technologies)	Eagle Firewall	info@raptor.com
Ringdale	Proxy Router	rnall@hbmuk.com
SECANT Network Technologies	CellCase45—Encryption hardware for ATM networks	info@secantnet.com
	CellCase155—Multimode Encryption hardware for ATM networks	info@secantnet.com
	CellCase155—Single Mode Encryption hardware for ATM networks	info@secantnet.com
Signal 9 Solutions	ConSeal PC FIREWALL for 95/98/NT	sales@signal9.com
	ConSeal Tunnel	sales@signal9.com
SOLsoft	Net SecurityMaster	info@solsoft.com
Sonic Systems	SonicWALL	sales@sonicsys.com
	SonicWALL DMZ	sales@sonicsys.com
	SonicWALL PRO	sales@sonicsys.com
Sterling Commerce	CONNECT: Firewall	connect@stercomm.com
Sun Microsystems	Solstice Firewall-1	tony.lo@corp.sun.com
Technologic, Inc.	Interceptor Firewall Appliance	info@tlogic.com
Trusted Information Systems	Gauntlet Firewall for UNIX	sales@tis.com
	Gauntlet Firewall for W/NT	sales@tis.com
Ukiah Software	Netroad Firewall	sales@ukiahsoft.com
V-ONE Corporation	SmartWall	sales@v-one.com
WatchGuard Technologies	WatchGuard SchoolMate	info@watchguard.com
	WatchGuard Security System	info@watchguard.com

Company	Product	Web Site/Contact E-Mail
WebTrends Corporation	WebTrends for Firewalls and VPNs	info@webtrends.com

Intrusion Detection Systems, Software, and Services

♦ AAFID (Autonomous Agents for Intrusion Detection)
  www.cs.purdue.edu/coast/projects/autonomous-agents.html
  Purdue University, West Lafayette, IN

♦ ACME!
  www.acme.ibilce.unesp.br/
  University of Sao Paulo, Brazil

♦ AFJ (Anzen Flight Jacket)
  www.anzen.com/afj
  Anzen Computing Inc., WA

♦ AID (Adaptive Intrusion Detection system)
  www-rnks.informatik.tu-cottbus.de/~sobirey/aid.e.html
  Brandenburg University of Technology at Cottbus, Germany

♦ AIMS (Automated Intrusion Monitoring System)
  www.access.gpo.gov
  U.S. Army

♦ ALERT-PLUS/ Protect 2000
  www.compsec.com/html/products_and_services.html
  Computer Security Products Inc., Mississauga, Canada

♦ ARMD (Adaptable Real-Time Misuse Detection)
  www.isse.gmu.edu/~jllin/system/
  George Mason University, Fairfax, VA

♦ ARMOR (Adaptive Risk Management, Observation, and Response System)
  www.hiverworld.com/armor.ice
  Hiverworld, Inc.

♦ ASAX (Advanced Security audit trail Analyzer on uniX)
  www.info.fundp.ac.be/~amo/publications.html
  www.ja.net/CERT/Software/asax/
  University of Namur, Belgium

♦ ASIM (Automated Security Incident Measurement)
  www.access.gpo.gov
  U.S. Air Force Information Warfare Center and Trident Systems

♦ BlackICE
  www.networkice.com/html/products.html
  Network ICE Corp., San Mateo, CA

- Bro
  `www-nrg.ee.lbl.gov/nrg-papers.html`
  Lawrence Berkeley National Laboratory, Berkeley, CA

- Centrax
  `www.cybersafe.com/solutions/centrax.html`
  Centrax Corp., San Diego, CA; now CyberSafe

- CERN-NSM (Network Security Monitor)
  `www.zurich.ibm.com/pub/Other/RAID/Prog_RAID98/Full_Papers/`
  `moroni_manual.html`
  CERN, Geneva, Switzerland

- Cisco Secure IDS
  `www.cisco.com/warp/public/cc/cisco/mkt/security/nranger/`
  `prodlit/netra_ds.htm`
  Cisco Systems, Inc., San Jose, TX

- CMDS (Computer Misuse Detection System)
  `www.ods.com`
  ODS Networks, Inc. Richardson, TX

- Computer Watch
  `www.att.com/press/0293/930202.fsa.html`
  `www.att.com/press/1192/921116.fsa.html`
  AT&T Bell Laboratories, Whippany, NJ

- CSM (Cooperating Security Manager)
  `www.cs.tamu.edu/people/efisch`
  U.S. Air Force Academy, Colorado Springs, CO
  Texas A&M University, College Station, TX

- CyberCop Monitor
  `www.pgp.com/asp_set/products/tns/ccmonitor_intro.asp`
  Network Associates International, Santa Clara, CA

- CyberTrace
  `www.cybertrace.com/ctids.html`
  Ryan Net Works, LLC Fairfax, VA

- DIDS (Distributed Intrusion Detection System)
  `seclab.cs.ucdavis.edu/`
  University of California at Davis, CA

- DPEM (Distributed Program Execution Monitor)
  `seclab.cs.ucdavis.edu/~ko/papers/thesis.ps`
  University of California at Davis, CA

- Dragon
  `www.securitywizards.com/`
  Network Security Wizards, Rochester, NH

- EMERALD (Event Monitoring Enabling Responses to Anomalous Live Disturbances)
  `www.csl.sri.com/emerald/index.html`
  (further development of NIDES)
  SRI International, Menlo Park, CA

- ERIDS (External Routing Intrusion Detection System)
  `www.ir.bbn.com/projects/erids/erids-index.html`
  BBN Systems and Technologies, Cambridge, MA

- eTrust Intrusion Detection
  `www.cai.com/solutions/enterprise/etrust/intrusion_detection/`
  Computer Associates International, Inc., Islandia, NY

- GASSATA (Genetic Algorithm for Simplified Security Audit Trail Analysis)
  `www.supelec-rennes.fr/rennes/si/equipe/lme/these/these-lm.html`
  SUPELEC, Cesson Sevigne, France

- GrIDS (Graph-Based Intrusion Detection System)
  `olympus.cs.ucdavis.edu/arpa/grids/welcome.html`
  University of California at Davis, CA

- Hummer
  `www.cs.uidaho.edu/~hummer`
  University of Idaho, Moscow, ID

- IDA (Intrusion Detection and Avoidance system)
  `agn-www.informatik.uni-hamburg.de/people/fischer/eng.htm`
  University of Hamburg, Germany

- IDA(3) (Intrusion Detection Agents Systems)
  `www.ipa.go.jp/STC/IDA/index.html`
  Information-Technology Promotion Agency, Tokyo, Japan

- IDES (Intrusion Detection Expert System)
  `www.csl.sri.com/intrusion.html`
  `www.csl.sri.com/trlist3.html#1992`
  SRI International, Menlo Park, CA

- IDIOT (Intrusion Detection In Our Time
  `www.cerias.purdue.edu/coast/coast-tools.html`
  Purdue University, West Lafayette, IN

- ID-Trak
  `www.axent.com/Axent/Products/Framesection`
  `www.internettools.com`
  Internet Tools, Inc., Fremont, CA; now AXENT

- Intruder Alert
  `www.axent.com/product/smsbu/ITA/default.htm`
  AXENT Technologies, Inc., Rockville, MD

- JiNao
  `www.mcnc.org`
  MCNC, Research Triangle Park, NC

- KSE (Kane Security Enterprise)
  `www.intrusion.com/Products/enterprise.shtml`
  Intrusion.com, Inc., New York, NY

- KSM (Kane Security Monitor)
  `www.intrusion.com/Products/monitor.shtml`
  Intrusion Detection, Inc., New York, NY

- MIDS (Master Intrusion Detection System)
  `seclab.cs.ucdavis.edu/projects/idip.html`
  University of California at Davis, CA

- NADIR (Network Anomaly Detector and Intrusion Reporter)
  `seclab.cs.ucdavis.edu/cmad/4-1996/session2.html`
  Los Alamos National Laboratory, Los Alamos, NM

- NetProwler
  `www.axent.com/product/netprowler/default.htm`
  AXENT Technologies, Inc., Rockville, MD

- NetStalker
  `www.haystack.com/netstalk.htm`
  Haystack Laboratories, Inc., later TIS, now NAI, Santa Clara, CA

- NetSTAT (Network-Based State Transition Analysis Tool)
  `www.cs.ucsb.edu/~kemm/netstat.html/projects.html`
  University of California at Santa Barbara, CA

- NFR (Network Flight Recorder)
  `www.nfr.net`
  Network Flight Recorder, Inc., Rockville, MD

- NID (Network Intrusion Detector)
  `ciac.llnl.gov/cstc/nid/nid.html`
  Lawrence Livermore National Laboratory, U.S.A.

- NIDES (Next-Generation Intrusion Detection Expert System)
  `www.csl.sri.com/nides/index.html`
  SRI International, Menlo Park, CA

- PRéCis
  `www.bellevue.prc.com/precis/`
  Litton PRC, McLean, VA

- POLYCENTER Security Intrusion Detector
  `www.digital.com/info/security/id.htm`
  Digital Equipment Corporation, now COMPAQ, Palo Alto, CA

- RealSecure
  `www.iss.net/prod/rs.html`
  Internet Security Systems, Inc., Atlanta, GA

- RID (Reactive Intrusion Detection for Gauntlet Firewalls)
  `www.lurhq.com/rid/rid20info.pdf`
  LURHQ Corp., Conway, SC

- SecureNet PRO
  www.mimestar.com
  MimeStar, Inc., Blacksburg, VA

- SecureSwitch
  www.ods.com/
  ODS Networks, Inc., Richardson, TX

- SHADOW (Secondary Heuristic Analysis for Defensive Online Warfare)
  www.nswc.navy.mil/ISSEC/CID
  Naval Surface Warfare Center, Dahlgren Division, Dahlgren, VA

- Snort
  www.snort.org
  Snort, Boston, MA

- Stake Out
  www.stakeout.harris.com
  Harris Corporation, Melbourne, FL

- Stalker
  www.haystack.com/stalk.htm
  Haystack Laboratories, Inc.; later Trusted Information Systems, Santa Clara, CA

- Tivoli Cross-Site for Security
  www.tivoli.com/products/index/cross-site_sec/index.html
  Tivoli Systems, Inc., TX

- T-sight
  www.EnGarde.com/software/t-sight/index.html
  En Garde Systems, Inc., Albuquerque, NM

- UNICORN (Unicos Realtime NADIR)
  www.EnGarde.com/~mcn/unicorn.html
  Los Alamos National Laboratory, Los Alamos, NM

- USTAT (Unix State Transition Analysis Tool)
  www.cs.ucsb.edu/TRs/TRCS93-26.html
  University of California at Santa Barbara, CA

- VisionIDS
  www.whitehats.com/ids/
  WhiteHats, Inc., NV

- WebStalker Pro
  www.haystack.com/webstalk.htm
  Haystack Laboratories, Inc.; later Trusted Information Systems, Santa Clara, CA

Magazines and News

- Data Storage (ds.pennnet.com/home.cfm)

- InfoStor (www.infostor.com)

◆ iSCSI Storage Magazine Search Engines (www.iscsistorage.com)

◆ Mass Storage News (www.massstoragenews.com)

◆ Storage Magazine (www.storagemagazine.com)

◆ Storage Management Solutions (www.wwpi.com/sms.shtml)

◆ Storage Virtualization News (www.storage-virtualization.com)

Search Engines

◆ www.SearchStorage.com

◆ www.StorageSearch.com

Storage Network Software

Company	Product Name	Web Site/Contact E-Mail
ATTO Technology	ATTO AccelNet	sls@attotech.com
Digital Equipment	FDDI Server	info@digital.com
IBM	HACMP/6000 High	askibm@info.ibm.com
Impactdata	Common Peripheral Interface	info@impactdata.com
Luminex	LSX SCSI Expander	info@luminex.com
Mercury Computer	SuiteFUSION	suitefusion@mc.com
Network Storage	SPANStor	srleads@nssolutions.com
Programmed Logic	StackOS—Stackable	info@plc.com
REALM Information	REALM Universal Server	sales@realminfo.com
Seagate Software	Seagate Backup Exec	info@moguls.com
StorageTek	Client System Component	desk@stortek.com
	Enterprise Software	desk@stortek.com
	LibAttach NT Servers	desk@stortek.com
	Removable Media Lib. S/W	desk@stortek.com
Transoft Technology	FibreNet, FibreNetLite	salesinfo@transoft.net
Vinca	StandbyServer	info@vinca.com

Virus Control

Company	Product	Web Site/Contact E-Mail
Command Software Systems	F-PROT Professional Anti-Virus	sales@commandcom.com
Computer Associates	eTrust Antivirus	info@ca.com
Finjan, Inc.	SurfinShield Xtra	info@finjan.com
ForeFront Group	ForeFront Anti-Virus	productinfo@ffg.com
IBM	AntiVirus, Enterprise Edition	askibm@info.ibm.com
Intel	LANDesk Virus Protect v1.7 for Windows NT	support@cs.intel.com
	LANDesk Virus Protect v4.0 for clients and PCs	support@cs.intel.com
	LANDesk Virus Protect v4.0 for NetWare	support@cs.intel.com
McAfee	Ontrack Virus Scan (2.2)	support@mcafee.com
	NETSHIELD	support@mcafee.com
	ROMSHIELD	support@mcafee.com
	VIRUSSCAN	support@mcafee.com
	VirusScan Deluxe	support@mcafee.com
	WebScan v 1.04	support@mcafee.com
NetZ Computing	InVircible	netz@actcom.co.il
Novell	ManageWise	sales@ontrack.com
ON Technology Corp.	Macro Virus Track	info@on.com
	Virus Track	info@on.com
Ontrack Computer Systems	Ontrack NetShield	sales@ontrack.com
	Ontrack VirusScan	sales@ontrack.com
	Ontrack VirusScan 95	sales@ontrack.com
PC Guardian	Workstation Manager Plus	pcg@pcguardianmail.com
Quarterdeck	ViruSweep	info@quarterdeck.com
	ViruSweep Extra Strength	info@quarterdeck.com

Company	Product	Web Site/Contact E-Mail
SecureNet Technologies	AVAST! Antivirus for DOS/Win	sales@securenet.org
	AVAST32 Antivirus for Win 95/NT	sales@securenet.org
	V-Net Gold with MACROBLASTER	sales@securenet.org
SOFTEAM	VirusCOP	viruscop@softeam.com.co
Sophos, Inc.	Sophos Anti-Virus	sales@sophos.com
	SWEEP	sales@sophos.com
Stiller Research	Integrity Master	wolfgang@stiller.com
Symantec	Norton AntiVirus for Netware	webmaster@symantec.com
Trend Micro, Inc.	InterScan WebProtect	sales@trendmicro.com
	PC-cillin 6	sales@trendmicro.com
	Trend InterScan 3.0 with eManager	sales@trendmicro.com
	Trend InterScan AppletTrap 1.0	sales@trendmicro.com
	Trend InterScan VirusWall	sales@trendmicro.com
	Trend PC-cillin 3.0	sales@trendmicro.com
	Trend ScanMail for Lotus cc:mail	sales@trendmicro.com
	Trend ScanMail for LotusNotes	sales@trendmicro.com
	Trend ScanMail for MicroSoft Exchange	sales@trendmicro.com
	Trend ScanMail for MicroSoft Mail	sales@trendmicro.com
	Trend ScanMail for OpenMail	sales@trendmicro.com
	Trend ServerProtect for NT, for NetWare	sales@trendmicro.com
	Trend Virus Control System	sales@trendmicro.com

Company	Product	Web Site/Contact E-Mail
Wolf Computer Systems	InVircible Antivirus Software with Disk Crash Recovery	sales@wolfcomputer.com

White Papers

This section contains free technical papers and reports on storage networks and security. You'll also find documents from leading IT analysts.

♦ HP/Compaq Storage White Papers
  (www.compaq.com/storage/whitepapers.html)

♦ iSCSI White Papers
  (www.iscsistorage.com/iscsiwhitepapers.htm)

♦ ITpaper Technology Guides
  (www.itpapers.com/resources/tech_guides.html)

♦ Network Buyers Guide Industry White Papers
  (www.networkbuyersguide.com/search/105003.htm)

♦ searchStorage White Papers
  (searchstorage.techtarget.com/whitepapers)

Index